Technology
and
Teaching

Technology
and
Teaching

Les Lloyd, Editor

Information Today, Inc.
Medford, NJ
1997

Copyright© 1997 by: Information Today, Inc.
143 Old Marlton Pike
Medford, NJ 08055

Printed in the United States of America.

Library of Congress Cataloging-in-Publication Data

Technology and teaching / Les Lloyd, editor.
       p.   cm.
    Includes index.
    ISBN 1-57387-014-5
    1. Education, Higher--United States--Data processing--Case studies. 2. Educational technology--United States--Case studies.
3. Computer-assisted instruction--United States--Case studies.
I. Lloyd, Les.
LB2395.7.T425 1997
378.1' 73--dc21
                                                           96-45083
                                                           CIP

ISBN: 1-57387-014-5

Price: $42.50

Cover Design: Jeanne Wachter

DEDICATION

This book is lovingly dedicated to my father who spent his life teaching and working with young people. It was his enthusiasm for his work that led me to follow in his footsteps.

CONTENTS

Preface xiii

PART ONE: GENERAL

1. When Everyone Buys in: A Case Study
   of Technological Change 3
   Carole Carmody, Director of Information Technology,
   Bloomfield College

2. The Affect of Computers on College Writing:
   A View from the Field 13
   Jo Ellen Winters, Senior Associate Professor of English,
   Bucks County Community College

3. A Professional Development Needs-Assessment of
   Computing and Information Technology:
   A Case Study at Lock Haven University 23
   Punnipa Hossain, Assistant Professor and Technology Consultant,
   Lock Haven University
   Robert O. Little, Computing Center Director,
   Lock Haven University

4. Computing in the Curriculum at Wellesley College 35
   Alan Shuchat, Professor of Mathematics,
   Wellesley College

PART TWO: MULTIMEDIA

5. Some Experiences Integrating Electronic Media
   into the Art and Design Curriculum 43
   Wayne Draznin, Computer Arts Program Coordinator,
   Cleveland Institute of Art

6. Developing a Multimedia Computer/Video Environment in a
   Comprehensive Community College 49
   S. James Corvey, Director of Educational Computing,
   Mountain View College

7. MacCycle: An Extensible Multimedia for Teaching the Physiology
   and Histology of the Menstrual Cycle 63
   James F. Aiton, Physiology Lecturer,
   University of St. Andrews
   Susan Whiten, Senior Demonstrator in Anatomy,
   University of St. Andrews
   Nils S. Peterson, Instructional Software Designer,
   Washington State University

8. Multimedia: A Systematic Approach to its Placement in
   Education 73
   Robert A. Saldarini, Assistant to the President,
   Bergen Community College

PART THREE: SOFTWARE

9. Software for Sociology: A Tool for a More Effective Learning
   Paradigm 85
   Christopher Sullivan, Director of Information Services,
   Baldwin-Wallace College

10. DATASIM: A General Purpose Data Simulator 93
    Drake R. Bradley, Professor of Psychology,
    Bates College

11. An Integrative Approach to Writing with Computers 119
    W. Brett McKenzie, Instructional Support Specialist,
    Bryant College

12. Chronicles from a U.S. Department of Education
    Title III Grant 129
    Jeanne Buckley, Adjunct Professor of Instructional Technology,
    College of Textiles and Sciences
    Marilyn Puchalski, Director of Academic Computing,
    Bucks County Community College

13. Learning Information Systems Through a Mail-Enabled Business Simulation: The Case of Trent Engineering 139

*Clive Holtham, Professor of Information Management,
City University Business School
Martin Rich, Lecturer in Information Management,
City University Business School*

14. Integrating Technology into the Health Information Management Curriculum 157

*Dorine Bennett, Instructor, Medical Record Programs,
Dakota State University
Paulette Wiesen, Director, Medical Record Programs,
Dakota State University*

15. The Computer-Mediated English Department 165

*Patricia Ericsson, Instructor of English,
Dakota State University
Eric Johnson, English Professor and Dean of the College of Liberal Arts,
Dakota State University*

16. Using Technology in a Computer Concepts Course 175

*James S. McKeown, Instructor of Information and Business Systems,
Dakota State University
Lynette Molstad, Assistant Professor of Business and Information
Systems, Dakota State University*

17. Energies Plus, Inc. 185

*N. Faye Angel, Assistant Professor of Business,
Ferrum College*

18. TransIT and Refocused Strategies in Teaching Advanced Translation 197

*Doug Thompson, Professor/Reader, Modern Italian History and
Literature, University of Hull*

19. Chemistry and Art: Developing a New Course with NSF Grants 207

*John L. Bordley, Jr., Professor of Chemistry and Computer Science,
Johns Hopkins University*

20. Evolution of the Classroom with New Technology 213

*Abigail M. Thomas, Associate Professor of Mathematical
and Computer Science, Lyndon State College*

21. **CAL Heuristics in the United Kingdom's UMIST** 217
   Marie C. Hayet, Lecturer and CAL Project Officer,
   University of Manchester Institute of Science and Technology

22. **Medaille College: Integrating Computers into Course Syllabi** . . . 237
   Donna Marie Kaputa, Chair of Computer Information Systems,
   Medaille College, in collaboration with Douglas Anderson,
   Carol Harrison, and Janice Schlegel

23. **Computer Information Systems and Art: The Development**
   of a Symbiotic Relationship 241
   Ellen M. Dauwer, Assistant Professor of Computer Information
   Systems, College of Saint Elizabeth

24. **Student Information Skills Project** 247
   Susan P. Fowell, Project Leader, Information Skills Project,
   University of Sheffield

25. **A Case Study in the Use of Union College's**
   Teagle Writing Lab 255
   Najmuddin Shaik, Associate Professor of Computer Information
   Systems, Union College
   Dianne Ferris, Chairperson, Humanities Division,
   Union College

26. **Using Computer Software in a Literature Class: Rereading a Text**
   with SEEN by Conduit 269
   Nancy Enright, Seton Hall University

PART FOUR: SOFTWARE/HARDWARE

27. **Professors as Developers: Exploiting the NeXTstep**
   Environment 275
   Joel Smith, Director of Academic Computing and Information
   Technology, The Claremont Graduate School, Allegheny College

28. **Establishing a Networked Lab with Focus on Integrating**
   Computers into the Writing Curriculum 287
   Constance Chismar, Associate Professor of English Education and
   Computer Writing Center Director, Georgian Court College

29. The Value of Portable Computers in the Classroom 295
   Garrett Bozylinsky, Associate Vice President for Computing,
   Indiana University of Pennsylvania
   William Creighton, Director of Academic Computing,
   Indiana University of Pennsylvania

30. Music, Computers, and Learning at New England
   Conservatory 303
   Paul Burdick, Music and Computer Studio Director,
   New England Conservatory
   Lyle Davidson, Theory Department Chairperson,
   New England Conservatory

31. Academic Computing Case History: Establishment of
   Microcomputer Access at a Community College 317
   Dick W. Birkholz, Coordinator, Academic Computing,
   Sheridan College

32. Development of an Advanced Technology Classroom 325
   Eugene P. Buccini, Professor of Management,
   Ancell School of Business, Western Connecticut State University
   Ronald G. Benson, Professor of Management and Chairperson of
   Management Department,
   Ancell School of Business, Western Connecticut State University

33. The Advanced Technology Classroom 333
   Marla J. Fischer, Professor of Management Information Systems,
   Ancell School of Business, Western Connecticut State University

PART FIVE: THE WEB

34. A Syllabus for a World Wide Web Writing Workshop 347
   Jack R. Kayser, Education Technologies Specialist,
   Lafayette College

Notes on Contributors 351

Index 361

PREFACE

During the past fifteen years, working with computers and other technology in the classroom has changed dramatically. Early on, it was the computer science and other technically minded faculty who programmed their own demonstrations and struggled to find equipment that adequately displayed the work for their classes. Typically, they would expect to spend ten or twenty hours in preparation for every hour of materials actually used in class.

Since then, programming languages have been replaced by authoring systems and the World Wide Web, and projection of computer images is almost akin to using an overhead projector (though adequate financial resources for this equipment are not necessarily in place at every college). Students are often employed to assist faculty members with the design of classroom materials, so we've progressed somewhat from a faculty-intensive process to a collaborative one—one that enhances learning not only for those in the class but also for students working closely with faculty on these projects.

The evolution is certainly not complete. Anyone who has used multimedia resources in a classroom knows that one piece of equipment will fail during the most crucial part of the semester (this is Murphy's Law of multimedia). And while the preparation time has been reduced somewhat, it still takes a substantial time commitment to develop these materials for classroom and remedial use. But if anything is certain with technology, it is that things change, and it is likely that the time ratio between preparation to demonstration will continue to decrease.

The faculty who have contributed to this volume come from a variety of disciplines and have used different techniques to help enhance the classroom experience for their students with multimedia technology. And while they might not consider themselves pioneers any longer, they are still among the leaders on their respective campuses in this process. A similar volume in five years would certainly show the strides they will make in the years to come.

I hope you will be able to draw on the experiences of these faculty to enhance your own research and teaching.

Part One: General

Chapter

1

When Everyone Buys In: A Case Study of Technological Change

Carole Carmody

Director of Information Technology
Bloomfield College, Bloomfield, New Jersey

Bloomfield College, a small liberal arts college with limited resources, has begun an academic computing program, and its experience is an example of what can be done with careful planning and a universal effort on the part of faculty, students, and administration. Examining the goals set for faculty and student literacy and the hardware and software purchased and allocated in ways that helped us achieve our goals provides a study of a planned, campus-wide change.

Bloomfield College is a private, liberal arts college in northeastern New Jersey, one-half hour from New York City. It has a full-time faculty of fifty-three and a combined day and evening student population of 2,100. The college was founded in 1864 as a seminary of the Presbyterian Church preparing first a German-speaking, and later a multilingual, multicultural student body for the ministry. Today, as a nonsectarian, four-year college, its mission is "to prepare students to function at the peak of their potential in a multiracial, multicultural society." This is more than a mission statement; Bloomfield College provides its students with a multiracial and multicultural environment in which to study and live: 46 percent of its student body are African-American and Afro-Caribbean, 39 percent are Caucasian, 11 percent are Latino, and 3 percent are Asian-American; 69 percent are women. As part of our commitment to educate students who have traditionally been underrepresented in higher education, we attempt to prepare our students to participate in a workforce in which technological competence is a necessity.

To achieve this mission, central to the academic life of the college, we have focused our energies on faculty development and renewal; curricular change to incorporate issues of race, ethnicity, and gender; the integration of computer-assisted instruction across the curriculum; and the building of a technological environment to support these changes.

IN THE BEGINNING

Prior to the fall of 1989, computing facilities and programs at the college were limited. Virtually no money had been spent on academic computing equipment or facilities in a number of years. There was one public access computer lab with sixteen Apple IIEs and ten dual-drive IBM PCs. The college's only software holdings were AppleWorks, several copies of DOS, WordStar 3.3, and Lotus 1-2-3. Students enrolled in computer information systems classes checked out software for use in the lab. The lab was barely able to support these classes. Students received instruction in computing only in programming courses or in Computer Literacy, a course required of all business majors. A small number of students used the Apples for word processing. About one-third of the faculty had some level of computer literacy ranging from word processing to Lotus 1-2-3, statistical applications, or programming languages, but only a few of the science faculty had Apple or Mac computers in their offices.

THE PROGRAM

In 1989, the college received a three-year Excellence Initiative grant (formerly called a Challenge to the Independents Grant). This $1.8 million grant from the New Jersey Department of Higher Education recognized and supported the college's mission. Initially, $198,167 was awarded to the Information Technology program to purchase hardware and software to support programs for faculty and student training. Over the three years of the grant this amount was increased to $317,470. These grant monies served as the wellspring for the metamorphosis in technology at Bloomfield College.

The Information Technology program had two central goals: (1) to assist students who have been traditionally underprepared in computing and its application in the workplace—computer literacy—the "fourth basic skill" and (2) to help faculty become computer literate and integrate computer-assisted instruction into their classes. Our challenge was to plan for the development of computing across the campus and provide a range of constituencies with enough equipment and software to get them started, involved, and excited about the possibilities of computing for teaching and learning.

All of our planning, including the purchase of hardware and software and the development of a technological environment, was driven by these two goals and by the mission of the college. Several questions had to be answered:

1. How could we provide as many of our students with computing facilities and training that would allow them to develop basic skills in

computing, to prepare them to pursue college work, and to become competitive in the workplace?

2. How could we involve the faculty, provide them with basic computer resources and training and hook them in so that they would play with the computer and see its possibilities for instruction, and prepare them for more sophisticated involvement in computer-assisted instruction in the future?

3. How could we gain the interest of the whole campus, including administration and staff and help them see that technology was central to the life of the college both in teaching and learning and in the creation of an effective informational base for the institution?

These questions led us to make the specific plans and decisions that shaped academic computing at Bloomfield and to make the choices in hardware and software that would best support these programs.

The decisions that we made to purchase specific types of hardware and software and the ways in which these resources were distributed around the campus were based on these goals and on the underlying idea of giving access to computers and software to the greatest number of people. Instead of providing state of the art equipment for a limited number of users (e.g., computer information systems faculty and students), we chose to distribute less expensive equipment to a larger number of people in public access facilities and in faculty offices for the first stage of our development. As additional funding became available, we upgraded equipment and software.

PROGRAMS FOR STUDENTS

To provide access to the largest number of students, we focused our development efforts on public access labs. During 1989-1990, the first year of the grant, twenty-four 286 AT-compatible computers were installed in the main lab. The old Apple IIEs were given to psychology and biology for use in their labs. During the second year, 1990-1991, we added ten computers to the computer lab. We developed a second public access lab in the library, using fifteen older IBM PCS and XT clones, outfitted with additional memory and hard cards.

As additional funds became available during 1991, we began the process of upgrading our existing lab equipment from 286s to 386SXs. We replaced twelve computers in the lab and moved them to faculty offices and to minilabs for learning support and nursing. An additional ten machines were upgraded by the addition of SX cards and additional hard drives. The new 386SX machines all had larger hard drives and 3 megabytes RAM to accommodate the packages that we had started using in graphics and desktop publishing classes.

In 1991, AT&T awarded the college a networked lab consisting of eighteen computers and a server running UNIX which provided a more sophisticated environment for our computer and information systems majors.

During the 1991-1992 academic year we continued to add to our holdings and to expand our services. In January 1992 we opened an Advanced Technology Center in the library which had a 386 computer and full page monitor (both pretty powerful at that time), a scanner and postscript, and color printers. In this facility, administration, faculty, and advanced students could use a variety of software for graphics, art, and desktop publishing. It also was used to publish the campus literary magazine, *Common Ground*. During that year we also began to purchase 486 technology for the main lab. We also branched out providing computers to the Learning Support Center and the nursing labs where we created mini-labs for student use in tutoring.

During 1992-1994, we began to upgrade our holdings in the main labs to 486 computers that could support a library of packages for graphics and desktop publishing. We are presently upgrading our existing hardware and adding new equipment that will accommodate Windows-based packages which will form the basis for our revised computer literacy curriculum. Presently, we have close to 140 PCs in four labs, two minilabs, and in faculty offices.

To support students and computer-assisted instruction in the disciplines, a library of current software for use in the labs was developed. These holdings include WordPerfect, Windows, WordPerfect for Windows, MS Word for Windows, Corel Draw, Ventura, Aldus PageMaker, PhotoStyler, OmniPage Professional, Lotus 1-2-3, Pascal, C++, Kwikstate, and SPSS. We have also obtained a number of specialized packages for individual divisions including nursing, math, biology, chemistry, and business.

The college emphasizes programs for freshmen to assist in retention. These include programs for Education Opportunity Fund (EOF) students; orientation for freshmen and new students; a semester-long academic skills course, Human Communication and Development (IDS 161), for freshmen enrolled in academic foundations programs; and a growing English as a Second Language program (ESL). To meet our goal of helping students achieve basic computer literacy, we integrated training in the use of computers and word processing into these programs.

The thrust of these activities is to provide training for all first-year students to help them become comfortable with the technology, to assist them in making the computer an integral part of the learning process, and to prepare them to use the computer in more advanced courses that have computer-assisted learning components. Achieving the basic skill of using the computer for papers and assignments gives beginning students, especially those who are underprepared, a sense of accomplishment early in their college careers. Since most of the academic programs for freshmen emphasize writing and revision of written work, the use of computers enhances the work done in these courses. We originally used WordStar for this training, but the institutional standard is WordPerfect. Depending on the requirements of the specific program, the training ranges from one to four hours of hands-on work at the computer, and each student receives a manual, *An Introduction to the Computer and Word Processing*, which we wrote and distribute to all students using the computer labs.

Computer workshops are now a part of every freshman orientation. Between September 1990 and September 1991, 345 freshmen received a one-hour introduction to the lab; of these 240, 85 percent of the freshman class, were part of the fall 1991 freshman orientation workshops in computing. During orientation, new students were given diskettes to use during the training and on return visits to the computer labs. We have found that when students are given a diskette it encourages them to return to use the lab for papers and assignments. The more they use the lab the more comfortable and proficient they become. More than 200 students in the EOF, ESL, and academic foundations and IDS 161 classes received an additional two to four hours of training in the lab during the 1990-1991 academic year and a similar number received this training during 1991-1992. In August of 1992, we trained about 250 students in the freshman orientation and 270 students in the August 1993 orientation.

Besides the workshops for first-year students, other workshops in the use of word processing have been offered in the lab to both day and evening students. This training has also been provided to several sections of our English core courses.

In the five years since we began the development of our computing facilities, the level of lab use has increased significantly as measured by lab sign-in logs in the main computer lab. Students take advantage of the facilities even when they are not required to do so for specific course work. One faculty member has commented that the computer lab is more of a meeting place for students than the campus center and is usually more crowded. There is often a waiting line to get a computer in the evening.

FACULTY DEVELOPMENT

The second goal of making faculty computer-literate drove our program of providing computers and software to faculty. During the first two years of the program, computers were provided to the fifteen faculty in the Seminar in Computing, to the offices of the CIS faculty, and to divisional offices. Later, computers were placed in additional faculty offices and in the offices of the deans and associate deans who were working on special projects supporting student learning and assessment. Presently nearly every full-time faculty member has a computer or shares an office with someone who has a computer and therefore has access to it.

To stimulate faculty awareness and interest about the possibilities of computing and computer-assisted instruction, the Faculty Seminar in Computing was offered. Fifteen full-time faculty and administrators, six the first year and nine the second, participated in this program. Nearly all of the faculty who participated in the seminar were novices to computing and several were avowed computer-phobics. In the seminar, they developed basic computer literacy, learning to use DOS and WordStar in hands-on lab sessions; a few explored Lotus 1-2-3, BASIC, or SPSS. In return for participating in the seminar and revising a course to integrate computer-assisted instruction, each participant received a computer, printer, and software for use in his/her office. A number of disciplines were represented: chemistry, biology, math, nursing, management, accounting, psychology, philosophy, history, learning support and social work, art, and ESL. The administrators who participated, including the ESL director and the assistant dean of advising, also teach and used the computer for administrative projects, for program development, and for course revision.

Discussions in the seminar centered on educational issues and concerns involved with integrating computing into the curriculum as well as the practical problems of learning a new skill. Their own difficulties in learning to use the computer gave them insights into the problems their students have in learning new and often difficult material. They no longer took for granted the assumption that if students worked hard they would "get it." Both in the seminar, and with the information technology director individually, faculty explored areas for development of computer-assisted instruction, researched software available, and began the preparation of the course that they would teach using software appropriate to their disciplines.

By the fall of 1992, most of the fifteen participants had completed their required projects. The projects have used software ranging from word processing to discipline-specific applications, and the length of time devoted to the module varies from several days to one day a week for the entire semester for writing classes. Some examples of the projects include lab modules in experimental psychology and cognition; mathematics for nurses; legal aspects of nursing; clinical simulations in nursing; accounting packages and Lotus 1-2-3; biology tutorials; nuclear magnetic resonator simulations in organic chemistry; project management software in business; in class writing and revision on the computer in academic foundations, ESL, and freshman skills development classes.

The ongoing work on curricular integration beyond the required project is a sign of the seminar's success. Faculty continue to explore software for use in other classes. The department that has made the most significant changes in the use of computing in its curriculum is nursing. Nursing faculty are using a variety of packages in both their theoretical and clinical classes, which include clinical simulations in medical/surgical nursing and maternal and child health, pharmacology programs, case studies in renal dialysis, programs to tutor in the use of EKG, packages on nutrition, and analysis of blood gases. The nursing faculty is now using computer-assisted instruction where possible. One of the nursing faculty in the seminar, who taught the legal aspects of nursing using a computer-assisted instruction module, found that students have learned more using this modality. The nursing faculty is also preparing students to use computers for the nursing boards and is hoping to acquire an interactive laser disk system to add to the learning lab.

The impact on faculty members is evident both in what they have produced in course revision and in a fundamental shift in attitude toward using this technology in teaching, as well as in their own feelings toward the computer and their ability to learn to use it. There have been a range of responses as they engage in the learning process. One faculty member was extremely resistant and computer-phobic at the beginning of the seminar. By the end of her first year, she was using the computer for some of her own work and engaged in planning the use of computers in her writing class. She thought it would work but wasn't completely sure. Her students were required to write in-class papers in the computer lab once a week for a semester. I interviewed her students at the end of the semester; all but one was enthusiastic about using the computer for the writing process, and several no longer wanted to compose using pen and paper.

A second "conversion" is a nursing faculty member who slowly learned how to use the computer and word processing software. The success of her curricular revision, in terms of her students' learning, has led her to request that the college purchase authoring software so that she can try to develop modules in her field. A third, a member of the business faculty, has learned to use SPSS to assist him in his dissertation research. A fourth has made much slower progress but for him it was tremendous, a real "wow." He now does much of his work using a word processing package; he has also purchased a computer for home since he now uses it so much. Each of the fifteen participants has learned, explored and experimented, and is committed to seeing computer-assisted learning as part of the curriculum.

Other faculty members, not part of the seminar, have been exploring the use of computing in their courses. The head of the freshman core program in English has brought his students to the lab for their weekly in-class writing assignments as have several of his adjunct faculty. Biology faculty is using software packages for anatomy and physiology. A theater arts professor with a personal interest in desktop publishing has offered informal sessions in DTP for administrators and staff and currently offers a popular course in this area. He, along with an art professor and a seminar participant, have designed a curriculum for a new computer-based major in creative arts technology. This program has been approved and is currently enrolling majors. They have also received two grants for equipment for the program.

The seminar had a life span of two years. Although no additional funding was available to continue the program, other efforts have been made to provide faculty with equipment and with workshops to increase literacy.

Training for Faculty, Administration, and Staff

As part of our effort to serve the entire college community and to continue to develop literacy among faculty, administrators, and staff, we have offered a variety of open workshops including word processing, DOS, and Lotus 1-2-3 to the community. Workshops have also been offered to full-time and part-time faculty and academic support staff during the college's annual January faculty development workshops. Sessions have been offered on Introduction to the PC, WordStar, Lotus 1-2-3, SPSS, and Introduction to Graphics, WordPerfect, Desktop Publishing, and Corel Draw. In the years since the first Faculty Development Workshops in Computing, the level of sophistication of the faculty has increased and their interests have expanded. We anticipate that we will offer workshops for faculty and staff that meet their changing interests.

NETWORKING

A campus network is key to the growth and expansion of both computing efforts and the ability to collect and analyze information vital to the academic life of the institution. In September of 1992 we installed the first phase of our academic network. It was partially funded by a grant from the Teagle Foundation which the college received to support its Student Advancement Initiative and work in student assessment. This small network connected faculty, academic advising, and student affairs staff and supports the Noel/Levitz ActionTrack enrollment management software, which is designed to track student retention. The initial phase of networking supported the pilot project designed to track fifty students during the first year with increasing numbers in subsequent years.

In the summer of 1994, the college planned for the installation of fiber-optic wiring and a full campus network which would bring together three networks—the DEC administrative network, the PC LAN supporting the Student Advancement Initiative, and a small network in the Office of Development. During the winter of 1995, an automated library system will be installed and this network will be connected to the other three through the fiber backbone. Faculty will be able to access the online public catalog from their offices and conduct individualized bibliographic instruction with their students. Shortly after this we hope to install a CD-ROM server that will allow us to use the various indexes on CD-ROM through the main library system. The final step will be to network the main student labs and connect those to the fiber, allowing students and faculty to communicate with each other by e-mail. During the same period. we hope to find funding to install our own Internet gateway.

CONCLUSION

The Information Technology program at Bloomfield has had an impact on the campus over a period of five years and has assisted faculty, students, administration, and staff in developing computer literacy and becoming comfortable with technology. It has provided support for teaching and learning at Bloomfield College. In a very short time, we have come to think very differently about technology and its impact on how we teach and learn. It has made students and faculty more productive. It has given students an important tool both for the classroom and for the workplace. We have now all become more sophisticated in the use of technology and our expectations have been raised. Our task in the future is to try to meet these expectations and to continue the work already begun of integrating computing and computer-assisted instruction across the curriculum and across the campus.

Faculty, students, and administration have accepted the process of change and have helped to make it happen. Students' enthusiastic use of the lab facilities and the success that they have experienced in using the technology as part of the learning process encouraged faculty. Faculty members are pleased with the rapid transition in technology and with the training that has prepared them to use this technology. Curricular integration has been started and for some, (e.g., nursing) it has enabled them to teach some material more effectively and with students learning collaboratively. For others, it has challenged traditional assumptions about the way they and their students learn. It has made them personally and professionally more productive. The reason for the success of these efforts with faculty, both in the seminar and on the campus as a whole, is that they feel that they "own" the project and that they have been involved with planning and implementing technological and curricular change. The college has not mandated computing across the curriculum but has fostered the environment in which this change can take place. While not every faculty member has participated directly in the process of change, even some of the self-confessed Luddites have begun to use computers for their own work and accept technology as necessary for the growth of the institution. Today a number of faculty are eager to explore the use of multimedia and interactive video for the enrichment of their classes.

The administration has not only promoted the change, but a number have participated in various programs including the Faculty Seminar in Computing and training workshops. They provide on-going support and participate in planning activities. They recognize that information technology is now essential to all sectors of the college and have made the improvement of information technology a goal in the college's strategic plan.

Technological change is not always easy to effect, especially in an academic environment. Administration can mandate computing across the curriculum, but if faculty, staff, or students don't participate willingly or do so in small numbers, then campus-wide change never becomes a reality. Alternatively, if the faculty seeks technological change, desires computers, curriculum revision, and a networked environment, but the administration does not support the change, then the faculty is frustrated. Bloomfield College provides an example of what can happen when administration and faculty agree on change and use limited fiscal resources wisely. The integration of computing across the curriculum, supported by the acquisition of hardware and software and fostered by programs for faculty development, has been successful because everyone—faculty, students, and administration—has "bought in."

Chapter

2

The Affect of Computers on College Writing: A View from the Field

Jo Ellen Winters

Senior Associate Professor of English
Bucks County Community College
Newtown, Pennsylvania

I have been teaching Introduction to Composition (CMP 107) as a computer-augmented course at Bucks County Community College (BCCC) for three years. The course explores developmental composition through selected readings, all essays, to which students respond by discussion and expository writing, first in developmental paragraphs and later in multiparagraph essays, all composed and revised on a word processor. Since I began offering CMP 107 as a computer-augmented course in 1989, I have been rethinking several philosophical and pedagogical issues in order to understand the impact of computers on the teaching of writing.

All students at Bucks must take a holistically graded essay placement test by the time they have completed twelve semester hours; they are encouraged to take it on entry into the college. Students placed in CMP 107 can write sentences, spell, and punctuate correctly much of the time, but in general they have no experience with paragraph development, thesis statements, coherence, unity, or extended use of concrete detail. They are not ready to write essays. As a result, the CMP 107 departmental writing requirement consists of ten 150 to 200 word paragraphs and at least three multiparagraph essays in the second half of the semester to prepare students for the traditional English Composition I course.

I teach two sections of CMP 107, and each fifteen-student section is scheduled for the computer lab once a week. In addition to the eighty machines in the four writing labs, there are about one hundred word processors, Macs and IBMs, available on campus for student use throughout the day and on weekends, which utilize a wide range of programs from Lotus to WordPerfect. The word processing program I use in my 107 course is Professional Write; it is both easy and efficient. Although students enrolling in computer-augmented courses are not required to have word processing skills, I devote only one fifty-minute meeting in the lab to orientation, distribute a three-page handout with basic Professional Write commands to each student, and have never in three years had a student who could not keep up with the typing or with the word processing program itself, with the exception of a young man who was always late, frequently forgot whether we were meeting in the classroom or the lab, and regularly and quite deliberately threw himself on the mercy of the more computer-literate females in the room. (Even during the final, for which he actually wrote a semi-distinguished essay, a young woman stopped revising to help him move text, and several of us insisted on saving his work for him as the test period reached an end. It worked just the way he'd hoped it would.) Last semester, on the other hand, a Russian student and a Japanese student, neither of whom spoke fluent English, both learned Professional Write as a third language quite rapidly.

In the weekly lab period, my students work on brainstorming, outlines, rough drafts, and revisions, sometimes individually but more often in groups. Occasionally I devise an exercise or drill for them, but for the most part I am interested in their performing writing tasks in the writing lab. It is the process of writing, of moving fluidly from idea to textual embodiment of that idea, which a word processor seems made to enhance; it is the process of writing on a word processor which invites collaboration, in prewriting, invention, development, and revision, and which allows us together to literally see how we are shaping our texts even as we shape them.

COMPUTERS AND COLLEGE WRITING

When the BCCC *Staff Bulletin* confused "affect" with "effect" and announced that I would be speaking in November 1991 at Myrtle Beach, South Carolina, on "The Effect of Computers on College Writing," I had to laugh. When we speak of "effect," we of course mean change, to accomplish or execute a result; when we speak of "affect," we mean influence, to influence, incline, or dispose (psychology understands "affect" as the manifestation of a strong feeling or emotion as distinguished from thought or action). As I have no clear idea how writing is actually learned or its skills quantified, I do not pretend to know how to assess the effect of computers on writing skills, and I have seen enough studies and statistics to know that others too are troubled by the question of measurement (Dobrin, Bridwell and Beach, Herrmann, Gordon). However, from here in the field I can speak as to the influences computers have had on the attitudes of beginning college writers whom I and my colleagues at Bucks have observed and instructed, and on the attitudes of writing teachers as well.

Recent studies in computer-augmented composition instruction suggest that student writing composed on a word processor may be longer, more coherent, and better developed than writing done with pen and paper, or even typewriter (Anhorn, Turner). There have been studies, too, which examine errors in grammar, spelling, vocabulary, and sentence structure in student papers produced by a word processor; some studies prove conclusively that these errors are reduced by word processing (Stanton, Hawisher, Southwell), some prove they are unaffected (Collier, Watkins, Gordon), and some prove the errors increase, that writing at the developmental level at which I teach may actually deteriorate with a word processor (Mendelson, Halio). All the test results seem inconclusive (and often contradictory) thus far.

My interest, however, lies in changed student *attitudes* toward writing, especially writing in the computer lab. I believe that student attitudes have everything to do with success in a writing course: by success I mean that students recognize the need to write clear English, become active learners/participants in the process, and develop genuine enthusiasm for the task. I contend that the impact of the word processor on student attitudes toward writing is wholly beneficial.

Utilizing observation and structured interviews with beginning composition students and faculty who teach writing in a computer lab, I have found a range of positive attitudes toward writing with a word processor. When I arrive at the lab, typically my students are already there, PCs turned on, typing. Attendance in my classes is consistently better on the day we meet in the writing lab and so is promptness; they don't want to lose any time. "Using the word processor takes your mind off having to rewrite the paper," wrote one student. "You will be able to put more energy into the work." Students arrive with all the materials they need for a given assignment—lists, drafts, books, disks—almost without exception. They settle down to work rapidly, pausing only occasionally to engage my attention as I move around the class, because this way, as another student expressed it, "You can get it all down without losing it." Also typical in a lab period is the presence of two or three students from the previous class who will stay and continue their work if permitted. Similarly, when my class is over and I return to my office for an appointment or a meeting, I generally leave behind a handful of my students still working in the lab. And since I have a computer in my office, I am often accompanied there by a disk-toting CMP 107 student who wants to discuss an assignment.

THE COMPUTER LAB ENVIRONMENT

I have always used a workshop approach to teach composition, but workshops that center around a screen of developing text seem to me unexcelled in their ability to stimulate students' creativity and independence from authority. For example, exchanging seats in the lab, viewing an isolated developmental paragraph of a classmate, and composing new paragraphs to precede and follow the original provide students with a liberating exercise in finding an appropriate voice; the returning writer receives a valuable lesson in audience. The resultant collaboration is real: when I approach a group, individuals are talking about their work, not chatting about the weekend. They move easily from screen to screen, laughing and arguing, sharing ideas and developing skills, without seeking direction from me. In the spring 1992 semester, only one student out of thirty I interviewed responded negatively to what a satisfied student called the "laid-back collaborative environment" of the lab, although another complained that there was sometimes "too much going on" for full concentration. Enthusiasm for the lab as workshop was echoed in comparable surveys conducted by four colleagues at Bucks who also offer computer-augmented CMP 107.

I step back sometimes and observe my students: they don't watch the clock. The sounds of zippers and velcro, advance notice that composition class is nearly over, are almost never heard in the computer lab before the end of the period. When I inform students that the class period has ended, I am more likely to hear moans than sighs of relief. They have let go of time.

LEARNING IN THE COMPUTER LAB

My students resent "teaching" in the lab—they resist analyzing an essay from our anthology there, or discussing the merits of conjunctive adverbs vs. subordinate conjunctions. They have been empowered as writers in that room, they and their peers, and seem at times to be part of a strongly united community, unwilling to be distracted from their writing by what they perceive as petty voices or petty concerns, even if the voice or the concern belongs to an instructor.

It would be shortsighted to neglect the positive *effect* of computers on basic writing. For example, I believe my students' work—paragraphs first, and then essays—is longer and better developed than that of developmental writing students who do not compose on word processors. But word processing influences much more than measurable composition skills. Many of my students stumble onto the statistics feature of Professional Write early on and discover to their surprise that their paragraphs and essays expand and grow dramatically as the semester proceeds. They are impressed. A student whose placement in CMP 107 seemed largely based on an inability to generate sufficient words in response to assignments reported with delight at midterm that he was consistently "over the limit," certainly not a problem for him or for me. In addition, computer-augmented developmental writing encourages a far stronger sense of audience than does comparable writing produced by traditional methods, and it should, considering its development. Students interact with their computers, with their writing, and with each other. Sometimes they write alternate endings to the same piece, or scramble the introductory, developmental, and concluding paragraphs of several authors writing on the same topic and evaluate the results;

sometimes they write peer evaluations of their classmates' work, alone or in groups; sometimes they all contribute to one piece of writing projected by liquid crystal display (LCD) onto a screen (no networks here yet). In the lab, they are active learners, writers before students. They write more drafts—four or five is not unusual—and they spend longer on each assignment. It is not unusual for a student to continue to revise a paper long after a "final" draft has been submitted and graded.

Three years ago when I, as a computer novice, first walked into the lab I'd been assigned, a roomful of PCs clustered in groups of threes and fours, I asked, "Where's the front?" In spite of having used a workshop or group approach for many years, I still knew where the front of a classroom was and how to get there and just what that position signified. But in the lab I suddenly felt dislocated and downright nervous about teaching something I had so recently and so incompletely mastered, especially in such a nontraditional setting. Admitting that I didn't know where a student's text had gone or why it wouldn't print out would be easier if I could hold on to at least the literal position of authority, I imagined. Understand that from the front, I could imply, no, I *don't* know what happened to your text, but I'm sure it's something *you've* done.

However, a wonderful thing happened to me in that nontraditional front-less lab. In every class, someone knew more than I about computers. *I* didn't change the student-teacher relationship in the lab; even more than the radical physical layout, my students effected the change, and I gratefully surrendered my absolute authority, first to teach the operation of the computers themselves, and then, quite naturally, to teach the process of student writing. I instead became a kind of coach in the lab, moving from group to group, working with whatever spirit seemed to move a student or collection of students, helping them to help each other. And a second wonderful result followed: if I could reveal my occasional ignorance and accept correction in the lab, so could they. My students seemed to grow less defensive about their work, less fearful of making errors. They cheerfully helped me, they helped each other, and they allowed me to help—but not correct—them. This discovery of our mutual fallibility, our interdependence, set the whole tone of the experience.

Giving up the symbolic position of power and some of the trappings of supreme knowledge that lent me authority in the classroom wasn't easy—but when I saw how much more I could accomplish in this new role, how much more trusting my students were of me, and willing to listen, I happily gave up almost all the props. Sometimes now I sit and write at a machine of my own when my students are writing, and I welcome their visits and their comments. We write together.

I am in a new lab now. The machines are arranged in a W formation with screens facing the center of the room, instead of in clusters, so that students can easily see a monitor screen projected onto the wall by an LCD panel on an overhead projector. I'm not sure I'm as comfortable with this new seating arrangement, but the results still seem remarkable. Any configuration that makes collaboration among students so natural also allows for increased individualized feedback from an instructor. Because each student's work is displayed on a screen, it is completely natural for me, teacher/coach/mentor, to wander around the room, helping students to find new ways of looking at what they have composed, learning myself how different the creative process is for each of them. It is also natural for my students to expect and even desire that I look at their work; the glow of the screen draws me to each of them even as they are drawn to each other's screens. (Privacy, in the sense of the private act, the concealed act, has been wiped out by the word processor. Composing in a word processing lab becomes something of a spectator sport—it's a screen, isn't it? Watching someone write this way is like watching TV or a video game: nothing private about that. Ask any student.

CONCLUSION

My expectations of student work are much higher than in the past. Papers are more coherent and more carefully and thoughtfully developed. One composition student said simply, "Instead of just writing, I think of what I want to say." Papers are long, often very long. Of course I expect papers which look better and I get them. Obviously, no one says, "I can't copy this over one more time." when working on a word processor. Because working with individual students is such an integral part of teaching in a computer lab, I am better able to develop different expectations for each student rather than hold a generalized expectation related only to the assignment. Thus not only do the papers read better, but I am also a better reader of the papers.

A satisfying development here is that I find my students relentlessly critiquing their own work. A common occurrence at the end of a class is a student request to keep the paper, make some changes, and hand me the paper at the end of the day. Instead of gratefully parting with a painfully composed (albeit flawed) paper, the student eagerly transfers his/her disk to the Writing Center to incorporate the ideas of peers and instructor and to revise until he/she is satisfied. One student remarked recently that he could "only see on the screen the direction in which a paper is headed"; he added that he was only able to actually take the paper in that direction after a lab workshop.

Having a computer in my office makes student conferences there very effective; to some extent we can recreate the collaborative mood of the computer lab. It's encouraging. The student sits at the computer and I sit nearby, as we read through the paragraph or theme together, changing and rearranging. Sometimes two or three students come in to work together. Even as I struggle to draw breath in the soda-and-potato-chip-laden air, I continue to marvel at the phenomenon of collaborative writing demonstrated over and over in my office, just the way it occurs in the lab.

What seems especially important in the computer-augmented writing experience is less what the machine or program can do for students, and more what they can learn to do for themselves with its encouragement. I realize that I have made teaching writing with a word processor sound like a religious experience. It isn't. Negative reactions from students in computer-aided sections of composition do occur: "I still have to see it written before I can just type it. I can't type from my head." Also, "I can't really concentrate in the lab because when I write I have to be by myself, and it has to be quiet." And some complain that, unless they have a machine at home, it's often very difficult to get to a computer on campus when it is convenient for them. Objections like the ones above recorded in student conferences aren't common, but they are certainly valid. The one-hour lab isn't always long enough to really benefit some students, especially those with developing typing skills. One tradition-based student finds it "difficult to focus on the teacher" in the lab situation. As noted, many students worry about the unavailability of computers on campus during midterms and finals and about how to coordinate their free time with free machines. Moreover, students swear that certain machines in the library have voracious appetites, consuming valuable documents at a clip. Viruses lurk. From a pedagogical perspective, I still receive papers with run-on sentences and fragments, as well as some beautifully presented papers which somehow manage to be very long, heavily detailed, and completely incoherent.

No matter. I still believe that I am in the midst of an experiment that is going to prove successful. Teaching college writing on a word processor is not traditional in any way: the physical space is different, the tools are different, the student-teacher relationship is different, and the products of the experience—the text and the writers themselves—are different. The advantages of the computer for students of writing are easy to see: it's fast, fast enough to keep pace with their thoughts; it shows them what they have written in a mode that enables them to anticipate their reader's response to that writing; it allows them to make changes without having to either throw away the original or erase until the paper is covered with smudges and holes. Though not discussed here, modems and special software programs can rapidly connect students to networks of information and information collection once thought beyond the reach of the beginning writer and researcher.

But there's more. There is the affect I have been speaking of, the influence of the word processor on the attitudes of beginning writers of college composition and their teachers. In a room in which teachers have chosen to surrender traditional authority, students feel safe to view each other as peers, to collaborate, not to compete. They are able to function along with the instructor as a community, united in their use of an efficient and nonjudgmental writing tool: "My true feelings come out when I type on the screen." I have seen them convinced to give up the notion of paper and pencil as holy objects, of their text as sacred writ: "I can think better when I can rearrange sentences." I have seen them convinced to give up their reliance on a red-pen wielding teacher in the front of the room, even as the teacher gives up the red pen itself in exchange for the motivating power of the computer monitor. I have seen them let go of traditional notions of time and privacy. I have even seen them, some of them, give up their anxiety about writing: "I am not afraid to mess up."

It is the word processor which has converted them to active learners, people who want to write, and the writing instructor who is willing to function as a facilitator may be left nearly breathless by the changes. I still don't know about the *measurable effect* of computers on college writing, because clearly even improvement of the particular text a writer produces is not a measurement of his/her real growth as a writer, but I do know that the change from passive to active learning, from indifference to concern, from dependence on authority to collaboration and self-reliance, is a good one. At least it seems so, from the field.

REFERENCES

Anhorn, Judy. "Collaborative Learning Games for the Computer-Based Writing Course." Computers Across the Curriculum: A Conference on Technology in the Freshman Year. NY, May 29-31, 1992.

Bridwell, Lillian, and Richard Beach, eds. *New Directions in Composition Research.* NY: Guilford, 1984.

Collier, R. "The Word Processor and Revision Strategies." *College Composition and Communication* 34 (1983): 149-55.

Dobrin, David N. "A Limitation on the Use of Computers in Composition." Holdstein and Selfe 40-58.

Gordon, Barbara L. "A Comparison of 3 Style-Checkers for Improving Students' Compositions." Computers Across the Curriculum: A Conference on Technology in the Freshman Year. NY, May 29-31, 1992.

Halio, Marcia Peoples. "Student Writing: Can the Machine Maim the Message?" *Academic Computing* Jan. 1990: 16.

Hawisher, Gail E. "Studies in Word Processing." *Computers and Composition* 4(1986):6-35.

Herrmann, Andrea. "Computers and Writing Research: Shifting Our 'Governing Gaze.'" Holdstein and Selfe 124-135.

Holdstein, Deborah H., and Cynthia L. Selfe. *Computers and Writing: Theory, Research, Practice.* NY: MLA, 1990.

Mendelson, E. "How Computers Can Damage Your Prose." *Times Literary Supplement* 22 February 1991: 28+.

Southwell, Michael G. "The COMP-LAB Writing Modules: Computer-Assisted Grammar Instruction." Wresch 91-104.

Stanton, D. "Discoveries." *Compute!* Sept. 88: 80.

Turner, J. A. "Use of Computers Can Improve Students' Writing Ability, Study Shows." *Chronicle of Higher Education* 7 November 1990: A13+.

Watkins, B.T. "Computer Notes: Word Processors Don't Improve Students' Writing, Study Finds." *Chronicle of Higher Education* 17 April 1991: A19+.

Wresch, William, ed. *The Computer in Composition Instruction: A Writer's Tool.* Urbana: NCTE, 1984.

A Professional Development Needs-Assessment of Computing and Information Technology: A Case Study at Lock Haven University

Punnipa Hossain

Assistant Professor, Foundation Studies and Technology
Consultant, Computing Center
Lock Haven University, Lock Haven, Pennsylvania

Robert O. Little

Computing Center Director
Lock Haven University, Lock Haven, Pennsylvania

This chapter reports on a study conducted in November 1991 at Lock Haven University (LHU). The study had two fundamental objectives: to profile the current state of computing affairs of Lock Haven University (LHU) and to identify the professional development needs with regard to information technology of the LHU faculty and staff. A survey instrument was employed, and the resulting data formed a reference point upon which professional training programs for the academic year 1992-93 were based.

BACKGROUND

The application of advanced technology is a hotly pursued objective in higher education. Being true to the objective, integration of computers into the curriculum is uppermost in the minds of many policy makers and planners. Discovering a kaleidoscope of computerized solutions has led to the hope that technology will be the ultimate panacea for all of the problems in education. Pouring moneys into computing, higher education institutions set aside an average of three percent of their total budgets for the acquisition of information technology during the 1980s (McClure and Williams 1992).

The continued integration of computers into the educational process is also seen as the natural progression of the historical development of society. Alvin Toffler's seminal work (1984), *The Third Wave,* outlined historical change in three distinct waves: the agricultural wave, followed by the industrial revolution, and then the information society (the final culmination). Each one of the evolutionary stages is characterized by distinct social, economic, and cultural traits. The final stage will be revolutionized by microelectronics innovations such as computers, networks, and other major technological forces. As a result, the widespread use of computers is viewed as a consequence of historical inevitability.

The proliferation of microcomputers in the last decade has utterly revolutionized the education system. According to Siegal (1986), the availability of the microcomputer has empowered individuals and small groups to move away from total dependence on big institutions for their computing needs. Flexibility inherent in the use of microcomputers has allowed small work groups and institutions to innovate and design their own computing facilities, thereby being more responsive.

The integration of computers in higher education can be seen from two distinct vantage points. One perspective is that of the institution and the other is from the individual's standpoint. According to Gillespie (1983), institutions have gone through various well-identified stages: (1) computers as substitutes for functions performed manually; (2) computers as tools with new capabilities to perform various innovative tasks; and (3) computers becoming an integral part of the system and forcing the evaluation of an institution's goals and objectives. It is apparent that the implementation of computers in the workplace is a direct result of policy decisions. Modianos and Harman (1991) attempted to identify the four developmental stages of individual adaptation to the computer. According to their work, the four stages are awareness, access, mastery, and application. In other words, incorporating computers into one's work is a conscious and deliberate choice an individual makes.

Over three decades, our continuous experimentation with instructional and administrative computing has produced some encouraging indicators. However, it is argued that educational application of the microcomputer is not without its problems (Tolman and Allred 1984). Critics believe it is time for us to stand back and evaluate both the accomplishments and the failures of this innovative technology in education.

There is no uniformity of opinion among researchers concerning the impact of computers in education. According to some (Bracy 1989; Sloan 1985) computers have fallen short of anticipated outcomes. On the other hand, some educators (Alson 1985; Olson 1988; Kulik et al. 1983; Bright 1983; Kearsley et al. 1987) have noted the effectiveness of the computer as an instructional tool. However, while sorting through the literature, a careful reader can easily isolate a group of educators who are dissatisfied with the outcome of computing, but their criticisms are not directed against the technology per se, but aimed toward the processes of innovation. It is argued that, during the integration of computing into the curriculum, policy planners have frequently neglected the needs of the potential users. As a result, either expensive computers have languished, or the technology was not exploited to its full potential.

Hakken (1992) noted that, in designing an instructional and information system, there are two options to be considered—machine-centered and human-centered approaches. With the machine-centered approach, most basic decisions are about hardware and software. Contrastingly, the human-centered approach focuses on the needs of potential users and the impact of the system on its clients remains central to decisions of the planners. It can be argued that an overemphasis on the machine-centered approach, in planning for an instructional and information system, can alienate potential users.

Stockdill and Morehouse (1992) emphasized that the most frequently overlooked aspects of newly established computer-based learning systems are the needs of potential users. Experts are most often eager to implement technology for experimentation without paying sufficient attention to the users' fundamental needs. Overlooking such a critical factor often results in a dismal outcome. As a result, Riesenberg (1984) concluded that the first and foremost responsibility for the designer of a computer-based learning and information system is to define the needs of the potential users.

THE PRESENT STUDY

In line with the literature in the field, this study presupposed that an objective assessment of the computing needs of LHU's faculty, administrators, and staff was a compulsory prerequisite to establishing a technology agenda. The study also attempted to form a profile of the existing computing environment at LHU. It was the contention of this study that, against the backdrop of the current state of computing affairs, the faculty, administrators, and staff needs assessment would form the catalyst necessary to enable a concurrent financial investment in computer-based instructional and information systems.

Objectives

The study set out to accomplish the following objectives:

1. To establish a baseline view of computing affairs at LHU
2. To identify professional development needs of LHU faculty, administrators, and staff, so that an effective training program could be developed

Rationale

The incorporation of computing, both for learning and for administrative purposes, is a dominant priority set forth in the LHU Strategic Plan published in October 1991. By gauging the computing and training needs, this study provided a foundation for an institutional computing and information technology agenda.

Limitations

The study included only faculty, administrators, and staff as respondents. The exclusion of the student population left a void in the generalizations made in the study. Limited resources and time constraints did not allow for the inclusion of students in the sample. However, it is expected that students will form an essential component of future research endeavors.

A PROFILE OF LHU COMPUTING AFFAIRS

The LHU Computing Center plans and manages the use of information, networking, and data communication technologies for both the main and satellite campuses. The center has been making efforts to provide a rich, computer-based environment for teaching, learning, and research at LHU. The LHU Strategic Plan, spanning 1991-96, places enormous importance on the incorporation of computing and provides for comprehensive training and consulting services to students, faculty, administrators, and staff. The objective is to empower the LHU community, via technological knowledge and skills, so that the university can play a key role in training society for the coming information age. The existing computing environment of LHU is discussed below.

Computing laboratories. LHU has seventeen student computing laboratory facilities, comprising 190 personal computers (fifty Apple IIs, twenty-four Apple Macintoshes, and 116 DOS platforms). Installation of networked computing facilities in student residence halls has just been completed. Among the other laboratory facilities, four are used for instructional purposes.

Software and video library. The library has established a software and videotape lending service to promote computer literacy and usage among students, faculty, and staff. The videos include a series on computer learning.

Technology support group. Campus management has helped to launch a Technology User's Group (TUG). TUG is a campus organization made up of students, staff, and faculty to share ideas about innovations in computing and information technology.

Newsletter. The center publishes a newsletter entitled *The Bridge.* This newsletter informs the university community of the advances in the use of information technology, both in instruction and administration.

Training workshops. The center has organized various training workshops to facilitate the use of computers on campus. The following are some of the workshop training sessions held during past academic years:

- Computer Intimacy Seminars: A series of half-day workshops was conducted on topics such as PC-DOS, Quattro Pro, and Microsoft Word.
- Brownbag Series: From September through December, the center conducted a series of twelve Friday lunch seminars, showing tutorial video materials and demonstrations of PC usage. Subjects included DOS Levels I, II, and III, Windows 3.0, MS Word 5.0, and Quattro.
- Getting Started with E-Mail: Multiple sessions were organized to familiarize faculty and staff members with the network and electronic mail systems.
- Guest Lectures: LHU hosted two distinguished speakers on information technology. The speakers emphasized the multimedia applications in language learning and the use of Internet in professional development.

Professional development. LHU faculty and staff members have attended important national and regional conferences on information technology in education, such as CAUSE, EDUCOM, and the annual West Chester University Connectivity Symposium.

The Writing Center. The Computing Center has assisted the Writing Center in the selection and implementation of additional computing equipment.

Demonstration facility. A demonstration area has been established in one of the computing laboratories, in order to encourage vendors to showcase their technology.

Library automation. The Stevenson Library automation system from Dynix Corporation has been installed. The system will enable public access to the bibliographical database. Instantaneous searches may be conducted according to author, title, subject, and keyword(s).

Connectivity. The campus fiber-optic network is completed. All twenty-five campus buildings are connected to the Computing Center. There are six major campus-wide servers on the 16MB token ring. LHU is poised to connect to the Pennsylvania State System of Higher Education Network (SSHE-net) which will yield Internet access for this rural campus.

Student Information System. The implementation of the CARS Student Information System has just been completed. This application maintains admissions, academic records, schedules, and related information.

Alumni/development. The implementation of the CARS Alumni/Development system has just been completed, allowing for efficient correspondence and fundraising capabilities.

Faculty computers. During the past three years, over sixty computers have been procured for faculty use. Through institutional support for network connections, other faculty members are attaching computers that they own personally.

COMPUTING AND TRAINING NEEDS ASSESSMENT

An objective assessment of computing needs was key to establishing a technology agenda at LHU.

Methodology

A mail questionnaire was developed to collect data. The questionnaire contained both open-ended and closed-ended questions. The questionnaire was pretested among some of the faculty/administrators and staff in the fall of 1991. The pretesting helped to improve, change, and determine what pertinent information was necessary to accomplish the objectives of the study.

LHU had a total of 289 faculty/administrators and 187 staff members. The questionnaire was sent to all of this population. A little over one-half (51 percent or 147 respondents) of the faculty and administrators and one-fourth (25 percent or 46 respondents) of the staff returned the questionnaire. The 25 percent response rate for the staff can be explained by the fact that, even though the questionnaire was sent to all staff, many do not use computers in their work. The total response rate of the questionnaire is 41 percent (see Table 3.1).

Findings

The findings can be broken down into two categories: the current state of computer usage/knowledge and computing and training needs assessment.

Current state of computer respondents' usage/knowledge. Data indicated that an overwhelming majority of the respondents (85 percent) use a computer in their work. Among those users, three-fourths (75 percent) use IBM or IBM compatibles. The remaining respondents (25 percent) use Macintosh and Apple computers. Three-fourths of the computer users (75 percent), operate computers owned by the university. Conversely, one-quarter (25 percent) use personally owned

Table 3. 1 Distribution of Questionnaires

	Faculty/ Administrators	Staff	Total
Questionnaires sent out:	289	187	476
Questionnaires returned:	147	046	193
	(51%)	(25%)	(41%)

machines. Data on participant skill level indicates that over two-thirds of the users (67 percent) rated their skills as intermediate or advanced. Another 28 percent believe that they are beginners.

Word processing is the most widely used software among the respondents (93 percent). Among the other applications used are spreadsheets (46 percent), database (42 percent), communications (27 percent) and desktop publishing (22 percent). More than one-third of the respondents (35 percent) were linked up with the LHU Network (see Table 3.2).

Computing and training needs assessment. Over two-thirds of the respondents (65 percent) who are not linked up with the LHU network would like to connect. The respondents also noted a list of workshops and seminars they wish to attend. The top ten training topics requested were access to campus network (40 percent), electronic mail (37 percent), orientation to Internet (28 percent), Microsoft Windows (28 percent), getting started with IBM and compatibles (24 percent), Microsoft Word for Windows (23 percent), Microsoft Word (22 percent), desktop publishing software (22 percent), using DOS (22 percent), and Statistical Analysis System (20 percent).

A traditional group session was the preferred learning method for over one-half of the respondents (51 percent). Another 32 percent noted individual tutoring and tutorial software as their preferred method. Tutorial videotape was chosen by another 19 percent of the respondents (see Table 3.3).

CONCLUSIONS AND IMPLICATIONS

This assessment of LHU's current state of computer knowledge and usage at work was greatly encouraging. A significant majority of the faculty, administrators, and staff already use a computer at work, and over two-thirds perceive their skills to be at intermediate or advanced levels. In other words, the respondents are well prepared and are willing to accept the challenges of some of the newer technology. A closer look at the application software indicated an encouraging level of computer use for both administrative and instructional purposes. The computing and training needs assessment data show that the respondents are further willing, even anxious, to incorporate various other aspects of the technology into their work. To grow academically and also to foster administrative efficiency, computer "knowledge workers" *must* network. Educators are vocal in their opinion that the future needs of academia are dependent on the movement toward campus, intra-campus, and extra-campus network connectivity. In that scenario, computing and communications resources are openly accessible by faculty, staff, and students. Confirming this, the study showed the top three training topics requested were pertinent to computer networking.

The respondents' interest in training for statistical packages, authoring tools, desktop publishing, spreadsheets, word processing, and other application

Table 3.2 Current State of Computer
Usage/Knowledge of the Respondents

a) Computer usage in work:

	% N=193
Users	85
Non-users	<u>15</u>
Total	100

b) Types of *most* frequently used computers:

	% N=165*
IBM or IBM Compatible (DOS only)	41
IBM or IBM Compatible (Windows Capable)	34
Macintosh	22
Apple IIe	<u>03</u>
Total	100

*Only the users are included here.

c) Ownership of the computers used by the respondents:

	% N=165*
University property	75
Belongs to the respondents themselves	44
Others	06

* Some respondents reported using university-owned as well as self-owned computers.

d) User skill levels as stated by the respondents:

	% N=165
Intermediate	50
Beginner	28
Advanced	17
No response	<u>05</u>
Total	100

e) Types of applications used by the respondents who stated using computers in their work:

	% N=165*
Word Processor	93
Spreadsheets	46
Databases	42
Communications	27
Desktop Publishing	22
Test Bank	18
Presentation Software	11
Authoring Tools	07
Others	32

* Most respondents reported using more than one type of these applications.

f) Connectivity of the respondents' computer to the LHU network:

	% N=165
Yes	35
No	64
No response	<u>01</u>
Total	100

software points to the fact that there is a strong desire on the part of the respondents to increase their individual productivity and quality.

Table 3.3 Computing and Training Needs Assessment

a) Respondents willingness to link with the LHU network:

	% N=106*
Yes	65
No	08
Do not know	25
No response	02
Total	100

*Only those who were not connected with LHU network are included here.

b) Workshops and seminars respondents wish to attend:

	%* N=188**
Access to Campus Network	40
Electronic Mail	37
Orientation to Internet	28
Microsoft Windows	28
Getting Started with IBM & Compatibles	24
Microsoft Word for Windows	23
Desktop Publishing Software	22
Microsoft Word	22
Using DOS	22
Statistical Analysis System (SAS)	20
HyperCard (Macintosh authoring tool)	17
ToolBook (IBM authoring tool)	14
Quattro Pro	12
System 7.0 for Macintosh	11
Presentation Software	11
LinkWay (IBM authoring tool)	10
Getting Started with Macintosh	09
Paradox	06
Others	14

*Some respondents stated their needs to attend more than one seminar or workshop.

**Five respondents did not respond to this question.

c) Respondents' preferred learning method:

	%* N=188**
Group Session	51
Individual Tutoring	32
Tutorial software	31
Videotape	19
Others	09

*Some respondents have more than one preferred learning method.

**Five respondents did not respond to this question.

As a result of this study, we have hastened to design an effective training program for LHU faculty, administrators, and staff. The conceptual basis of the training program stems from Hazari's (1991) Content Area Training Model. According to the model, the content area of the proposed model is organized in a hierarchical structure with the following three levels:

1. Awareness
2. Development of skills
3. Application of knowledge

The awareness about the technology and its application will create an itch of curiosity among the potential users. The consequence of this awareness will result in computer literacy through hands-on training. Ultimately, this will result in the application of knowledge in work situations. Faculty familiarity with computers is an essential prerequisite to their incorporation into the teaching-learning process. Fleit (1987) noted that the more faculty members become aware of the potential of computers and acquire the skills, the more students will benefit from their education. In other words, faculty motivation and utilization of computing are necessary preconditions for increased computer literacy among students. However, critics argue that institutions of higher education have been slow to incorporate computers into their curriculum. Greene's (1991) findings of a recent survey of college faculty at three medium-sized colleges do support the assertion that only a minority of faculty has integrated computers into their teaching. Universities and colleges throughout the country are reorganizing their computing environment so that an effective and efficient computing and information system can be developed.

Only a few months after the needs assessment, the Computing Center began implementing a detailed plan for workshops, training sessions, brown-bag discussions, etc. All the workshops and training sessions for the coming academic years are based on the academic and professional development needs of LHU faculty, administrators, and staff.

LHU is assigning vast importance to computing and information technology as it relates to academic and administrative effectiveness. The relative importance placed on technology in the university's Strategic Plan speaks directly to the perceived essential value. The information technology milieu of LHU shows great promise and is generating high levels of excitement and anticipation in the community. The Computing Center can capitalize the momentum and provide leadership in preparing the community for versatile electronic and information technology.

ACKNOWLEDGMENTS

The authors would like to express their appreciation to the faculty and staff of Lock Haven University for their gracious cooperation in this project.

REFERENCES

Alson, D. R. 1985. Computers as tools of the intellect. *Educational Researcher* 14:7.

Bracey, G. 1989. Individual learning styles disregarded by computer-based instruction. *Electronic Learning* 8(7): 16-17.

Bright, G. W. 1983. Explaining the efficiency of computer assisted instruction. *AEDS Journal* 16(3): 144-152.

Fleit, L. H. 1987. Computing America's campuses. *Electronic Learning* 6(6): 18-23.

Gillespie, R. 1983. Computing and higher education: The revolution is through the gates. *Forum for Liberal Education* 5(6): 2-8.

Greene, B. B. 1991. A survey of computer integration into college courses. *Educational Technology* 31(7): 37-47.

Hakken, D. 1992. Culture-centered computing: Social policy and development of new information technology in England and the U.S. *Human Organization* 50(4): 406-423.

Hazari, S. 1991. Microcomputer training for higher education faculty. *Educational Technology* 31(10): 48-50.

Kearsley, G., Hunter, B. and Siedel, P. 1987. Two decades of computer-based instruction projects: What have we learned? (Part II). *Technological Horizons in Education Journal* 10(4): 86-96.

Kulik, J. A., Bangert, R. L. and Williams, G. W. 1983. Effects of computer-based teaching on secondary school students. *Journal of Education* 75(1): 19-26.

McClure, P. A. and Williams, P. 1992. Metamorphosis in computing services at Indiana University. *Cause/Effect* 15(1): 15-25.

Modianos, D. and Harman, J. 1991. Computing in the curriculum: A case study. *Collegiate Microcomputer* 9(4): 193-201.

Olson, J. 1988. *Microworlds: Computers and the Culture of the Classroom.* New York: Pergamon

Riesenberg, B. 1984. Selecting computer hardware and software. In *Enhancing Student Development with Computers.* C. Johnson and K. Pyle (eds.). San Francisco: Jossey-Bass Publishing. pp. 35-43.

Siegal, L., 1986. Microcomputers: From movement to industry. *Monthly Review* 38: 110-117

Sloan, D. 1985. Introduction: On raising critical questions about the computer in education. In *The Computer in Education. A Critical Perspective.* D. Sloan (ed.). New York: Teachers' College Press. pp. 1-10.

Stockdill, S. H. and Morehouse, D. L. 1992. Critical factors in the successful adaptation of technology: A checklist based on TDC findings. *Educational Technology* 32(1):75-58.

Toffler, A. 1984. *The Third Wave.* New York: William Morrow.

Tolman, M. and Allred, R., 1984. *The Computer and Education.* Washington, DC.: NEA Association.

Chapter

4

Computing in the Curriculum at Wellesley College

Alan Shuchat

Professor of Mathematics
Wellesley College, Wellesley, Massachusetts

This chapter describes the efforts made at Wellesley College over the past few years to broaden the use of computing by faculty and students and to extend computing applications across the curriculum. It discusses ways Wellesley has found to help faculty members overcome some of the barriers they face in introducing computing and other technologies into their courses and gives examples of curricular projects across a range of disciplines within the liberal arts. It also touches on issues of the faculty reward structure that will need to be resolved before curricular computing can become more widespread.

SUPPORT FOR COMPUTING IN THE CURRICULUM

Wellesley College is a selective, independent four-year liberal arts college for women located in Wellesley, Massachusetts, a suburb of Boston. There are approximately 2,200 students at Wellesley and a 10:1 student to faculty ratio. The faculty is divided about evenly between women and men.

In order to help make curricular computing a reality, Wellesley seeks to provide easy access for faculty and students to appropriate equipment and software, training to use these resources, assistance to faculty in identifying potential applications of computing in various disciplines, and technical support to help bring an idea to fruition in the classroom.

Wellesley has chosen a two-pronged approach of supporting students and a broad base of faculty at a reasonable but modest level, while providing more substantial resources for a small number of faculty innovators. Desktop computers have been provided to nearly all faculty members who want them, with a mix of Macintoshes, IBMs and compatibles, and UNIX workstations connected to a campus-wide network. Faculty and students have free accounts on the main academic VAX cluster and several departmental machines, and an ever-increasing number of classrooms, laboratories, and study areas are equipped with computers. The library and course catalogs are available over the network, and E-mail, bulletin boards, and the Internet are now a part of campus life. Students and faculty have access to a range of hardware and software at attractive prices at a campus computer store. Over 60 percent of the students now have their own computers and soon each dormitory room should be connected to the network. Easy access to computing in the dorms, as well as in the academic buildings and libraries, is needed for faculty to be able to give extensive course assignments that require computers.

The Office of Information Technology Services (ITS), which addresses the needs of both academic and administrative users, holds extensive training classes, and every college computer comes with a coupon that can be redeemed for one-on-one help. A telephone hotline is available and advice can often be given without delay. ITS staff liaisons help faculty learn about the range of curricular software that is available, solve technical problems, and offer assistance to those faculty members who wish to create their own software. Curricular applications, including interactive audio and video, are available for exploration, and a new Learning and Teaching Center have expanded the resources on which faculty can draw. A newsletter updates the community periodically on the computing resources that are available and on innovative work in progress.

Faculty members, rather than the computing staff, are often the ones who can best explain to other faculty how a particular technology or application can be valuable in teaching and research. "High-tech" teaching talks and an annual Computer Fair bring faculty from many disciplines together to demonstrate work and share ideas. At the fair, a free lunch and vendor giveaways attract many members of the college community.

Faculty members with curricular projects that involve instructional technology and require a significant investment of time can apply for summer stipends to assist them in their work. While the stipends are modest in size (up to $2,500), they provide an incentive for faculty to devote some effort in this direction as they balance the competing demands on their time. They may be used to compensate faculty time or student assistance or to purchase software and materials. Stipends are awarded for projects having a direct impact on a particular course but are also used to support more general proposals, especially in departments that are new to technology in the curriculum. About five to ten faculty members per year have received support through stipends funded by the Dean's Office and grants from the Howard Hughes Medical Foundation and the New England Consortium for Science Education (NECUSE). Some projects make use of existing commercial, shareware, or freeware programs. For others no suitable software exists and faculty are developing their own programs, sometimes with student programming assistance.

Technology is most likely to be an effective teaching tool when it is easy to use and available on short notice. Wellesley has outfitted two classrooms in the Science Center with computers for each pair of students and with computer and projection equipment for the instructor. Each room has a whiteboard and a large projection screen and lighting that makes both easy to read at the same time. The rooms are used mainly for lectures and lab activities in mathematics and computer science and are available after hours for student assignments. Funding from the National Science Foundation's (NSF) ILI program, Apple, and IBM, together with college matching funds, was used to outfit these rooms. Computing equipment for science laboratories has been upgraded with the addition of workstations and higher-end PCS and Macintoshes used by students in chemistry and the other physical sciences. This equipment was funded by grants from NSF and AT&T. A computer-equipped writing classroom has been used extensively by more than a dozen writing instructors, as well as by foreign-language instructors. An improved computer lab for the social sciences is used frequently in economics and sociology. Similar facilities will be installed shortly for the humanities. Computers with liquid crystal display (LCD) projection pads can be wheeled into classrooms that do not have permanent installations, and a few notebook computers are available for faculty borrowing. The college is promoting the use of software that runs on all major platforms, so that it will be easy for faculty and students to use the same applications regardless of the machines they use and to exchange files without difficulty.

EXAMPLES OF COMPUTING IN THE CURRICULUM

A range of curricular computing activities exists at Wellesley. The examples presented in this section are only meant to be representative, and several interesting projects must be omitted because of space constraints.

Physicist Ted Ducas combines video and computer technology in Project AVID (Active Video Instructional Development), a winner of EDUCOM's Joe Wyatt Challenge Award. Students record physical phenomena on videotape in the lab or in the field and use the tapes as a source of data for calculations and testing hypotheses. Computers are used in conjunction with the video technology for data analysis and extracting information from digitized images. For example, in studying the laws of motion, a student may use MathCad to make calculations from a videotape of a falling apple. In mathematics, Patrick Morton has worked with Professor Ducas to have students use these techniques to connect calculus with real world phenomena.

In chemistry, William "Flick" Coleman uses spreadsheets and mathematical software to explore a greater variety of examples than is possible in a text and standard problem sets. Depending on the level of the course, this may be done by the instructor as a demonstration or directly by the students. In addition to using Quattro Pro for spreadsheet calculations, Professor Coleman uses PC programs such as MathCad for preparing interactive documents mixing text, calculations, and graphics, Derive for doing algebraic manipulations, and MINSQ for curve fitting. Adele Wolfson's biochemistry students use software from Molecular Simulations on Silicon Graphics workstations for molecular modeling projects such as protein design.

In economics, Ann Witte's students use SAS on the VAX or Excel on the PC to analyze economic data with econometric methods. They use data sets available at Wellesley and also download data from remote sites such as Data Resources, Inc. Students have direct access to up-to-date and detailed information on the U.S. and international economies. All assignments in the econometrics course are distributed across the network, and much of the interaction outside of class between the instructor and students takes place electronically.

Sociologist Tom Cushman's students in popular culture and mass communications courses make extensive use of a lab of three Macs with video digitizers, funded by NSF. Students incorporate digital video clips of television news, movies, and advertising into their papers, which are submitted on magneto-optical disks. Project topics have included comparisons of news coverage of the Vietnam and Gulf wars and comparisons of "buddy films."

Several faculty have written their own software, some of which has been published. Most are using HyperCard for the Macintosh or ToolBook for the PC, since these development tools are generally easier to use than other languages.

Classicist Ray Starr has written *Latin 201*, a ToolBook program for students to use on the PC when studying Vergil's *Aeneid*. Students can read passages from the Latin text and click on hotwords to see English definitions, which are visible only briefly to help keep the focus on the original language. Clicking on buttons brings up quotations from related Latin texts and questions for guided study. Students can get general help with the literary and historical background of Rome in Vergil's time, as well as look up points of grammar.

Ma and Robert Smitheram used HyperCard to write HyperChinese, a program for elementary and intermediate language instruction that received an EDUCOM Distinguished Humanities Software Award. The program uses graphics, digitized sound, and animation to help students learn grammar patterns and vocabulary. A modular design makes it possible to use the program in a flexible way and adapt it to many texts. HyperChinese uses built-in sound to speak preprogrammed words and phrases and also accepts sound input from students. *HyperChinese* is published on CD-ROM by Cheng & Tsui (Boston).

In mathematics, Alan Shuchat and Fred Shultz have written *The Joy of Mathematica* for use alongside Mathematica in calculus, linear algebra, and differential equations courses. This Mac program is written in SuperCard and provides a point-and-click interface to accompany Mathematica's command-line interface. Using *Joy*, students generate Mathematica commands without needing to learn the proper syntax in advance, but they can learn it as they go. They can perform routine tasks such as graphing, algebra, differentiation, integration, and

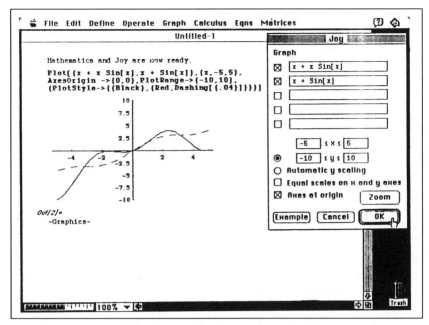

Figure 4.1 Students point-and-click in *The Joy of Mathematica* to create commands for Mathematica to execute.

matrix operations more rapidly and accurately than by hand, leaving more time to focus on underlying principles and on richer problems. Figure 4.1 illustrates how *Joy* is used. *Joy* is published by Addison-Wesley (Reading, MA).

In computer science, Eleanor Lonske, Director of Information Technology Services, uses HyperCard stacks to illustrate fundamental notions such as queues and hash tables and to animate algorithms. These stacks, written by ITS Instructional Technology Specialist Ken Freundlich, are designed for the instructor to use in demonstrations rather than for students to use in assignments. For example, one stack uses graphics, animation, and sound to show how the length of a queue changes over time.

Physicist Yue Hu has written HyperCard stacks to illustrate projectile motion and Gauss's Law. Students use these stacks as aids for understanding principles of motion and of electric fields. For example, students can simulate the flight of a projectile and see how varying the flight parameters affects the flight path. Graphics show how the horizontal and vertical components of the velocity vector behave as the projectile moves along its path.

In Russian, Tom Hodge uses Pesnia, a ToolBook program that he and ITS Instructional Technology Specialist Susan Hafer have developed. With Pesnia, which means "song" in Russian, students control music CDs of Russian songs and study their texts in English or in the original. Many of these songs are musical settings of Russian poems, and Professor Hodge uses Pesnia in both elementary language and upper-level literature classes.

Other curricular uses of computing are found in courses in anthropology, astronomy, biological sciences, classical civilization (using the Perseus interactive database), geology, Italian, language studies, music, philosophy, political science, psychology, studio art, and writing (using Daedalus).

Many of the departments in which these activities are now taking place have cost very little to run in the past, apart from compensation. The startup costs for computerization and the continuing costs for training, maintenance, upgrading hardware and software, etc., will make it more expensive to operate these departments in the future. Wellesley has already begun to incorporate the costs of more widespread curricular computing into the budget and planning process.

THE FACULTY REWARD STRUCTURE

One question about all such activities is how they fit into the institutional structure for tenure, promotion, and salary increases. Wellesley College values both teaching and research very highly when evaluating faculty work, and the most successful faculty members have significant achievements in each domain. Adapting the curriculum to take advantage of new possibilities in ways that are effective in promoting student learning is, of course, a strongly positive factor in evaluations of teaching. Such innovation helps to demonstrate that a faculty member will remain vigorous and productive in his/her teaching over the long span of a tenured appointment.

Like many other institutions, Wellesley will need to decide how to "count" software development when evaluating scholarly activity. Both untenured and tenured faculty are involved in computing projects and as they devote significant time to writing software, it will be important to have clear policies on how to evaluate this work. Of course, this is particularly important for faculty without tenure. For example, if the software is in support of research, will it be treated as the equivalent of a research paper or monograph? If it is in support of teaching, how will it compare to a textbook? What forms of publication and peer review should be expected? What institutional support should be provided and what should the institution's role be in any commercialization of the results? Institutions should recognize the legitimacy and importance of these activities as they evaluate the work of their faculty members, and to establish clearly formulated guidelines for doing this.

In order for curricular computing to become more widespread, faculty will need to be assured that the time they spend perfecting their command of the new technology and its use in the classroom will be considered and rewarded appropriately. Colleges and universities, in turn, must communicate clearly the ground rules for tenure, promotion, and salary increases. They will also need to help provide support in time, equipment, and technical assistance to enable faculty to meet the institution's expectations during the evaluation process.

Part Two: Multimedia

Chapter

5

Some Experiences Integrating Electronic Media into the Art and Design Curriculum

Wayne Draznin

Computer Arts Program Coordinator
Cleveland Institute of Art, Cleveland, Ohio

Founded in 1882, Cleveland Institute of Art (CIA) is a small independent college of art and design, offering the Bachelor of Fine Arts degree. CIA is well-known for its emphasis on the basics; the mandatory two-year foundations program focuses on the development of skills in painting, drawing, and design. Upon completing foundations, students enter into one of fifteen independent, medium-based courses of major study in areas ranging from ceramics to industrial design.

By the mid-1980s, it had become clear that the now ubiquitous computer could not be ignored in providing an education in the arts. Design shops were increasingly turning to computers as their main production tools, desktop publishing and CAD quickly replacing X-Acto knives and modeling. The non-applied, or "fine," arts were not ignored by this revolution. The versatility offered by designing on computer, combined with powerful yet easy to use software, appealed to many artists working in traditional forms such as sculpture and painting. Other artists were finding, in electronic media itself, a unique way of commenting upon contemporary culture. If an arts education was to remain relevant, these realities had to be reflected in the curriculum.

INTEGRATING THE COMPUTER INTO COURSES

In 1984, an ad hoc faculty committee was formed to look into approaches to academic computing at CIA. It determined, in keeping with the school's general practice, that the first step was integration of computer applications within the foundations program. This would set the basis for further developments within the major departments. The committee began looking for a versatile platform which could prepare students for future work containing the following:

- an easy-to-learn interface
- color-capable paintbox software
- word processing software suitable for English Composition courses
- relatively inexpensive hardware and software, so that multiple stations could be purchased

Shortly afterwards, Commodore introduced the Amiga A1000. This machine seemed to fit the bill, and the school purchased five units on a trial basis. (Although it was initially believed that these machines would be quickly outmoded, several continue in use.)

At the time, all of CIA's administrative functions were still being done manually. Working with members of the faculty committee, the development department applied for a Federal Department of Education Title III (Institutional Strengthening) Grant, which was awarded in 1985. Over three years, the grant provided for these activities:

- computerizing the administration
- establishing a first-year computer course within the foundations program and developing related computer-based assignments in second-year foundations design classes
- educating the faculty in computer applications

With the Title III Grant funds, a student computer lab was established containing seventeen Amigas (a mix of older A1000 and newer A2000 machines), digitizing stations and a large-screen monitor for instruction. A one-semester, 1.5 credit Computer Basics course became part of the first-year foundations curriculum. During the second year of the grant, computer arts faculty began working with other foundations instructors in developing class assignments. Over the summer, faculty workshops were conducted to develop familiarity with the system and software, and they were continued with funding from a Lilly Foundation Incentive grant.

CIA's approach has always emphasized accessibility. The ad hoc faculty committee initiated this approach when it decided that many low-end units were preferable to a few high-end ones. While a standard Amiga does not have the capabilities of, say, a Silicon Graphics workstation, many more students can be taught with a roomful of Amigas. The skills they develop are easily transferable to other platforms. Also, particularly important for artists, they learn that the computer is an approachable, usable medium which will remain within reach upon leaving school. An open lab policy was established in the beginning, which remains in effect today. Staffed by student work aides, the lab is kept open at least forty hours per week for use by any CIA student. (Lab work outside of class time is also a required part of the Computer Basics course.)

The Title III Grant provided further funding for the purchase of equipment for an intermediate level lab: three Macintosh II CXs, several more Amigas, and an Amiga-based animation/video editing station. This lab was established when I joined the faculty of CIA in the fall of 1989, and a part-time lab manager was hired to coordinate the functioning of the two labs.

As first conceived, the Computer Basics course tried to be everything for everyone, providing an overview of paintbox, image manipulation, and word processing applications. While this emphasized the "meta" character of the tool, it did not lay a strong basis for continued work. Concepts flew by so quickly that students had little opportunity to consider how these concepts might fit in with their own approach to art and design. They found it hard to focus on and retain the information, and the planned-for integration of computer assignments in the sophomore year proved to be difficult.

Further, it had been presumed that the foundations computer study would be added to once students began their major studies. But, as yet, there were no concrete plans for how this was to take place. When the Title III Grant came through, the original ad hoc faculty committee was disbanded.

COMPUTERS IN ADVANCED COURSES

It was clear that the institution was ready for a more organized strategy for dealing with new technology. The first step was reorienting the Computer Basics course. CIA was an art and design school; the class needed to center on that aspect of the computer. Computer Basics was restructured to take students through working with RGB color, image digitization, and paintbox work, and then touch on animation and multi-image presentation. A broad overview of the tool's imaging capabilities is presented, while elements such as word processing are not discussed.

Additionally, CIA added two intermediate-level elective courses: Experimental Computer Imaging and 3D Modeling and Animation. Experimental Computer Imaging extends the knowledge gained in the Computer Basics class, further exploring image manipulation, hard-copy alternatives, the computer/video interface, and contemporary issues in the medium. The 3D Modeling and Animation course is an introduction to modeling, rendering, and animation software, taught by an experienced sculptor. Both of these courses are repeatable, and they often focus on a particular topic. (One semester, for example, Experimental Computer Imaging addressed Art in Cyberspace: Using the Telecommunications Networks as an Art Form.)

With the cooperation of the photography department, in October 1989 a proposal was developed for an extended electronic arts curriculum involving computer arts and video arts. The video program, under the aegis of the photography department, had, for complex reasons, become moribund. CIA viewed the advances being made in the computer area as an opportunity to bring this critically important medium back to life at the college. The institute's underlying philosophy was stated in the proposal's opening:

> Over the past two decades electronic media have moved from the peripheries of art-making into the mainstream. These art forms have a unique capacity to speak to the era which created them; their exploration is an exploration of our times. They have come to function as basic tools for contemporary artists.
>
> Electronic art forms display an inherent refusal to recognize the traditional boundaries separating one medium from another, bringing an interdisciplinary approach to the forefront. This presents new challenges and opportunities to traditional arts education. We must look to teaching these new forms in a manner which recognizes both their unique characters and their inter-relationships with traditional disciplines.

The proposal addressed immediate equipment needs of the computer and video areas, suggested specific curricular developments for the next two semesters, and offered, as a long range perspective, a belief that, "student interest will eventually lead to implementation of a major in these areas. This would include a range of subject-oriented studio classes, many of which would involve coordination with other departments."

COMPUTING AND TRAINING NEEDS ASSESSMENT

Rather than acting directly upon this proposal's recommendations, the administration decided to expand on the concept, applying it to the entire institution. In November, the vice president for academic affairs organized a Computer/Video Committee which included faculty from computer arts, foundations, industrial design, graphic design, photography, and metals/jewelry. Key administrative personnel were also involved so that the curricular recommendations could be developed with an understanding of budgetary and fundraising realities and so that the implementation of those recommendations could be facilitated. The committee was charged with developing an overall understanding of the institute's electronic media needs and providing detailed recommendations regarding curriculum, equipment, and structure. It thus found itself faced with a number of questions:

- What was the attitude of the faculty towards new technology?
- In which departments was rapid progress most critical?
- What areas could be pushed forward to serve as models?

CIA decided to begin with a simple survey of the entire faculty. The response (or lack of response) would demonstrate intensity of interest, and, hopefully, turn up additional resources. A questionnaire was distributed, asking the following:

- How would you see using computers in your area? Would this take the form of occasional workshops or regular class usage?
- How important a role does the computer play in your field? How important is it for your classes to involve computer usage?
- Do you currently use or do you plan on using computers in your own work? If so, how?

While the response rate was only about twenty percent, those who did respond were quite helpful. (An occasional disgruntled traditionalist did take the trouble to answer the questions. My favorites were the terse "None. Not at all. No." from a soon-to-retire studio professor, and the "I prefer the students to work in longhand" from a writing teacher.) Most respondents were enthusiastic but clearly not very knowledgeable about computer applications. Several, however, offered detailed suggestions, including hardware and software recommendations.

As committee chair, I held meetings with most of the department chairs to gain a more detailed understanding of their views. After analyzing the survey responses, we met individually with faculty who had offered concrete suggestions for progress. A number of students brought their concerns to the committee, as well. We also reviewed the course offerings at other art and design schools, to learn how they were offering electronic media.

It was immediately clear that the most pressing needs were, in addition to video, in the applied arts areas of graphic design and industrial design. Computer knowledge was critical for students entering the job market in these fields. It was also clear that concrete possibilities existed in a number of other areas. Based on the survey responses and subsequent discussions, we worked with key personnel from each of these areas to develop a detailed proposal encompassing the particular importance of electronic media to that area, curriculum changes required, and equipment needs. These proposals served as our final report, issued in January 1990.

The proposals from computer arts and video echoed (with further detail regarding faculty and equipment needs) those made in the October 1989 proposal. The graphic design department, noting the primacy of the computer in that field, concluded that "while this does not require changes in our course offerings, it does require a re-orientation of those courses" around computer usage. They proposed the outfitting of a Macintosh II-based lab for students in that department. Industrial design felt that curricular changes could best be developed over time based on concrete experience. They also proposed, as an interim solution, a Macintosh II-based lab for their students, with further training for faculty.

A detailed proposal for a CAD/CAM station came from the metals and jewelry department, with a similar proposal for a computerized loom from the fiber department. Liberal arts proposed reintroducing word processing through their first-year English Composition courses, utilizing the computer arts equipment. The library, responsible for instructional media, sought an Instructional Media Center "for general equipment, technical support, and improved video and computer use in instruction."

The committee's report provided concrete direction, and Robert Mayer, the institute's president, now took direct personal charge of the efforts to implement it. Development of grant proposals had been paralleling our investigations and were meeting with success. (These proposals were developed by the president with the vice-president for external affairs, in consultation with committee members.)

As a result, immediate steps were taken regarding the applied arts and video areas. The computer arts Macintosh systems were transferred to graphic design and industrial design. Additional equipment was purchased for full-scale dedicated labs in each of these areas, for the exclusive use of their students. The video program was reestablished, with up-to-date cameras and editing equipment (an SVHS manual editing station and an SVHS computer-controlled editing station).

With the support of Commodore Business Machines and a local funding source, we added eleven Amiga A2000HD machines to the computer arts intermediate lab. Several of our original A1000s were sold at that time, while others were given to departments within the school for student access.

The fiber department was in an excellent position to serve as a model for integrating traditional and contemporary techniques. The institute's women's committee raised the funds for a Macintosh-based computerized loom. The department was also given two of the Amiga A1000s, obtaining weaving design software for these machines.

CONCLUSION

With these advances, computer usage has been increasing steadily on campus and new inroads into the curriculum continue to develop. In the spring 1992 semester, word processing became a part of the first-year English Composition course. During 1993, I undertook a study aimed at expanding the Computer Basics course. Based on faculty recommendations, this became a two-semester course in the fall 1993 semester, with students taking one semester each of their two foundation years. The class now spends more time on issues which this tool brings to the fore, as well as creative approaches to output forms, animation, multimedia presentation, and desktop publishing. The graphic design Macintosh lab has quadrupled in size, the photography department has added a Macintosh for photo manipulation/retouching, and there was discussion of updating the Computer Basics lab. It is clear that at Cleveland Institute of Art, the computer has begun to play the integral role of contemporary practice in art and design demands.

Chapter

6

Developing a Multimedia Computer/Video Environment in a Comprehensive Community College

S. James Corvey

Director of Educational Computing
Mountain View College, Dallas, Texas

Mountain View College (MVC) is the community learning center for thousands of people in southwestern Dallas County. Opening its doors in the fall of 1970, MVC is the second of seven colleges in the Dallas County Community College District. Located in the southwestern section of Oak Cliff in Dallas, the college serves residents of South Dallas, Oak Cliff, Duncanville, Cedar Hill, and parts of Grand Prairie.

The various programs at MVC are designed to meet a broad range of educational needs. Students may elect to complete their first two years of study leading toward a bachelor's degree or to prepare for a career in an occupational or technical area. Many students attend Mountain View to train for an entirely new career opportunity. Noncredit courses are also available for people of all ages seeking personal enrichment, cultural awareness, or participation in productive leisure-time activities.

The Mountain View student body of more than 6,500 students is composed of people of all ages and all backgrounds representing a cross section of the community which the college serves. This rich opportunity to interact with people from all walks of life is an important part of the educational process and is well established in the Mountain View tradition.

RECOGNIZING THE CONSTRAINTS

Introducing the use of a broad-based technology into a comprehensive community college presents several fundamental constraints which must be addressed. Perhaps the number one constraint is budget. Colleges across the nation are facing budget reductions, making paradigm shifts in instruction very difficult. The president of MVC knew, up front, that technology costs money—big money! To move to technology-based educational programming, an institution must be prepared to shift priorities in order to insure funds are available to implement both the hardware and software components.

Securing faculty commitment and support is a second major constraint when introducing technology. Even for faculty members who have grown up with multimedia applications as a part of their program, the transition to modern computer-based interactive video is significant. Learning the new skills and developing instruction based on "smart" technologies require a major commitment to both learning and development on the part of faculty and support staff.

Part-time teaching faculty make up a significant portion of most community college faculties, often with only limited on-campus time. Integrating these adjunct faculty members into the mainstream of technology-based instruction is a major challenge to overall effectiveness which must be taken into consideration in the planning process.

The following are major planning categories and questions that require consideration:

1. Budget

   - Can the college support the transition to a multimedia technology-based instructional mode?
   - What level of transition can be made?
   - With dollars available, what implementation time frame is feasible?
   - What new production and support facilities will be needed?
   - What type and number of support personnel will be required?
   - Can the college commit to upgrading equipment and software as newer technologies become available?
   - Can the college support all faculty who want to become involved in making use of technology?

2. Faculty

   - How will faculty be identified to participate in implementing programs?
   - How will support and training for faculty be provided?
   - How will teaching workloads be determined for faculty members who are making extensive uses of technology?

Leadership at the top is critical to the success of any major initiative, cutting across broad areas of the college. It is important for the president to clarify and focus the vision of the institution as it relates to instructional quality and the pursuit of excellence. Direct involvement in the planning process, support of budgetary changes necessary to fund the projects, and the removal of roadblocks are important roles for the president to orchestrate. In addition, the president needs to be "on record" as supportive and committed to the success of the shift to a technology-based instructional concept.

INTERACTIVE LASER DISC DEVELOPMENT FOR SOPHOMORE LITERATURE INSTRUCTION

While computer applications in the classroom have impacted selected disciplines in higher education in dramatic ways, the use of computer-assisted support produced by professors for use in the humanities and social sciences has rarely and only incidentally progressed very far beyond word processing. In composition courses, a few English instructors—students in tow—have braved the aisles of the computer labs where students have been introduced to the rudiments of word processing. Still rarer (and usually in journalism), others have led their students into the domains of desktop publishing. For the most part, however, English instructors have been reluctant to upgrade their own computer experience beyond selectively mandated electronic mail use and the development and storage of syllabi. Even more remote has been the development of computer-assisted applications for sophomore literature studies.

The introduction of authoring programs in the college's Office of Educational Computing during the past three years provided opportunities for addressing specific semantic problems students exhibit universally in sophomore-level literature classes. Symptomatic of both perceptual and conceptual reading difficulties are such student expressions as "I don't know what I'm supposed to get out of this reading" or "I don't see where the instructor gets that; I never saw that in the passage." More to the point, such frustrated confessions reflect, in part, students' inability to distinguish with confidence the differences between stated, implied, and inferred meaning in both imaginative and nonfiction literary selections.

With the introduction of authoring capabilities in educational computing, complemented by a full-production video studio, a small team of faculty and staff began to explore ways that applications might be developed for individual student use that would augment more traditional classroom instructional methods. Since it seemed certain that the development of new computer-assisted applications would be time-consuming and relatively expensive to develop, the educational team realized from the beginning the importance of thorough planning. Whatever applications might be possible, they would need to reflect careful analysis of student needs. The lead instructor spent several hours talking with students from various classes about content and learning problems they faced as sophomore literature students. Student needs were as follows:

1. Many returning students are insecure readers; earlier experiences in academic reading and writing were only marginally successful, and they are intimidated by new academic demands or requirements which may expose their weaknesses in class.

2. While public school students have been introduced almost universally to the basic elements and motifs of literary analysis, many community college students express reluctance in transferring what they have learned in the past to college settings.
3. They have forgotten—or think they have forgotten—what they learned previously.
4. They are sophisticated enough to withhold commitments of past knowledge until they are familiar with the points of view, interests, or idiosyncracies of the instructor; in other words, even if they are confident in prior knowledge, they are reluctant to apply it in a new instructional context.

Improved reading skills are the key to more confident learning as well as to the enjoyment of imaginative literature. Being able to recognize intended implications or to be able to construct appropriate inferences from texts are skills important to that learning and enjoyment. Nevertheless, during inquiries, many students expressed considerable distress when asked to do so in class discussions or on essay examinations.

It was clear from some student comments that more and even better lectures weren't necessarily the answer. Neither were improved study guides for independent study and class discussion. While both of these options are valuable support for many students (not to mention the quality of instruction and the credibility of the instructor), they don't resolve the primary need of every student: at one time or another, every student will need to build confidence independent of the traditional lecture/classroom context if the value of holistic reasoning and critical thinking skills that are addressed in literary analysis are to be transferred into the students' worlds outside the academic community. A program intended for independent student use in the Learning Skills Center seemed ideal to address these reading needs.

Our staff, including the lead English instructor and the director of educational computing, determined to develop a laser disc and computer-assisted program for use in the college's Learning Skills Center.

As it has evolved, the program, Solving Literary Problems: Recognizing Meaning in Literature, assists students in developing more confidence in distinguishing between stated, implied, and inferred meaning in selections of literature. The program consists of two basic components: a computer-controlled laser disc and a set of computer-generated and managed reading exercises. In these exercises, students enter the program through a batch file that automatically downloads the program when the computer is turned on. Students proceed through the program by watching graphic displays on the computer screen and by watching segments of a video program on a video monitor mounted next to the VGA computer monitor. They respond to questions and tasks displayed on the computer monitor with the use of a mouse. Those new to the computer mouse have the option of entering an instructional program loop by keying an entry command before entering the actual program.

The video component, digitized on the laser disc, introduces a reading selection and basic commentary for each of six study units. The selection is a passage from Mark Twain's *Life on the Mississippi*, his well-known romantic/realistic description of the river. To create interest in the passage, the video includes scenes from the Mississippi River area and Mark Twain sites in and around Hannibal, Missouri, and features a dramatic appearance of Mark Twain in a white suit in an interview with the instructor. The video commentary presents basic terms, concepts, and illustrations of stated, implied, and inferred meanings. Each of these video segments is about three to ten minutes long; the whole video component is exactly thirty minutes. After viewing each segment, the student may choose to return to any portion of the video by selecting from an activated, highlighted index or may proceed to the unit exercises. At the end of the video segment or a review of any parts of it, the student turns to the unit exercises displayed on the computer monitor.

Following an animated Mark Twain cartoon announcing each unit, the student moves through the exercises with the use of the mouse, selecting from activated, highlighted text or multiple-choice answers and Go! boxes at the bottom of the screen. Each exercise is short, never more than five minutes long. Times for each exercise are announced at the beginning so that students understand the time constraints and can work more comfortably. Typically, an exercise will require the student to analyze a sentence or two from the *Life on the Mississippi* passage or from some other brief reading on the screen for stated, implied, or inferred meaning. Options are offered after each passage. A screen of commentary follows each selection, complementing a correct response and providing additional concepts, or there is an explanation of a wrong selection with directions to loop back through the exercise or to proceed to optional exercises in order to develop more basic concepts or reading strategies.

At the end of each segment of the exercises, the student has an option to select I Quit!, Return to Menu, or otherwise loop back through any part of an exercise. A Return to Menu selection allows the student to move forward through the program units sequentially or at random.

The decision to videotape the presentation of basic comments and to transfer them to disc was important: students may move at random through the disc to review information that will never change. Most importantly, however, was the decision to use the computer to drive the exercises; these may be augmented or changed at any point with relatively little effort, once the program developer (we didn't say "programmer") is familiar with the authoring software, the essential software component that drives the whole educational program.

The production of Recognizing Meaning in Literature has been an exercise in rather sophisticated staff development for an English instructor. It must be noted at the outset of the project, the instructor was already heavily involved in video production as an educational producer and scriptwriter and had at the time some three years experience in computer graphic development and 2-D animation. From conceptualization through post production, the instructor worked closely with the director of educational computing to discuss the designs of exercises, interfaces between the video and computer components, and the various options available in the authoring program.

At the beginning of program development, several production issues had to resolved:

1. What should be laid to tape and hence to disc? On the other hand, what program elements would be designated to the computer? We had elected to use thirty-minute analog glass discs. The video segment filled the disc without room for exercises, and the delegation of computer-based components was settled by definition of physical space.

2. What authoring system would provide us the "friendliest use" and, at the same time, the most flexible options for development of both the program components and graphic capabilities? We chose ICONAUTHOR, an authoring software program that includes both a program development component (called ICONWARE) and a graphics design component (called ICONGRAPHICS) that enjoys a variety of text fonts and size options. The limitation of the sixteen-color palette used in the creation of PCX graphics files is offset, in part, by a gradient function that allows a simulated spread of any one color from dark to light within an area. The program also includes both smart-text options and user response tabulations which track and record student progress through the exercises. Most useful, the program generates a printout of the structure of the program that can be assembled to show the complete branching of every segment of each unit and its individual functions. Such a reference is indispensable when trying to edit any part of the program.

3. What authoring program would be most "transparent" to the student using it? We wanted the student to be able to move through Recognizing Meaning in Literature unaware of the operational program driving it. Again, we chose ICONAUTHOR. The student is never exposed to any of the program's operations with the exception of brief periods of no more than two or three seconds when the ICONWARE program "dumps" screen images to access the laser disc player and the animation segments.

4. Should we program for mouse or key entry of information? We chose mouse entry to reinforce the student's interaction with the screen image in making selections of information, an important function in developing retention.

5. How much storage memory would we need? What we dismissed fairly early as only a minor factor, storage memory would become the single most significant question in the development of the program, dictating ultimately both content and style of the computer component.

At first we assumed that we might need only 20 megabytes to 30 megabytes of memory, anticipating perhaps 200 to 300 PCX graphics files at most. We were wrong. Student piloting of the beta version of the program was disheartening but very revealing. Weak readers and hesitant computer users simply weren't reading the screen. Clearly, they weren't reading even the simplest of instructions (Now, select Go).

The reason was soon clear. Sluggish or reluctant readers weren't being led into the on-screen text. A colleague suggested that the program wasn't using the full capacities of the authoring program when displaying only a static screen. Why not "scroll on" the text, line by line, or in short, two or three-line paragraphs at most? So we tried that, scrolling on the text, pacing between each entry, and forcing the reader to select Go! at the end of each "page" or screen in order to advance through the exercises. The implication for memory was soon apparent. Text which, at first, could be introduced on a single screen in only one PCX file might now require as many as ten different full-screen PCX files in order to effect the scrolling texts. Memory requirement for just "one" image jumped from 20,000 bytes of memory to 200,000 bytes and more. The graphics for just the first two revised units jumped from sixty to more than 400, more than 80 megabytes of storage memory. To complete the entire revision might require as much as 500 megabytes of storage, a capacity only acquired in the most powerful PCs on campus. It looked as though we would be committing a 486/35 PC to just this program alone. Clearly, we were reaching just about every production and budgetary limitation for only one application! What might be the answer?

Advanced image compression and a software solution called "smart text" are two options we are currently investigating as we continue to work on the program. As this study is being prepared we have learned of a 30:1 compression algorithm demonstrated in California for the first time during June 1992 which may hold a key to our dilemma. What may be the more reasonable option in the short term, however, is the use of "smart text." Through the use of "smart text," that is, activated text controlled by the computer that can be entered over a particular selected PCX file, the file size can be controlled. Although less graphic in nature, this accommodation will provide a "fix" for the immediate future. It remains for us to see what stylistic revisions we may be forced to accept by using "smart text" for our projected text files.

Clearly continued development of increasingly powerful hardware and revised software techniques will be brought to bear on problems encountered in advanced multimedia program development.

BUSINESS MEDIA LAB

An interactive laser disc orientation developed for the business division was funded by a small development grant to the faculty members through the college's Instructional Development Grant Program. The overall direction of the project including coordinating the video production, pressing the disc, and providing training and support for authoring came through the Office of Educational Computing. Delivering the finished program to students takes place in a mid-management lab devoted to the delivery of video and computer based instruction in an open lab individualized format.

The self-paced business lab at MVC has evolved over a ten year period to effectively serve thousands of students. The business lab addresses the community college challenges of part-time students and courses not offered because of low student enrollment. It provides flexibility and opportunities that would not otherwise be available to these students. The faculty, administration, and support staff recognize the potential of technology and multimedia applications for improving learning and achieving student success.

The self-paced lab began in 1982 in a renovated classroom equipped with four 3/4-inch video cassette players and monitors. Three courses (Introduction to Business, Introduction to Computer Science, and Principles of Marketing) were the initial offerings.

Today the lab is equipped with VHS videotapes, video laser disc, CD-ROM, plus microcomputer, and appropriate software to control and integrate it all. The lab serves 500 to 600 students per year with ten to twelve courses offered per semester.

Self-paced, individualized business courses are built around a syllabus, a textbook, a study guide, and audiovisual programs. The courses are individualized because the student may study, read, watch, and listen to the tapes of the course at a pace suited to his/her personal priorities. Even though the student studies independently, an instructor for the course is available during posted office hours or other times by appointment to assist students.

The courses are self-paced because the student may complete the course on or before the final deadline established for the semester. Students are evaluated by means of tests (taken in the testing center) and a class project.

Our vision of the lab for the future is one linked by high-speed fiber-optic technology and multimedia applications. Students will be connected to the lab by an interactive computer network. Learning will be expanded with distance learning, electronic simulations, and personalized education.

BIOLOGY OPEN LAB FOR NONSCIENCE MAJORS

When MVC opened in 1970, the biology department divided the introductory courses into classes for major and nonmajor students. Research at El Centro College of the Dallas County Community College District (DCCCD) had shown that combined classes of biology majors and nonmajors were detrimental to both groups. Nonmajor students were exposed to material only needed as a basis for future biology courses and missed the enrichment to be found in involvement in environmental and lifestyle issues. In mixed classes students majoring in biology were unable to receive the in-depth experiences that would help them determine the future direction of their studies in biology.

In the DCCCD, classes for students majoring in biology, pre-med, pre-dental, nursing, and other related fields were traditional lecture/lab courses. These classes were exact replicas of their counterparts at local universities with the exception that classes are generally small and the lab portion was taught by senior faculty.

The DCCCD nonscience major classes were based on the Postewaite model with general assembly sessions, small assembly sessions, and independent study. At Mountain View College, a college-wide testing center was created and for a short time was used as a site for testing biology students. The number of biology students and the frequency of tests for biology students, however, soon overwhelmed the testing center, and a revised testing procedure was instituted in the biology lab. The introduction of scantron to PC hardware and the use of powerful PC-based software (ParScore and ParTest) allowed the lab staff to handle the more than 1,800 tests and credit-generating exercises each semester. In time the general assembly sessions lost much of their impact and were supplanted by additional small assembly sessions. Eventually, the small assembly sessions were replaced by video presentations and one-to-one instruction or by traditional lectures. Much of the Postewaite model was retained, however, and is still in use over twenty years later. The program has proven to be very popular with students, and the classes have been a "sellout" virtually each semester.

During this period, the staff continued to produce audio and video presentations. Video topics included basic genetics, photosynthesis and respiration, metric system, scientific notation, buffers, succession, relaxation techniques, microscope, and cell processors. While many of these early attempts were "talking head" presentations, some involved field experiences that proved to be very useful. It was determined that extra experiences in these areas were needed. The new videos produced used the college's studio and 3/4-inch editing capabilities. Many of these videos have since been revised or replaced with new materials. As more commercial videos, tapes, and video discs have become available, the need for additional local productions has changed in nature. Currently productions are more closely focused on local issues of health, the environment, ecology, and biology of North Texas. For example, a recent tape that will be transferred to disc format for use in interactive instruction involves the field identification of wild flowers indigenous to the Dallas area.

Audiotapes have also been an important component of the instructional offerings in biology and still tend to be an integral part of the program. Students may obtain a copy of the instructor-produced audiotapes for study at home or in the car while commuting to Mountain View. The audiotapes are constantly reviewed and revised. The audiotapes cover all topics presented in the course with extensive examples and references to the students' lifestyles and current events.

During the late seventies, an Apple II computer was obtained and several stand-alone biology programs were purchased. The Apple programs were used as supplements to the lecture materials, and students could choose to utilize the programs if they wished. Due to the large number of students seeking access to the one computer available, the system was overloaded. Students were unable to gain access to the programs and became frustrated. As a consequence the project was abandoned.

The acquisition of an IBM-PC with extended memory and EGA graphics was the next step in the evolution of the nonmajor program. While this system was used mainly for instructor development and the implementation of computer management in the lab, several Show Partner and Dr. Halo projects were completed using the system. However, the lack of speed and the low resolution of the graphics produced did not appeal to students used to playing arcade games such as Pac Man and Donkey Kong. Faster systems and better graphics were needed to entice students to use the computer to expand the study of biology.

In 1986 an extensive review of the state of computer-aided instruction was instituted at the college. Mountain View College President Dr. William Jordan and Jim Corvey, director of educational computing, along with a faculty team including biology instructor Larry Legg, conducted site visits, scheduled demonstrations, and reviewed the literature in the areas of desktop video production and interactive instruction. Following this process Dr. Jordan, at the recommendation of Larry Legg, authorized a complete remodeling of the nonscience labs and the purchase of two MS-DOS 386 development stations and sixteen MS-DOS 286 student stations for use in the biology department. This was the beginning of multimedia interactive instruction for nonscience major students in biology at MVC. The development stations have recently been replaced by 486 systems and plans include upgrading student presentation stations to 486 machines in the near future.

Multimedia in use at the lab encompasses a great variety of instructional materials, each serving a specific purpose. The materials used in the course can be rated from lowest to highest according to the level of student interactivity. The lowest level is found in tutorials purchased from a variety of sources. These include standard topics such as the heart, genetics, and evolution. Comprised mostly of textual material, the units are linear and progress only when the student gives the correct answer. No directions or hints are offered when incorrect answers are chosen. The tutorials are inexpensive and usually have low-level graphics or no graphics. These tutorials have been used as models in some cases to create similar programs with higher levels of graphics. Both 2-D and 3-D graphics have been incorporated into updated linear programs. These programs currently run as stand-alone parts of the multimedia system.

The 2-D and 3-D animations produced by the biology department staff are vital to the understanding of molecular, chemical, cellular, and physiological processes. They are also beneficial, helping the students understand complex processes such as evolution, geology, and aspects of embryonic development among others.

Several commercial laser discs have been repurposed for use in the lab. For example, four copies of Biosci II are used in interactive instruction and traditional lectures. Chapters (segments) from laser discs, as well complete programs on disc, are also used in this way. The CLV video discs are often used in a pause-and-play mode. Students are asked to view a specific segment, then to pause the tape with an on-screen command, and to answer questions or propose a hypothesis that will best suit the situation presented on the video disc. Discs that may be used in this manner can often be obtained very inexpensively.

The use of the Ventura Publisher Desktop Publishing package to produce lecture/lab guides to assist the student was the next obvious step in a total system. Specific behavioral objectives, self test, lecture notes, and lab activities are included in each 400-plus page guide produced using Ventura Publisher. Scanned and computer-generated graphics are used in illustrations. Two high-level drawing packages, Arts and Letters and Corel Draw, are used. Arts and Letters offers a large number of biology and science clip-art graphics that have been redrawn and labeled to meet specific needs. Corel Draw and several other clip-art suppliers also offer outstanding biology graphics that have been used in whole or in part. Picture Publisher is used to produce high-level grayscale artwork. Additional graphics were attained from students willing to share their artistic talents. In addition, some graphics were repurposed from government sources.

Desktop publishing is also used to produce transparency masters and computer-generated graphics presentations used in the traditional lecture. Signs used to alert students to special information are generated using Ventura Desktop Publishing or other drawing packages. Handouts are produced using WordPerfect for Windows and Ventura for Windows. Additionally, an environmental newsletter *Ecobytes* is published on a semi-monthly basis using scanned articles and graphics. All orientation materials are produced using graphics, drawing packages, WordPerfect, and Ventura.

Original videotapes have been mastered for eventual transfer to a digital format. They include original color clip-art, line drawings, 2-D and 3-D graphics, 2-D and 3-D animations, and text. These tapes will be mastered, with audio, in a small format disc, the most likely candidate being CD-ROM.

At Mountain View, 2-D animations have a history that dates back to the early 1980s. Show Partner was used to produce several EGA-level tutorials. One program on photosynthesis did such an outstanding job of instruction that it was in use for ten years. Autodesk Animator, a program currently in use, has proved to be a much more versatile and useful tool than previous systems. With current programs, 2-D animations can be created in a short time and are especially useful for creating lessons rapidly when students fail to understand a topic currently being studied.

Computer graphics and animations have also proven very useful to students lacking developed skills in visualization. Visualization, a skill honed by reading and conceptualizing images, is necessary in order to understand many of the processes that are not directly observable in biology. While the production of graphics and animations have sometimes proved difficult and time-consuming, the students have benefitted from the effort. The animations apparently have the same appeal as cartoons and animated movies, thus many students see the process of learning as fun.

Several 3-D animation segments are currently in progress or are being planned. In one, the biochemical cycles interacting in an ecosystem are used to teach the basic principles of chemical interactions. Typically, illustrations in textbooks show each cycle as a separate illustration. Students often find it difficult to combine the illustrations into a coherent whole and visualize all the cycles influencing each other as seen in Liebig's law. In another, the concept of recessive genes, difficult for many students to grasp, is taught, and the program follows such a gene through many generations. The movement of each of the food molecules from ingestion to utilization and the movement of an oxygen molecule from inhalation to excretion will follow the food processing cycles with animation bringing the process to life.

Another component of the total system is based on computer-generated games. All major topics have interactive crossword puzzles which can be solved using the vocabulary of biology. Word Search is also currently under development. Both games help build the students' biology vocabulary. Several memory matching games have been developed. One game, matching a graphic of the stages of mitosis and meiosis with their names, has proven very popular. Additional turn-over and match games are planned for chemistry, anatomy, and diversity.

The development of multiple information and visualization sources produced, managed, and delivered by computer has provided a unique opportunity to make a major transformation in the nature of the way biology for nonscience majors is taught. The conversion of the fact-giving approach utilized in most biology courses to one of discovery and inquiry is under development by the biology faculty. Many have lamented the inability of students to apply critical thinking to problems encountered in and out of the academic setting. It is true that students have had little practice in critical thinking. Only a few courses and teachers take the time and effort to foster such an approach. If students have not practiced this technique, how can they be expected to apply it in their course work?

Due to the large number of students and limited number of faculty and staff, the program will employ a multimedia interactive approach. Much of the literature shows that most critical thinking endeavors have utilized small numbers of students or large numbers of faculty and staff. Since such a pattern is not economically possible, we have chosen to rely heavily on our experience with technology as one solution. It is anticipated that the majority of previously produced materials will be used in the critical thinking exercises. These materials will be used to present situations upon which the student may base a hypothesis or aid in proving a hypothesis.

The use of sophisticated authoring and presentation programs in the development of multimedia offerings allows for the inclusion of student input and record keeping as a part of the program. Students may try different paths or experiments until they can prove their hypothesis or suggest an alternative hypothesis. When the student chooses a hypothesis or test not anticipated by the instructor and consequently not programmed into the lesson, the instructor will act as a mentor to help the student rechannel his/her efforts. Should the student present a valid alternative view, it can quickly be programmed into the system.

Various levels or starting points of the critical thinking system can be programmed. At the simplest level, students can be given a hypothesis and asked to select data that will prove the hypothesis. At a more challenging level, students may be given data and asked to form a hypothesis. The most rigorous level will provide the students with data, have them form a hypothesis, design experiments to support their hypothesis, and form a conclusion based on the process. All of these methods are programmed into the multimedia interactive system by combining various authoring systems and by a profusion of media.

This system allows students to practice critical thinking methods in a non-threatening environment. Several authors have suggested that practice is the missing ingredient in the inability of students to use critical thinking processes. Multimedia interactive instruction overcomes this hurdle in a relatively inexpensive and student- centered fashion. Multimedia interactive instruction offers the instructor the ability to quickly adapt to the students ever changing needs and yet utilize many of the existing materials.

FUTURE DIRECTIONS

The base of Mountain View instructors who want to become involved in using technology, at some level, is growing. Within the past three years all full-time instructors have been provided with a PC in their offices. Soon all faculty members will be networked and have access to databases which will expand their ability to team with other faculty to do joint programming.

As our faculty members gain experience and confidence in the utilization of the technology available to them, we are likely to see an explosion in adaptation and usage. Our instructors are just beginning to see the possibilities that exist. Through computer-generated animation they are now able to visually demonstrate dynamic processes that in the past could only be discussed or diagrammed. For creative instructors, technology can now support their ability to enhance the learning process. We are truly on the threshold of significant breakthroughs in the learning process. Those instructors who master the art of the new technologies will be the superstar instructors of tomorrow.

Educational computing at MVC, particularly in the area of developing programs for multimedia delivery, finds its focus in the Educational Development Demonstration and Development Suite. This unique facility, established with the appointment of a director of educational computing in fall 1987, provides a college-wide laboratory for developing and demonstrating the latest in technology. Designed to provide the equipment and training necessary to promote technological development by faculty and staff, the suite contains state-of-the-art programs in video graphics production, video digitizing and manipulation, 2-D and 3-D animation, color and black and white scanning, optical character recognition, desktop publishing, authoring for multimedia applications, support for laser disc and CD-ROM production, and faculty research, as well as support for faculty-produced video in the S-VHS format. The production aspects of the suite are complemented by a 3/4-inch and S-VHS video production and editing studio that has gained recognition in nationwide video competition each year since opening its operation in September 1987.

The planning and budgeting for the development of multimedia programs follows a pattern that promotes the integration of developed programs and systems into the ongoing operations of the college. Typically there is a three-pronged approach that includes the active participation of the instructional division, the Office of Educational Computing, and an administrative support component providing initial development funding in the form of internal faculty grants or released time.

The case studies offered are three that illustrate the range of development underway at MVC. It is important to note that systematic instructional development has been an integral part of all development at the college for two decades. Faculty experience in establishing, developing, and enhancing multimedia instruction prior to the introduction of personal computers has also had a long and successful history. In many ways the advent of computer-based multimedia instruction is a natural extension of an active development effort. The rapidly expanding capabilities of hardware and software and the recent adoption of specific standards related to multimedia offerings have accelerated the pace of development and opened new opportunities for faculty-based multimedia instruction.

Future directions for Mountain View College in the area of multimedia computer-based instruction are integrated in the total college plan and are based on identified needs by the instructional divisions of the college. At the same time, we have found it imperative that the college not just react to technological advances but anticipate and direct those advances. A team effort is required to effectively react to changes in technology, to commit the necessary financial resources, and to allocate significant amounts of faculty and staff time. The team involves college administrators, including the president, the director of educational computing, members of the president's planning group, and a knowledgeable faculty.

Chapter

7

MacCycle: An Extensible Multimedia for Teaching the Physiology and Histology of the Menstrual Cycle

James F. Aiton[1]

Physiology Lecturer
School of Biological and Medical Sciences
University of St. Andrews, St. Andrews, Fife, Scotland

Susan Whiten

Senior Demonstrator in Anatomy
School of Biological and Medical Sciences
University of St. Andrews, St. Andrews, Fife, Scotland

Nils S. Peterson

Instructional Software Designer and Owner
Center for Development of Educational Technologies
Washington State University, Pullman, Washington, USA

The development of MacCycle, a multimedia visual database of the female menstrual cycle, stemmed from two related events. Firstly, the School of Biological and Medical Sciences at St. Andrews University, Scotland, began to make contingency plans to update a computer classroom which had been used to teach physiology for about five years. Secondly, staff retirements were about to change the profile of the school's teaching coverage in the key area of pre-clinical medicine. We anticipated that the introduction of a more flexible delivery system for the histology course might offset potential staff shortages.

These factors led us to examine the feasibility of adapting parts of our histology course to a computer-based system. The major constraint was that software would have to be delivered on student workstations which, while low-cost, would be able to provide acceptable image quality.

At St. Andrews, histology is taught to ninety science students and 200 preclinical medical students, though at any one time the numbers in the practical classes are approximately fifty. In designing a computer-based teaching system for histology instruction, four important technical and strategic criteria emerged as being central to the success of the project. Any solution we adopted would have to be

- an integral and compulsory component of the course
- capable of accommodating 100 students per week
- part of a general-purpose solution to other computing requirements of the school
- able to provide good image quality at an affordable price

We were already aware of the existence of other computer-based teaching programs for histology and pathology, particularly laser disc-based systems.[2] While these had some features that impressed us, laser disc technology requires dedicated hardware; it is rather inflexible and is also expensive to implement for teaching large numbers of students. More importantly, the NIH syndrome (Not Invented Here) all too readily afflicts academics asked to develop a course using someone else's material. A software-based, digital image storage and display system offered a less expensive and more flexible solution to our specific problems.[3]

After evaluating a number of hardware configurations during the summer of 1991, we selected the Apple Macintosh LC 6/80 (6-megabytes RAM, 80-megabytes hard disk) running System 7 as our basic student workstation. For display, we chose the Apple-12 inch color monitor (512 x 384 pixels) with 512K expansion VRAM (video RAM) added to each machine. This gave 16-bit color capability with images displayed from a palette of 32,000 colors. Although the pixel resolution of the 12-inch Macintosh screen seemed relatively low, in practice the ability to display images at 16-bit color depth proved to be a crucial factor in successfully displaying high-quality histological images, and we concluded that for the type of images we used, increased color resolution could be offset by lower spatial resolution. By October 1991, we had completed the installation of a teaching laboratory of thirty Macintosh LC computers connected by an AppleTalk network to a LaserWriter IIg for printing and to a Webster Multigate for access to the university Ethernet network. The lab is equipped with HyperCard 2.1, QuickTime 1.6, and standard productivity software (word processor, spread sheet, graphing, and statistics packages etc.). At the time of this writing, we are in the process of upgrading the computer laboratory, and even the current United Kingdom entry level Macintosh (LC 475) will offer a significant improvement in performance over our original hardware choice.

TEACHING BACKGROUND AND AIMS

Histology is taught as an integral component of the preclinical Human Function course and consists of thirty-five lectures followed by thirty-two hours of practicals. The range of subjects covered includes all the major body systems (respiratory, cardiovascular, reproductive, and nervous system, etc.). The students examine a collection of approximately 100 microscope slides which are fully described in a weighty course booklet. Although sections are demonstrated on large color TV monitors via a video camera linked to a teaching microscope, students sometimes experience difficulties both with microscope technique and the individual identification of relevant structures. We hoped to overcome these and other difficulties by using computer-based technology to accomplish the following:

- Integrate the teaching of physiology and histology by emphasizing the structural and functional relationships of cells and tissues in the body systems
- Introduce a wider range of human material than would have previously been used in our histology classes, e.g., endoscopic and other medical imaging techniques
- Enhance the student's opportunity to see and understand the relevant microscopic detail, firstly by eliminating the frustration and limitations of the student microscope and secondly by making available explanatory diagrams

At the start of term in January 1992 we committed ourselves to replacing a time-tabled practical unit on reproductive physiology with a computer-based histology unit (MacCycle). This gave us approximately eight weeks to develop our first histology program for student use.

The complexity of the interactions between the four major female reproductive hormones and the cyclical changes in the structure of the ovary and uterus meant that this topic was well suited to the integrated approach that we felt was important to student understanding of dynamic biological processes. Conventional treatment of the subject in lectures, laboratories, and textbooks often fails to convey the very dynamic nature of the menstrual cycle, and we felt confident that the subject material would lend itself to the approach we envisaged. Three other important factors influenced decisions on program content and timing of introduction:

1. Students would already have had thirty hours of scheduled computer practicals. These practicals not only familiarized students with general purpose software packages but also included a number of physiological

simulations implemented in HyperCard. Students already had adequate skills to cope with instantiation of the computer-based histology practicals (mouse technique, file handling, etc.).

2. We anticipated that the development process would require considerable input not only from a software developer but also from a domain expert. Most staff in the school had no software development skills; therefore, we relied upon the expertise of a visiting research fellow (NSP) who had been involved in the development of educational software for several years. The domain expert had only limited computer skills at the beginning of the project but was enthusiastic about the concept.

3. Technological advances in digital image handling and storage (QuickTime) on personal computers had made feasible our idea of storing an extensive visual database of images on each workstation.

The QuickTime system extension and its associated image compression and decompression capabilities (codecs) permits the efficient storage and display of still and moving images. QuickTime is best understood as a storage technology for a collection of time-based data. The data file is called a "movie" because it is typically used to store a series of still images (frames) with an optional audio channel. The file may be incorporated into many different applications and played in a number of ways, including forward and reverse motion sequences, stop action, and random access of individual frames or segments.

QuickTime provides a software-based solution for displaying digital video and sound on any color-capable Macintosh (PowerMac, Quadra, II series, or LC models) with 4MB of RAM and System 6.0.7 or later. The QuickTime codecs compress the large data files that are normally needed to store complex visual images in digital form and automatically decompress them only when they are being viewed on screen. A typical, full-screen, 24-bit color image can be compressed and stored as a 35K file. When the compressed image is recalled, there is no apparent loss in the quality of the color or spatial resolution. In our work, we used the Video, Animation, and Photo (Joint Photographic Experts Group) compressors to store and display short movies, diagrams, and high resolution 24-bit color pictures. Apple's PICT Compressor is a software implementation of the Joint Photographic Experts Group (JPEG) standard and can be used to open and compress any PICT file. JPEG can achieve compression ratios of between 10:1 and 50:1, depending upon image complexity and degree of compression chosen. Thus, with QuickTime, not only were we able to think in terms of creating a database containing many images, but we were also able to modify the content of the image library as and when needed.

We chose to implement MacCycle in HyperCard (as opposed to other authoring languages such as Guide or Authorware) for four reasons:

1. It was well-suited to rapid prototyping, having facilities for both navigation and computation.

2. It came free with all Macintosh computers and this avoided licensing problems.[4]

3. Version 2.1 was fully QuickTime compatible.

4. It was capable of displaying 24-bit color images in separate windows.

IMAGE CAPTURE

Four image capture technologies were used during the development of the program:

1. A VideoLogic DVA-4000 full-motion digital video adapter was used to capture and display live video images on a standard Macintosh 13-inch color monitor. The DVA-4000 board can accept input from analogue sources (e.g., videotape and video cameras) in a number of different video input formats including composite video (PAL or NTSC), RGB, and S-Video. The analogue images are dynamically resizable and single frames can be saved as 24-bit PICT files.

2. VideoSpigot boards (SuperMac Technology) were used to capture still and moving digital video images from composite video sources. The VideoSpigot displays the incoming signal in a live window and can store both sound and video data directly to RAM memory or disk at up to 24-bit color depth. The VideoSpigot can also be used for making QuickTime movies directly.

3. A 24-bit color flatbed scanner (LaCie SilverScanner) was used for the digitization of drawings and photographic prints. We normally scanned at seventy-two/dpi (maximum screen resolution) to minimize file size.

4. A Microtek ScanMaker 1850s was used to scan 35mm photographic slides. Slides were scanned at 1850 dpi and 24-bit color depth, then scaled to produce the appropriate screen-sized image.

Both the flatbed and slide scanner have software plug-ins for Adobe Photoshop which also provides JPEG compression. The images were archived at 24-bit color depth on a 128-megabyte, 3.5-inch rewritable, optical floppy drive and catalogued using FileMaker Pro.

DESIGN AND CREATION OF MACCYCLE

The menstrual cycle is usually described as a series of phases based on hormonal and structural changes. In the MacCycle stack, individual cards were used to give details of different phases. The title of the card appeared in the upper left-hand corner. Some significant days, such as the day of ovulation (day 14), required an individual card, whereas other phases could be described as a group of days (days 18-24). Pictures were attached to the cards to illustrate significant structural and hormonal changes. As the students used MacCycle they were able to call up the attached illustrations using the Figures pull-down menu (see Figure 7.1).

Most of the histological sections in the image database were captured using the Microtek slide scanner from 35mm slides taken with a Nikon 35mm camera attached to an Olympus BH2 Microscope. Some sections were digitized using the DVA-4000 board with an S-video signal input from a Sony 3 chip video camera (DXC 325p) attached to the Olympus BH2 microscope. Subjects too large for microscopy were photographed with a macro camera (Leitz Dialux 20), then printed (5 x 7-inch) and scanned with the flatbed scanner. The images were edited (color balance adjustment, cropping, rotation, etc.) with Photoshop and compressed at medium quality.

Initial prototypes of MacCycle had up to three fixed windows on each card (to show the endometrium, the follicle, and the hormone levels); however, this approach was abandoned because of the size restrictions imposed by the screen. The final card design (Figure 7.2) had a fixed, scrollable field set aside for text, but the visual images were displayed in freely movable windows. Students were therefore able to choose which images to view on screen, where the image would be located and, in most cases, what size of image was displayed. When using MacCycle, we found that the students appreciated the freedom to control the screen configuration.

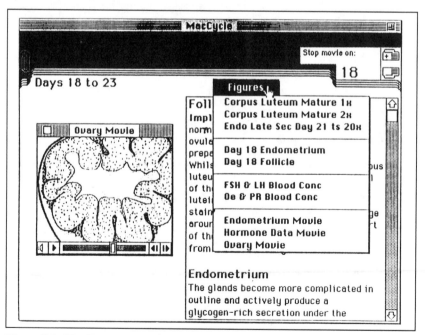

Figure 7.1 The Figures pop-up menu displayed over the fixed, scrollbar text field during the process of selecting a new image for study. Note the navigation tool at the top right-hand corner.

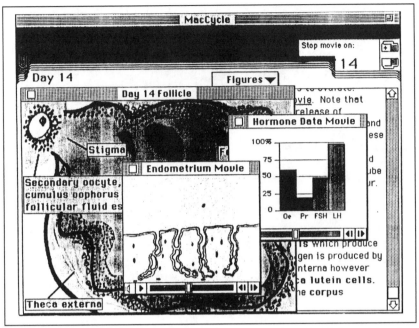

Figure 7.2 A MacCycle card for Day 14 showing text overlaid with 2 movies and an annotated diagram.

Four types of images could be viewed and selected from the Figures pull-down menu seen in Figure 7.1:

1. Color photomicrographs obtained by the image capture techniques described above.
2. Line diagrams highlighted the key structural elements in the photomicrographs. These diagrams were originally drawn by hand, scanned, and colored using the paint tools available in Photoshop. Labels were subsequently added in Canvas 3.0.
3. Graphs showed the changes in blood hormone concentrations through the cycle.
4. Movies showed the cyclical changes in the endometrium, follicle, and hormone levels (Endometrium Movie, etc.). The individual frames for the endometrium and follicle movies were drawn by hand, scanned, and saved as PICT files. The hormone data movie was created from a series of histograms generated by DeltaGraph Professional. These series of PICT files were assembled into movies by using either Apple's PICTtoMovie application or Adobe Premiere. A movie, showing the actual moment of ovulation, was created by frame-grabbing key frames from a videotape recording and linking the frames using the PICTtoMovie application. Though these movies firmly belonged in the

flick-book school of animation, they provided convincing evidence of the dynamic nature and integration of the physiological and histological changes which occur during the different phases of the menstrual cycle.

AUTHORING OF MACCYCLE

MacCycle is a HyperCard stack with an index facility which allows rapid navigation through the different phases of the menstrual cycle.[5] The MacCycle stack also includes integral editing tools which make simple the assembly of the text with relevant illustrations. To create MacCycle, the domain expert typed text directly into the scrollable field on the card, where it was automatically saved. Appropriate images were selected from the database to illustrate the text, and these were attached to the card. Attaching the pictures to the cards was achieved by using the Add Open Figures option from the File menu (Figure 7.3). Titles of the selected illustrations then appeared in the Figures pull-down menu. The list of figures appearing in this menu was therefore unique to each card and easily modifiable.

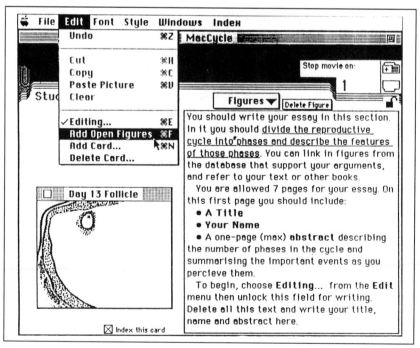

Figure 7.3   The first card of the Student Essay with Editing enabled, the scrollable text field unlocked, and an open figure being added to the card (Day 13 Follicle)

STUDENT USE

After an introductory lecture on gametogenesis, students used the MacCycle database to investigate the menstrual cycle. They were able to read a short, explanatory text and examine digitized images of histological specimens, graphs, and movies. Since the number of images which can be displayed at any one time is only limited by computer memory, the student could, for example, view on one screen, text, dynamic changes in hormone levels, and the related structural changes in both the ovary and the uterus (see Figures 7.1 and 7.2).

For assessment purposes, students submitted an "electronic multimedia essay" in which they synthesized structural and hormonal information by defining significant phases of the menstrual cycle (Figure 7.3). Using the MacCycle editing tools and instructions for editing, students composed their essays within the program, creating their own multimedia by illustrating important points with graphs and images drawn from the database. On average the essays took two hours to write and the total time spent in the computer lab studying MacCycle was between four and five hours.

STUDENT EVALUATION

Students enjoyed the innovative approach to the practical teaching of histology, and they appreciated the opportunity to view a great variety of images. They also found animations a valuable aid to understanding dynamic biological systems and consequently had a better understanding of the integration of physiological and structural changes than has been achieved by previous methods of teaching the subject. Results of student evaluations from three classes, each of 100 medical students, show *average* scores in the top twenty percent for enjoyment, ease of use, and acceptance of new technology. One interesting development we had not anticipated was that after using MacCycle, students would look at histology sections under the microscope. A number expressed the view that, after having studied the computer images, they had gained the necessary confidence to be able to identify the key structures in the normal histological sections. We are conscious of the "novelty effect" that the introduction of new teaching technology has and think students would enjoy a mix of technologies with some practicals being taught in the traditional way and some on computer.

CONCLUSION

QuickTime image compression makes image-intensive projects, such as MacCycle, feasible on inexpensive student workstations. MacCycle provides a wide selection of materials which enhances the students' opportunity to see important histological details. It is also a rich computer database (not a page-turning tutorial) containing both histological and physiological information and thus can be used to set open-ended research problems which the students can complete within the same environment in which they view the material. We found that students enjoyed the materials and appreciated seeing the greater variety of images than are normally available for viewing in a traditional microscopy classroom setting. Animations were also a valuable aid for illustrating dynamic changes in biological systems. Having assessed the essays, we felt that the students who had used MacCycle had a clearer understanding both of the dynamics of the changes and also the *integration* of physiological and structural events than had been achieved by previous methods of teaching this subject. Our experience has led us to believe that it is possible for university staff with little or no prior experience of computers to use, with a minimum of outside expertise or assistance, the MacCycle HyperCard authoring shell in order to construct practical multimedia for teaching.

NOTES

1. Requests for additional information can be addressed on the Internet to jfa@st-andrews.ac.uk.

2. Two systems are the U.K. Path disc available from Cambridge Multimedia Systems, Burwell, Cambridge, U.K., and Keyboard Pathology from Keyboard Publishing, 484 Norristown Road, Blue Bell, Pennsylvania 19422.

3. Hanka, R., Stephens, C. and Thompson, P. "Networked implementation of a computer-aided learning system using digital images," *The CTISS*, 11, 10-14 (1991).

4. Version 2.2 of HyperCard allows developers to create stand-alone applications, thus avoiding the need for licensing agreements, etc.

5. Whiten, S. Peterson, N. and Aiton, J.F. (1993). "MacCycle: a computerized visual database for studying the female reproductive cycle." *J. Physiol.*, 459, 2P.

Chapter

8

Multimedia: A Systematic Approach to Its Placement in Education

Robert A. Saldarini

Assistant to the President
Bergen Community College, Paramus, New Jersey

Too often in education a technological advancement is integrated haphazardly. This is especially true when there are multiple vendors in the marketplace offering different products that perform what one would believe is a similar task. A propensity to repeat this behavior exists when one addresses multimedia, particularly when the term itself has many definitions. Multimedia means anything from the smallest interactive computer-assisted instruction (CAI) module to the most elaborate audiovisual presentation platform. For successful integration of this instructional technology into education, it is imperative that a systematic approach be applied.

USES OF MULTIMEDIA WITHIN EDUCATION

Multimedia may be either an object or subject of instruction; therefore, there are three uses for this technology:

1. A CAI learning platform where the student uses the computer as his/her training source, interacting with the multimedia software
2. A presentation tool where the instructor uses the multimedia platform in an unobtrusive manner enhancing his/her teaching
3. A course of study where the principles of multimedia development and authoring are taught

In most cases, educators focus their initial efforts on using multimedia as an object of instruction for CAI purposes. From an instructional technology point of view, many would argue that there is no better individual learning environment.

The ability to mix motion video, animation, sound, and text with user interaction provides superior flexibility over the past generation's linearly designed CAI sessions. It is in this area of multimedia applications where the vendors use all the marketing force Madison Avenue can muster.

For the inexperienced educator, the smoke, mirrors, and glitter surrounding products like IBM's *Illuminated Books and Manuscripts* can be overwhelming. Although impressive at the onset, needs analysis may yield that a simple Level I laser disc package without computer assistance can do a quality job and for a fraction of the cost. Regardless of product selection and promotion, one should keep in mind that most applications augment or remediate instruction and are not intended to replace it. For example, while there are powerful multimedia chemistry packages, there is no substitute for hands-on training within a laboratory.

When using multimedia as a presentation platform, the instructor should make the processing environment as unobtrusive as the overhead projector is today. The students' attention should be drawn to the images and away from the computer. The use of an active matrix liquid crystal display (LCD) panel on top of the overhead projector will lighten the hardware load and avoid the need for large monitors.

As a subject of instruction, multimedia is truly interdisciplinary. It can be successfully taught within the disciplines of information science, marketing, broadcasting, and the communication arts. Despite the discipline responsible for training, a careful balance between design and technology must be sought. The most successful educational experiences occur when multimedia courses are team taught (e.g., among information science and broadcasting faculty). To teach students an authoring package without the proper design perspective will result in an education of skill and no talent.

NEEDS ASSESSMENT

The educational institution must identify the need for multimedia specific to its goals. Depending on the organization, there may be a coordinator of academic computing or possibly a media utilization advisor under whose purview multimedia may fall. Someone must take the initiative or be charged with the task of spearheading a needs analysis. If the multimedia integration is not coordinated properly, the institution runs the risk of having a variety of processing platforms, applications, and peripherals that prove to be incompatible. This incompatibility ultimately leads to a waste of resources and communication breakdown between faculty as efforts become concentrated in completely different directions.

Creating a task force is one of the best ways to control multimedia's integration. History has shown that when administration purchases instructional technology without faculty input, faculty fail to apply it. It becomes imperative to have faculty involved in the decision making process. The teaching faculty on the task force will ultimately become some of the innovators, using multimedia in their classrooms and assigning multimedia CAI modules to their students. In higher education, the task force may consist of a group of teaching faculty, a reference librarian, a technical assistant, and a dean. In secondary or primary education, the principal should select a task force of interested teachers from various grades or subject areas.

The first requirement of the task force is to establish a mission. The mission may be simply the evaluation of current multimedia products and services in addition to the possibilities of using multimedia within the institution. If economic resources are available, the task force may have the mission of establishing a pilot program on campus. Also, it is not unreasonable for the task force to have the mission of preparing a grant proposal to secure funding for multimedia technology.

When the task force clearly understands its mission, it can then start working on the identification of target objectives. By defining these objectives, needs analysis begins. The task force's objectives should be straightforward and focus on three tests of feasibility, namely technical, operational, and economic. Although technical feasibility holds with it an implied importance over the other two, nothing is further from the truth. Technology is often readily available, yet it cannot be purchased within economic constraints, or worse yet, it can be purchased but not operated.

TESTS OF FEASIBILITY

Technical Feasibility

When assessing technical feasibility, the task force must focus its efforts on the issue as to whether the needs of the institution can be technically satisfied. The technical feasibility test is twofold. First, the most obvious consideration when addressing technical feasibility is to identify if an appropriate hardware and software computer configuration exists that supports the desired level of processing. Yet, the technical level of understanding of the processing configuration must be of equal interest.

State-of-the-art multimedia, leading-edge applications are using digital video interactive (DVI) technology. At the time of this writing, there were only a few DVI commercial applications available for education. It must be addressed, however, that DVI has exceptional promise. The visual quality of digital motion imaging is increasing while the disk space required for saving material is decreasing due to the advancement of the compression/decompression algorithms. The reader is counseled to seek the latest information regarding DVI when involved in the multimedia decision-making process. For education, the future use of DVI will simplify multimedia local area network (LAN) applications, as the laser disc drive can be removed from the configuration.

When investigating technical feasibility, the task force should overcome the initial desire to assess hardware platforms. In some institutions the vendor is predetermined, depending on the "political climate" of IBM or Apple shops. If the task force has the option to make independent hardware decisions, equipment analysis should follow, in turn, after software or development considerations are completed.

If the need is to use multimedia for CAI training, the develop-or-design decision must be made. From a technical standpoint, development is a much more comprehensive process, one that requires a superior knowledge of analysis and design. It is almost impossible for one individual to produce a quality product. At the very least, the designer must consult continuously with the subject expert and have complete command over the hardware and authoring package. A thirty-minute presentation could take a small development team one year to complete. Yet, development of a multimedia training package has the distinct advantage of providing the institution with a customized training application.

Purchasing an application is the most expedient way of introducing multimedia into the curriculum. There are hundreds of packages available on a countless number of subjects from AIDS to zoology. *The Videodisc Compendium for Education and Training* provides an excellent starting point when searching for application packages. The *Compendium* furnishes information specific to the product including a brief description, appropriate grade level, processing constraints, and price.

When considering multimedia packages, one should review processing levels and standards. The industry grades multimedia training packages from Level I to IV. With only a few exceptions, education takes advantage of Level I and Level III applications. Level I applications allow the learning experience to be completed with only a video disc player and, of course, an appropriate monitor. Level I packages do not take advantage of computer power. One would find a considerable amount of Level I applications for use in grades K through 12.

Level III applications require the use of a computer. These packages come with laser discs and software. In most cases, with minimal installation time the products are up and running. The fact that these purchased products are general and not tailored to the needs of the faculty proves to be a major limitation. As a technical note, Level II applications have a computer code strategically placed on the laser disc itself, on one of the audio tracks, providing commands in a specific processing environment. Level IV applications require hardware modifications, e.g., EPROM chips inserted into the laser disc player.

The MPC standard continues gaining popularity. The standard, set by Multimedia PC Marketing, Inc., sets the minimum criteria for multimedia applications. The standard requires that the hardware platform consist of a 386SX processor, 2 megabytes of RAM, 30-megabyte hard drive, CD-ROM drive, front panel volume control, a two-button mouse, keyboard, 3.5-inch disk drive, as well as serial, parallel, joystick, and MIDI ports. It is interesting that when the standard was set both Apple and IBM platforms did not meet it. Apple violated the mouse requirement and the IBM M57 SLC did not have a joystick port. If the product carries the MPC endorsement, it is guaranteed to run "without a problem" on the standard hardware configuration.

When the need is to provide faculty with a presentation platform, technical considerations regarding authoring packages become paramount. There are pure presentation-authoring products such as PODIUM. PODIUM was designed by Fred Hoffstetter at the University of Delaware. Its major draw is its simplicity. A computer-literate faculty member should be able to author in PODIUM within an hour. The power of the package lies in Dr. Hoffstetter's use of external products to embed PODIUM links. One can author in PODIUM using a word processing package (e.g., WordPerfect or simply the Windows Notepad). The simplicity of PODIUM does confine it to its purpose; therefore, it is not conducive for authoring small classroom CAI modules for an instructor's use.

When authoring both classroom CAI exercises and presentation abilities are desired, low-end production packages such as Asymetrix's Toolbook may be appropriate. Toolbook is a powerful multimedia development product that is well entrenched in the education arena. Low-end development packages require a small degree of technical literacy; still, a dedicated faculty member should have no problem mastering these products. One should not underestimate the power and potential of the multimedia extensions embedded within a Windows processing environment.

High-end production level authoring packages like IBM's Audio Visual Connection (AVC) yield studio quality results. These products require programming knowledge and are not well suited for general lesson preparation and presentation.

Sources of information for multimedia presentations are abundant. Again, the *Compendium* details a large variety of prepared video discs for classroom use, e.g., *Sightlines: A Visual Database*, an ocular interdisciplinary encyclopedia. Presentation discs are generally inexpensive, usually with a price tag between fifty and 100 dollars. Publishers are now beginning to add laser discs to the litany of ancillary support materials. It is important that the presenter make sure that the disc is pressed in CAV (constant angular velocity) format. CLV (constant linear velocity) format is widely used in the production of entertainment discs, especially films. Except for the rarest configurations, authoring software can only successfully capture images from CAV pressed discs.

Should the need be to add multimedia to the curriculum and make it the subject of instruction, the dimension of laser disc creation is added. Multimedia applications are usually dependent on analog motion segments or a bulk amount of still images that require an author to cut a laser disc. Creation of a laser disc is not feasible within a training environment, as a master tape must be sent to a service company (e.g., the 3M Corporation). The turnaround time from the point of production to the pressed disc can be weeks, leaving an unacceptable time lag between the completion of the design and authoring.

To bypass the laser disc dilemma, the institution may opt to purchase an optical read/write drive. The Panasonic LQ-4000 drive can easily simulate a laser disc as it provides thirty minutes of motion on one platter or it holds the standard 54,000 still frames. Using an optical drive of this type will enable the students to work with a rough cut emulation that delivers the necessary frame stops needed to author a multimedia presentation. When simulating laser discs, it is imperative that the authoring software accept the optical drive as though it were the laser disc drive. If this important issue is not resolved, the incompatibility problems may make authoring impossible.

Once application decisions are made, the next step is to consider the physical processing environment. During the technical feasibility study, the task force should not attempt to select a processing configuration. At this time identification of equipment that will satisfy organizational needs is of prime importance.

When looking at processing platforms, the task force will find that Apple, Commodore, and IBM are the major players in the marketplace; yet, DEC, Tandy, and Sun Microsystems offer a multimedia product line. Apple and IBM are the most common computing environments, as most institutions either expand or upgrade existing facilities. It is unfortunate that Commodore carries with it the past "home" computer reputation, causing some to ignore this vendor. The Commodore Amiga line is outstanding and probably one of the greatest values for education.

As previously mentioned, technical support must be an item of concern for the task force. Who will support the multimedia applications, make recommendations, install software, and be available for consultation? It is not uncommon for an educational institution to receive funding for new technology and have no funds for technical support. During the planning process, technical support must be addressed. Multimedia is highly dependent on peripheral equipment. Hand scanners, flatbed scanners, digitizing monitors, touch screen monitors, and an LCD active matrix projection systems are just a few of the peripherals that may be called upon to prepare multimedia presentations. All peripherals must successfully conform to the processing platform; some devices require daughterboards, others switch boxes, and yet others require software drivers. It is unfair to burden teaching faculty with the responsibilities of technical support for the institution's commitment to the integration of multimedia.

Operational Feasibility

The focus of operational feasibility is to determine if people will use the system; in this case will the faculty incorporate multimedia into their lesson plans? The personality of educators run the gamut from dynamic and innovative, doing whatever it takes to enrich their course, to individuals who just chalk and talk. There are some faculty who are unreachable. The task force should view these educators as a controlled constant and make decisions that will best benefit the majority. A plan that requires the entire faculty to incorporate multimedia will most likely fail. Many can recall the past generation of an unused microcomputer in an elementary classroom, or further back, the unused piano in the kindergarten room.

As previously mentioned, involvement of faculty is a key for the successful integration of any new teaching methodology. Although a dean or principal cannot have every faculty member on the task force, those who do not participate must be kept informed. There is a tendency in education for administrators to select committee members from a list of "those who do." If the general faculty are not kept informed, the perception about multimedia's integration may be skewed by the excitement of the task force.

Task force members should poll other teaching faculty concerning the use of multimedia. If the institution is very large, a questionnaire on this topic may be appropriate. If the faculty does not know the power and potential of multimedia, a demonstration is necessary. Without the general faculty's understanding of this technology, the knowledgeable task force members will be as effective at conveying their message as the town crier shouting doom at Pompeii.

The task force can anticipate three major concerns from the faculty. The first concern will relate to the location of the equipment. The best case scenario, if funds were unlimited, would place a processing platform in each classroom. As this is an unrealistic plan, the task force must address the placement of the equipment within the instructional area. Multimedia processing platforms can be portable; however, due to the need for peripheral equipment, they are often cumbersome. If an active matrix LCD project panel is not part of the configuration, large monitors will be necessary for classroom viewing. Quickly, the multimedia equipment can generate the need to make two or three trips to its storage location prior to setup, thus making its use operationally infeasible.

A second concern will be the training issue. Most vendors offer training for faculty at either their location or at an in-house training session. Many institutions find it most successful to train one or two faculty members, and then conduct faculty development workshops to train others.

The third concern relates to technical support. Problems with scanners or systems that fail to access laser disc materials properly instill technostress in faculty members and therefore make them apprehensive to use highly technical presentation aides. The task force needs to address technical support as a key operational issue.

Economic Feasibility

Some states (e.g., Florida) require that a laser disc player be part of the instructional technology for each school district. For these institutions, appropriations for purchase of multimedia processing platforms become part of their capital budgets. In higher education and for school districts not required to purchase laser disc technology, multimedia is yet another contender for financial resources.

Reviewing multimedia, the task force must weigh the cost of this processing platform against other uses of the capital budget. Care must be taken to assess the intangible benefits of the increased quality of education when multimedia is successfully applied; however, it is the direct benefits of its use that jockey multimedia back into a competitive position.

Most multimedia processing platforms host a general purpose computer, one that can be used for other purposes. Laser discs store enormous amounts of material: the entire collection of the Louvre can be found on three discs. The discs include a descriptive frame following a photograph of each piece of art and a complete motion tour through the museum. Using laser disc players to present material linearly can ultimately replace the need for unwieldy film projectors. Unlike other instructional technology aids, the parts of a multimedia configuration can be used independently.

Incorporating multimedia-based training into a grant proposal is an excellent starting point to secure the technology without competing for existing resources. Funding sources are often interested in leading-edge training environments, and there are several commercially available packages on large volume grant areas such as ESL and vocational education. Some "bricks and mortar" grants will only allow funds to be spent on equipment. Should this be the case, the institution must be prepared to match funds for training and technical support.

IMPLEMENTATION

Once the needs analysis is complete, the task force should turn its attention to implementing its findings. If equipment must be upgraded or acquired, purchase requisitions or bidding RFPs (request for proposals) need preparation. During the time lag between the request and receipt of the physical configuration, faculty readiness should be underway.

If the institution is very large, a pilot group of faculty may be recruited to be the innovation team. For the sake of morale, it should not be assumed that the task force members arbitrarily become the team. If the needs analysis was performed successfully, teaching faculty who originally had little or no knowledge of this instructional technology may, at this point, be anticipating its implementation. They may be anxious to participate and would like to be considered as part of the innovation team. To maintain the multimedia integration's momentum, interested faculty should in some way be involved.

Administrators may want to ask faculty to attend special interest committees that assess the appropriateness of multimedia CAI packages. Most of the organizations producing these products have some type of review policy and often they do not charge for review. No application should be purchased without a rigorous review. Often overlooked, a review committee is essential when writing grant applications. An educational institution should not be locked into making a blind purchase of a product if the funding agency approves the proposal.

Faculty development workshops on the topic of multimedia should be scheduled. As a first session, a workshop on the design of multimedia lessons will prove to be very popular. This topic appeals to those using multimedia in the classroom and to individuals involved in the development of CAI modules. If necessary the class can be taught without multimedia technology.

A quality design workshop should be a minimum of three hours of theory. Topics should include the use of color, special effects, music, and animation. The copyright issue also must be addressed, as most items brought into a multimedia presentation are copyright protected. The faculty should also be made aware of video disc resources and, more importantly, how to secure them.

Once equipment is received and software is installed, faculty development should include hardware training. Faculty should not need to learn operating systems software (e.g., DOS or OS/2). One technical individual should document the necessary steps to get the users right where they want to go. When faculty members are using multimedia for classroom instruction, they require training on an authoring package.

Applications purchased for CAI training must be installed and user-tested. It is highly recommended that teaching faculty complete the entire training program prior to assigning it to their students. Select packages require user password access and provide the capability to test students as they venture through the experience. When students are tested, faculty must make value judgments on the impact these examinations will have on the student's overall course grade.

At the conclusion of the implementation, equipment should be in place and the participating faculty trained and ready to use this instructional technology confidently. The chair of the task force may want to be present during its initial use, to handle any last minute "fires" that may arise. Too often, unfortunately, the task force is disbanded at this time. To ensure a quality integration of the technology, a post-implementation review by task force members is necessary.

POST-IMPLEMENTATION REVIEW

After multimedia lessons are taught and students have worked through learning modules, the task force should reconvene to assess the integration effort. Appropriate statistics should be gathered on the various learning experiences. Faculty who taught using multimedia should be interviewed and qualitative data collected. At this time, problems must be reviewed and corrected before making additional multimedia-related decisions. The institution that conducts a comprehensive post-implementation review places itself in a highly competitive position for future grant acquisitions that will enrich the school's use of multimedia technology.

Part Three: Software

Chapter

9

Software for Sociology:
A Tool for a More Effective
Learning Paradigm

Christopher Sullivan

Director of Information Services
Baldwin-Wallace College
Berea, Ohio

In 1989 the sociology department of Baldwin-Wallace College left the comfort of traditional classroom lectures, braving the perils of new technologies, to bring their students to both a larger understanding of sociological principles and an earlier mastery of basic research skills.

In-class computing became the vehicle for revolutionary change in social science learning. No longer is it possible for students to passively absorb lectures as a body of facts to be recited at a future date. The introduction of in-class computing has transformed the classroom into an active learning environment in which students are immersed in the milieu of the sociologist.

The new environment provides the faculty member with opportunities to model those activities that are the essence of social science: the observation of a social phenomenon, development of a hypothesis to explain the phenomenon, experimentation to confirm or reject the hypothesis, and use of quantitative measures. More than just modeling the behaviors of the social scientist, faculty are able to involve students in these activities as social scientists. A mentor/protégé relationship develops between a faculty member and a student, encouraging the student to explore sociological concepts beyond textbook presentations. Students discover that the scientific method applies to a much wider field of inquiry than the hard sciences and that social sciences are much more than a collection of field observations.

PROBLEM DEFINITION

During the late 1970s it became clear to the faculty of the department of sociology that the traditional approach to introductory sociology was not as effective as it had once been. The traditional paradigm of faculty lectures to expand upon student reading of assigned materials was not eliciting the depth of student inquiry that was desired.

Several causes for decreasing student achievement were identified: deficiencies in high school preparation for college both in terms of quantitative skills and in social studies background, increasing off-campus employment competing for student time, a social environment that placed decreasing value on academic achievement (except where it lead to foreseeable economic advantage), and submersion in an entertainment environment that was simultaneously sensory-rich and intellectually nondemanding. In short, the printed medium of textbooks was boring and required an intellectual discipline which students had inadequately developed.

TRIAL ONE: ELECTRONIC REVIEW—A MIXED SUCCESS

The first attempt to use software to stimulate learning in sociology was the development of a set of review questions that were presented via a computer terminal; this work began in the late 1970s. For each chapter in the textbook the faculty designed a set of multiple-choice review questions which students could execute one or more times. Correct responses were acknowledged and incorrect responses resulted in the student being referred to a specific section of the text. When students felt comfortable with their understanding of the material, they would go to the department secretary and arrange to take the chapter test, which also was administered via computer terminal. Students who diligently used the review questions were well-prepared for the examinations and scored well.

Two groups of students seemed to benefit the most from this innovation: those students with lesser academic histories and the very best students. Both groups found working at their own pace to be more attractive than working at the pace dictated by the middle of the class. The most pronounced benefit was experienced by the weakest students. The opportunity for multiple reviews and the tutorial aspect of the program certainly contributed to the success of these students. Perhaps equally important for the weakest students was the excitement that was generated. Mastering the use of the computer increased self-esteem and the willingness to invest time in an academic pursuit. Frequently students would take parents to the computer labs on Parents' Day and Homecoming to show off their new skills.

The increased achievement of students was encouraging but at the same time was recognized as not yet achieving all the faculty's objectives. Students were able to better recite the facts, but they were not necessarily closer to understanding the basic nature of social science. The deficiency in quantitative skills had not yet been addressed. For those at the extremes of the academic spectrum some goals had been reached, but for the majority in the middle of the academic spectrum there had been little change. A good start had been made, but clearly something more was needed.

REVOLUTION IN THE SOCIOLOGY CLASSROOM

A close student/faculty relationship is the hallmark of a Baldwin-Wallace education. If information technologies could somehow be used to amplify the one-on-one relationship of student with faculty member, then the sociology faculty believed more progress could be made toward addressing the previously mentioned problems.

The ideal environment would be one in which students and faculty would work together to investigate sociological situations which students would regard as "real" and having relevance to their lives. The introduction of quantitative methods in these investigations was also highly desirable.

Several changes needed to take place to develop the desired learning environment. Some portion of the traditional lecture time would need to become interactive laboratory sessions. A lab environment would need to be created, with this lab containing information processing equipment. Datasets and software would be required to describe and investigate the sociological situations. Students and faculty would need to change their expectations of their interactions, responsibilities, and goals.

The decision was made to have three hours of lecture per week and two hours of lab. All students would meet with the instructor for the three hours of lecture, but each student would attend only one hour of lab. Classes were divided into two lab groups of approximately fifteen students each, with each group having an assigned lab day.

A lecture room in the sociology building was converted into a computer-equipped sociology laboratory. Each student would have a workstation to use during lab sessions. Arranged in small clusters to promote interaction among students and to facilitate the instructor's movement from student to student, workstations were sufficiently spacious to allow students to have texts and reference works at hand. The computers in the lab were 80286 DOS machines with color monitors and dot-matrix printers. Key to the success of the lab environment was the instructor's ability to move quickly from student to student.

Two additional features were borrowed from the laboratory environment of the physical sciences. First, lab assistants were utilized. Sociology majors with junior or senior class standing were invited to become lab assistants and were given responsibility for helping with problems related to the use of hardware and software. Questions related to sociological issues and the use and interpretation of statistical measures were the realm of the faculty member. Second, the faculty created worksheets which students used as a guide for the lab sessions. Worksheets provided a basic introduction to a topic from which students could launch their own investigations. As students completed the worksheets during lab sessions, the instructor could verify basic understandings and then either answer questions from the students or suggest possible areas for investigation. The worksheets were also designed to take the student through the logic of problem formulation and problem solving. Complexity, in the form of control variables and in sophistication of statistical analysis employed, increased throughout the academic term.

Software selection was the single most important step in creating a new learning environment in sociology. The activities that would bring students and faculty together were defined by the software. The degree to which both student and faculty could concentrate on sociology rather than issues of hardware or software would determine the success of the project. The more transparent the operating environment the better. The result of an extensive evaluation process was the selection of MicroCase as the software environment.

MicroCase distinguished itself both in terms of form and function. MicroCase is menu driven, has easy-to-read screens that are not overly "busy," provides a help function, and is bug free and devoid of such irritations as unexpected and unexplained termination. MicroCase provides aggregate data by geographic units (precincts, counties, states, nations) and displays that data both in tabular form and as maps. Maps can provide insight into relationships that may not be evident in tabular representations (e.g., differences between rural and urban populations). MicroCase can be used to introduce various statistical measures over the course of several lab sessions.

Of equal importance with the software itself are the individual case-level datasets used by the software. MicroCase prepares the General Social Survey (GSS) for all available years, 1973-1991. This annual sample presents the diversity of the United States' population. MicroCase datasets include variable descriptions that are very useful to students in selecting variables for study. In addition to providing datasets, MicroCase allows for the generation of institution-specific datasets. At Baldwin-Wallace students generated a dataset for Cuyahoga County (in which the college is located) with the same variables as are found in the distributed dataset for Seattle. Since most Baldwin-Wallace students come from a five-county area surrounding the college, there is familiarity with the neighborhoods described in the Baldwin-Wallace generated dataset.

During laboratory sessions the faculty member works with fifteen students on a specific project. Students are given a worksheet that leads them through an introduction to a population and a project. Upon completing the worksheet, students continue to investigate the population independently. The faculty member is available to answer student questions and, more importantly, to stimulate inquiry. These are frequently heard faculty comments: "That's an interesting relationship, what do you suppose is the cause?" "Have you thought how that might relate to . . .?" "What other variables do you think might distinguish these subpopulations?" "What statistical measures could be applied to . . .?" The faculty member moves around the classroom, looking over shoulders, encouraging, prodding, stimulating—often in one or two minute bursts of one-on-one interaction.

Students are encouraged to expand their work on projects outside the scheduled lab sessions. The sociology lab is used daily from 9 A.M. until 3 P.M. for classes but is open for drop-in student use until the building closes at 10 P.M. The MicroCase software is installed in general usage labs around the campus but primary use is in the sociology lab.

As students progress through the courses in the sociology curriculum, the lab is used increasingly for small group projects. The use of small groups of two or three students simulates a professional work environment and provides students with experience in peer tutoring. Recent graduates report that the tutoring experience, both with the introductory course and in group projects, has been valuable preparation for graduate school assistantships.

MEASURES OF SUCCESS

No formal, controlled studies have been performed to measure the impact of the change in instructional paradigm on student achievement, but there is a plethora of observational data confirming the desirability of the use of a computer-based laboratory in social science courses. Most obvious has been the increase in student participation in class. Students take greater responsibility for their learning and become more imaginative and effective in generating inquiries as part of the weekly projects. Unlike the computerized review, which had greatest impact at the ends of the achievement spectrum, the sociology lab has positively affected students across the full spectrum of academic achievement.

The number of sociology majors has steadily increased since the implementation of the sociology laboratory. Not only has the number of majors increased, but the quality of work has shown a marked improvement. The faculty attribute the increased numbers of majors to the more apparent relevance of the coursework. The improvement in the quality of student work is attributed to higher faculty expectations of students and earlier communication of those expectations to students and to the recognition by the most talented students that the social sciences can be intellectually challenging and worthy of their talents.

A level of comfort with introductory statistics has been another outcome of the use of MicroCase software. Students are introduced to statistics as a tool for understanding relationships. Bypassing the theory and mechanics of statistics allows students to begin applying statistics and using the software to calculate statistical measures at an earlier stage of their academic careers than would otherwise be possible. While having the software select and perform the statistical tests does not resolve the students' quantitative skill deficiencies, it does allow them use of the tool in much the same way a student uses an automobile without understanding the chemistry of internal combustion or the physics of inertia. That students recognize the value of statistics is evident in the increased use of statistical measures in student papers and presentations outside the sociology department.

The enthusiasm for social science research engendered by the sociology lab can be seen in two student initiated projects. After assisting the introductory class, one upperclass student decided to take a published study from the 1970s and replicate the study using 1990 data; this project eventually resulted in a senior honors thesis and a presentation at a national conference. The second project involved several students creating a local dataset for the same variables found in the MicroCase dataset for Seattle, Washington. The local dataset project provided students an opportunity to practice data collection skills, learn more about their neighborhoods, and contribute to the relevance of the course for future classes.

Perhaps the strongest recommendation for the use of computer-augmented classrooms/laboratories comes from outside the sociology department. Seeing the success of the sociology laboratory, faculty in a number of departments have copied the instructional model. In 1991 major new curricular innovation took place in the departments of psychology and mathematics. In the psychology department the major new emphasis is on undergraduate research and in-class use of statistical tools. The department of mathematics developed two computer-augmented classrooms where students use Mathematica to improve their understanding of the foundations of calculus. Use of real-world problems as a basis for student investigation is a significant component of the mathematics labs.

CRITICAL SUCCESS FACTORS

What facilities and actions were instrumental or necessary for the success of the shift in instructional paradigm? The genesis of the project was a faculty desire to improve student learning; the project would not have begun without a faculty accepting of change and willing to embrace technology. In addition to an academic climate supportive of change in general and technology in particular, several critical success factors were identified at Baldwin-Wallace.

First and foremost on the list of critical success factors is the selection of student-friendly software. Software must require the least possible amount of training for its use and, to the greatest degree possible, use of the software should be transparent. Students should not need to learn a set of commands to invoke software functions; rather, those functions should be presented in a menu for selection. Software should be resistant to student errors; data entry errors and inappropriate function selection should result in diagnostic messages, not program termination. Output should be easy for students to read and screens should not be overcrowded with information. The existence of a context-sensitive help function is very valuable. Selection of software which is difficult for students to use or requires faculty to devote instructional time to teaching its use will doom the project to abandonment.

Implementors must focus on the interaction of student and faculty and develop a physical environment that promotes that interaction. Easy circulation of the faculty member among student workstations is essential. Placing student workstations around the perimeter of the room was found to facilitate faculty movement.

Using datasets that have interest and relevance to students overcomes the age-old student question: "Why do I need to study this?" Faculty inform classes that the projects they undertake are like those that might be done by an urban planner or a marketing department in a corporation. Students quickly relate to the need to study income and age distributions in making decisions regarding the placement of specialty retail stores.

With students increasingly career-oriented, it is valuable to maximize the relevance of core curriculum courses. An example of the impact of relevance on student usage is found in the case of the sociology lab experiencing a dramatic increase in usage when, on the first day of the Persian Gulf War, the Islamic Nations database was installed.

Location of the laboratory relative to faculty offices is also a critical success factor. Work on weekly projects is meant to stimulate student inquiry and that inquiry is restricted if the student can not share both problems and discoveries with the instructor in a timely manner. It was found that students working during the open lab periods would often seek out their instructor to share a particularly interesting relationship—it was exactly this sense of discovery that faculty most wanted to stimulate. Having special purpose labs as close to faculty offices as possible is highly desirable.

WORDS OF WARNING AND ENCOURAGEMENT

Warning—be prepared for success! The Baldwin-Wallace experience is that students and faculty embrace the more active learning style and that technology is now a facilitator rather than an impediment. Success in one academic discipline will generate demands for resources in others, with significant budgetary consequences.

Be encouraged by the potential for improving student learning. What began as a trial in one academic department has lead to greater student understanding of social interactions, earlier and more widespread student use of statistics, and expanded opportunities for undergraduate research. You can make a difference!

ACKNOWLEDGMENT

The curricular innovations described in this chapter were the result of the insight and efforts of Dr. Margaret Brooks-Terry and Dr. David Treybig, both distinguished faculty of the department of sociology. It was their concern for students, eagerness to embrace technology, and sheer hard work that made these changes happen. The author is pleased to have had the opportunity to provide encouragement and technical support for their efforts and to report their success.

Chapter

10

DATASIM:
A General Purpose
Data Simulator

Drake R. Bradley

Professor of Psychology
Bates College, Lewiston, Maine

Without question, analyzing data is one of the most important activities undertaken by researchers in the social and life sciences. Because of this, most undergraduate departments devote considerable staff time to teaching courses in statistics and research methodology. The key role played by computers and statistical software in the analysis of data requires training in these areas as well. All of this points to a classroom environment in which computer demonstrations are used on a routine basis to supplement the standard lecture.[1]

The ability to easily display and manipulate datasets in class (interactively) represents an important application of computer technology to teaching. Specially designed datasets are often essential for illustrating key points in a lecture. For example, datasets having values of r ranging from the extremes of ± 1.0 on down to 0 (in .1 or .2 increments) are very useful for clarifying the concept of correlation. Other datasets might be developed to illustrate the effects on r of outliers, heterogeneous subgroups, nonlinearity, range truncation, and third variables (partial correlation). To give a last example, consider the two-way analysis of variance. When teaching this topic, it is very instructive to have datasets which clearly depict the various patterns of main, simple, and interaction effects which can arise. The concept of interaction, in particular, is one which requires many instances and counter-instances to fully understand.

Unfortunately, constructing datasets by hand is a tedious and time-consuming process because a fair amount of trial and error is required in order to successfully incorporate the desired characteristics and trends in the data. Suppose, for instance, that you would like to create two columns of data having specific means and standard deviations. By making up and adjusting (as necessary) the data values for the two columns, it is not too difficult to achieve the desired result. Certain "anomalies" may well arise, however, because altering data values selectively can produce outliers, non-normal distributions, sequential dependencies, and other non-random elements in the data.[2] To complicate matters further, suppose you would like to create two columns of data which have a specified degree of linear correlation as well. Juggling data values so as to simultaneously achieve particular degrees of central tendency, variability, and intercorrelation turns out to be quite difficult. Even if successful, the result would most certainly *not* represent a random sample from a bivariate normal distribution. To do this right requires a computer program employing rather sophisticated data generating algorithms.

Moreover, once a dataset has been created, there needs to be some convenient way to display, plot, and analyze the data in class. This chapter describes a software package, called DATASIM, which greatly simplifies the process of creating and analyzing customized datasets (Bradley, 1988; Bradley 1991b). The name DATASIM is short for *data simulator*, which aptly describes the primary function of the program. Creating a customized dataset with DATASIM is quite easy. The instructor simply initializes the relevant population parameters and then generates one or more random datasets from the population. Allowing for sampling error, the datasets will more or less reflect the trends and characteristics specified for the population. Each dataset can be displayed, plotted, and analyzed. When a dataset is found which closely models the desired characteristics, the simulation can be saved and subsequently retrieved for class demonstrations.

BIVARIATE CORRELATION

To illustrate, suppose an instructor would like to create a dataset showing the bivariate correlation between intelligence (IQ) and grade point average (GPA). To generate the data, DATASIM needs to know the research design, sample size, and population parameters. This is done by entering commands after the DATASIM command prompt (©), as shown in Figure 10.1. For the present example, the Design command specifies a multivariate design with $k = 2$ variables, Nobs sets the sample size to $n = 10$, and Mu, Sigma, and Rho specify the values of the relevant population parameters. In addition, the Decimal command sets the number of decimal places to the right of the decimal point in the data, and the Labels command provides labels for the two variables. Note that the commands entered to this point simply *initialize* the simulation. That is, they configure DATASIM to generate random datasets from the appropriate population.[3]

Once the initialization is complete, the Data command may be used to generate the data. This command causes DATASIM to compose a randomly selected

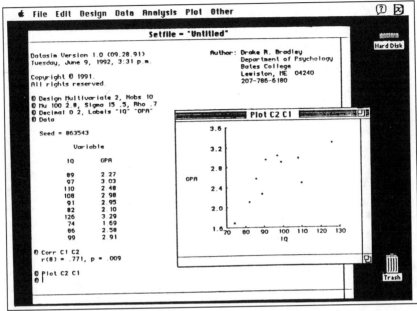

Figure 10.1   DATASIM initialization and simulated data for a bivariate correlation problem

six-digit "seed" for initializing the random number generator, to generate a dataset based on this seed, and to display the resulting data. Figure 10.1 shows a dataset which was generated using a seed of 863543. Once this (or any) dataset is "resident" in DATASIM, the data can be analyzed and plotted. As shown in the figure, Corr computes the sample correlation, and Plot displays the corresponding scatterplot. The difference between the sample and population values of r (.771 vs .7) is simply a reflection of sampling error. Indeed, the sampling distribution of r derived from a large number of DATASIM simulated datasets follows a theoretical distribution of r with n-2 df (Bradley, Senko, and Stewart, 1990, p. 243-244). The fact that DATASIM randomized datasets show the expected amount of sampling variation is important because many instructors will want to use the program to teach sampling theory (Bradley, Hemstreet, and Ziegenhagen, 1992).

Since the $n = 10$ pairs of IQ and GPA scores in Figure 10.1 are completely determined by the value of the seed, this particular dataset can be reconstructed at any time. To do this simply re-enter the initialization commands in Figure 10.1, and then the command Seed 863543 (rather than Data). This would regenerate the original dataset.[4] Hence, there is no need to store customized datasets on disk. Of course, it would be very convenient if we did not to have to re-initialize the simulation again. As it turns out, DATASIM provides a way to save both the initialization of a simulation and the seed value associated with the current dataset. To do this, simply enter Simsave followed by a filename: for example, entering Simsave R-Demo at the cursor position (|) in Figure 10.1 would store the following commands in a file called R-Demo:

```
DESIGN MULTIVARIATE 2, NOBS 10
LABELS "IQ" "GPA"
MU 100 2.8
SIGMA 15 .5
DECIMAL 0 2
RHO .7
SEED 863543
```

Excluding the last command, these commands are simply those entered in Figure 10.1 to initialize the simulation. The last command (Seed) stores the value of the seed for the current dataset. It should be obvious that R-Demo is just a DATASIM command macro. When the time arrives for the classroom demonstration, the instructor can run the macro by entering Execute R-Demo. DATASIM will then execute each command line in R-Demo just as if it had been entered manually. In the present case, the effect would be to restore the original initialization of Figure 10.1 and to regenerate the dataset associated with seed 863543. The instructor could then proceed to display, plot, and analyze the data.

All of this assumes that the original dataset generated in Figure 10.1 does, in fact, possess the right characteristics for the demonstration. Suppose, however, that this is not the case. Perhaps the instructor would like the sample correlation to be very nearly $r = .70$, rather than $r = .771$, or perhaps the shape of the scatterplot is not ideal in some respect. In this case the instructor would simply generate additional datasets until one is found which is just right. An easy way to do this is to enter the following on one command line: Data, Corr C1 C2, Plot C2 C1. This will generate a new dataset, output the correlation, and display a scatterplot. Since DATASIM provides a way to recover the last command line which was entered (pressing F6 on the IBM or the up arrow key on the Macintosh), it is easy to execute this command line over and over again until an ideal dataset is obtained. The Simsave command would then be used to save the initialization commands and the specific seed assigned to that dataset.

OTHER RESEARCH DESIGNS

The discussion so far has focused on the generation of a customized dataset for a simple problem involving bivariate correlation. As illustrated in Figure 10.2, datasets for other research designs can be generated as well. Figure 10.2a, for example, shows how to generate data for a 2x3 contingency table. Ntot specifies a total sample size of $N = 100$, and Cprobs assigns the probabilities that observations will be allocated to the six cells of the table: .10, .20, .30 (row 1); .25, .10, .05 (row 2). Following the initialization, the Data command generates a random dataset from the population. Allowing for sampling error, the observed frequencies of 13, 21, 29 (row 1), and 23, 11, and 3 (row 2) are consistent with the cell probabilities. Although not shown in Figure 10.2, one-way tables are possible as well: Design Table 1x7, for instance, could be used to create a table containing the frequency of heart attacks by day of week.

Figures 10.2b-e illustrate the initializations and simulated datasets for several experimental designs. Figure 10.2b represents the simplest case, a one-group

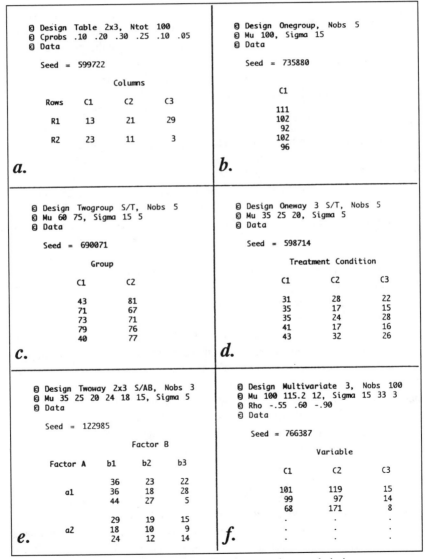

Figure 10.2 Initialization and simulated data for several research designs

design. Such designs are rare in practice, although they are sometimes appropriate when an experimental treatment is applied to a random sample drawn from a population with known parameters. For the present example, suppose that $n = 5$ children are given nutritional supplements for a period of six months. The researcher then administers a standard IQ test in an attempt to assess whether or not the supplements increase intelligence. From the initialization in Figure 10.2b, we see that the null hypothesis is true because the population mean specified is 100 rather than a higher value, such as 106. We would expect, therefore, that a one-sample *t* or *z* test computed on the simulated data would result in a decision *not* to reject the null hypothesis. If the test *did* result in a decision to reject, this would represent a Type I error. Since the datasets generated by DATASIM faithfully model the sampling variation which would actually occur, the probability of committing a Type I error will be equal to the alpha-level employed for the statistical test (usually .05).

Figure 10.2c presents the initialization and a simulated dataset for a two-group experimental design. For this example, assume that students prepare for an examination using either a "massed" or a "spaced" study strategy. The data in the two columns are the resulting test scores. Since the population mean for the massed condition is less than the spaced condition (60 vs. 75), the null hypothesis is false. A failure to reject the null hypothesis would therefore represent a Type II error. Note also that the massed condition has a much higher standard deviation than the spaced condition (15 vs. 5). This was done for two reasons. First, it shows that an experimental treatment can affect the variability as well as the central tendency of the data. Second, it violates the homogeneity of variance assumption of the *t* test, and this will need to be considered when analyzing the data.

Figure 10.2d shows the initialization for a one-way experimental design with $k = 3$ conditions and $n = 5$ observations per condition. In this example, the independent variable is the fin angle of the Mueller-Lyer illusion (30, 45, or 90 degrees), and the dependent variable is the amount of illusion expressed as a percent.[5] The population means show that the amount of illusion decreases as the fin angle increases. Since only one value is specified for the population standard deviation, DATASIM will use this value for all the conditions of the experiment. The same is true for Nobs; since only one value is specified, all three groups have the same sample size ($n = 5$). If unequal n's are desired, then three separate sample sizes can be listed (e.g., Nobs 5 3 7).

The token S/T in the Design statement of Figure 10.2c and 10.2d requires special comment. This tells DATASIM that the observations across conditions are statistically independent or uncorrelated. When this is true, the experiment is said to have an "independent groups" or "between groups" design. Experiments employing repeated measures, randomized blocks, matched groups, or pretest-posttest designs, on the other hand, produce correlated observations across conditions. Such experiments are said to have a "correlated groups" or "within groups" design. The token TxS is used to initialize designs of this type, and Rho is entered to specify the correlation across conditions. Explicitly declaring the design as S/T or TxS allows DATASIM to select the proper error terms for various statistical analyses.[6]

Figure 10.2e represents an extension of the one-way design to a 2x3 factorial design with $n = 3$ observations per cell. Factor B, the column factor, is once again fin angle (30, 45, and 90 degrees). Factor A, the row factor, is fin length (long vs. short). To provide continuity, we will assume that the "long-fin" variant of the Mueller-Lyer figure is the same figure that was used in the preceding one-way design. The population means specified for the three cells of the first row of the 2x3 design are therefore unchanged (35, 25, 20). The population means specified for the second row are new, and reflect the generally weaker illusion observed with "short-fin" variants of the Mueller-Lyer figure (24, 18, 15). Computation of the row and column marginal means for the 2x3 matrix reveals that factors A and B have non-zero main effects. Likewise, the cell means within the rows and columns of the matrix reveal non-zero simple effects for A and B, as well as an AB interaction. Of course, any pattern of main, simple, and interaction effects can be achieved by specifying appropriate values for the population cell means.[7]

Figure 10.2f shows the initialization and a portion of a simulated dataset for a multivariate design with $k = 3$ variables and $n = 100$ observations per variable. The three variables are IQ, F-score (a measure of authoritarianism), and Years of Education. To initialize the simulation we need to obtain (or contrive) estimates of the population means and standard deviations for each variable. Furthermore, in contrast to the bivariate correlation illustrated in Figure 10.1, designs with $k > 2$ variables require the specification of a correlation matrix after Rho. The three values listed in Figure 10.2f specify r_{12}, r_{13}, and r_{23}, respectively. The value of $r_{12} = -.55$ is the correlation between IQ and authoritarianism and is based on actual values cited in the literature. The values of r_{13} and r_{23} were selected in order to demonstrate the concept of partial correlation, as shown below.

Several other commands are useful for initializing simulations: Decimal controls the number of decimal places in the data, Lower and Upper prevent the generation of off-scale values, and Lambda or Catvar generate data having non-normal distributions. Also, various commands are available for labeling the conditions and/or variables of the design. An example of a labeling command was provided in Figure 10.1 (Labels). Such labeling helps to document the displays, plots, and analyses of the data. When labels are not specified, as in Figure 10.2, DATASIM uses "default" labels appropriate for each of the respective designs.

The examples in Figure 10.2 show how easy it is with DATASIM to generate customized datasets for various research designs.[8] Of course, this is just the first step; once a dataset is resident in DATASIM, the next step is to plot and analyze the data. Doing this helps to confirm whether or not the dataset closely models the patterns or trends desired for a particular demonstration. Figures 10.3 and 10.4 present examples of graphical and statistical analyses of the datasets generated in Figure 10.2.

Figure 10.3a expresses the cell frequencies of Figure 10.2a as percentages relative to the column totals. The percentages suggest that the two variables making up the 2x3 table are not independent, and this is confirmed by the corresponding chi-square analysis in Figure 10.4a. Figure 10.3b presents a histogram of the IQ

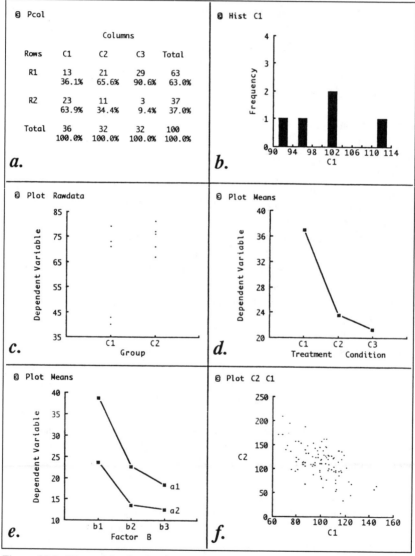

Figure 10.3 Plots of the simulated data for the design in Figure 10.2

data for the onegroup design of Figure 10.2b. Given the small sample size, this histogram is not particularly informative. However, we can see that the center of the distribution is relatively close to 100, so there would seem to be little reason to doubt the null hypothesis. This is confirmed by the one-sample t test shown in Figure 10.4b; the sample mean of 100.6 does not differ significantly from 100. This produces a correct decision to not reject the null hypothesis.

Figure 10.3c plots the test scores for the massed and spaced conditions of Figure 10.2c. The lower mean and greater variability of the test scores in the massed condition are apparent from the plot. A two-sample t test comparing the means, shown in Figure 10.4c, is not significant ($p = .1599$). Given the initialization, this would be a Type II error. An F ratio comparing the sample variances shows that the massed condition produces significantly greater variability in the test scores ($p = .0191$). While this is of theoretical interest in its own right, it also raises the issue of the effects of violating the homogeneity of variance assumption on the previous t test. As it turns out, a t test which adjusts for heterogeneous variances yields a similar nonsignificant result ($p = .1856$).

Figure 10.3d plots the means for the one-way experimental design, and Figure 10.4d shows the results of pairwise comparisons of the means. Although treatment 1 differs significantly from treatments 2 and 3, the latter do not differ from each other ($p = .5611$). Since all three population means differ (Figure 10.2d), the nonsignificant result for T2 vs. T3 is a Type II error. Of course, the small difference between the population means for these two conditions would lead to relatively low power in tests involving this comparison. Figure 10.3e plots the cell means for the two-way design, and Figure 10.4e presents the results of a two-way analysis of variance on the simulated data. The significant main effects for A and B are correct decisions, whereas the nonsignificant AB interaction is a Type II error.

Figure 10.3f plots the scatterplot between the IQ and authoritarianism data for the multivariate design. Figure 10.4f shows the sample correlation matrix, part and partial correlation analyses, and a multiple regression solution for predicting F-scores (C2) from IQ (C1) and Years of Education (C3). Allowing for sampling error, the sample correlations reflect the values specified for the population in Figure 10.2f. Since the correlation between IQ and F-scores is $r = -.552$, it is tempting to argue that high intelligence leads to a less authoritarian personality. However, the part and partial correlations between IQ and authoritarianism, with Years of Education held constant, are $r = -.076$ and $r = -.094$, respectively. This illustrates the problem of inferring causation from correlation: the fact that the relationship between IQ and F-scores is highly attenuated when education is partialed out suggests that the relationship is mediated by this third variable. Perhaps self-selection factors lead more intelligent people to attain a higher number of years of education, and this in turn reduces authoritarianism due to the "liberal" value systems prevailing at institutions of higher learning. This interpretation assumes no direct causal link between intelligence and authoritarianism. One way to test this idea would be to regress the IQ and F-score variables against Years of Education individually, obtain the residual errors, and then plot the F-score residuals against the IQ residuals (as in Figure 10.3f). With the effects of education removed, we now get essentially a circular scatterplot. Of course, the correlation between the residuals is simply the partial correlation noted above ($r = -.094$).

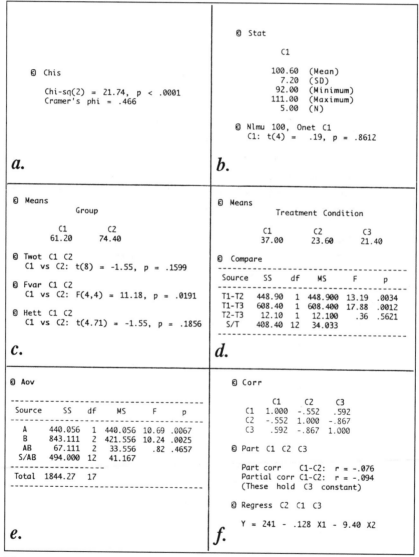

Figure 10.4   Some sample statistical analyses for the designs in Figure 10.2

The last example is a good one for illustrating how DATASIM can be used to develop creative demonstrations for class. Manually constructing datasets to illustrate the concept of partial correlation is extremely difficult. With DATASIM, however, it is simply a matter of experimenting with different correlation matrices, generating simulated datasets, and analyzing the results. Similarly, creating datasets which illustrate "suppressor" variables in multiple regression is usually quite difficult, but with DATASIM it is simply a matter of selecting the right pattern of intercorrelations among the variables. The program will then generate (and analyze) the data for you.

GENERATING INDIVIDUALIZED DATASETS

Another important application of DATASIM is for generating "individualized" datasets for students to analyze and interpret. The datasets can be used for homework assignments, laboratory projects, or take-home tests.[9] To illustrate, suppose you have twenty-five students taking a course in statistics and would like each one to practice the computation of r. To generate the datasets you would initialize a simulation as in Figure 10.1, open the printer for output (Open Printer), and then enter the Data command twenty-five times. Entering Eject after Data would force each dataset to be printed on a separate page for ease of distribution. An even more convenient way to generate the datasets is to enter the following commands on one command line:

OPEN PRINTER, REPEAT 25, DATA, EJECT; CLOSE PRINTER

The Repeat command repeats, a specified number of times, all of the commands listed between it and the semicolon delimiter (if any). In the present case, DATASIM will generate and display a dataset (Data) and force a new page (Eject) during each repetition cycle. The twenty-five pages of output can then be detached and the "individualized" datasets distributed to the students.

When the students return the completed assignments, some way must be found to verify if their answers are correct or not. One way to do this would be to re-initialize the simulation, enter Seed followed by the appropriate value, and then Corr. This approach is best if the instructor intends to check only those answers which are pretty clearly in error. If all of the students' answers are to be checked, however, a better approach is to have DATASIM output the correct answers "on the fly" with the datasets:

OPEN PRINTER
REPEAT 25, DATA, EJECT, INFO, CORR, EJECT
CLOSE PRINTER

In this case, each page containing a dataset is followed by a page containing information about the current initialization (Info) and the value of the correlation coefficient (Corr). The output of the Info command includes the seed for the dataset currently resident in DATASIM. This is needed to match up the "answer" pages with the datasets returned by the students.

While the preceding methods work well enough, there are more efficient ways to have DATASIM generate individualized datasets and the corresponding solution sets. In fact, the entire process can be automated through the use of special macros which generate and print the descriptions, simulated datasets, and solution sets for an entire selection of problems. Using these macros, the instructor can easily create booklets of problems covering all of the topics in the course. The books are distributed during the first week, and each week thereafter the student simply detaches the problem description and dataset to be analyzed for that week, completes the assignment, and hands it in. Course assistants then compare the students' answers to the solutions generated by the macro.

THE DATASIM LIBRARY

One of the main advantages of DATASIM is that it allows instructors to easily design their own problems. Nevertheless, it was anticipated that many instructors would prefer to have a selection of representative problems provided with the software. This has been done through the incorporation of a special library, DATASIM.LIB, which stores prepackaged problem descriptions and initializations in individual files. Datasets for homework problems can be generated from this library, and entire books of problems created and printed using the Book command. If desired, instructors can easily augment the library with problems of their own devising.

In selecting problems for the DATASIM library, an attempt was made to include a large number of classic studies published in psychology. The rationale for this was simple: if students are going to learn to analyze and interpret data, they might as well do so for problems based on actual studies published in the literature. That way, they are introduced to the content of a particular discipline as well as to the statistical procedures used. Of course, problem libraries based on studies in biology, sociology, economics, market research, and other areas could be developed as well.

The initialization files in the DATASIM library are similar to those illustrated in Figure 10.2. Labels for the conditions and variables are provided, and sample statistics from the original study are used to estimate the population parameters (e.g., Mu, Sigma, Rho). Any number of simulated datasets can be generated for a problem, and each dataset can be regarded as an independent replication of the study on which it is based. In addition to the initialization file, each problem has a description file summarizing the research hypothesis being investigated, the variables and/or conditions of the study, and other pertinent information. The description concludes with a complete reference to the original study.

A listing of very brief descriptions of the problems in the DATASIM library can be produced by entering Help Problems or by selecting Other ==> Problem ==> Review All from the menu bar. As shown in Figure 10.5, this causes DATASIM (for the Macintosh) to open a scrollable window containing the problem descriptions. Scrolling through this list reveals some forty problems in the built-in library. After reviewing the list, suppose you would like to obtain a detailed description and a simulated dataset for the problem Adapt. This is done by entering Describe Adapt, Initialize Adapt, Data. An alternative approach is

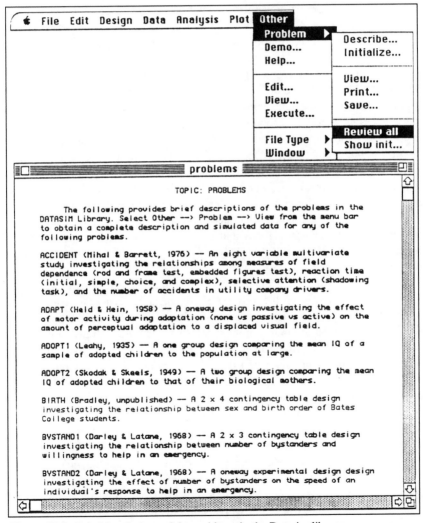

Figure 10.5 Brief descriptions of the problems in the Datasim library

to have DATASIM open up a "view" window containing the description and simulated dataset.

Sometimes a study has more than one variant in the DATASIM library. Bystand1 and Bystand2, for instance, are both based on the well-known bystander intervention study by Darley and Latané (1968). These investigators examined the effect of group size on the willingness of a subject to help a fellow student in an emergency. Subjects participated in either two-, three-, or six-person discussion groups using an intercom system. One of the students (actually, a confederate of the experimenter) had a "seizure" during the discussion. The dependent variable of the experiment was assessed in two ways. First, a dichotomous measure was obtained in which subjects were classified as having helped or not helped. A subject helped if he/she reported the emergency to the experimenter prior to the end of the victim's seizure. The results showed that eighty-five percent, sixty-two percent, and thirty-one percent of the subjects in the two-, three,- and six-person groups, respectively, reported the emergency. These differences were significant: chi-square = 7.91, $p < .02$. The DATASIM problem Bystand1 generates simulated data for this measure. A second measure, assessing speed of response, was computed by taking the reciprocal of each subject's latency (in seconds) in leaving the cubicle, and multiplying the result by 100. (Subjects never leaving the cubicle were assigned a maximum latency of 360 seconds.) The mean speed scores for the two-, three-, and six-person groups were .87, .72, and .51, respectively. An analysis of variance showed that these differences were significant: $F(2,49) = 8.09$, $p < .01$. The DATASIM problem Bystand2 generates simulated data for this measure. Note that both the chi-square analysis and the Anova supported the researchers' hypothesis that subjects are less likely to assist a victim if others are present during an emergency.

Figure 10.6 shows a convenient way to obtain a detailed description and a simulated dataset for the problem Bystand1. The menu bar is used to select Other ==> Problem ==> View, and when the file dialog box appears, Bystand1 is selected from the list of built-in problems. DATASIM initializes the simulation, generates a dataset, and then opens a scrollable view window containing the problem description and simulated data. The contents of this window can be printed or saved to disk. The description concludes with a reference to the original study (Darley and Latané, 1968), and that the simulated dataset is preceded by the value of the seed (211935) used to generate the data. This particular dataset can be regenerated at any time by entering Initialize Bystand1, Seed 211935.

Once a simulated dataset has been generated, we can close the view window and analyze the data. Figure 10.7 shows the results of percentaging the cell frequencies relative to the column totals (Pcol). We see that 100 percent, 69.2 percent, and 38.5 percent of the subjects helped in the two-, three-, and six-person groups, respectively. The chi-square analysis shows that these percentages differ

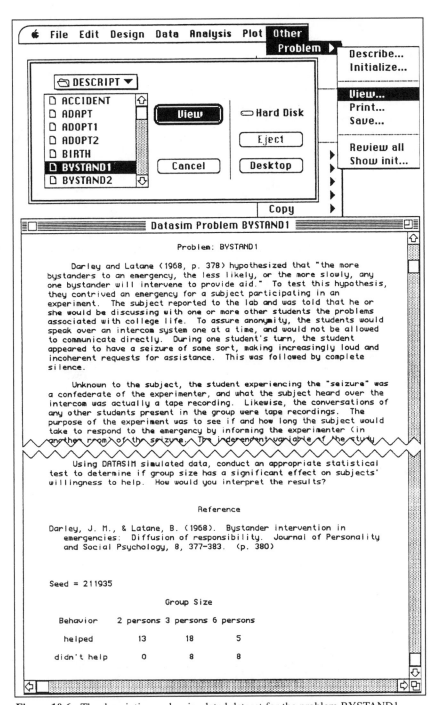

Figure 10.6   The description and a simulated dataset for the problem BYSTAND1

significantly ($p = .0031$). In the present context, the chi-square statistic provides a test of the homogeneity of proportions across the three experimental conditions. Since $p < .05$, we reject the null hypothesis that group size has no effect on willingness to help. Given the initialization for Bystand1, this is a correct decision.

The initialization files for DATASIM problems are stored in the subdirectory DATASIM.LIB:PROBLEMS. Inspecting the contents of these files can be quite helpful to instructors designing their own problems, because the files provide ready-made templates for initializing simulations of various studies. As illustrated in Figure 10.7, the Show command is used to display the contents of an initialization file. It is apparent that the Bystand1 file is simply a DATASIM macro for initializing a simulation of the Darley and Latané (1968) study; entering Initialize Bystand1 or selecting Other ==> Problem ==> View from the menu bar (as in Figure 10.6) causes DATASIM to execute the commands stored in the file.

The commands in Bystand1 specify the research design, the labels for the rows and columns of the table, and the probabilities of sampling observations in the 2x3 cells of the table. The cell probabilities are estimated by dividing each of the cell frequencies in the original table (Darley and Latané, 1968, p. 380) by the total N of the table (52). Also, rather than using Ntot to set the total

```
════════════ Simfile = "Bystand1" ════════════ ▣▤

⊟ Pcol

                          Group Size

    Behavior    2 persons    3 persons    6 persons       Total

      helped        13          18           5             36
                 100.0%       69.2%        38.5%          69.2%

   didn't help       0           8           8             16
                    .0%        30.8%        61.5%          30.8%

     Total          13          26           13            52
                 100.0%      100.0%       100.0%         100.0%

⊟ Chis
   2x3 chi-square:  Chi-sq(2) = 11.56, p = .0031
   Cramer's phi = .471

⊟ Show "BYSTAND1"
   design table 2x3, cfix 13 26 13
   rmain "Behavior", rlabel "helped" "didn't help"
   cmain "Group Size", clabel "2 persons" "3 persons" "6 persons"
   cprobs .212 .308 .077 \
          .038 .192 .173
   reference: Darley & Latane (1968). JSPS

⊟ |
```

Figure 10.7   Analysis of the simulated data and a listing of the initialization file for BYSTAND1

sample size to $N = 52$, Cfix is used to set the sample size of each column of the table to $n_1 = 13$, $n_2 = 26$, and $n_3 = 13$, respectively. (These were the sample sizes employed by Darley and Latané for the two-, three, and six-person groups.) Constraining the column totals in this way is necessary because Bystand1 is an experiment in which fixed numbers of subjects are assigned at random to each of three conditions. Consequently, although the row totals are free to vary in the simulated datasets, reflecting as they do the overall willingness of people to help or not, the column totals are fixed by the design of the experiment. By way of comparison, the initialization in Figure 10.2a sets no constraints on the row or column marginals. Since only the total sample size is determined (Ntot = 100), both the row and column marginal totals are free to vary across the simulated datasets.[10]

Before considering the related problem, Bystand2, we should digress briefly to demonstrate a unique feature of DATASIM; i.e., its ability to perform *repetitive* simulation. In this mode, multiple datasets are generated and the statistics computed on the data (z, t, F, r, etc.) are used to form empirical sampling distributions. DATASIM provides ways to direct the statistics to a file, and to subsequently process the file so that the statistics of interest can be extracted and read into DATASIM as data (Bradley, 1989a, p. 105; Bradley, 1991a, p. 199). One can then plot the sampling distributions, compute the means and standard errors, or tabulate the number of times a particular statistic exceeds a critical value (for assessing Type I error rates or power, as appropriate). The Simulate command is used to perform repetitive simulation in DATASIM.[11] Figure 10.8 shows an example based on Bystand1: Simulate 10 generates ten randomized datasets, and Display and Chis tell DATASIM to display each dataset and to compute a chi-square analysis on the data. The results are output as the simulation proceeds. Note that since the seed used to generate each dataset is displayed, we can regenerate and analyze in greater detail any particular dataset of interest. Entering Seed 826856, for example, would regenerate the third dataset shown in Figure 10.8.

Students can attain a good appreciation for sampling error by inspecting the variation in the cell frequencies and chi-square statistics of Figure 10.8. Relative to the value of 7.91 reported by Darley and Latané, the values of chi-square range from a low of 2.60 ($p = .2725$) to a high of 19.99 ($p < .0001$). Tabulating the number of datasets with $p < .05$ provides an empirical estimate of the power of the test: since eight of the ten tests are significant, the empirical power is .80. (The two cases in which $p > .05$ are Type II errors.) Although not the focus of the present paper, it should be noted that the repetitive simulation in Figure 10.8 constitutes a small-scale Monte Carlo simulation or *sampling experiment*. Large-scale simulations are also possible, involving 1,000 to 10,000 simulated datasets. Now, suppose we initialize the simulation in such a way that certain assumptions of a statistical test are violated. We can then perform a sampling experiment and tabulate the number of Type I (or II) errors which occurred for the test. The

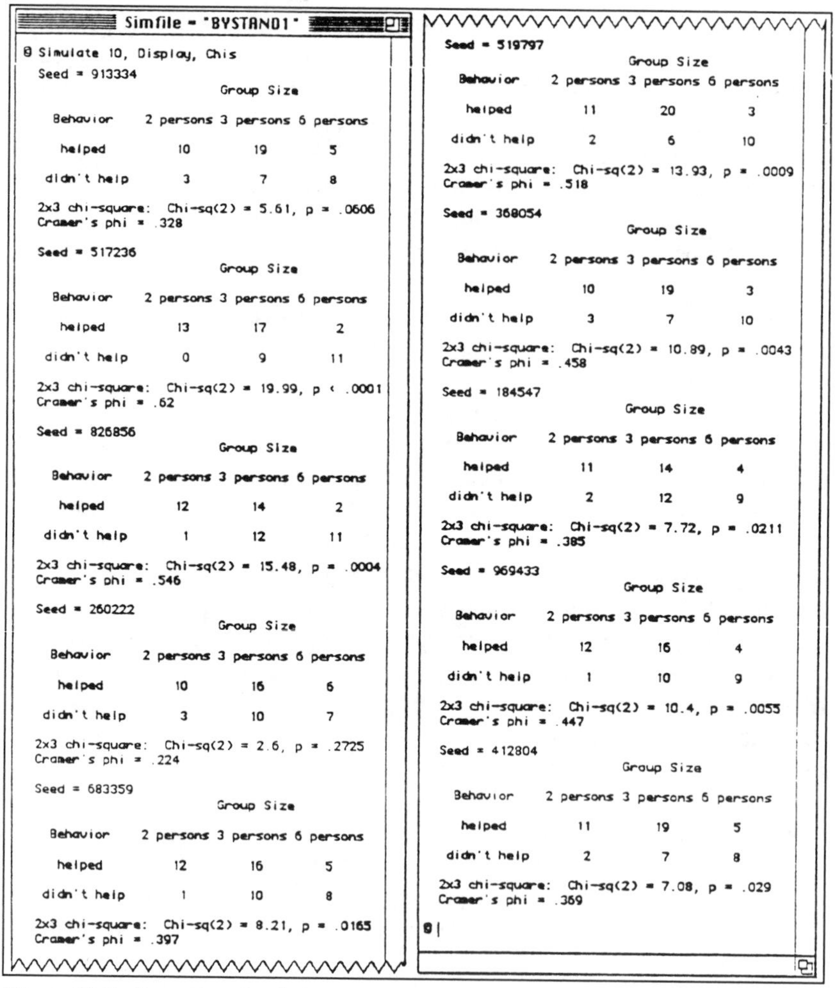

Figure 10.8 Repetitive simulation with the problem BYSTAND1

empirical error rate can then be compared to the nominal error rate in order to assess the consequences of violating the assumptions. We can also have DATASIM compare the cumulative distribution function (CDF) of the empirical sampling distribution to the corresponding theoretical distribution (Bradley, Senko, and Stewart, 1990). As an exercise, students can calculate the theoretical power by referencing a non-central chi-square distribution.[12] This value can then be compared with the empirical estimate obtained through simulation.

Consider now the problem Bystand2, which was designed to generate simulated data for the speed measure employed by Darley and Latané (1968). Show Bystand2 displays the contents of the initialization file:

DESIGN ONEWAY 3 S/T, NOBS 13 26 13
MAIN "Group Size", LABELS "2 persons" "3 persons" "6 persons"
YLABEL "Mean Speed\(100/latency)", XVAL 2 3 6
MU .87 .72 .51, SIGMA .3249, DECIMAL 2, LOWER .277777
LAMBDA C1 -.906 .1455 .0207 .1794
LAMBDA C2 -1.001 .0855 .004546 .0991
LAMBDA C3 -.993 -.001081 -.00000407 -.001076
REFERENCE: Darley & Latane (1968). JPSP

```
═══════════ Simfile = "Bystand2" ═══════════

 ⊟ Initialize BYSTAND2
 ⊟ Data

   Seed = 800853

                    Group Size

     2 persons  3 persons  6 persons

          .64        .54        .33
          .75       1.45       1.30
         1.11        .53        .37
          .68        .71        .69
          .62        .43        .95
          .53        .70        .61
         1.16        .49        .28
         1.20        .39        .28
          .86        .56        .28
          .90        .54        .55
         1.11        .63       1.30
          .56        .72        .40
          .50        .49        .30
                     .69
                    1.01
                     .53
                     .88
                     .49
                     .72
                     .82
                     .68
                     .54
                     .71
                     .56
                     .76
                    1.22

 ⊟ |
```

Figure 10.9 Initialization and simulated data for the problem BYSTAND2

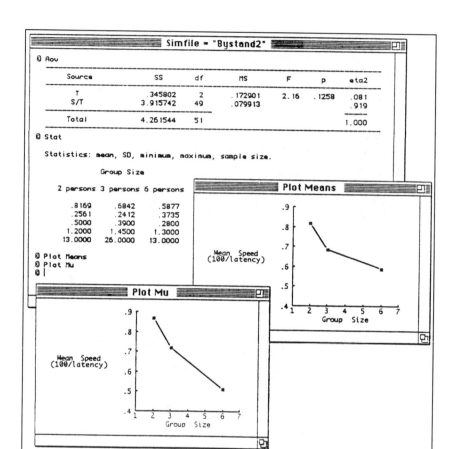

Figure 10.10   Analyses and plots of the simulated data for BYSTAND2

Note that the Lambda command is used to generate non-normal distributions (Bradley, 1989b, pp. 162-168). Figure 10.9 illustrates a simple and direct method for generating the simulated dataset: Initialize Bystand2 executes the commands in the initialization file, and Data generates the data. (The description is displayed by entering Describe Bystand2.) An analysis of variance and descriptive statistics for the simulated data are shown in Figure 10.10. Since the differences among the means are not significant ($p = .1258$), this would lead us to commit a Type II error. Comparing a plot of the sample means (Plot Means) to a plot of the population means (Plot Mu) reveals the reason: sampling variation has resulted in relatively small differences among the means. Ten additional datasets for Bystand2 were generated using the Simulate command, and a one-way Anova and plot of the means were obtained for each. The results are presented in Figure 10.11. The seed, F, and p values for the datasets are shown

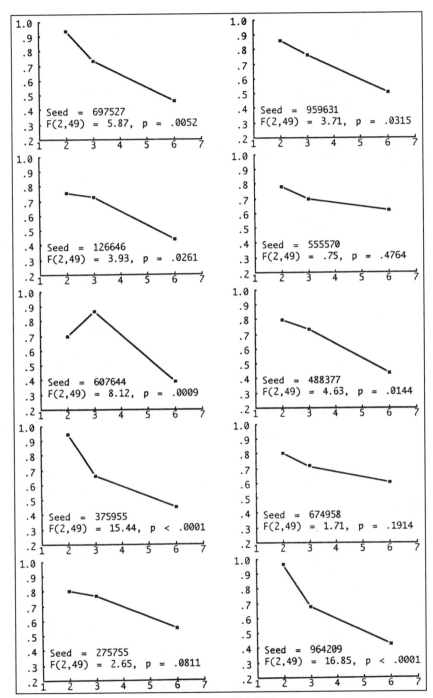

Figure 10.11   Repetitive simulation with BYSTAND2

in the insets of the plots. Tabulating the number of cases where $p < .05$, we find that seven of the ten F ratios are significant. As in Figure 10.8, the variation in the results reflects the effects of sampling error.

Bystand1 and Bystand2 illustrate the kinds of problems that have been included in the DATASIM library. The instructor can augment the library by installing additional initialization and description files in the appropriate sub-directories of DATASIM.LIB. The built-in problems are designed to sharpen students' skills in analyzing data and interpreting results. The required analyses range from simple descriptive statistics and inferential tests (mean, SD, correlation, one- and two-sample t tests, etc.) to relatively complex statistical procedures (repeated measures Anova, two-way Anova, pairwise comparisons, linear contrasts, multiple regression, partial correlation, etc.). Students in a statistics course would typically be assigned one or two problems from the library each week.

Of course, the problems in the DATASIM library are also quite useful for online demonstrations in class. Using simulated data for well-known studies is certainly more effective and involving than using the "trumped-up" and highly artificial datasets provided in textbooks. Furthermore, by reinitializing the values of certain parameters, it is quite easy to answer a variety of "what if" questions. Consider, for instance, the power of the F test: *what if* the sample size is made larger, the means more dissimilar, the standard deviation smaller, the correlation (for repeated measures designs) larger, or the alpha level more liberal? By altering the appropriate parameters, generating a number of simulated datasets, and tabulating the number of correct rejections ($p \leq$ alpha), it is a simple matter to illustrate the answers to these questions in class.

CONCLUSION

This chapter has reviewed a general purpose data simulator called DATASIM. The program can generate datasets for table, experimental, and multivariate research designs. By initializing simulations with properly chosen values for the population parameters, it is easy to create customized datasets which have particular characteristics of interest. In addition, the repetitive simulation capability of DATASIM is useful for demonstrating sampling variation, Type I and Type II decision errors, and various principles of sampling theory. The examples presented in this chapter give a reasonably good indication of how DATASIM is used to facilitate teaching. Additional information may be found in publications reviewing the basic design and capabilities of the software (Bradley, 1989a, 1989b), the accuracy of the random number algorithms (Bradley, Senko, and Stewart, 1990), the methodology for simulating two-way factorial designs (Bradley, 1991a) and multivariate designs (Bradley, 1993), and the use of DATASIM for conducting computer-based laboratory assignments (Bradley, Hemstreet, and Ziegenhagen, 1992).

NOTES

1. Classroom demonstrations require some means of projecting the output of the computer to a large screen. A panel projection system, used in conjucation with an overhead projector or a multisync data projector can be used to do this. A less satisfactory solution is to mount several large monitors throughout the class.

2. These anomalies can be avoided by applying systematic scale-changing procedures to a random sample of standard normal deviates. In doing this, however, one is well on the way to creating a data simulator of the sort described in this chapter. Furthermore, the generation of correlated observations requires matrix operations which are simply too tedious to perform by hand (see Bradley, 1989b. pp. 168-171).

3. By default, DATISIM will generate normally distributed data. However, it is possible to specify non-normal distributions using the Lambda or Catvar commands.

4. Unlike the Data command, the Seed command does not display the data. This is useful when generating large datasets. The data currently resident in DATASIM can be displayed at any time by entering Display.

5. In the Mueller-Lyer illusion, a shaft flanked by out-going fins appears longer than a shaft flanked by in-going fins:

>---< vs. <--->

The strength of the illusion can be measured by having the observer adjust the shaft with the out-going fins until it appears equal in length to the shaft with the in-going fins (the so-called method of adjustment).

6. There is a rationale for using the tokens S/T and TxS to represent independent and correlated groups designs, respectively. In the analysis of variance, whenever the levels of one factor are not crossed with those of another, the levels of the former are said to be "nested" within the levels of the latter. Independent group designs necessarily have different subjects serving in each treatment condition. Therefore, if we regard subjects as a factor in the design, then we would say that the subjects are nested within treatments. The token S/T, short for "subjects within treatment," represents this case. In a repeated measures design, on the other hand, the same subjects serve in all conditions, and therefore the subject factor is fully crossed with the treatment conditions, and therefore the subject is fully crossed with the treatment factor. Since all levels of the subject factor are combined with all levels of the treatment factor, this is sometimes referred to as a treatment by subjects (TxS) design. The token TxS is used by DATASIM to represent this case. Similar logic applies to multifactor designs: the token BxS/A, for example, indicates that the observations are correlated across the levels of factor B, but independent across the levels of factor A. In this case, different groups of subjects are nested within each of the levels of A, but the subjects in each such group serve in (or are "crossed with") all the levels of B. This is commonly referred to as a split-plot design. DATASIM can generate and analyze the data for this and many other designs: AxS/B, AxBxS/AC, BxS/C, S/AB, S/ABC, etc.

7. Although not shown in Figure 10.2, DATASIM can also generate and analyze the data for three-way factorial designs. The initialization would then need to take into account a third factor (C) and its levels (c_1, c_2, etc.) in specifying the population cell means.

8. Although the datasets in Figures 10.2 are relatively small, no limit is imposed by DATASIM on the sample size. The maximum size is therefore dictated by the amount of primary storage. To cite an extreme example, multivariate datasets with

$k = 8$ variables and $n = 100,000$ observations per variable have been generated on a Macintosh IIci with 16 MB of RAM.

9. The use of independently randomized datasets for a given problem ensures that students will do their own work. Since the correct solution for an analysis is unique to each dataset, the student must check his/her work carefully for internal consistency, and for the presence of transcription, data entry, computational, and other errors. Unlike textbook problems, this process cannot be short-circuited by comparing solutions with a classmate, because each student analyzes a different dataset. Moreover, because of sampling variation in the data, it is possible (even likely) that some students will obtain significant results whereas others will not. Consequently, even the most general conclusions about the data (e.g., whether the experimental treatment had an effect or not) must be tailored to the particular dataset the student is analyzing. The fact that students arrive at different conclusions for one and the same problem has important pedagogical implications: the astute instructor will see this as an opportunity to clarify the meaning of Type I and Type II decision errors (Bradley, 1991b, p.18).

10. DATASIM allows you fix the row marginals (RFIX), column marginals (CFIX), or both. Otherwise the marginals are free to vary in the sampling scheme.

11. The Simulate command assumes that a simulation has been initialized. This is done by entering commands manually, as in Figure 10.1, or by executing an initialization file in the DATASIM library. The latter is accomplished by entering Initialize followed by the problem name, or by generating a description and dataset for the problem as in Figure 10.6.

12. Although not the focus of the present chapter, the repetitive simulation in Figure 10.8 constitutes a small-scale Monte Carlo simulation or *sampling experiment*. Large-scale simulations are also possible, involving 1,000 to 10,000 simulated datasets. Now, suppose we initialize the simulation in such a way that certain assumptions of a statistical test are violated. We can then perform a sampling experiment and tabulate the number of Type I (or II) errors which occurred for the test. The empirical error rate can then be compared to the nominal error rate in order to assess the consequences of violating the assumptions. We can also have DATASIM compare the cumulative distribution function (CDF) of the empirical sampling distribution to the corresponding theoretical distribution (Bradley, Senko, & Stewart, 1990).

REFERENCES

Bradley, D. R. (1988). *DATASIM*. Lewiston, ME: Desktop Press.

Bradley, D. R. (1989a). Computer simulation with DATASIM. *Behavior Research Methods, Instruments, & Computers, 21*, 99-112.

Bradley, D. R. (1989b). A general purpose simulation program for statistics and research methods. In G. Garson & S. Nagel (Eds.), *Advances in social science and computers* (Vol. 1, pp. 145-186). Greenwich, CT: JAI Press.

Bradley, D. R. (1991a). Anatomy of a DATASIM simulation: The Doob and Gross horn-honking study. *Behavior Research Methods, Instruments, & Computers, 23*, 190-207.

Bradley, D. R. (1991b). *Datasim for the Macintosh*. Lewiston, Maine: Desktop Press.

Bradley, D. R. (1993). Multivariate simulation with DATASIM: the Mihal and Barrett study. Submitted for publication.

Bradley, D. R., Hemstreet, R. L., and Ziegenhagen, S. T. (1992). A simulation laboratory for statistics. *Behavior Research Methods, Instruments, & Computers, 24*, 190-204.

Bradley, D. R., Senko, M. W., and Stewart, F. A. (1990). Statistical simulation on microcomputers. *Behavior Research Methods, Instruments, & Computers, 22*, 236-246.

Darley, J. M., and Latané, B. (1968). Bystander intervention in emergencies: Diffusion of responsibility. *Journal of Personality and Social Psychology, 8*, 377-383.

Winer, B. J. (1971). *Statistical principles of experimental design* (2nd ed.). New York: McGraw-Hill.

11

An Integrative Approach to Writing with Computers

W. Brett McKenzie

Instructional Support Specialist
Bryant College, Providence, Rhode Island

This chapter presents the design principles that guided the integration of computer technology into a first-year writing program at Bryant College. The discoveries made by the faculty and staff are presented as a narrative in the hope of demonstrating that the design principles applied to this course are general principles. As general principles, these design principles could be applied in any subject area.

This chapter also describes the curriculum that resulted from combining these elements. This curriculum has all the contingent characteristics of a work in progress. It grew from discussions during a long car ride and conversations between, or in response to, conference presentations. While the new writing program has been successful since the first trial in the 1990-91 academic year, the group who designed the course does revisit those issues that demanded a new course. We also learn from the results of classroom practice. Perhaps like a machine or computer program, we are tweaking the course to fix the bugs caused by unanticipated conflicts with student and faculty, student and student, and student and machine interactions.

DESIGN PRINCIPLES

The chairperson of the English department had come under pressure to computerize the English writing program. This pressure came from the promise of improving writing with computers, from following a fad, and from confusion about how computers would be integrated into the lives of the graduates in their work environments. In a business school, which emphasizes the utility value of knowledge, many of the courses tilt toward providing students useful skills for the day after graduation. Committees, dean's councils, and administrators had considered curriculum initiatives for integrating computers into most academic departments. Nothing had caught the attention of the faculty sufficiently to effect the design of any course, let alone the required writing course which seemed peripheral to the computer's heritage as a computational device. As a consequence of the lack of action, the chairperson of the English department asked two faculty members and an instructional designer to devise a course to integrate computers into the first-year writing sequence. The faculty members were known to be interested in innovation, and the instructional designer had taught composition and wanted to promote computer use in the humanities.

The first-year writing program that exists at the college follows a model commonly found in post-secondary education. All students must take an introduction to writing during the first semester. All students (except a handful of advanced-placement students) take the second-semester course which focuses on writing analytically about literature. This skeleton would be preserved in our program design because our primary goal was to evaluate an alternative model that could become institutionalized. Our full program had a three-phased approach: first, introduce the new curriculum and teach it for two years without substantial change to a select group of first-year students; second, expand to a larger segment of the first-year population and introduce more instructors to the methods; and finally, move the whole writing program over to this model. To date, we have completed the first phase and are currently working on expanding into the second phase.

Along with the two-semester sequence, the English department has institutionalized the process model as the instructional pedagogy for teaching writing. All classes require multiple drafts and revision of student essays. Instructors, however, are free to select their own texts, write their own syllabi, and employ their favored instructional techniques, such as peer review or conferencing. The only other departmental requirement is that during the first semester students must gain research and documentation skills.

The habit of the institution, when confronted with technology issues, has been to use as low a technology solution as possible. There was no campus-wide network. There would be no special funding for this course. There was, and would be, no writing lab. While these constraints might seem overly restrictive, they did force the course design to focus on writing and to concentrate on using the technology as a means to improving writing. These restrictions have caused us to downplay technological wizardry. Sometimes they have forced us to devise a mechanical or physical solution when, with greater resources, we might have plunged more quickly into electronic and digital solutions. In retrospect, the course design focuses on the learning environment brought about by the technology. The designers discovered in developing the course that the ways computers change the social interactions of writing and the construction of meaning are more important for students to understand than the mechanics of writing with a different stylus.

The funding restriction meant that no new equipment could be bought for this course. Any computers and peripherals dedicated to this program would have to be cadged from an existing source at the college. If we could not get dedicated computers, the course would have to be planned around scheduling class hours in the existing labs for teaching courses that used PC-based software. These computer labs were already so heavily scheduled (on a cycle of decreasing availability during the term) that only one recitation period per week would be the most the instructors could expect of these rooms. The first course design principle evolved from this problem:

> If the technology was not available on demand by the faculty and students during their scheduled classes, then the technology would never become integrated into the course but would remain an adjunct component. As an adjunct component, the course would fail in its objective to computerize the writing program.

The need to have the technology on demand meant that the course required its own computers. The traditional model for a class that uses computers has been "one-student-one-computer." Computer boosters have reinforced this model; comparative statistics of different school settings detailing student-to-computer ratios to measure a school's status has reinforced this model, and the apparent antisocial computer culture embodied in the "geek" or "nerd" has also reinforced this model. Using a computer is most often seen as a solitary activity, like reading a book or writing on a piece of paper. Without outside funding, the course would not have the resources to purchase computers for everyone in the class, nor could it expect to compete with other subjects to have so many computers for its own use. The issue of having computers on demand without a large hardware commitment would have to be resolved.

Our second design principle resulted from how we viewed the computer, how it had changed our activity as writers, and what level of intrusion we wanted the technology to make into the process of writing. Echoing the concerns of the institution for skills, suggestions for integrating grammar or style checkers had been urged. Likewise, suggestions to use special software for brainstorming or the other phases of the writing process had initially seemed worthwhile. Our own attempts to design sophisticated macros to aid the revision process, such as selecting the first line of each sentence or having the computer follow a formalized rubric for good writing, had left us feeling dissatisfied. Our reviews of specialized software packages, our trials, and a cursory examination of the literature made us decide on our position from which to view the technology. This led to our second design principle:

> Computers would be communication devices not symbol manipulating devices. Students would discover those techniques of using

the computer to write which suited them best. Just as some wrote from an outline in the pencil and paper world, some might brainstorm with the screen turned off. In our course design, the computer would help all students in the program converse with each other—sometimes electronically, sometimes in hard copy.

In practice, this principle removed a burden from the faculty to instruct students in how to use the computers. This had the advantage that faculty could concentrate on the writing of their students, an activity for which they were well trained and an activity in which they had developed considerable skill in their years of teaching. Furthermore, without funding for software purchases, we would be unable to purchase an expensive integrated system such as Daedalus from the University of Texas. Those special software considerations might influence our decision when we consider the structure of the course for the entire first-year class because we have learned that there are network elements in those programs that we might like to explore.

In case I appear to have overemphasized the lack of funding, its absence made accepting the ramifications of our third design principle easier. We realized, about the time we recognized the importance of technology on demand, that we wanted to shift the balance of power between the instructor and the student in the classroom. First, we were committed to the principle that the teacher-centered classroom had severe limits for teaching at this level. Second, we knew that we had to learn from our students. We could speculate on how they regarded technology. We could be awed by how effortlessly they learned software with which we struggled. If we maintained the posture of presenting an all-knowing curriculum to the students, we would never learn those elements that would improve the course. The third course design principle reflected this issue:

> Much of the burden of learning would be put on the students. They would become resources for themselves to negotiate the territory of their investigation as well as to determine among themselves the level of technical knowledge they would need to succeed.

This third principle ripples throughout the design of the curriculum. Some of its instances may have little direct impact on the application of technology. However, a course that proposes to fully integrate the computer becomes a different course if a division is made between the territory where students can use the computer and the territory where the computer has no place. In an organic system, much as this course has become, the curriculum elements create a larger entity than they would as separate modules.

CURRICULUM DESCRIPTION

The two faculty members involved in this program each taught two sections of the first-year writing program for both semesters of the academic year

1990-91. The program had four sections of approximately fifteen students—two on a Monday-Wednesday-Friday schedule and two on a Tuesday-Thursday schedule. We selected the students for these classes because they either showed a greater interest in writing based on an pre-major selection, or their records indicated a greater aptitude for writing. We neither designed nor implemented any formal experimental protocols to measure the effectiveness of the program. First, the instructors had embarked on a curriculum for which we had found no precedents. We felt the challenge of introducing a new course and simultaneously determining benchmarks would be more than the small staff could do. Second, even today, we have yet to settle on how to measure a student's performance in this different environment. The course generates an overwhelming amount of data from student drafts and final copies, student and faculty journals, and the student online journals. We need to develop a framework to winnow the vast pile of text the course generates. Finally, we had a commitment to run the program without substantial change for two years. This was to ensure that the instructors would become familiar and comfortable with the technological environment and the emphasis on collaboration by the students. We were confident that the structure of the program made sense based on the promise of the program elements from individual studies. What made this program unique, however, was that no one had combined these course components with students at the college level.

We built the course on the following components:

1. confrontation and investigation of a significant intellectual issue using student research teams
2. publication of all students' final work
3. use of computers to record conversations/dialogue about issues of their own choice

RESEARCH GROUPS

The faculty determined a global issue for the students to investigate. In the first year, we chose the topic "Computers in Society." We selected this topic because we hoped that by forcing the students to wrestle with the ramifications of computers in society, we might learn more about how they understood and related to computers. Our expectations of how students would integrate the technology into their writing was speculative. Surveys of student attitudes toward computing had not given us much insight into designing the course. The results of those surveys, including an in-house survey, had given us no clear direction about how students confronting an increasingly computerized society felt about becoming dependent on computers. Discovering very quickly that students in fact have little interest in examining computers, in subsequent years we have changed the investigation to issues of ethnicity and cultural origins. This change in topic provides better preparation for the second semester and parallels issues that students will confront in other classes in the first- and second-year sequences, such as the core introduction to the humanities. Furthermore, I now suspect that students may not be intellectually ready to distance themselves from technology to comment upon it while they are reconciling themselves to using it.

We divided the students in each of the sections into research teams of four to five members. Within the global topic a research team decided on a more narrow topic, and within that group, each student chose a more focused aspect of the group's topic. For example, one group in the first year selected the topic of "Computers and Government." Individual research areas were "Government Spending on Computers," "Effects on Political Campaigns," "Government Support of Computers in Space," and "Computers and the Military-War Games." For the final essay, the students in a research teams gathered elements of the individual essays into a combined essay.

From the first year we learned that the ideal size of the research group was smaller than we had anticipated. Because of the size of the computer screen and to encourage interaction with the computer as a group, three people to a research team has become our standard. With more than three, those students who are not either sitting at the keyboard or to the left and right of the keyboard operator are relegated to a back row. Consequently, they become excluded. We have avoided collaboration about a larger computer screen because the size of text on the screen becomes more critical as the group increases in size and moves further away from the screen to accommodate the larger number. Additionally, we wanted the technology in the classroom to mirror the technology in the public labs to minimize dissonance between writing in one environment in the classroom and a different environment on their own time.

CLASSBOOK

Through the first half of the term the students worked on individual essays. Members of the research team critiqued the essay, and the student whose essay was being reviewed made modifications online. Shortly after midterm, the research teams presented their findings in an oral presentation for critique by their classmates in their section. Following this larger critique, the students in a research team combined their individual essays as a collaborative essay. This collaborative essay then became the research team's contribution to the classbook.

We have attempted to have upper-division students who have taken a desktop publishing course serve as the classbook's publishers. Our aim has been to make the students, both lower and upper division, responsible for the final product. As most student writing is for an artificial audience and is returned to the students with instructor comments and corrections, publishing is an attempt to urge students to establish a professional standard for their semester's work. The college's print shop prints and binds the classbook. Each student receives a copy of the classbook and a copy is catalogued in the college library. We hope that future students will refer to the books of the previous years to challenge or support the ideas presented by the earlier classes. Until we have more experience on the same topic, we will not be able to evaluate this recursive social process.

ONLINE JOURNALS

The course elements described so far take maximum benefit from collaboration among the students with the computer as the mediator and means of production. To aid in creating a community of thinkers and writers about an issue, we have also used an online journal to promote an exchange of ideas among the students. While we would like to establish a network that allows synchronous communications over the network so that the conversations become "live," we have been forced to limit ourselves to asynchronous entries.

The purpose of the online communications, or online journal, is to encourage exchange of ideas about the general topic. First, we wanted to extend the boundaries of the classroom beyond the specific meeting times. Second, we wanted students who were analyzing the same problem from a different perspective to stimulate others to see different aspects of the same problem. As such, we required the students to make a minimum of a weekly entry into the online journal, and we had Group A from one section conversing with Group A from another section. The effect of this arrangement meant that a research team whose topic was "Effects of Computers in Education" might converse with a group whose topic was "Computers in Entertainment."

We gave students the option of using a "handle" or pseudonym for their online contributions. This was designed to give those who were shy, or who might take a stance against the prevailing opinion of their conversational partners, the chance to voice their concerns. When we first tried the online journal, faculty made some comments and attempted to nudge the conversation in a direction they felt would help the students. As much as faculty tried to disguise their presence through pseudonyms, students quickly recognized the origin of their comments. As such, the faculty now no longer participates in the student dialogue and monitors it only to ensure that all students participate in the exchange. This leads to a totally self-regulated electronic conversation.

An analysis of the electronic conversation has shown that students used this means of communication differently from our anticipation. Our expectation of a sophisticated epistolary exchange about the issues of the course or the class has not occurred. Rather, students use the exchange mostly for social purposes, such as suggestions for where to find materials at off-campus libraries, end of semester gatherings, escape mechanisms from the academic burdens, and generalized complaints about the institution and the course. Interspersed with these entries, however, are exchanges about larger social issues such as abortion or the campus attitude towards sexual orientation. These exchanges often do echo issues from the classroom.

Our most recent analysis of the online journals gives us the sense that students are creating their identities through their entries. It is not unusual to find a student contradicting or modifying a stance between the opening and closing of an entry. We have found it interesting that the students will leave these contradictory entries. On the computer, they could easily erase or revise their entry to make it consistent. The area of online communications in the classrooms, the corporate realm, and society in general is beginning to attract more attention. The online journals have been our most direct application of technology to the writing classroom and have been the element most easily transferred to other classes. One of the instructors from this program has recently been working with introducing the concept into her senior-level literature classes with promising results.

TECHNICAL CONSIDERATIONS

When we first established the course, we agonized over the choice of software for the students' use. The college has only DOS machines in the public labs and has not promoted computer purchases by the students. Our software choices, therefore, had to work with the public resources and were limited to character-based DOS software. The college has adopted WordPerfect as the standard word processor and has developed noncredit modules to establish student proficiency. These modules, however, run throughout the first semester with the result that many of the students in this program have not developed proficiency early enough in the term. Expecting all students to use a complicated word processor might impede some students from writing well.

To alleviate the problem of teaching the software, we chose Collegiate Writer, an easy-to-learn and inexpensive word processing software, developed at the University of Western Washington. We required the students to purchase the word processing software. Our primary reason for the purchase was to test the notion that the structure of public labs and standardization of word processing essentially rationed the technology to the students. With students owning their word processing software, they would have access to their writing tools on any DOS computer. This would include computers they may have at home, at a job, or that a fellow student might have brought to campus. A secondary reason was that the software we chose included a bibliography formatting module. This module allowed students to create bibliographies merely by entering the necessary elements, such as author name, title, and so on. Minimizing class time devoted to teaching this mechanical process seemed an unanticipated benefit of the class.

When we asked students whether owning the word processing software seemed significant, few students felt that it gave them a particular advantage. We have since dropped the software purchase as a requirement. Besides the lack of student interest, the cost of software competed with book purchases. Buying books and software makes the course more expensive than any other course. We have, however, kept the word processing software for this course because of the advantage in having students use the software from the first week without extensive instruction by the writing faculty. When word processing programs become less idiosyncratic, this will no longer be an issue.

In retrospect, the required features for the word processing software for the collaborative phase of the program would be an easy import/export of text so that students can combine essays easily and prepare text for desktop publishing and multiple document editing with a simple cut-and-paste feature between documents so that students can combine parts of their individual essays for the collaborative essay.

We have used the same word processing software to make entries into the online journals. Our mechanism for the online journal has required a sneaker-net. The journals are maintained on separate disks for each group and a student checks out the diskette to make an entry. This procedure is not ideal. As expected, it sometimes causes frustration when more than one person wants to make an entry to the same journal at the same time. Our attempts at working around using a network version of word processing software with a public file have not succeeded. We will need to incorporate bulletin board software with its concomitant administrative overhead and different interface to use the online journal in an expanded way. We have developed sufficient interest and experience in electronic communication so that these needs will be considered in the design of a campus-wide network.

To accommodate the instructors' requirement to have technology on demand, we made a separate facility available for teaching these classes. This facility was designed primarily as a language lab to support foreign language self-study. The layout of the facility, however, includes carrels designed as collaborative workstations. As this facility also houses some computers, we could use the space during class meeting times to support this course. We are currently seeking funding to purchase the technology to equip dedicated classrooms for the second phase of the project. The requirements will include seven networked CPUs for students. We are still debating whether to include a workstation for the instructor. At this time, we are leaning away from that proposal because tying an instructor to a computer might diminish the interactions between the student and the instructor. At no point in our course design or consideration of technology have we wanted to substitute electronic communication for social interactions. For us, technology has been used to augment the means for the students to communicate among themselves and with the larger community of the college.

CONCLUSION

Writing with computers has become fully integrated into the writing program at Bryant College. Because funding had an effect on the integration of computers into the program, the design principles of the program had to be carefully thought out to get maximum benefit with limited hardware and software. Through the initiation of the program, students developed their own techniques for using the computer to write and became their own resources in its utilization. With the program's focus on student research groups, a classbook was created that future students could access. An added communication benefit was the establishment of an online journal for maximum collaboration of the students. Succeeding phases in the program will continue the commitment to increase communication and computer accessibility while retaining social interactions.

ACKNOWLEDGMENTS

Dr. Mary Prescott and Dr. Nora Barry are owed thanks for taking the risks of teaching the course. Dr. Mary Lyons, chairperson of the English department, is also owed thanks for having faith in the program we designed.

RESOURCE BIBLIOGRAPHY

A. L. Brown and J. C. Campione, "Communities of Learning and Thinking or A Context by Any Other Name." In D. Kuhn (Ed.), Developmental Perspectives on Teaching and Learning Thinking Skills [Special Issue]. *Contributions to Human Development*, 21, 1990:108-126.

Collegiate Writer, computer software, Bellingham: Western Washington University, 1990.

M. M. Cooper and C. L. Selfe, "Computer Conferences and Learning: Authority, Resistance, and Internally Persuasive Discourse." *College English* Vol. 52, No. 8, Dec 90:847-869.

M. L. Heim, *Electric Language*, New Haven: Yale University Press, 1989.

W. B. McKenzie, "Application of Conversation Theory to Writing Curriculum Design." Conference on College Composition and Communication, 21 March 1991.

W. B. McKenzie, N. Barry and M. Prescott, "Thinking and Collaboration in the First-Year Writing Curriculum." *Proceedings of the 8th International Conference on Technology in Education*, Toronto, 1991:633-635.

S. Papert, "New Theories for New Leanings." Conference on National Association of School Psychologists, 18 April 1984.

J. A. Rheither and D. Vipond, "Writing as Collaboration." *College English,* Vol. 51, No. 8, December 1989:855-867.

T. Winograd and F. Flores, *Understanding Computers and Cognition: A New Foundation for Design*, Norwood: Ablex Publishing Corporation, 1987.

Chronicles from a U.S. Department of Education Title III Grant

Jeanne Buckley
Adjunct Professor of Instructional Technology
Penn State Great Valley and Philadelphia
College of Textiles and Science

Marilyn Puchalski
Director of Academic Computing
Bucks County Community College
Newtown, Pennsylvania

The introduction of educational technology into the teaching and learning process often results in profound changes in an institution's faculty, students, and a school's established curriculum. The adoption of technology appears to create systemic change in the education process, causing teachers who use new technologies to analyze how students learn and how they themselves teach. This self-reflection process ultimately affects the content and philosophy of an institution's curriculum.

At Bucks County Community College (BCCC) in Newtown, Pennsylvania, this process of rethinking teaching, learning, and the curriculum has drastically accelerated over the last three years, due mainly to an influx of resources from a U.S. Department of Education Title III ("institutional strengthening") grant. This grant supplied thirty-one faculty with computers, release time, training, conference travel funds, and the support of an educational technologist. In turn, these faculty, who represented all major programs of study, were required to select one of their courses and to identify or develop a technological application specific to their students' needs.

This case study chronicles the specific activities of three faculty members participating in this grant who were particularly successful in their technological intervention attempts: an English professor who is investigating the nature of collaborative writing via computers and the software program Aspects; a statistics teacher who is using the package Minitab to teach introductory statistics; and an accounting professor who experimented with Ready-to-Run, an integrated ledger accounting system that runs on top of Lotus 1-2-3.

Before describing the activities of these three educators, a brief synopsis of the history of technology use at Bucks County Community College is provided. This contextual information should help readers more fully understand the impact that the success of the grant has had on the institution.

HISTORICAL PERSPECTIVE

BCCC is a two-year, fully accredited, higher education institution located in Newtown, Pennsylvania, about twenty miles northeast of Philadelphia. The college enrolls over 11,000 full- and part-time credit students in more than seventy-five transfer, occupational, and certificate programs of study. BCCC employs approximately 200 full-time and 400 adjunct faculty members, and a staff of 325.

Recognizing the increasing importance of technological literacy, the college designed and conducted a bifurcated research study in the fall of 1988. The first, or external study, assessed entering students' computer literacy and the expectations of future employers and/or transfer institutions regarding students' computer skills. The results of this external study indicated that the institution was not meeting the needs of either interest group (students or employers). In addition, an internal evaluation of BCCC faculty and programs of study revealed a lack of technologically trained faculty, as well as insufficient computer resources for instructional purposes.

To address these problems, a grant proposal was submitted to the U.S. Department of Education in the spring of 1989. The primary focus of the grant was on developing the technological competency of the faculty, with their students as the ultimate beneficiaries of discipline-specific exposure to the use of computers in their program of study. The following rationale supported this approach:

> The average age of the 200 faculty members at the college is forty-nine years. Since the average faculty member completed his/her undergraduate education well over a quarter of a century ago, they have had little or no personal exposure to many of the instructional methods which are widely used in contemporary educational institutions. Their professional development activities have emphasized the updating of subject matter expertise rather than developing alternative instructional delivery methods. Consequently, the traditional instructional styles of the universities—lecture/discussion, presentations, and formalized laboratory experiences—dominate the college's classrooms. Faculty who wish to develop new methodologies

find little assistance or expertise within the institution. There is no instructional development person in their subject discipline to help them develop the sophisticated skills needed to implement new teaching/learning strategies which may require them to make substantial changes in their thinking as well as acquire new capabilities. Faculty interest in developing new methods is high and administrative support is strong. The tangible resources, however, are not present . . . funds have never been budgeted for providing an integrated and systematic approach to computer-augmented instruction[1] across the major disciplines at BCCC.[2]

In October of 1989, grant funds were allocated for faculty development activities and computer resources for faculty and students. Computer resources included open access laboratories, a classroom lab for teaching purposes, and individual computers for faculty participating in the grant.[3]

Resources for faculty development activities included computer training, one course release time for four semesters, funds to attend conferences, and the support of a full-time educational technologist.

The four-year project consisted of three discrete phases. In the first phase, the faculty received "minimal competency" training in computer comfort and basic skills, general purpose and specific software, computers as instructional delivery systems, and educational computer resources. In the second phase, the faculty designed, implemented, and evaluated a course-specific computer activity plan that was pertinent to their specific disciplines, students, and teaching style. The third phase required faculty to serve as resources to their colleagues, sharing the skills, knowledge, and expertise they had gleaned from their participation in the project with others.

Almost all faculty involved in this project have been extremely successful in implementing discipline-specific activities. Many of these activities are creative, pedagogically challenging, and stimulating and have had beneficial results for both teacher and students. To illustrate the diverse Title III activities, we have summarized the efforts of three specific faculty members who have been particularly successful in their efforts.

COMPUTERS AND COLLABORATIVE WRITING

John Strauss, a member of the language and literature department at BCCC, teaches a combination of beginning and intermediate writing and literature courses. His interest in the collaborative, or, to use his term—"peer responding"—writing process predates his use of computers. Before his involvement in the Title III project, Strauss organized his writing classes so that students actually commented on each other's essays during class time and incorporated peer comments into their revisions. Strauss strongly supported this *interactive, nonjudgmental approach* to writing, and believes his students benefitted from both processes: learning from their peers' comments, as well as developing their own abilities to critically evaluate writing. He comments, "People learn by doing, not by hearing about it . . . if I want them to be critical, I have to let them do it!"[4]

During Strauss' participation in the Title III project, he introduced his students (and himself) to the computer-as-participant in this collaborative approach to writing. The first year he held classes in the MS-DOS computer lab using Professional Write.[5]

In the second year of the project, Strauss switched to the Macintosh lab and had his students using Microsoft Word on Macintosh LCs. It was during this second year that Strauss realized the power of the Macintosh to facilitate both his own and his students' commentary on assignments. When students turned in their work, Strauss would collect it on disk and using his own Macintosh, would proceed to insert his comments directly into student essays using a different (enlarged, stylized, etc.) font than the student had used. In this way, Strauss's comments were immediately visible to the student as well as "place-specific" when he returned their work to them. In this way, students *had to deal* with Strauss's comments in order to complete their revisions.

Students were also required to give feedback to each others' papers, and Strauss prepared a list of questions for them to follow (e.g., what is the main point of this essay, what is the theme, how is the theme developed, etc.). Student feedback was either inserted in the text or it appeared as answers to questions at the end of the essay.[6]

Strauss became interested in the software package Aspects because of its ability to connect writers to each other in a networked environment, and thus allow several students to work on the same document simultaneously. For Strauss, this would increase student interaction about class assignments in real-time writing situations. Using Aspects, several people could actually carry on a dialogue about a particular point or critical comment, further increasing the interactivity and collaborative nature of the writing process. In addition, the instructor could use Aspects to "distribute" work for collaboration or comment.

Strauss believes the computer has had a profound effect on both his teaching and student learning. His students have developed more fully as writers through an easier revision process; they also increased their analytical skills through responding to their peers' work. The quality and quantity of revisions increased dramatically, particularly in the intermediate writing classes. While Strauss feels that he now puts more time into commenting on students papers (often papers become twice as long when his comments are added), he also believes he receives more polished papers because they are peer-reviewed before being handed to him. Students also seem to have no problem meeting the 500 or 1,000 word minimum assigned to them although this was not the case before. Strauss believes students now feel more responsible for their own and their peers' work, thus increasing student "ownership" of their writing.

This method of collaboration and peer-review clearly requires a teacher who is comfortable sharing responsibility and authority with his/her students. Strauss actively solicits student input and comments, firmly believing that writing is not a solitary or singular activity.

Strauss "pilot-tested" Aspects during the spring semester 1992 and planned to implement it more fully during the 1992-93 school year. In addition, Strauss's plans for the future are to continue to explore the computer-as-participant in the writing process and to find a way to provide feedback on student feedback to their peers' writing.

COMPUTERS AND STATISTICS INSTRUCTION

Elizabeth Farber teaches introductory and intermediate statistics at BCCC. During the first year of the Title III grant, she reviewed various statistical software packages to determine which one would best suit her teaching requirements, and her students' needs. Farber ultimately selected the program Minitab and, in the spring of 1991, pilot-tested it with her introductory statistics class. Their response to the program was so positive that she opted to fully integrate Minitab into the course, and in the spring of 1992, she held all of her course sessions in the Macintosh lab.

Farber's case is unique to our faculty development effort for several reasons. The first is that in 1991, she was contacted by the Addison Wesley Company to write the *Student Edition of Minitab*, a tutorial for the Minitab program. Therefore, at the same time that Farber was incorporating Minitab into her teaching, she was also creating a text on this program for national publication. This situation presented her and her students with the unique opportunity for the formative evaluation of problems and exercises that would eventually be more widely distributed.

Second, because of a sabbatical vacancy, Farber was asked to teach two sections of statistics in the spring of 1992; one was a computerized course, and one was the "traditional" course. Although one course used Minitab and one didn't,[7] the content to be taught was basically the same. Thus, Farber had the opportunity to collect some original "data" on the use of Minitab with three important variables held constant: the teacher, the content and students from the same sample audience.[8]

Farber found that the students who used the Minitab software package when learning statistics could concentrate more on the statistical concepts than on the computation of numbers, a time-consuming mental and physical activity. Students who did not have access to Minitab spent more time computing the answers to exercises and problems than they did assessing what those answers meant in terms of "real-world" cause and effect. Thus, one of the benefits of using Minitab was that it allowed students to ask "what if?" questions about samples and/or statistical tests, quickly perform those tests, and compare results. This development of higher-order thinking skills about statistics was a pleasant, unexpected outcome of using Minitab for both the students and the instructor.

On the negative side, however, Farber does admit that the computerized section of the course was much harder to teach—it required more one-on-one contact with students and much more physical movement around the computer lab than was usual in a traditional lecture course. In the beginning, students had problems learning the computer and the Minitab program itself; thus, Farber found herself spending more time than she would have liked on fundamental skills. In addition, preparation for the class required a great deal of time, as Farber could not depend on already published sources for problems and examples; rather, she had to construct her own for each session. Of course, these are now included in the *Student Edition of Minitab* that Farber authored, so other faculty will not suffer from the same problem.

In spite of the above problems, Farber is committed to using Minitab and the computer to teach statistics in future classes. She believes the benefits of reduced computation time and increased concept development far outweigh the drawbacks of increased time for course development and increased individual attention, and on-the-spot problem-solving in the classroom.

COMPUTERS AND THE ACCOUNTING CURRICULUM

Tom Zaher is a member of the business studies department and a practicing CPA. He and his colleagues have struggled with the issue of how to appropriately integrate microcomputers into the accounting curriculum for many years. The following questions confronted Zaher when he agreed to participate in the computer-augmented instruction project:

- Which course should be targeted?
- What computer skills will students bring to that course?
- If hands-on instruction is built into an already rigorous syllabus, which topics get less attention or get dropped altogether?
- Should Lotus 1-2-3 be used with exercises the instructor develops or a commercial application package used by professionals, or materials that accompany a textbook?

Zaher found a commercial package with educational applications. Ready-to-Run is an integrated general ledger package which runs on top of Lotus 1-2-3. A student version is produced by Addison Wesley which includes both the software and a tutorial with cases. In addition, problems are keyed to the most popular texts used to teach the first course in accounting principles. Ideally, the software could be used throughout the entire accounting course sequence. The decision was made in the spring of 1991 to pilot test the software in all the sections of Accounting I that Zaher was scheduled to teach the following fall.

Zaher spent half of his three-credit release time that spring learning to use Ready-to-Run. The remainder of his release time was spent determining how to adjust an already packed syllabus so that he could devote one class period per week in this four credit course to using the software and exercises in class. Zaher felt strongly that he should be present when students were working with the software because of possible student frustration; thus, he did not assign out-of-class work that required use of Ready-to-Run.

The tutorial which accompanies the Ready-to-Run software uses a case study which is similar to a practice set to introduce the operation of the software. The same case is used throughout the five chapters with a lab that the student completes at the conclusion of each chapter. An alternate case is provided for variety. Initially, Zaher planned to assign all five parts of one of the cases for the pilot; however, he has subsequently revised his expectations.

The fall of 1991 was the first semester of implementation for the project. This is what Zaher reported about the experience:

> Only the first three lab assignments were completed due to in-class time constraints. It was felt that supervision of the students' time and software usage was more critical than completing all assignments. A survey of students confirmed my observation that the software was too complex to attempt out-of-class assignments. However, the students were enthusiastic about the opportunity to use a commercial accounting package. The case study approach did reinforce accounting topics covered in the textbook for both experienced and inexperienced computer users.

Zaher used student surveys and his own teaching experience with Ready-to-Run to modify his approach for the second semester of the pilot. Results of student surveys revealed that while Ready-to-Run was difficult to use, students felt that the integrated approach did improve their understanding of accounting concepts. Zaher found student interest increased with Ready-to-Run, and his initial concern about varying levels of student computer skills lessened as the more experienced students coached the computer-naive users. He did have problems incorporating the computer exercises into his grading system since the students often collaborated on assignments, and individual assessment was difficult. Both Zaher and his students found time to be a factor in using the program; students wished they had more time to spend with the software and Zaher found that it took more time then he had expected for the students to complete assignments.

Because of these findings, Zaher altered his plan for using Ready-to-Run in the second semester of the pilot. Zaher introduced the software later in the semester, after students had gained some basic accounting concepts, and he reduced the number of computer assignments for the students to complete. These adjustments alleviated some of the stress he experienced in his first semester of using the software. His future plans include continuing to use Ready-to-Run in this course, as well as experimenting with its use in an accounting applications course and other upper-level accounting courses. The following statement summarizes Zaher's assessment of using Ready-to-Run with his students: "This professional software package presents a unique opportunity to enhance the teaching and understanding of the basic principles of accounting."

CONCLUSION

The influx of Title III-sponsored educational technology has had a profound effect on Bucks County Community College's faculty and students. There have been faculty transformations regarding the use of computer technology, and because each of the thirty-one faculty participating in this grant began at a different point in their computer education, each faculty member actually personalized his or her own development process. This process involved not only increasing technological skills but also discovering a computer activity that reflected individual pedagogical approaches to teaching and learning.

While this case study has highlighted three particularly successful Title III participants, many more could have been selected. For instance, one biology teacher, Esta Schwartz, is writing HyperCard programs for use with videodiscs to teach her students anatomy and physiology. Another teacher, Dr. Maxine Hirsch, has used young children to help preservice teachers evaluate age-appropriate software. Yet another, Dr. Ray O'Brien, has his students generating population density maps with the computer to illustrate trends in ethnic population distribution. Because the structure of the grant encouraged it, each faculty member has personalized his/her activity, and we feel this personalization has contributed greatly to the success of our project.

An unanticipated result of BCCC faculty participation in this grant is that the thirty-one faculty involved have really coalesced as a *team*. Because of the grant's requirements (faculty must attend monthly meetings), a forum has been created that has not previously existed at the college. These monthly meetings have allowed the group to explore common concerns, successes, and failures, and has created an interdisciplinary structure that has transcended technology-only issues.[9] In addition, because of their increased expertise, grant participants have become recognized by the institution as community leaders in the use of technology.[10]

As of the writing of this article, it was year four of the grant with the external resources ending the next year. These resources—release time, equipment, and personnel—have been instrumental in the success of all these efforts. The challenge that lies ahead for Bucks County Community College is to continue to provide faculty development support for *all* of its faculty after the Title III grant. The long-range planning process of the college includes specific recommendations for sustaining technological growth, and the commitment of the thirty-one participating faculty will support the growth of educational technology at our institution. Finally, these four years have taught the college a great deal about faculty development, integrating technology across the curriculum, and the effect of computers on teaching and learning. Some lessons have been learned about the effect of the computer on a teacher's role; the effect of the computer on students' interaction with each other and their teachers; the individualization of the integration process; the adaptability of the computer to suit varying pedagogical styles; the creativity of faculty in devising course-specific technological interventions; the computer's ability to perform routine tasks empowering students to master content at a higher level; and the motivation of faculty and students to explore new methods of teaching and learning through the use of educational technology.

NOTES

1. The term "computer-augmented instruction" was selected to describe the pedagogical philosophy of the project instead of "computer-assisted instruction," a term more commonly used in education and industry. By using "augmented instruction," the grant writers placed more emphasis on the faculty member's role in the learning process, not the computer's. In this approach, the computer does not serve as the paragon of instructional but as tool for facilitating learning.
2. Bucks County Community College. (1989). *Application for Support: Strengthening Institutions' Program, Title III of Higher Education Act.*, Newton, PA: Committee for Preparation of Title III grant.
3. Faculty could opt for either MS-DOS or Macintosh computers . . . surprisingly, the preferential split was almost fifty-fifty with individuals in business and the humanities opting for MS-DOS, and those in science and the art selecting Macintosh.
4. Telephone interview with J. Strauss, July 13, 1992.
5. Professional Write is a word processing package (MS-DOS) adopted by the writing faculty because it is very easy to learn; thus, it is used by most students at BCCC.
6. Paper authors were required to ask for specific feedback as well as obtain more reader-directed feedback.
7. Farber did introduce the noncomputerized section to Minitab at the end of the semester.
8. Examples, problems, and tests for the two sections were necessarily different.
9. Interdisciplinary "teams" have come together to work on various projects, involving communications faculty with artists, scientists with social scientists, and mathematicians with psychologists.
10. Several faculty members have made presentations at national conferences based on their Title III activities.

Chapter

13

Learning Information Systems Through a Mail-Enabled Business Simulation: The Case of Trent Engineering

Clive Holtham
Bull Information Systems Professor of Information Management
City University Business School, London, England

Martin Rich
Lecturer in Information Management
City University Business School, London, England

MANAGEMENT EDUCATION AND INFORMATION TECHNOLOGY

There is discussion in most societies of the problems of management education, concerning its nature, quality, or quantity, and in particular whether it is relevant to the global and regional challenges faced by most industrial and commercial based societies. Most societies perceive they face nothing short of a crisis in the education of their managers. Increasing international competition and rapidly changing market technologies, customers, and workforce all contribute to a feeling that management is constantly trying to catch up, with many of the areas involved being largely outside its direct control.

In particular societies or organizations, there are a whole variety of solutions advocated and this is not the place to debate their merits. Two fundamental threads however are likely in redeveloping management education:

1. It will have to be achieved in most societies without significant (or any) increases in per capita funding of management education; indeed per capita funding may fall in the United Kingdom, for example, because all political parties are committed to much higher participation rates in higher education as a first priority.
2. It will have to be based on the principle that managers and prospective managers will behave differently (i.e., "better") as a result of their management education, compared to what they would have done had they not received it.

Since this latter statement appears trite or even trivial, what it is attempting to stress is that management education cannot be seen *solely* as a further stage of the general education process. It cannot and should not serve only this purpose. It must also serve more instrumental goals.

There is considerable debate about precisely what managerial skills can or should be taught or learned. For present purposes it is assumed that there is some definable group of management competencies, in which managers can increase their skills through management education. It is not difficult to identify clear-cut areas such as negotiating, marketing, planning, and financial management where such competencies are definable and where specific education goals can be set.

What then is the potential for information technology (IT) in this? It is argued in this chapter that its major potential comes from its ability to create an artificial environment in which students of management can develop and test their skills and can experiment and make mistakes.

It is the ability of IT to process information in increasingly vast quantities and rapid speeds that offers the greatest opportunities in management education. This represents a significant extra dimension, on top of the largely ad hoc use of specific PC-based packages that characterizes most business students' use of IT at present.

There is current software that can be used to assist in this, but which—because it is based on what *was* possible or available in the past—may be misleading as to the future. There are, for example, many computer-based business games and simulations. These (as well as noncomputerized games and simulations) clearly provide an important opportunity for creating an artificial environment. The computer-based business game will continue to be useful for developing skills in specific, often quantitative, areas. But the term "business game" is far too limiting to describe the concept of the artificial environment.

Much closer to the concept of the "artificial environment" is the flight simulator training given to airline pilots since the World War II. These have become increasingly expensive but working with them can, for certain purposes, be deemed a substitute for actual flight experience. The flight simulator is a totally artificial environment except for the cabin unit which is a replica of the real aircraft cabin. The simulator provides external graphic displays (the view out of the cabin) which have become increasingly lifelike. There is a monitoring, recording, and assessment system so that student and tutor can replay the flight and analyze what happened.

OBJECTIVES OF CASE

Even the most sophisticated and expensive flight simulators cannot cope with every possible situation. At present neither can any business simulation, and it is not claimed that the one discussed here—Trent Engineering—is able to do so. It is, in fact, geared to analyzing one specific area, namely the more effective use of information systems in business. However, it is argued that there is an increasing need to develop material which can provide those in management education, and specifically MBA students, with a much more realistic type of artificial environment than has typically been available to date, even if this relates to specific areas.

The Trent Engineering case has been specifically developed to meet two parallel objectives:

1. To test business studies students' understanding of information systems and technology concepts and to test their ability to relate these to real-world problem situations.
2. To involve students directly in the use of electronic mail, nonpaper-based communications, and remote database access, since these are of increasing potential for business efficiency and effectiveness, but often underutilized.

The distinctive feature of this case study is the way that it is substantially based around electronic mail ("mail-enabled") in such a way as to simulate some of the real managerial interactions faced by senior executives.

There has been a wide variety of experiences in using electronic mail in distance education, including in management education: Mason and Kaye, 1989; Hardy, Hodgson, McConnell, and Reynolds, 1991. However, there is much less application to full-time courses, as outlined in this chapter.

THE IMPORTANCE OF MANAGEMENT SIMULATIONS

The concepts involved are not in themselves new. The case study model addressing the first objective has been in use since the early days of formal management education at the Harvard Business School (McNair, 1954). There are also an increasing number of mail-enabled simulations.

Rawson (1989) describes the International Business Negotiation Simulations (IBNS) project, developed by the University of Maryland. It involves three half-day workshops "built around a country-specific simulation which allows U.S. business executives acting as members of a mock U.S. company, to perform a negotiation (via computer conferencing) of a specific business venture with their peers from a chosen foreign country."

The International Negotiation Project uses electronic mail to conduct simulated legal negotiation exercises between students from around the world. It originated in the Universities of Warwick and Hawaii (Clark, 1990). The approach taken was to create message files using the standard word processing package on the law school network and then transfer these files to the UNIX system for onward transmission via JANET and BITNET to Hawaii.

IMI-Geneva has developed an extensive simulation (Smiley, 1989):

> In the Integrated Management Exercise, there is no written case study providing pre-digested "knowledge" of a given situation. There is, however, a vast amount of company and industry information and data contained in a computerized information file. The "infofile" not only includes the "numbers," but also narrations which can unfold the history, background, and culture of the organization plus descriptions of the people within it. All are taken from a real international company.

In the United Kingdom, Shaoul (1991) has pursued an accounting-oriented simulation at Manchester University:

- A computerized simulation of the management accounts, production plan, and budgets of a carpet manufacturing company over a five-year period
- The contextual information relating to the industry, market trends, the company itself, and its competitors

Perhaps the major business simulation that also has a strong mail-enabled element is the Proteus simulation, initially funded by IBM. This work was focussed on a group of universities: Aston, Sheffield, Strathclyde and Manchester Business School. Subsequent development work to translate the software to a local area network (LAN) environment has been continued at Manchester Business School, based on funding from the Department of Employment, entitled Network Proteus.

The Proteus simulation has considerably advanced the British business academic community's experience and understanding of the capabilities of this type of holistic simulation and gave direct inspiration and insight to the developments of the Trent Engineering case. We would like to note the stimulus provided by Dr. Raul Espejo of Aston University, who with colleagues has developed the use of Proteus in a particularly imaginative way for the Aston M.B.A. course.

There has also been a wide variety of experiential learning simulations for management development based on "in-tray exercises," some of which have been developed into computer-based formats.

THE CITY UNIVERSITY BUSINESS SCHOOL AND INFORMATION SYSTEMS

Each academic institution has its own needs, environment, and resources. The Trent Engineering case has developed out of the specific situation at City University Business School, whose driving forces may (or may not) be relevant to other institutions.

The school has a very large full-time, one year M.B.A. course (the Day M.B.A.) with over 200 students from a very wide range of backgrounds, and with a strong international dimension. The Day M.B.A. is organized around five specialisms: finance, human resources management, information technology management, international business and export, and marketing.

All the core courses and the Business Policy course are taught to the combined student body, but because of the centers of gravity provided by the specialisms, it is always important to look for devices which provide integration of disciplines within the core courses. This has always been done through the creation of teams for group work, with members from each specialism involved. However, given the intense pressures and heavy workloads faced by the students, not all group exercises have really succeeded in combining disciplines synergistically. Work is perhaps totally delegated within the group and simply assembled together to produce the final product.

There is also an intrinsic problem in team structures that it is rarely possible for marking schemes to reflect the differential efforts of individual team members. Various techniques have been developed to address the problem of the under-participating team member (the "free-loader"). For example, systems have been created in which students can allocate a fixed quota of marks differentially to individual team members depending on perceived quality of individual inputs. However, such schemes are not always easy for students to manage; there is a natural tendency to support individual group members, especially if their chances of graduating may be affected.

The school, unlike several other leading business schools, has for many years had a compulsory core course in computing for all M.B.A. students. This is in addition to the formal hands-on training in Term 1 to ensure that the basic ability to use essential software packages is present. Virtually all the M.B.A. students have access to a PC at home as strongly recommended by the business school.

The compulsory M.B.A. core course is a eight-week course taught in Term 2. Although this course is entitled Core Computing, it has paid decreasing attention to the mechanics of computing as such and has increasingly addressed the issue of successful application of information technology and systems at the strategic level.

As with almost all the taught courses, student feedback concerning these M.B.A. courses suggested an increasing need for less time in the lecture theater (the one used for core courses is the university's largest) and more on group and experientially based work. At the time of this writing, Core Computing took a slot every Friday morning in tandem with Core Operations Management, and after the January-March course in 1991, it was decided by the two lecturers to teach these two courses in a more integrated fashion, using a combined case study. Unfortunately due to a lengthy absence of one of the lecturers in the second half of 1991, it proved to be physically impossible to collaborate on the revision of the case, so a decision was made in late November 1991 to continue to teach the courses separately.

University Information Technology Strategy

City University has, across all its schools, one of the highest proportions of its academic staff teaching IT or closely related subjects and also has a heavy use of IT in teaching and learning in virtually all its academic disciplines.

In 1989 the university reviewed its IT strategy as part of the review by the government funding body, the Computer Board. Three key decisions were made by the university and supported by the Computer Board:

1. The central IT service would support the needs of virtually all disciplines, not the few who had tended to predominate in its use before.
2. The service would be decentralized physically to four "clusters," each cluster to be in one of the university's major buildings and to consist of one or more servers and a group of high-powered workstations. This was the procurement funded by the Computer Board, and for approximately £1m the university obtained the servers plus nearly 200 scientific workstations and associated peripherals.
3. The university itself would fund the installation of a high-speed backbone campus network across all the campus except in some of the outlying buildings.

One cluster was located in the business school and had twenty-nine DOS/UNIX workstations, one SparcStation and two file servers. Unfortunately, these fell short of the specification set by both the university and the school in a key respect. This was that the business school was some 1 kilometer from the main campus, and its old 9.6-kilobyte link was only upgraded to a 64-kilobyte line. The main campus used a fiber-optic backbone, capable of 10 megabytes routinely. Given the integrated nature of the network, this meant that the response times of the workstations were significantly slower at the business school than at the main campus.

Initial use of electronic mail had been piloted in the winter of 1990-91 with a group of forty students and proved generally satisfactory. However, the mailer used—cmail—proved to be unstable, and the quality of the link to the main campus also made use of the system too slow.

However, the electronic mail front-end—elm—adapted as standard by the university for 1991-92, required the use of the UNIX vi or similar text editor. This proved to be a major deterrent and difficult even for IT professionals who were by now used to PC-type packages.

The Decision to Introduce the Simulation

Against this background the prospects of using a simulation-type exercise for the 1992 Core Computing class looked slim. However, perhaps by some good fortune, and despite the decision in November 1991 not to innovate, several events in December 1991 proved to be pivotal in enabling the simulation to proceed:

1. A new member of staff was appointed who was an M.B.A. by background and able to make an immediate and direct impact on the development of the material, as well as the training that was necessary.
2. Investigations of another mail front-end, mailtool, proved very positive and even though it was not "supported" by the university computer unit, a decision was made to abandon elm, except for these who needed access via modems, and to focus on what was hoped to be a more acceptable front-end.
3. As part of the implementation of a new telephone network for the university a 2-megabyte link was installed to the main campus, and from January 1992 there was a dramatic improvement in the speed of accessing the network, particularly the e-mail element of it.
4. A decision was made by staff of the accountancy division of the business school in December to use the Plan-It business simulation for undergraduate teaching. This had been in use for two years with only eight copies of the software. The decision triggered the need to upgrade to a site license, which in turn meant that the simulation could be available in the numbers required for M.B.A. group work.
5. At a meeting of the M.B.A. Staff-Student Liaison Committee in December 1991, the student representatives made a strong call for more experiential learning situations. Because by now it seemed that this was logistically possible, this meeting finally precipitated a decision to proceed with the simulation, which had by then been made physically achievable.
6. Due to a reorganization of the M.B.A. core courses, one of the other courses had reduced its class contact time by a half-day per week. This happened to be on a Friday afternoon, while the Computing Core was on a Friday morning. This meant it was possible to schedule the additional training sessions as well as the three half-days needed for the Plan-It business simulation, without causing other courses to be disrupted.
7. A suitable case had already been developed in a traditional format (Holtham, Slattery and Watson, 1990), which could, with only minor

amendments, serve as the basis of the new business simulation, entitled Trent Engineering, and based on a valve manufacturing company in the English Midlands.

Training

The first major hurdle to overcome was training some 200 students in routine use of the workstations, particularly electronic mail. Their initial brief introduction in October had in most cases been insufficient to develop actual skills, and many had been deterred by the unfriendly mail system then used.

Work started in December to develop new training material, based around a 2.5-hour "crash course." Two pilot sessions were held with students in the week before term started, and even further simplification and focus was made, plus the development of a worksheet which literally showed step-by-step what to do.

The great bulk of students were trained over five sessions in weeks one and two of the term. Positive feedback resulted from these sessions:

1. The groups were "streamed" by self-selection into more PC-literate and less PC-literate. Although in practice there appeared to be relatively little difference between the two groups, students clearly perceived they were being allocated to an appropriate level of class, and this perhaps improved their confidence before they even started. With four to six tutors per class of twenty to thirty students there was a reasonable level of direct moral and physical support.

2. Much had been learned from previous experience about how to teach the workstations both in detail, and by setting their use within an overall environment. In detail, the worksheets had been redesigned so students in a large class could work at their own pace to some degree. Also, it had proved impossible, for technical reasons, to project the workstation image on a large screen monitor; therefore, a video camera pointed at the tutor's workstation screen, which could be connected to the large monitor screen, was used. Despite flicker and the illegibility of much of the text even on the large screen monitor, this at least gave a reference point to students. High-quality OHP slides were made of points requiring detailed explanation and reproduced in the worksheet.

The pilot sessions provided good insight into what students actually found useful. They wanted not only to use the workstations in themselves, but also to see how they could be an adjunct to their home PCs. In this respect a PC was used in the class to simulate a student's home PC, and output from that was saved to floppy disk to be either mailed from the workstation or used as input to WordPerfect and then either printed on the network PostScript printer, and/or mailed.

3. Use of e-mail was compulsory in the Core Computing course. There was relatively little interest in using mail when it was not a necessity to do so.
4. The mailtool mail front-end proved not only easy to use but even quite popular.
5. For some students the prospect of e-mail to other universities nationally and internationally was very highly valued, but the problem of discovering remote e-mail addresses quickly (and other than by phone or mail) became a disincentive.

THE TRENT ENGINEERING CASE STUDY

At first sight the Trent case looks like a conventional business case study, with a written case description setting out the background to the company, its personalities, problems, and opportunities (Holtham, 1992). The case is indeed rooted in the "classic" case study tradition, and the underlying content is no different from a more conventional case. Trent Engineering is a company faced with a number of difficult strategic and operational problems, many of which in fact impinge on information technology potential and problems.

There are, however, major differences in presentation and processing of the case material, because the case is essentially rooted in an electronic infrastructure, with a particular emphasis on the use of electronic mail for communication between the instructors and students, (and vice versa) and between the students themselves. Of critical importance is the executive chairman of Trent Engineering's (Dr. Peter Green) method of working.

Dr. Peter Green

In the case, Green was educated as an engineer and became a lecturer in engineering after completing his Ph.D. He moved to the United States to teach, but then took on an increasing amount of business-related consultancy, eventually leaving the academic world to become a management consultant to poorly managed U.S. engineering companies. He then took an M.B.A. at the MIT Sloan School of Management.

Green spends a considerable amount of time traveling within the United Kingdom and internationally. Although Green is a full-time executive chairperson, as a result of his large amount of time away from the company offices, he has decided, for the moment at least, to allow the executive directors to create and allocate roles among themselves, in particular: the managing director, finance director, sales and marketing director, and the production director.

These four posts constitute the current management team of executive directors of Trent Engineering, and students in their groups allocate themselves to the roles.

Green has made it clear that if they are not able to change their approach they will be early targets of an efficiency savings program.

Communicating with Dr. Green.

Dr. Green can be very difficult to get in touch with. He usually attends the Friday morning meeting of executive management but this is the only time board members can see him. However, despite his physical absence, he is a very active communicator both inside and outside the company, generating large quantities of typing and numerous memoranda, notes, and phone calls, especially to the directors.

When he was working in American universities and consultancies, he became a user of electronic mail. When he arrived at Trent, he immediately instructed the IT department to install an electronic mail system. A system that was already in use for some staff was chosen, based on a UNIX minicomputer. This is accessed over the company network and can also be accessed by dialing using a modem.

Green has particularly requested the executive directors to use e-mail to receive communications from him and as the normal method to reply to him. This has not been popular with the executive directors, some of whom had limited experience using PCs, but no experience with a network.

Basic Operation of the Case

Students are allocated into groups before term starts; groups must reflect a mix of disciplines/backgrounds and require a core of at least four full-time students (part-timers and occasional students must be additional). If it were a course where all the students were part-time, it would be essential to try to ensure that there are at least four students per group with the resources and skills to participate actively in the case.

The case description and case instructions are issued in paper format in the first week of the course, and an oral briefing is given at this time to set the scene, explain the marking system, etc.

The case description looks complete but is not. The whole point is that further information about the company emerges gradually week by week, sent by the case administrators by e-mail. It would be possible to dispense with the written case and instructions entirely, but this will not necessarily create immediate confidence among the less IT-literate students.

The Nature of the Information Provided

The information provided electronically falls into several categories:

Actions. Actions are a specific instruction to be carried out in a defined time scale. This is the marked course work. These relate to subjects being taught in the parallel lecture course, (e.g., how to design more effective systems, whether executive information systems need to be developed, how the IT-related skills of the company could be improved).

Relevant Background Information. This material provides relevant data about the organization, its environment, people, or problems. Relevant background information may well be a prelude to a later action.

Case Administration. There are a variety of ad hoc matters relating to the procedure of the case that are independent of the actual "running" of the company (e.g., location and timing of briefing sessions).

Noise. A proportion of the communications are in fact irrelevant to the specific areas to be covered; students are not, however, able to tell at the time whether an apparently irrelevant issue will turn into a subsequent action.

Team members need to share information (quickly) to be able to carry out the case study (or even to know what the questions are). Some information may be sent to every group up to every three days during the specific periods.

Students only have to respond to "actions" by using one of the following:

- e-mail to specific mailbox, confirmation of receipt or substantive content
- paper to specific staff member
- attendance at a meeting (e.g., all forty students, one from each group, at a particular time to get oral briefing)

Communications

Some items are communicated simultaneously to all students in the whole class. Others are only communicated to one member of each team. Different members of a team may receive information about separate parts of a problem. Teams that are poor at intercommunications will be at a disadvantage.

It is not essential or even necessary for the case administrators to know the formal role of each team member. Mailing lists can therefore be created arbitrarily so that communications on a given day are, for example, all sent to the first person listed in the group schedule. The ability to create a variety of different mailing lists is a powerful feature of a mail-enabled simulation.

Briefings and Videos

Briefings can be given via the case description (paper), the content of e-mail (electronic), or oral explanations (oral).

However, a potentially powerful medium for communicating a large quantity of information is a video. At the time of writing, three videos were available for the case representing Peter Green, executive chairperson (new broom); Derek Latham, group chairperson (group policy); and George Goldie, director (seasoned skeptic).

One of the advantages of the video is that softer, more subtle information can be given than is possible in a case. The videos were made to a specification, but the interviews were not scripted as such. The participants were expected to behave as the "characters" they represent and each of the participants in the video has actually held roles similar to that of their character.

The Haste LTD Business Game

By the third week of the course, groups were asked, in addition to their mail-enabled exercises, to work on a more conventional business game, using the Plan-It software from Understanding Systems Ltd. In the case, there was a subsidiary of the group called Haste Ltd., and the group chairperson had asked the directors of Trent to rework some of the previous management's decisions using the business game software.

In practice, the Haste exercise took on, in many student's minds, a dominant position, and many groups spent too much time on this exercise, perhaps because, being quantitatively orientated, it appeared to have specific correct answers.

Lessons: Prerequisite Infrastructure

The case, as written and used at City University Business School, has a number of essential technological prerequisites. All these features may not be easy to replicate in other environments, but the case may be adapted to fit within local constraints.

Adequate Communications Infrastructure

The case is predicated on access to an electronic mail system, with terminals or PCs in a quantity and location that make them convenient to use for both students and participating staff.

Individual Computer IDs for Each Student

It is very important in the case, as developed, that each student has an individual computer identity number (account/user name), so that mail can be pinpointed to individual students and also sent from individually identifiable student accounts. Since there is an individual element in marking, this tends to increase the significance of specific pieces of work being identifiable to that individual.

Software Ease of Use and Reliability

It is an absolute prerequisite that the electronic mail software be reasonably easy for the target student group to learn and to use and to offer a reasonably high degree of reliability. If the mailing system in use is archaic and/or oriented toward the needs of highly computer literate students, then the learning process will be one of considerable frustration for the business student, and valuable time will be wasted on technicalities which should be devoted to business thinking. The same applies to reliability. An unreliable system or one with very poor response times makes the whole exercise burdensome, a chore, time-wasting, and counterproductive. One of the aims of the case is to shift thinking about IT and encourage its creative use in business.

Adequate Training Capability

Most business studies students are, at the time of this writing, unskilled in the use of e-mail. Some have been users of electronic mail systems other than the system chosen: they face a "relearning" curve which may be just as steep as that of initial learning.

Much depends also on the general skill and hardware environment. If the students have a background that is 100 percent rooted in PCs, they may react negatively to the use of dumb terminals, for example, irrespective of the software in use.

An institution may have a general training capability in computing and electronic mail for students, but this has to be checked to ensure it is relevant to the expertise required for the Trent Case (reply to and compose simple e-mail messages) as opposed to more general, more expert, or more specialist needs. Since there is relatively little time available to teach business students the mechanics of computing, it is essential that this be done as quickly, relevantly, and effectively as possible.

Adequate Support and Advisory Services

The case as developed is fairly challenging to the computing services of the academic institution, because it may involve a large number of relatively inexperienced (in IT) students simultaneously using network and mail services with which they are not familiar.

Tutors will need support to develop and test both the case and supporting training and information materials. After initial tuition, it is also inevitable that some students will need continued advice and support. A major aim of the case is to ensure that students provide that support to each other; however, there is an inevitable minority who find the technology a barrier.

Adequate Computer Literacy of Instructors

Since the case is e-mail based, all instructors involved must, as a minimum, be able to use e-mail themselves, and ideally should be confident in file upload and download, and possibly access via a modem.

A subset of the instructors needs to be substantially computer-literate to provide academic leadership in the business use of IT, and to be able to deal with the inevitably broad range of student queries (and at least to know to whom some questions should be directed).

Because the case as developed involves a variety of software and remote databases, the functionality needs to be thoroughly tested before it is released to students, and this can be a lengthy and time-consuming process, especially when the case is initially developed.

Adequate Academic Resourcing

Due to the nature and incidence of interaction with students, this approach needs a more varied and greater volume of academic input. It requires several staff (two at the very minimum) to be involved, and even if some lecture time is eliminated or reduced, being able to marshall and sustain these resources is not a trivial exercise.

Infrastructure and Resources

A fairly elaborate and fairly interactive case study of any type, computer-based or not, is more demanding of an institution than any more traditional approach.

Certainly at the time of writing, a computer-based exercise adds further dimensions of complexity and resources. Even though it permits high-speed activity and can actually totally eliminate paperwork in certain areas, it requires a focused effort over many weeks of both preparation and delivery.

It is not the intention here to deter potential instructors either from this case or from devising their own. But it needs to be recognized that computer-based teaching methods are rarely a source of savings in staff effort, certainly when under development. Traditional lectures, especially where not amended from year to year, remain the least-cost approach in most areas. The idea behind more experiential and group-based work is to increase the quality of learning, and this is the goal that an innovative delivery method can address.

EXPERIENCES AND FEEDBACK

Feedback partway through the course and observation of students in groups showed some preliminary experiences:

- Students tended to print out hard copy as soon as they received their mail. This meant that usage of the network printer was very heavy, indeed far in excess of normal capacity.
- The distinction in roles between academic and computer support staff often appeared unclear to students; academic staff were queried on detailed technical problems, and computer staff were often asked for extensions to course work submission dates.
- The computer laboratory used offered too little space for effective group work.

Overall, an intensive exercise of this sort places severe demands on the university's network infrastructure. No one, it would appear, had ever tested the electronic mail system with such student numbers before. A fault was discovered in the mail system's software. When mail was sent to more than fifty people in a single mailing list, delivery was unreliable or failed after the initial fifty. Not all students saved their own mail, despite warnings to do so. Intensive use meant a few workstations became faulty. There were recurring problems with a printer, exacerbated by heavy use.

None of these would probably have been serious in themselves, but with a large group of highly stressed MBA students, any infrastructure failures that impinge on their ability to complete coursework causes strain and tension. In this context, minor technical problems are rarely trivial.

The single most vocal complaint in the early part of the course concerned the groups. Groups were not self-selected, as was school practice in Term 2. A noticeable minority of groups had some problems at a basic interpersonal level, and the level of tutorial monitoring and support was insufficient to deal with every case that needed help.

In the light of the student feedback on workload, and the greater-than-planned time spent by students on it, it has been decided to separate the Haste Ltd business simulation out from the Trent case study; this will probably be used in Term 1 in another course.

Although there had been strong pressure from students for more experiential learning, in practice some students found the uncertainties associated with a nearly real-time case study very different from what they had encountered in other courses and in other pieces of group work. It was not possible to plan much in advance, and there was a premium on excellent and fast communications within a group. Where the latter did not occur, frustrations began to build up.

Despite all the "teething," technical, and group problems, the overall evaluations at the end of term were favorable, with a marked increase in rating over the previous year's lecture-only course.

The major decision made as a result of the feedback, and of the staff's own evaluations, was to shift a significant proportion of the dissemination of material from the electronic mail system to a City University Bulletin Board and Conferencing System. Certainly in our environment, mass publication of material for large numbers of students is more appropriate through such a system. Mail will continue to be used for targeted mailings to subgroups of students and for student responses to staff.

AUTOMATE OR INFORMATE?

It is increasingly well-established that in the business and public sector environments, a great deal of computerization has simply replaced existing manual systems with computer-based ones: this can be described as automation. Several commentators, most notably Zuboff (1988), have argued that to achieve the potential benefits which could accrue is not enough. What is needed is not just to automate business processes but to reconstruct them in the light of the new technological potential: this is a process she describes as "informating."

The university sector and indeed the educational sector generally in the United Kingdom has been very heavily orientated towards the use of IT for automating existing educational processes. For example, the then Computer Board funded a Computers in Teaching Initiative in 1989, and a center specifically devoted to accountancy and business studies was set up. A journal, an annual conference, and regional events have developed from this. It is clear from these publications and events that there is an often enthusiastic minority of management education academics who are actively using or considering the use of information technology, but that much of this is automating-type activities. There are very few examples which go further.

There are some notable exceptions. A pioneering and particularly imaginative use of remote databases accessed via the United Kingdom academic network (JANET) to support the teaching of quantitative methods in economics has been created by Burley and Mabbett (1991). The Proteus simulation clearly developed a new approach to simulations. But these are essentially isolated examples.

THE DEVELOPMENT OF BROAD-BASED BUSINESS SIMULATIONS

In 1983 the Computer Board carried out a review of computer needs in universities over the following decade. The review painted scenarios of an "advanced" university in 1992 (Computer Board, 1983):

> New tutorial and simulation software is produced by small teams including lecturers, computer center programmer/analysts and educational technologists. . . Students studying vocational subjects (engineering, accountancy) use the communications network to use and carry out project work with contemporary applications software. . . In such an environment we envisage that all students would use their computers regularly to send and receive electronic mail, to house the library catalogue for source books in relation to their current studies, to write essays using word processing software, and to answer tests set on their courses.

The forecast was remarkably accurate in many respects, but overemphasized the degree to which students in subjects such as accountancy and business studies would be using networked services, even in the more "advanced" universities. A major part of the problem in the United Kingdom is that many business studies academics, even in leading business schools, are not physically connected to campus and hence national networks and thus are unable to develop suitable course material (Holligan, 1986).

ELECTRONIC CLASSROOM SUPPORT SYSTEM

After the Trent case had been completed, the tutors involved discovered from Internet discussion groups and their archives that Ralph Lewis, an academic at

California State University, Long Beach, had already been developing many of the concepts that had been worked on in the Trent Case Study.

Lewis's Electronic Classroom Support System (ECCS) is based around use of both electronic mail and bulletin board systems and represents a very significant use of electronic networks in teaching MBA courses:

> An electronic classroom support system has been developed based on Internet and CSUNET communications. It provides the student with online resources to select topic assignments, conduct bibliographic literature searches, access remote information servers, prepare written reports, review and comment on others' reports, conduct peer evaluations as well as receive input and feedback from the class instructor. A CoSy conferencing system is also utilized in a virtual work technology mode to provide the students with the experience of working in a decentralized, project-oriented, collaborative and distributed organizational environment. (Lewis, 1991)

FUTURE DEVELOPMENTS

It has been decided to apply the same approach to undergraduate teaching, but using a different case that is currently in preparation; it is not based around group work and follows the second-year Business Studies Information Technology syllabus. This case is called Sphere Consultancy. Support has also been obtained from several overseas business schools to organize collaborative case studies between their own students and those of City University Business School. Much depends in these circumstances on the communications infrastructure available. The simplest available is electronic mail. More advanced in the use of the Internet and direct log-on to remote machines (e.g., via telnet).

A longer-term objective of creating a more comprehensive "artificial environment" remains. Ideally this would be based on real company data, not at the relatively abstract level usually associated with business games, but literally in full detail—all transactions for a medium-sized company for a significant period (e.g., up to two years). This would be accompanied by as much softer data, including electronic and paper mail, as possible. The most feasible method of developing such a data resource would be as a national facility, accessible over the academic network. Such a resource would be valuable not only in learning about business information systems but also in many other business studies subjects.

Creating and developing the Trent Engineering case study was never easy, especially in the time scale available. In hindsight, the aims were perhaps overly ambitious and the staff input greater than expected. But the exercise was valuable for students (as shown in their assessments), and staff members have learned a considerable amount about how to use technology in the lifelike learning of technology in business.

BIBLIOGRAPHY

Burley, Tom and Mabbett, Alan (1991) "Has IT reached maturity?" *The CTISS File*, No.12, September 1991, pp42-48.

Clark, Andrew (1990) "Electronic Negotiation: The International Negotiation Project" *Law Technology Center and BILETA Newsletter*, Vol. 2 No. 4 Winter 1990, pp119-121.

Computer Board for Universities and Research Councils (1983) Report of a Working Party on Computer Facilities for Teaching in Universities (Chairperson, Ms. D. Nelson).

Hardy, Ginny; Hodgson, Vivien; McConnell, David; and Reynolds, Michael (1991) "Computer Mediated Communication for Management Training and Development" Research Report, Center for the Study of Management Learning, University of Lancaster.

Hiltz S.R. and Turoff, M. (1978) *The Network Nation*. Addison-Wesley, Reading, MA.

Holligan, Patrick J. (1986) *Access to Academic Networks*. Taylor Graham, London.

Holtham, Clive; Slattery, Dennis and Watson, Milton (1990) "The ABC Ltd Case Study" City University Business School Case Study.

Holtham, Clive (1992) "The Trent Engineering Case Study" City University Business School Case Study.

Keisler, Sara B. and Sproull, Lee S. (1987) *Computing and Change on Campus*. Cambridge University Press, Cambridge.

Lewis, Ralph (1991) "Education for the virtual workplace: The Electronic Classroom Support System (ECSS)" available from several Internet archives.

Mason, Robin and Kaye, Anthony (Eds)(1989) *Mindweave: Communication, Computers and Distance Education*. Pergamon Press, Oxford.

McNair, Malcolm P. (1954) *The Case Method at the Harvard Business School*. McGraw-Hill.

Rawson, James H (1989) "Simulation at a distance using computer conferencing" *Educational and Training Technology International*, Vol. 27 No.3 August 1990, pp284-292.

Shaoul, Jean (1991) "Management Accounting Database" *The CTISS File*, No.12, September 1991, pp21-22.

Smiley, Tex (1989) *An Experience in Integrated Management Learning*. IMD, 89/1 pp15-18.

Zuboff, Shoshana (1988) *In the Age of the Smart Machine*. Heinemann Professional Publishing, Oxford.

Chapter

14

Integrating Technology into the Health Information Management Curriculum

Dorine Bennett
Instructor, Medical Record Programs
Dakota State University, Madison, South Dakota

Paulette Wiesen
Director, Medical Record Programs
Dakota State University, Madison, South Dakota

Dakota State University (DSU) is a unique institution where scholarship and excellence embrace technology and innovation. The 1984 South Dakota Legislature and the South Dakota Board of Regents turned to DSU to educate leaders for the information age. In response to this need, DSU has become a leader in computer and information systems programs and pioneered the application of computer technology to traditional fields of academic endeavor. In recognition of its recent pioneering, innovative, and unique academic programs and outreach efforts, DSU was selected as one of the ten finalists for the 1987 G. Theodore Mitau Award. Computer laboratories with microcomputer, minicomputer, and mainframe access, from a variety of computer manufacturers, are located in every academic building on campus, as well as in the residence halls. Most computers on campus are linked together through a local area network (LAN) that provides campus-wide communication and easy access to software. Through connection to external academic networks (BITNET), the networked environment also provides communication between DSU computer users and computer users around the globe. A key to DSU's success in integrating computer technology throughout the curriculum has been the development and acquisition of software that allows professors who are experts in their subject area to use computers in appropriate ways to teach complex subject matter. Software evaluation, development, and support are provided through professional computer programmers and outstanding college students.

MEDICAL RECORD PROGRAMS AT DSU

The medical record degrees at DSU are designed as a "2 + 2" program. Students acquire technical skills in medical records during the first two years. At this point, they may choose to graduate with an associate degree in medical record technology or to continue their education for the baccalaureate degree in the medical record administration program, which emphasizes management skills. Integration of computers into the academic programs at Dakota State provides students the advantage of learning the latest in information systems technology as it applies to health information. Students also gain realistic experiences through directed practices and practicums at health care facilities.

According to the American Health Information Management Association, one of the most critical emerging issues in health care is the growing demand for accessing, processing, coordinating, analyzing, and communicating information. To remain financially viable and deliver high-quality patient care, health care executive management can no longer rely on past performance or incomplete data to guide its decisions. Now, more than ever, timely, reliable, accessible, and accurate health care information is needed to facilitate quality patient care in a cost-constrained environment. The medical record professionals, now defined as health information management professionals, through knowledge and experience, provide the key to managing clinical, financial, and diagnostic information required to meet this challenge head on. Health information management is the dynamic application of intelligence to medical data. The health information management professional is trained to gather, manipulate, and evaluate complex data from multiple sources and types of medical documentation while maintaining confidentiality of patient information, and to incorporate these findings into a knowledge base for the health care delivery system.

The faculty of the Medical Record Programs at DSU, encouraged by the commitment to technology from the American Health Information Management Association and DSU's support in terms of both hardware/software and computing expertise, has integrated computer software learning modules specific to medical record applications into the curriculum. Students in the medical record programs at DSU are required to take Computer Concepts, a course designed to provide experience in several "general" software applications, such as WordPerfect for word processing, Lotus 1-2-3 for spreadsheets and graphics, and dBase III Plus for database management, as well as an introduction to DOS. Students utilize these software applications in subsequent health sciences (medical record) classes. For example, Introduction to the Health Record Field teaches students how dBase III Plus could be used to manage a Master Patient Index

(MPI) and an abstracting system. Lotus 1-2-3 and Harvard Graphics are utilized in statistical compilation and data presentation in Basic Foundations of Health Data Systems. Harvard Graphics is also used in Management of Health Data to create organizational charts. Instruction in the Medical Terminology/ Transcription course employs WordPerfect for transcribing a variety of reports and requires students to use the advanced features of WordPerfect. Classroom simulations of medical record functions utilizing patient records and computer capabilities provide a hands-on approach to computerized health information processing and management to strengthen students' career opportunities.

INPUT FROM DSU'S SMALL BUSINESS INSTITUTE

Dakota State's Small Business Institute (SBI) students were utilized as consultants in selecting software specific to medical record applications to incorporate into the curriculum. SBI is a program sponsored by Dakota State in cooperation with the Small Business Administration Department of the federal government. Selected junior and senior students serve on teams assigned to assist a small business with marketing, advertising, accounting, inventory control, computing, and/or other areas as the business indicates a need. In this case, the "business" was the Medical Record Programs at DSU. The SBI team researched the health information management industry to identify the most applicable software within outlined budget limitations for the curriculum at Dakota State. The team completed a survey of area hospitals and clinics to determine which software is most commonly used. These common softwares were evaluated in the areas of number of medical record functions available, costs, required hardware specifications, and support. The decision was made to obtain the computer-based 3M Multi-Function Record Management System from 3M Health Information Systems of Utah. This system is a comprehensive tool which automates a number of tasks formerly performed manually in many hospitals and other health care institutions; tasks such as Master Patient Index (MPI), abstracting, ICD-9-CM and CPT-4 encoding, DRG and ASC grouping, record completion, record tracking, and ad hoc reporting are among the capabilities. Computer hardware was obtained and the software was installed on a file server. Eight 80386 microprocessor-based computer workstations were networked utilizing an 80386 computer as the file server and Novell networking software, with plans to expand to twenty-four networked workstations.

Beginning with the 1991 fall semester, many health sciences courses were revamped to incorporate the new technology into instruction. Classroom instruction included examples and demonstrations through use of computer software, both by student activities and by A-V projection of instructor use. Laboratory experiences were designed to demonstrate both manual and automated methods of medical record functions, thus allowing students an opportunity to evaluate the benefits of technological advances as well as enhancing their abilities to critique information provided by vendors. Critical thinking is developed through exposure to computerization of available functions which provoke thoughts for additional applications. There is also discussion as to the availability and/or timeliness of information on a manual system, as opposed to the benefits of automation.

INTEGRATING TECHNOLOGY INTO HEALTH INFORMATION MANAGEMENT

The faculty members in the Medical Record Programs at Dakota State University recognize the importance of integrating technology into all facets of the health information management profession. Students gain an understanding of the need for and benefits of automation in each of the functions of a medical record department. Each course incorporates use of the computer, particularly using the 3M Multi-Function Record Management Systems software where appropriate. As mentioned, students utilize actual medical records to perform functions commonly found in the workplace. Data from medical records are entered into the automated MPI just as data is entered into a hospital registration system. The MPI serves as a guide for locating records for all persons who have received health care at a facility. A selection of medical records is also used for entering the patient information from the records into a manual MPI to teach students the basic concepts and offer a realization of the benefits or drawbacks of each system. One feature of the software is the capability to print out index cards for the patients entered into the system to provide hard copy of the MPI. The students print out a sample of these cards to gain that experience; the cards are also used in later exercises.

Computer software applications used by students include the Chart Deficiency and Chart Location functions. Classwork is done in evaluating medical records to determine completeness of the charts and to identify deficiencies (including the person or department responsible for completion/correction of the deficiency). This information is entered into the automated system to be used in follow-up on the deficiencies and in generating reports. Students also create letters to be sent to the responsible person or department. Students use the system to check out charts and track the location of charts previously checked out. One function performed in a medical record department at a health care facility is the release of confidential information in response to authorized requests. At Dakota State, students in the Legal Aspects of Health Records course are instructed in evaluating and responding to requests for information. Requests have been created and are given to the students to deal with as they would in a health care facility. Students search the manual and automated MPI to determine the existence of the patient, the appropriate medical record number, and other demographic information such as birthdate, used in performing release of information. Dakota State also utilizes software demonstrations in the classroom to instruct students on automating a correspondence log to track the responses to requests, calculating charges, and maintaining accounts receivable records for correspondence; students also explore ways of using general software, such as dBase III Plus or Lotus 1-2-3, for this.

The 3M Multi-Function Record Management System software is also used to illustrate the use of the computer in the medical record functions of coding and grouping. Patient care information is provided by assigning a correct code number to each disease or disorder for which a patient receives treatment and to each operation or procedure provided to the patient. These codes are used for reimbursement by third-party payers for development of cost/quality payment systems and for facilitation of data retrieval (both internally by the facility and for external agencies). Some reimbursement systems, such as Medicare and Medicaid, utilize the codes for placing the patient into a particular "group" based on diagnosis and service to determine the amount of payment; this is called grouping. Students are taught the manual systems of coding and grouping to provide a basic understanding of the processes; the automation of these functions illustrates how the processes are accelerated. Demonstrations of other coding or grouping software packages permit the students to critique and evaluate software for the features that they expect and want available.

Just as the MPI is used as a guide for locating patients treated at a health care facility, the Diagnosis, Operation, and Physician Indexes are designed to locate information on a particular diagnosis, procedure, or doctor which is abstracted or collected from the patient's medical record. This process may be done with a manual system within the hospital, through a contract with an abstracting company (in which the data is collected on a paper abstract form or media and is sent to a company which enters the data into a computerized system with resulting reports returned to the health care facility), or with an in-house computerized system. At Dakota State laboratory exposure to all three forms of abstracting is provided with emphasis on the in-house abstracting system. Students are taught to pull charts and/or prepare reports for particular diagnoses, procedures, physicians, and combinations of these using each system.

Students also learn how to create ad hoc reports. For example, software is is used to abstract data from a number of actual patient medical records. After developing the database on patients, the students search for information on the database and generate reports. In one simulation, the marketing department requests information on where patients live (sorted by zip code) for use in analyzing the facility's market share or developing a customer mailing. Students prepare a demographic report from the 3M Multi-Function Record Management System software and provide this information, which can be displayed in either table or graphic mode utilizing other software applications.

Many health care facilities maintain a cancer data system, or tumor registry, to improve cancer management by collecting, organizing, analyzing, and interpreting cancer data. These data may be used for medical planning, physician education, and research. This function is also taught at DSU through the use of a manual system as well as through exploration of an automated system.

Building on the data entered in the abstracting function and determinations resulting for the DRG/ASC grouping feature, case mix (patient mix) information can be gathered and analyzed. Combined with financial information, case mix reports can be very powerful, eye-opening analysis tools. Case mix reports furnish valuable comparative insight on the overall performance of the facility, a service, or individual physician. The availability of case mix reports provides students with the opportunity to interpret, evaluate, and discuss the meaning of the data and to recommend potential avenues of corrective action, if warranted. Of even greater relevance to medical record/health information management professionals are the realization, experimentation, and demonstration of the impact code assignments and their connection to the case mix reports and resultant conclusions.

Case mix report findings may prompt the use of another capability of the 3M Multi-Function Record Management System—physician profiling. Physician profiles can also be constructed from the information already entered into the system through the abstracting function. These profiles differ from physician indexes (as they are typically defined) in that they report utilization related data (i.e., length of stay, case mix, financial information, etc.) rather than patients and diagnoses and/or procedures of those patients treated by the physician being queried. From these profiles practice-specific information on physicians in the same specialty can be compared. Classroom discussions are focused on a number of parameters, such as outliers in the areas of length of stay, charges, tests/exams performed, etc. Such dialogues can include brainstorming efforts on how any noted variations may be explained, learned from, and/or corrected.

All the functions cited so far culminate in a very important component and concern in today's health care environment—quality. The successful industrial models of "total quality management" and "continuous quality improvement" can be just as successfully applied within health care environments. Case mix reports and physician profiles may uncover opportunities for continuously improving the quality of health care rendered to patients—health care's primary customer. After implementing corrective action, subsequent case mix and/or physician profile reports will provide documented proof if desired outcomes were achieved. Additionally, through use of the optional data fields in the abstracting feature, important quality assessment information (i.e., clinical pertinence, therapeutic drug-level monitoring, indicator information, etc.) can be tracked for future analysis.

CONCLUSION

It is the intent of the faculty at DSU to prepare students to enter the field of health information management with an excellent understanding of functions to be performed in this profession and of utilization of computers to assist in those functions. Students are taught the manual systems of all functions to provide awareness of basic concepts, and the ability to perform the functions and automation of functions are introduced in a number of ways. Many of the courses utilize the 3M Multi-Function Record Management System software to allow students to realize the building or cumulative effect of a multifunction networked software package as opposed to multiple stand-alone software packages which would necessitate repeated record reviews and data entry. However, students do use stand-alone software packages, including demonstrations, so that this option of automation is also a part of their education.

Students and practitioners will find a variety of methods for performing the functions of health information management, many of which have incorporated technology or automation; that technology has also been integrated into the curriculum at Dakota State University in the Medical Record Programs.

Chapter
15

The Computer-Mediated English Department

Patricia Ericsson
Instructor of English
Dakota State University, Madison, South Dakota

Eric Johnson
Professor of English and Dean of the College of Liberal Arts
Dakota State University, Madison, South Dakota

A 1984 mission change for Dakota State University authorized and encouraged the development of new, technology-oriented degrees, and it mandated the widespread use of computers throughout the university. This mission change provided the impetus for development of unique English degrees at DSU, and it stimulated changes in many standard English courses. We believe that the university has developed both courses and degrees that truly prepare students for the technical world of the next century.

This chapter has three related subjects: the first section discusses the computer lab used for English classes, the second covers the computer-mediated courses taught in the English department, and the third explains DSU's English degrees.

THE COMPUTER LAB

Many students at DSU are surprised and shocked when they arrive at their first English class meeting and find that the assigned room is a computer lab. Computers are used extensively in writing classes as well as in literature classes, and they are central in many specialized courses required for English majors. We are convinced that computers are essential to the best teaching and learning in a range of English courses.

We firmly believe that English classes must meet frequently in a computer lab; composition classes must meet as often in a lab as in a traditional classroom. This belief is based on years of experience teaching classes in both situations. When a class is held in a traditional room, but the students are expected to use word processing, text analysis programs, and electronic communications to complete their assignments, we have met with considerable resistance and a myriad of problems. Students learn the computer applications faster and more eagerly when they can work in the lab with the teacher.

The lab used for most DSU English courses is equipped with thirty microcomputers that run Microsoft Windows. All of these machines are linked with the campus local area network (LAN), and servers on the LAN provide a great variety of word processing, communications programs, programming software, writing analysis tools, and various other programs. All English faculty have similar networked computers on their office desks.

The thirty computers in the lab are arranged in five clusters of six machines each; each cluster has a dot-matrix printer (networked laser printers can also be used). The previous arrangements of the lab had the computers in rows. The change from a traditional row arrangement to clusters was made on the basis of several pedagogical and practical concerns. In arranging the new lab, we were interested in de-emphasizing the traditional placement of the teacher at the front of the classroom. Even though the lab does have a teacher's desk, it is placed at the side, rather than in the front of the room, and, in any case, it is little used. Teachers are physically not at the front of this room configuration because they must move about the lab during the class sessions. In choosing this lab configuration, we also hoped to create a sense of small communities that would be more likely to work together in the classroom sessions. Additionally, we wanted to avoid the appearance of a traditional lab or classroom so that students would know immediately upon entering it, that this was a unique place where unconventional things could happen.

Practically, the cluster arrangement has several advantages. The backs of all the machines are turned toward the center of a cluster. Therefore all cords and cables are removed from traffic. In the traditional row arrangement, we had experienced problems when students would accidentally bump and disconnect power sources or printer connections of computers behind them. Monitors emit the greatest amount of low-level radiation from the rear; we shudder when we enter a traditional lab and find students relaxing by resting their heads on the backs of the monitors behind them. The arrangement of computers in clusters reduces the unobstructed distances between machines and thus makes moving around the lab much easier for teachers and students.

It is perhaps symbolically significant that the teachers and students are on the same side of the computers. The struggle to create and edit is before both of them (not between them), and they work together to increase the students' writing skills.

English faculty members have voluntarily assumed the responsibility of making minor repairs to computers in the lab. If a laser printer needs a cartridge installed or if the boot files of a hard disk have been erased, a faculty member can return the equipment to operation in a matter of minutes. Since the delay of waiting for technical assistance is often avoided, the operation of the lab is near optimal level.

Although most of the equipment in the lab was purchased only a few years ago, there are plans to update it. Processors, monitors, and printers will be faster and have more memory. Integration of graphic images and text is increasingly encouraged in composition classes, and it requires larger, faster hardware. Since color monitors are standard, it makes sense to have color printers available.

COMPOSITION CLASSES

Four kinds of writing classes are offered at DSU: (1) developmental writing, (2) freshman composition, (3) junior composition, and (4) advanced composition and technical writing courses. Freshman composition and junior composition are requirements of the general education core that must be completed by every student at the university. A course in developmental writing is required for students whose placement tests indicate that their writing abilities fall below department guidelines. A course in writing computer documentation is required for computer science majors; several advanced composition courses are required for English majors and may also be taken by other students as electives.

The first course to be taught in a computer lab was freshman composition. The choice to teach this class there first was not based on any philosophical or pedagogical strategy: the teacher willing to attempt using the lab simply happened to be teaching freshman composition. Eventually, all sections of freshman composition were scheduled in the lab.

Initially there was some concern about placing developmental writing classes in the lab. Some teachers were reluctant to add the burden of learning to use computers for writing with students who were already insecure in their writing abilities. Some of the classes were taken into the lab on a trial basis and the results were remarkably positive. The students seemed to enjoy the move from pen and paper to a previously untried writing tool. Their attitudes toward writing improved.

Understandably, students who had taken their first one or two writing classes in the lab expected to have the advantages of the lab for upper-level writing courses as well. Consequently, junior composition was moved to the lab.

With this migration of the three required writing courses to the computer lab, scheduling all meetings of each class in the lab became impossible. Most classes now use the lab on a rotating basis, which allows maximum efficiency of the facility. Even with this rotation, however, it is necessary to hold some of the classes in computer labs in other buildings.

SOFTWARE FOR WRITING

The most frequently used program in the computer-mediated composition classroom is the word processing package. The campus standard at DSU is WordPerfect for Windows. Students are taught the basics of this package in a computer applications course which most students take during their first semester at DSU.

At the beginning of courses in both developmental writing and freshman composition, students need to know little more than how to create, save, and print a file. Since these skills are taught in the introductory sessions of the computer applications course, writing teachers spend their time reinforcing, not teaching, these basic skills. Later in the course, students are shown how to use more sophisticated word processing functions as the teacher perceives the need.

For developmental writing, the students do not need to learn much more than the basics of word processing. Since these basic skills are taught in one course and reinforced and used in their writing course, students quickly become very adept with the basics of the word processing program.

Freshman composition requires that students go beyond the basics of creating, saving, and printing. Throughout the semester, assignments are designed to culminate in a final research paper. Students are encouraged to use pieces of previously written assignments to build new papers. The series of research assignments requires writing a variety of papers on the same topic. This series typically begins with a personal experience paper on the topic and includes several summaries of newspaper, magazine, or journal articles, a profile paper of a person involved with the subject, and an opinion paper. This approach immerses students in their topics which results in better quality research projects. It also uses the storage and retrieval facilities of computer technology effectively because students are encouraged to retrieve completed papers and to use information from these papers to build the final research assignment. To complete this research process, students must have more advanced knowledge of the word processing program. Students must know how to merge files and rearrange blocks of text and since they must also incorporate the work of other authors in their writing, they must know more advanced formatting techniques.

In junior composition the only students who need much assistance with word processing are transfer students. Even though these students are initially daunted, through the help of teachers and fellow students, they soon become proficient word processors.

Both students and teachers agree that the most entertaining and stimulating computer programs available for composition classes are those of the Daedalus Integrated Writing Environment (DIWE). The Interchange module provides students with synchronous communication, and it is by far the most frequently utilized program in DIWE. Interchange allows members of a class to conduct real-time conversations online. Students key in their ideas, comments, and concerns during an Interchange session and those remarks immediately appear on the screens of all students participating in the session. The Interchange sessions are typically activated by a teacher's prompt or question.

Students in all levels of composition appear to be motivated by this kind of class discussion. Frequent topics for discussion include choice of writing topics, dissection of the current assignment, and problems that students are encountering in a particular assignment. Even though the teacher may suggest a prompt for an Interchange session, the students themselves often take the lead and adjust or change the direction of the session to fit their needs.

Interchange is only one of the interesting modules of the DIWE package. It includes heuristics for prewriting and revision, an electronic mail program, a word processor, shared file capabilities, and several other modules. DIWE is used in all levels of composition at DSU. It is introduced immediately in Writing Development. For students who have trouble with written communication, this program appears an exceptional motivator. The informal atmosphere of Interchange sessions frees them from the constraints of formal discourse. Even though the atmosphere is informal, instant feedback from others in the session demands that they express themselves clearly.

DIWE is also used extensively in freshman and junior composition. Interestingly, even if students have used the program in previous composition classes, they do not seem to be bored with it—on the contrary, the more students have used Interchange, the more they seem to enjoy using it.

In addition, all writing students can use a networked grammar and style checker, StrongWriter, that was developed at DSU. The program analyzes student texts and points out blunders, and it suggests revisions that can strengthen and clarify writing. Based on its analysis, StrongWriter tells students to avoid words like "irregardless" and forms such as "has went," and it advises them to revise their writing to avoid passive construction and vague, colorless words.

NETWORK ACCESS

Students in composition classes can access the statewide online library system through the campus LAN. This capability makes research projects in any composition class much easier since all students in a composition class may access the online catalog directly from the lab. Teachers can assist students in choosing the correct search terms for their topics and can also help students eliminate sources that would not be appropriate for their particular research.

CD-ROM applications are also accessible through the LAN. The availability of research tools on CD-ROM from any microcomputer can greatly expedite the research process. Since the students can access these sources during a composition class, the teacher can be available to guide the student on a productive research path.

Through the DSU LAN, students have access to the Internet. Composition classes at all levels have used this international network to communicate with students in other composition classes. Students in Developmental Writing and Freshman Composition courses have carried on semester-long dialogues with students enrolled in similar courses in New Jersey, Alabama, and Michigan. Students in more advanced composition classes use Internet to link to research sources like Gopher, WAIS, the WWW, FTP, and Mosaic. Through these resources, students can conduct sophisticated research from the confines of the composition lab.

A graduate course in programming for the humanities has been taught by a DSU English faculty member via international networks. Students enrolled in the course lived in Canada, England, Finland, Hong Kong, and throughout the United States. There are plans to teach other courses, including composition classes, in a similar manner.

LITERATURE CLASSES

A literature class is required for all students as a part of the general education core, and, in addition, English majors must complete at least three surveys of literature and three specialized literature courses covering an author, period, or genre. As appropriate, computers are used to enhance the teaching of literature.

DIWE is used by students in literature classes. As a means of starting discussion (or continuing it, or completing it), an instructor may ask literature students to meet in a computer lab and respond to a prompt posted on Interchange about, say, characters in an Austen novel. Most literature students have had experience using Interchange in composition classes, but those who have not used it can be shown how to do so in a few minutes. As students read one another's Interchange comments and reply to them, discussion can become extremely animated.

Literary discussion using Interchange is different from oral class discussion in at least three ways. First, statements are more thoughtful. The nature of written expression encourages students to make qualifications and to select words more carefully. Second, some students who seldom contribute to oral class discussion may become intensely active on Interchange. Third, Interchange discussions can be more focused: all students normally begin in the same electronic group, but subgroups can be formed if some students wish to continue on a topic while others want to branch to another topic. For example, discussion of the plot showing the relationship between the hero and heroine in a novel may lead to a discussion of the character of the heroine, and that may lead to description of the theme of the role of women in the novel. Any student can create a subgroup and encourage class members to join it. Interchange sessions can be saved on disk and messages can be sorted by the students who originated them. Then students can be given their comments which may become the basis for a paper.

Whenever possible, the texts for a literature course are made available in electronic form to the instructor and students. Text analysis programs can then be used in the course. Sometimes a particular printed textbook is selected for a class because of its availability in electronic form; the Wells and Taylor edition of the works of Shakespeare was adopted because the DSU could purchase a site license for the electronic version of the text. If the copyright permits, a scanner can be used to create the electronic version of most texts, and some have been created by keying them. A variety of computer programs for the analysis of texts are on hand. Some have been written by university professors; others are commercial software. They can significantly assist teachers and students to examine a work of literature. Sometimes they allow literary study that would be highly impractical (if not impossible) without computer analysis: for example, using a word-frequency program and a key-word-in-context concordance generator, it is possible to make a study the use of color in Hawthorne's *The Scarlet Letter* that shows that in this relatively gray and colorless novel, the 115 occurrences of "scarlet" are always associated with the letter except for three, and they are references to Pearl and, thus, indirectly related to the letter.

Students in literature courses literally beg to take in-class examinations in a computer lab so that they can use word processing. In papers, and sometimes on tests, if the professor requires supporting quotations from a literary work, students use cut-and-paste techniques to obtain quotations directly from the electronic text of the work.

THE ENGLISH DEGREES

The nonteaching English degree at Dakota State University is a Bachelor of Science in English for Information Systems. It is designed to prepare graduates to write technical documentation, to create and edit many kinds of publications, and to use computers for analysis of texts and for information retrieval. It contains a core of courses in writing, language study, and literature that are traditional parts of an English major, and it adds specialized areas of study and computer programming courses that make it unique.

Students majoring in English for Information Systems must complete at least one of five options. The computer publishing option is designed for those who want to write, edit, and publish newspapers, magazines and journals, and books. It includes courses in journalism that give practice in writing, editing, and layout on large and small computers as it is performed by modern newspapers. Courses in desktop publishing teach the principles of computerized design, printing, and publishing as well as the use of specialized software and hardware. In addition, students take a studio art course in design and business courses in accounting, marketing, and advertising.

The documentation option prepares graduates to write technical manuals and user guides. The skills of writing clear and accurate technical documentation and genuinely helpful user guides appear to be more needed in the world of technology than any other skills. Basic and advanced courses in writing documentation teach the principles of description of computer programs, and systems and principles of instructing users, programmers, and managers. A course in computer-aided graphic arts presents the applications of computer-generated and controlled imaging including graphing, drawing, and animation. A course in grant and report writing teaches researching granting organizations, writing grant applications, and the preparation of reports on the use of grant funds.

Students in the computer programming option study programming languages in order to program computers for advanced literary and linguistic applications. They study the principles of programming (logical design and structured programming techniques) as well as systems analysis and design. They learn to program in C, COBOL and Pascal; they learn job control language and how to use system utilities. They also take a course in advanced documentation.

Students in the business option study accounting and management in order to operate their own business or to assume executive positions in corporations. They also study business law and marketing.

The text analysis option provides advanced courses in computer programming for text analysis, including corpora analysis. It requires at least six courses of additional literary study. Three of the courses are additional surveys of world, English, or American literature. Three of the courses are additional specialized courses in a period (such as Victorian literature), in an author (perhaps novels by George Eliot), and in a genre (for example, a course on the sonnet).

COMPUTER PROGRAMMING FOR ENGLISH MAJORS

In addition to a course covering basic computer use, at least one course in computer programming is required for all students at Dakota State. Students majoring in business or a related field normally take courses in C or Pascal. Students in other areas, including those majoring in English, complete a course in which they learn to program in QuickBASIC. In addition, English students are required to complete an additional class in programming for the humanities in which they learn to write programs in SNOBOL4 and a related language, SPITBOL (a more powerful superset of SNOBOL4).

SNOBOL4 was selected as the programming language of choice for English students because of its power and features. SNOBOL4 is designed to do exactly the kinds of things that English students want to do: to search for strings of characters and manipulate them. SNOBOL4 programs can pick out words, phrases, and sentences from a text and analyze them. Because SNOBOL4 will manage storage and make needed data conversions automatically, students can write more powerful programs with fewer lines of code using SNOBOL4 than with other languages.

Since English majors complete a minimum of two programming courses, they can write computer programs of considerable sophistication to produce word frequency lists, to generate concordances, to index texts, and to extract virtually any kind of information from texts. Even if they do not continue to create programs after the course requirements are met, these students have a profound understanding of the ways computer programs work—because they have experience writing them. Such understanding is essential for English for Information Systems majors who work with programmers in developing internal and user documentation for software.

The university also offers a teaching degree in English: the English major for Bachelor of Science in Education. The teaching program has the same requirements as the nonteaching degree except that students do not complete an option (such as those in computer publishing or documentation). An understanding of computer programming is important for English teaching majors as well as for the English for Information Systems majors. English teachers are regularly required to make decisions on software purchases for their classes. Reliable evaluations of software are more easily made when the teacher understands what kinds of decisions go into software programming. Teachers who understand programming can more easily discern the pedagogical and methodological underpinnings of the software being evaluated.

At least two programming courses are required for students who minor in English or who earn a specialization in English as part of a degree in elementary education. Principals and superintendents are extremely impressed when they discover an elementary teacher with a specialization in English who can write a computer program to calculate the readability level of a text.

CONCLUSION

DSU's integration of computers and related technology into the world of English is exceptional, and we believe that our teaching of English is unusually productive and effective because we use computers. Graduates of Dakota State University enter the workforce with technical skills that make them uniquely prepared for the twenty-first century.

Chapter

16

Using Technology in a Computer Concepts Course

James S. McKeown,

Instructor in the College of Business and Information Systems
Dakota State University, Madison, South Dakota

Lynette Molstad

Assistant Professor of Business and Information Systems
Dakota State University, Madison, South Dakota

All students at Dakota State University (DSU) are required to take Computer Concepts to complete part of the university's computer requirement. This course has been the primary vehicle for integrating computers into the curriculum on campus. The success of Dakota State's mission has come from its ability to create a computer-literate campus which is accomplished in the Computer Concepts course.

In 1984, the South Dakota Board of Regents changed the mission of DSU to "provide instruction in computer management; computer information systems; electronic data processing; application and systems training; and the preparation of elementary and secondary teachers emphasizing the use of computers and information processing." This mission has led to the integration of computers in all areas of instruction. Computer literacy is expected of all students. In their first semester, students take Computer Concepts, a course which serves as the introduction to computers, applications, and the campus computer environment. The college curriculum is structured around the skills acquired in Computer Concepts. These skills thus become survival skills for students as much as reading and writing skills do.

DSU'S COMPUTING ENVIRONMENT

DSU has approximately 1,500 students and over seventy faculty and is located in Madison, South Dakota. The campus has over 450 computers, most of which are available for student or faculty use. Almost all the computers are linked to various servers on a Novell network. In addition, there are Macintosh and Apple II labs. The campus also has an IBM 4381 mainframe with twenty terminals and a MicroVAX minicomputer with fifteen terminals. PC terminal emulation software allows networked computer users to access the mainframe environment from any PC. Off-campus users can dial in to the mainframe environment. Direct-line communication is granted to the Earth's Resource Observation Station (EROS) facility near Garretson, South Dakota, and to the university's facility in Sioux Falls, South Dakota. Both sites are over fifty miles from campus.

The computing environment has been designed to be almost completely open with free access to computer labs. Nine labs are dedicated to instruction and student use. This includes a controlled-access lab where students can work at any time of the day or night. Permission to use this lab is granted to those who, because of jobs or family commitments, find it difficult to work in a lab during regular hours.

The campus supports two electronic mail systems and has BITNET and Internet nodes. The campus is also part of the South Dakota Library System. Students and faculty can log on to the Project for Automated Library Systems (PALS) to conduct searches and reserve materials from the campus library or any other public or school library in the state system. From a networked terminal, users can also access a number of database systems as well as a nationwide interlibrary loan system. Some of these systems include ERIC, First Search, InfoTrack, and Computer Select.

Any dorm student can, for a fee, have his/her computer connected to the network. Network cards are provided in the $75/semester fee. This enables a student to enjoy the entire computing environment, including mainframe access, electronic mail, library and database searching capabilities, and applications software, from a dorm room.

THE COMPUTER CONCEPTS COURSE

Computer Concepts is designed to build a broad base of computer expertise for students. The fundamental skills acquired in Computer Concepts are used to enhance instruction in nearly every other course offered. These skills include the basics of word processing, databases, spreadsheets, DOS, electronic mail, and the DSU computer environment. All students are expected to gain mastery of these skills. Students may also take a second microcomputer course, Computer Software Applications. This is an advanced course which builds on the knowledge gained in Computer Concepts. It stresses advanced topics in selected applications and integration of various software packages. Both courses develop word processing, database, spreadsheet, and DOS skills using the campus standard software packages. The standard software packages currently used are WordPerfect 5.1, dBASE III Plus, Lotus 1-2-3, and MS-DOS.

Over twenty-five sections of Computer Concepts are offered each year, with the class being taught in various ways every semester. Most students take Concepts in their first semester on campus. One section of Computer Concepts is offered as part of an honors class that combines Computer Concepts with freshman composition. Evening sections are offered which are generally filled with individuals from the community who take Concepts to get an introduction to computers. It is also offered several times a year at the DSU facility in Sioux Falls. This facility has its own Novell server and has direct-line access to the computing network on campus.

All sections of Computer Concepts are taught in a lab setting with a 1:1 student-to-computer ratio. Most sections meet for one hour twice a week. The instructor is equipped with a networked computer and projection panel and uses a combination of lecture, demonstration, and hands-on practice. Each lab is equipped with at least twenty-four IBM PC or compatible computers. There are four to eight dot-matrix printers with switch boxes in each lab as well as network laser printing capabilities. Each lab is part of the Novell network with full access to applications software, the mainframe through terminal emulation, electronic mail systems, BITNET and Internet, the library, and a host of online databases.

The course stresses hands-on learning and applications skills. The hands-on approach currently used provides the students with important skills which can be utilized in other classes and on the job. Very little time is dedicated to teaching what could be called computer appreciation skills. Most of the course is dedicated to teaching applications and computer usage. Many topics, such as hardware, software, storage, and ethics, are integrated into the course material. Topics such as computer history, careers, software development cycles, computer crime, and future computer uses are not covered. Many topics, are changing so rapidly that much of the material is dated almost before it can be put to use. Other courses also exist to incorporate much of this material, or it has been integrated into other parts of the curriculum. Seminars and presentations have also been given to educate students and faculty in these areas.

Hands-on training is given in every class almost every day. The instructor lectures and provides explanations and examples and then walks students through examples and sample problems. Students are provided with time to work on assignments whenever possible. The instructor is available to answer questions and solve problems in class while the students are on the computer and working with an application. When possible, examples and problems are provided. Common mistakes and pitfalls are shown as well as ways to avoid or minimize these problems.

Weekly assignments are given to provide practice on the computer, and six tests are given during the semester. Three tests are standard objective question tests, and students use scannable forms on these tests, which makes correction faster, easier, and more accurate. Three tests are online tests in which students are given specific problems to solve that can demonstrate their mastery of the applications and concepts presented. These tests are given in the lab with the students using the computer. Students are also given a final project to complete on a topic related to their major or career. They complete written papers using a word processor and combine this with information gathered using a database or spreadsheet. This information is then compiled into a report. Topics used for these projects have covered a wide range of interests, and some have completed more traditional projects such as categorizing their baseball card collection, personal library, or stamp collection. Others have created spreadsheets to calculate student grades for a fictional class or to compile basketball or baseball statistics for their favorite team. Some of the more creative projects have included databases to track registered livestock, spreadsheets used for running businesses such as a pizza parlor or a funeral home, spreadsheets to calculate the results of chemistry experiments, and databases tracking waterfowl migration. The final project stresses integrating the data gathered in one application with information compiled from another application.

Development of Support Materials

Many support materials have been developed to enhance instruction in the course. Particular attention has been given to providing consistent instruction among instructors and for providing students who have been absent with class materials. An applications textbook is used which provides some of the student assignments as well as reference and supplementary materials for student use. The text provides student versions of the software for use at home during the course. Most of the student assignments have been developed and improved by the course instructors. Students are expected to purchase several disks for use in the course; one contains the software needed to log on to the campus network, and the others are for storing files and for making backup copies.

The course instructors have developed templates which are distributed to the students to assist them. These templates have also been converted to laminated posters which are placed on the walls of the labs for student reference. Other materials have been created and distributed to the students, including a reference sheet with an alphabetized list of WordPerfect commands, dBase command syntax and examples, DOS commands, DOS syntax and examples, common Lotus 1-2-3 commands, examples, menus, and information, and the steps used to integrate data between applications.

A commercial videotape series is on reserve in the library for students to use as a supplement to class instruction. It allows students who have been absent to keep up-to-date and those who want to can access more material.

Use of the Network

Student assignments are posted on the network along with the files needed to complete the assignment. Files posted on the network are stored on the file servers in a subdirectory that is accessible to the students. Students are expected to copy these files to their disks and complete the lab assignments. This has also been very valuable for students who have missed class because their assignments and files are waiting for them on the network when they are ready to complete them.

Also posted on the network are the files needed for taking a pretest prior to each set of exams. Developed by one of the faculty members, the pretest contains twenty-five true and false questions and twenty-five multiple choice. To run the pretest, which contains topics which are contained on the upcoming test, students use a utility program to copy it to a student data disk. As students answer the true/false section, responses tell whether the answer is correct or wrong, and students then select responses until the correct answer is found. Once a question is answered incorrectly, the student cannot skip the question. For both parts of the pretest, the program tracks student answers and keeps scores, and provides a printout of the student's score and response for each question. For questions missed, the program also provides the topic of the question and page numbers from the text or reference handouts to find the answer. Online help is also available to explain how to use the program and contains several sample questions. Students can retake the test at any time, and it has become an excellent resource for students while providing immediate feedback and an atmosphere similar to the testing situation.

Files are also posted on the network to provide students with helpful information regarding testing times, review sessions, assignments, assignment due dates, and other information important to a multiple-section course. Files which provide the students with helpful information and tips for completing lab assignments are placed on the network. These are referred to as "Tips and Tricks" files and are designed to help students with difficult points or to provide them with command syntax or examples.

Review Sessions

Prior to each online exam, review sessions are scheduled in the lab. Several instructors lead the students through activities similar to the upcoming online exam. Questions are answered and the important points from the lectures and demonstrations are reinforced. Students are given a hands-on opportunity to work with problems. Several student organizations supply volunteers to assist with the review, and students who cannot attend one of the review sessions can get a copy of the review materials from an instructor. These materials are available only from an instructor and are available only after the review sessions have been held to encourage students to attend a review session.

Normally about one-third of the students enrolled will attend one of the review sessions. These students have been tracked and average about four percent higher on the exams than the class as a whole. Whether the review sessions help these students has not been determined. The review sessions may help those attending or the students attending the reviews may be better, more conscientious students and thus score higher on the exams.

Computer Knowledge Survey

When they first enter the class, students are given a survey which gauges their general level of computer knowledge and their exposure to various software packages, and they must rate their keyboarding ability on the survey. This data is then compiled and used to judge the overall computer literacy of the students. A survey is also used at the end of the semester to assess what the students have learned in the course and how they rate various parts of the course. It allows them to write constructive comments about the course and the materials used in the course.

The Help Desk

Students have access to the course instructors and are encouraged to seek their help. A Help Desk has also been set up and staffed near the computer labs to provide assistance for students who experience problems with the computers or have questions regarding the software they are using. Funded with work study monies, the Help Desk is open afternoon, evening, and weekend hours and is staffed by students who have successfully completed Computer Concepts and other computer courses. The Help Desk can aid students with concepts problems as well as problems in several other courses in the curriculum. A log of student problems is kept and compiled for use by the instructors of each course that the Help Desk services. The Help Desk is also responsible for maintaining the labs; this includes such tasks as changing ribbons, providing paper for the printers, and doing general hardware troubleshooting. It also sells disks to the students, provides network access disks, attempts to recover student data when it is lost, and provides file transfers between 5.25-inch and 3.5-inch disks. The Help Desk staff is provided with limited training, while meeting weekly with their supervisor and the instructors of the courses they service. This meeting provides an opportunity for the Help Desk staff to share problems and concerns, allows instructors to gather information on student problems, and provides the Help Desk staff with possible solution strategies. Concepts instructors can also brief the staff on upcoming material and warn them of potential problems.

Topics Covered in Computer Concepts

In a typical sixteen-week semester the course is distributed as follows. The exact timing may vary somewhat as does the order of presentation.

Week 1. introduction, expectations, and the campus network (syllabus, grading, disk preparation, network access)
Week 2. word processing using WordPerfect (creating, saving, retrieving, printing)
Week 3. word processing using WordPerfect (spell checking, margins, block commands)
Week 4. word processing using WordPerfect (advanced topics)
Week 5. DOS (directories, copy, delete, wildcards)
Week 6. written and online exams over WordPerfect and DOS
Week 7. dBase III Plus (creating files, structures, lists, printing)
Week 8. dBase III Plus (reports, sorts, queries)
Week 9. dBase III Plus (reports, indexing, complex queries, deleting)
Week 10. DOS (subdirectories, labels, disk copying, function keys)
Week 11. electronic mail, mainframe access, library system (using e-mail, terminal emulation, library database searches)
Week 12. written and online exams over dBase III Plus and DOS
Week 13. Lotus 1-2-3 (creating, saving, retrieving, and printing)
Week 14. Lotus 1-2-3 (formulas, formatting, copying)
Week 15. Lotus 1-2-3 and Graphs (sorting, text files, graphs, graph files)
Week 16. written and online exams over Lotus 1-2-3

Computer Concepts has as many as ten instructors to cover classes at the various sites. These instructors range from term contract instructors to tenured Ph.D. faculty. Each section, however, completes the same assignments and receives nearly the same instruction although individual teaching styles will vary. An individual serves as the coordinator for Computer Concepts and for the Computer Software Applications course as well. The coordinator has several responsibilities, including handling some of the day-to-day chores which lightens the burden of the other instructors and allows more consistency among sections. With input from other instructors, the coordinator prepares tests and has copies of them printed and available on testing days; copies of disks needed for testing are prepared and are made available as well. Copies of the students' labs are available in advance and are posted on the network as needed. Room reservations are made by the coordinator who is also responsible for providing handouts, templates, and review sheets. The coordinator schedules review sessions and is responsible for overseeing them. Any files needed for lab assignments and the files needed for the pretest are also prepared and posted by the coordinator.

Class materials are made available in advance and are transferred via electronic mail to other instructors. Electronic mail is used as much as possible to update and inform the other instructors. Regular meetings are scheduled to discuss assignments, due dates, test dates, review dates, and other issues. These meetings are usually short but have proven an important medium for sharing problems, concerns, and strategies. They have been an invaluable means of sharing support materials and teaching techniques. The textbook used in the course is selected with the consent of all the instructors who will be using it.

Future Plans

No course is perfect and Computer Concepts has gone through many changes. Changes are always being implemented to improve the course. Currently there are several plans to improve instruction in the course. A keyboarding requirement would be very helpful for students entering the class. This could be a concurrent requirement. Many of the students who encounter problems in the course lack or have only minimal keyboarding skills. These students seem to spend so much time trying to enter data that they miss important concepts and techniques. It also seems to be a shame to teach computer skills and ignore the primary method for computer interaction—the keyboard.

A network package to allow the instructor's screen to project on the students' screens is planned. This would make it much easier for the students to see what is being demonstrated. This setup would also allow proper lighting in the room during class, something that is not currently feasible with a projection panel and overhead projector. A network instruction package would provide an instructor with more flexibility to teach. Students could have their screens frozen while the instructor is demonstrating a point leading to more efficient instruction. An instructor could also take a student's screen and project it on all the other students' screens.

Electronic submission of at least some assignments is possible. Instead of printing a copy of an assignment and handing it in during class, a student simply finishes the assignment and submits it electronically using the mail system. This saves paper and provides the instructor with a date and time stamp on the file and the mail message when submission deadlines are important. This creates problems for instructors, though because they would need a system to store the student files. Computer access while grading the assignment would also be necessary. Original and backup copies of the files would have to be kept to provide evidence a student completed an assignment.

Currently, students learn the applications which are considered standard on campus. These are WordPerfect, dBase III Plus, Lotus 1-2-3, and MS-DOS although consideration has been given to teaching other packages, especially an integrated package. While an integrated package offers several advantages, students who have completed Computer Concepts are expected to have acquired basic skills in the campus standard packages. This is important when students begin work in offices on campus and when computer work is required in other courses. One of the goals of Computer Concepts has been to develop a computer-literate campus where students can utilize the computer to speed and to ease work in other courses.

The ability to use a graphical user interface is becoming important. Students will need to know Windows or OS/2, probably both, to compete in the job market, but at the time of this writing, neither is installed. One or both will need to be available with time to teach them. Currently the course is so full that another topic will have to be dropped to incorporate new topics. In the future, it is hoped students will have more skills when entering the course, and the pace can be improved. As software packages and interfaces become easier to learn and more intuitive, the pace of the course can be accelerated.

Plans are be implemented to use the student identification card for a wide range of uses. It is presently used as a debit card for the campus bookstore and food service. It will soon be used for vending machines on campus. In the near future, it will also be used for gaining entry to controlled-access labs. This security measure will track who enters the lab and when.

CONCLUSION

Computer Concepts provides invaluable training for students at Dakota State University. The training students receive enables them to use computers in nearly every other course on campus. (We're still working on integrating them into the aerobics classes!) This also better prepares Dakota State graduates for careers in the information age. Much of the success can be attributed to the time and effort invested by the instructors and the students and the computer-rich environment created on campus. Normally students are expected to spend two to four hours a week studying outside of class. Surveys have indicated that concepts students spend nearly twice that amount of time. The payback has been the development of a computer-literate campus.

Chapter

17

Energies Plus, Inc.

N. Faye Angel
Assistant Professor of Business
Ferrum College, Ferrum, Virginia

Energies Plus, Inc. is the title of a case study which can be used in a management information systems class. As presented here, it is designed to fit well with the seven steps of the structured system-development life cycle (SDLC) approach to systems development which are listed in the objectives. Also included are a description of case, five report assignments, and several tables of information. The needs and reports discussed in this case study are independent of one another so they can be assigned separately, and only those reports that conform to course objectives need to be completed.

OBJECTIVES

1. To use the computer and supporting software for decision support
2. To write templates for spreadsheets that are user-friendly and that allow users with little knowledge of the software to use them effectively and efficiently
3. To develop and to use database programs and reports to meet anticipated and unanticipated information needs
4. To set up a meaningful, easy-to-use file organization
5. To conduct a cost/benefit analysis for a proposed computer system including tangible and intangible costs and benefits
6. To sharpen the application of quantitative skills by using spreadsheets to augment decision making
7. To promote the articulation and communication of information needs by developing a data dictionary, by writing a plan to ease the transition from a manual to a computerized information system, and by creating a training manual for using the new system

DESCRIPTION OF CASE

Energies Plus, Inc. was founded by Shelby Halin in June 1986. She holds fifty-one percent of the stock. She is CEO and makes all of the important decisions. The company specializes in diverse types of energy-generating products.

Ms. Halin requires financial information on a potential investment that involves the development of a solar cell for automobiles and needs maximum profit and product mix determined for three energy-saving devices. She also requires the development of several database programs with appropriate reports that will allow her to obtain data for both anticipated and unanticipated information needs.

Halin has been employing M.B.A. graduate students to calculate manually such financial information as projected cash flows, net present values, internal rates of return, and optimal product mix and maximum profit for various products. This has created several problems. The graduate students do not calculate the financial information the same way so Ms. Halin is never sure how to analyze the results. On one occasion depreciation expense did not get added back into the projected cash flow statement; Ms. Halin failed to take notice of this and decided not to pursue the project because the NPV was negative. However, this mistake was later discovered, and upon recalculation with the appropriate data, it was determined that the project should have been undertaken.

In addition, Halin is disorganized. She frequently has to search a long time for a report because she cannot remember where she filed it. Many times it has had to be redone manually, and this has resulted in her not having the financial information when it was needed. In fact, she has missed the deadline for making her decision on some profitable investments. She would like an information system that would allow her to quickly locate pieces of information and reports on various projects and a file management system that lets her recognize what is contained in the file by the filename.

Halin knows very little about what computers can do, but she thinks they must provide an improved way for obtaining information than the one she now has. Further, she does not have a business degree and does not understand how to calculate such essential things as NPV, IRR, and product mix. She knows they are important and understands how to use them but needs to have a system that can calculate these pieces of information for her.

Standardization of certain reports is also important to Halin; she does not want added-back depreciation omitted in any more cash flow statements. She wants to be able to conduct "What if" analyses by changing a few numbers and to have the spreadsheets automatically recalculate. This can be accomplished by setting up data entry areas that make data modification easy.

Halin is interested in buying a computer and appropriate software and employing someone, on a temporary basis, to develop standardized templates for the investment projects. However, depending upon which projects she decides to undertake, she has the potential for a cash flow problem because certain major investments have not started generating revenue. She only has $12,000 to spend on the entire information system including what she will pay the new employee. Before any purchases are made, Halin wants a cost-benefit analysis performed. This should include intangible and tangible costs and benefits. The training costs should be included. Based upon this analysis, various alternatives will need to be researched and one selected that will meet Halin's information needs.

There is also a strong need for database files to keep track of inventors under contract to her and to provide information about her investors. Presently, this is done with index cards that may or may not contain up-to-date information. If Halin wants to find out who invested how much and when, she has to search manually through and read all of the index cards. She has found this procedure to be extremely time-consuming. Further, all payroll calculations for the inventors are being completed manually and more errors have been made. This has upset the inventors who do not like being "shortchanged" or having to refund a payroll overpayment.

Halin has an office manager who does not want to give up her "trusty" typewriter. And, she certainly does not like the idea of using spreadsheets and database programs! Halin is pleased with the office manager's work and has no intention of replacing her so a way must be found to increase her willingness to use the system after it is developed. Halin thinks the move to a computerized system should not be abrupt. For example, she is not ready to trust the computer to write the paychecks for the inventors' fees although she does want computerized payroll calculations.

Spreadsheet templates and database files need to be developed to assist Halin in decision making and problem solving. As previously mentioned, this can be accomplished by setting up data entry areas that make data modification simple and by writing macros to print and to save the spreadsheets. Data entry areas and macros make software programs user-friendly and less intimidating. The templates for the spreadsheet should be protected except where data are to be entered to prevent accidental erasure. Database software can be made more user friendly by writing program (PRG) files to perform routine tasks.

Further, the resistance of the office manager to learning the computer and the application software threatens the implementation of the proposed computer system. In an attempt to counter this situation, a plan needs to be created for easing the transition for the entire office staff.

REPORTS NEEDED WITHIN THE NEXT THREE MONTHS

Five reports must be generated within the next three months. These reports are described in detail in the following pages:

Report #1

Develop a projected cash flow statement for the years 1993-2002 with the purpose of determining NPV and IRR for an investment that involves a solar panel. It fits on a car grill and provides energy for two hours of driving time (after a ten-hour charging period). This project is a joint undertaking of Energies Plus, Inc. and the inventor, who does not have the cash to finance the product. An agreement has been reached that would give the inventor a guaranteed fee per unit sold. Mr. Smither, the inventor, will get $.50 per unit regardless of the number of units sold. However, if the product sells well, the inventor gets an additional percentage. This will be the first time that Energies Plus has negotiated a bonus based upon number of units sold. If more than 12,000 units and less than 22,000 units are sold per year, Mr. Smither will receive an additional 2.5 percent of the selling price. If more than 22,000 units are sold annually, he will receive 4.5 percent of the selling price on all units sold. Nested IF functions can be used to determine the bonus pay. The required rate of return for this investment is 15.5 percent. The programmer will need to determine if the inventor's fee is to be calculated on gross sales or net sales.

Halin had a consulting firm conduct a marketing study on the solar panel. The results have been mixed. In some cities it has done well while in others it has "collected dust." Due to the mixed results, Halin wants to develop three scenarios on which to base the NPV and IRR values—worse case, most likely case, and best case. The initial investment will be $100,000 for machinery and equipment, $250,000 for marketing expense (test study and consulting firm), and $52,110 for miscellaneous expenses. The straight-line method of depreciation could be used; however, other methods could be employed as well.

The consulting firm projected demand for each scenario and established an initial price and annual price increases (See Table 17.1 and Table 17.2.)

Table 17.1	Forecasted Demand for Each Scenario		
Year	Worse	Most Likely	Best
1993	10,000	13,000	18,000
1994	11,500	15,080	19,025
1995	12,800	16,200	22,000
1996	13,100	18,000	23,061
1997	13,400	19,909	25,000
1998	13,490	22,001	26,100
1999	14,200	22,800	26,900
2000	14,220	23,010	27,500
2001	14,400	23,180	27,999
2002	14,000	23,760	28,310

Table 17.2 Forecasted Initial Price and Annual Increases for Each Scenario

	Worse	Most Likely	Best
Initial Price	$60.00	$72.00	$80.00
Annual Increase	3.2%	3.5%	3.7%

Advertising expense is determined to be 12 percent of the selling price for the worse case scenario, 17.5 percent for the most likely scenario, and 20 percent for the best case scenario. Returns of the product have been estimated to be 0.8 percent, 1.0 percent, and 1.2 percent, respectively. This is expected to remain constant throughout the life of the project. Sales commission will be 20 percent of the selling price per unit regardless of the number of units sold. Sales commission will not have an annual increase, for as the price increases annually, so will the amount of money obtained from sales commission. Halin's sales force for this product will consist of part-time individuals who will do this as a second job. They will be given certain regions that can be easily covered by spending ten hours a week on promoting the product. Sales commission may be calculated on gross or net sales. If it is calculated on net sales, some procedure will need to be developed to track which units are returned based upon the initiating salesperson.

Halin has a small manufacturing division, and it has reported the labor requirements for the production of one unit will be .05 hour. The average hourly wage in 1993 is projected to be $14. However, the union is posing a serious threat. In order to avoid unionization, Halin plans to increase wages by 6.79 percent yearly for the next eleven years. Materials for each unit are estimated to be $18. Materials are expected to increase at a rate of 6 percent annually. Table 17.3 provides for indirect and overhead costs. Tax expenses must be included.

Templates should be developed with cell addresses that contain functions and formulas so if any piece of datum were to change, formulas or functions would not have to be rewritten. Placing a number in either of these may make it necessary to rewrite a formula or function. Since many users are not familiar with template development, a number in a formula or function may render the spreadsheet useless. This may force the office staff back to using a manual system.

The completed spreadsheet is relatively large. In order to get it on one page, the print will need to be condensed. A macro should be written to print the spreadsheet so that Halin's office staff will find it easier to use. The spreadsheet must be protected, except for the data entry areas, so that the formulas and functions do not get accidentally erased.

Table 17.3	Indirect and Overhead Costs	
Costs	Amount	Annual Increase
Indirect Labor	$30,077	6.01%
Utilities	17,000	6.50%
Heat/Air	21,100	6.00%
Repair to Machinery	17,060	8.99%
Admin. Salaries	51,100	9.50%

Report #2

Set up a database file that contains payroll information for inventors under contract to Halin. She wants the database program to calculate each inventor's gross monthly pay and year-to-date earnings. This will require two files with identical file structures. One will store the cumulative information and one will store the monthly information. See Table 17.4 for payroll information for the first three months of 1993. Since fields can have mathematical operations performed upon them, use the Replace command with a mathematical formula to calculate monthly gross pay and place the calculation in a field for gross pay. After calculating the monthly pay, append the data from that file to the cumulative file.

Net pay can also be calculated by setting up additional fields for federal, state, and FICA taxes as well as net pay. Again, use a mathematical formula to determine net pay.

After appending the monthly information to the cumulative file, replace the information in the fields that contain units sold and gross pay with 0 (zero) for the monthly file only. Also, place the current month in the month field. Use the Replace command. This will ready the monthly file for new payroll information. Not all of the fields in the monthly file will need to be modified so do not zap the records. If you do then you will need to reenter much of the information.

Get a hard copy of monthly gross pay and year-to-date earnings for each employee. This can be accomplished by using the monthly and cumulative files individually or creating a view file to produce a single report. Use the Total command for the year-to-date earnings information. As this will be an ongoing procedure, write a program file to perform these tasks. The PRG file will make the calculations and report generation very easy for Halin's office staff.

Report #3

Set up a database file for the inventors based upon the data in Table 17.5. The payroll file from report #2 will also be needed. If report #2 was not assigned, refer to Table 17.4 to obtain data to create the payroll file for March only. The

TABLE 17.4　Payroll Information

January 1993

SS NUMBER	NAME OF INVENTOR	UNIT FEE	UNITS SOLD	PRODUCT TYPE
123456789	Saws, Joyce	$3.23	710	100
234556789	Dill, Virgil	.78	390	120
098765432	Mills, Dawn	.70	451	120
987654321	Cox, Will	2.50	39	120
876543211	Oakes, Barry	.65	119	120
765432109	Webb, David	.80	67	100
345678901	Myer, Wendy	1.10	592	120
456789012	Gibbs, Pat	1.45	611	120
567890123	Angle, Don	.67	305	120
678901234	Knowles, Bo	4.55	793	130
789012345	Hodge, Jerry	.80	503	110
654321098	Percy, Tom	2.33	93	130

February 1993

SS NUMBER	NAME OF INVENTOR	UNIT FEE	UNITS SOLD	PRODUCT TYPE
123456789	Saws Joyce	$3.23	609	100
234556789	Dill, Virgil	.78	292	120
098765432	Mills, Dawn	.70	336	120
987654321	Cox, Will	2.50	61	120
876543211	Oakes, Barry	.65	200	120
765432109	Webb, David	.80	92	100
345678901	Myer, Wendy	1.10	527	120
456789012	Gibbs, Pat	1.45	509	120
567890123	Angle, Don	.67	345	120
678901234	Knowles, Bo	4.55	997	130
789012345	Hodge, Jerry	.80	492	110
654321098	Percy, Tom	2.33	107	130

March 1993

SS NUMBER	NAME OF INVENTOR	UNIT FEE	UNITS SOLD	PRODUCT TYPE
123456789	Saws, Joyce	$3.23	693	100
234556789	Dill, Virgil	.78	401	120
098765432	Mills, Dawn	.70	297	120
987654321	Cox, Will	2.50	74	120
876543211	Oakes, Barry	.65	192	120
765432109	Webb, David	.80	127	100
345678901	Myer, Wendy	1.10	586	120
456789012	Gibbs, Pat	1.45	743	120
567890123	Angle, Don	.67	299	120
678901234	Knowles, Bo	4.55	999	130
789012345	Hodge, Jerry	.80	571	110
654321098	Percy, Tom	2.33	157	130

report that Halin needs requires obtaining data from the two database files and incorporating them into one report.

Halin needs a report that lists the inventor's first and last name, product type, unit fee, gross pay for March, and date the patent was granted. This will require

Table 17.5   Personnel Information for Inventors

PATENT SS NUMBER	NAME	ADDRESS	AGE	DATE
123456789	Saws, Joyce	10 Scot St Roanoke, VA 24151	27	06/08/86
234556789	Dill, Virgil	22 Mona Ave Ferrum, VA 24088	23	01/15/91
098765432	Mills, Dawn	12 Pell Rd Roanoke, VA 24151	37	06/21/86
987654321	Cox, Will	32 Cort St Rock, VA 22151	33	02/28/87
876543211	Oakes, Barry	5 Cary Ave Roanoke, VA 24151	54	04/23/88
765432109	Webb, David	191 Pen Rd Ferrum, VA 24088	31	10/02/90
345678901	Myer, Wendy	3 High Rd Roanoke, VA 24151	43	06/02/86
456789012	Gibbs, Pat	60 East St Roanoke, VA 24151	29	09/30/91
567890123	Angle, Don	24 Tana Rd Rock, VA 22151	19	11/06/92
678901234	Knowles, Bo	1 Mount Rd Roanoke, VA 24151	29	05/08/87
789012345	Hodge, Jerry	3 Henry Ave Ferrum, VA 24088	51	06/23/86
654321098	Percy, Tom	34 Oaks Rd Ferrum, VA 24088	35	08/19/91

the creation of a view file. She would like the report grouped by product type. She also wants an average payroll payment to inventors for March. This report will meet an unanticipated, one-time need. Use the personnel file for the inventors and the monthly payroll file for March to create the view file.

Report #4

Determine the optimal weekly product mix for and maximum profit from three related energy-saving products that attach to common home appliances. These products reduce energy consumption by 15 percent. There are three similar, but different products—one fits on a clothes dryer (Dri-'n-Save), one on a water heater (Heat-'n-Save), and one on a dishwasher (Wash-'n-Save). Halin plans on entering this market gradually since she has commitments to other products and limited manufacturing capacity. She has decided to launch the product in only two modest-sized cities.

Table 17.6 Profit and Minimum Demand for Each Product

Product	Profit	Minimum Demand
Dri-'n-Save	$45	30
Heat-'n-Save	85	50
Wash-'n-Save	45	25

Spreadsheet programs such as Quattro Pro can be used to determine optimal product mix. Use the Tools Optimization (version 3) or Tools Optimizer (version 4). If a spreadsheet program is used to determine the product mix, minimum demand should be used for the lower bounds, and the number 500 (for

Table 17.7 Resource Allocation

Resource	Dri'n Save	Heat'n Save	Wash'n Save	Total
Processing (hours)	.50	.70	.60	150
Labor (hours)	.20	.15	.15	40
Metal (pounds)	.40	.50	.25	100
Finishing (hours)	.10	.30	.25	60

each product) should be used for the upper bounds. Other linear programming programs can also be used. Depending upon the optimization program employed, rounding may be necessary in order to express the product mix in integers. Data for setting up the spreadsheet or formulating the model can be found in Tables 17.6 and 17.7.

Report #5

Set up a database file of investors that would allow Halin to obtain a list of investors based upon narrow criteria.

Table 17.8   List of Energies Plus' Stockholders

NAME	ADDRESS	INVESTMENT	DATE
Sam Petry	1152 Mill Ct Wyco, TX 23451	$15,600,000	01/09/87
Merle Howe	2110 Walnut Rd Austin, TX 23411	3,269,819	06/23/88
Selma Rite	214 Kratz Rd Selvin, IL 45214	22,129,000	06/30/86
Wilard Ash	146 Fount Ave Dale, IN 34512	9,099,899	07/05/86
Barb Goes	710 Caborn Rd Jasper, IN 34980	6,983,221	06/04/86
Alan Golds	920 Oakley St Dale, IN 34568	43,900,456	08/17/90
Chuck Hams	766 Melody Ln Adams, AL 45678	9,549,780	07/01/90
Leah Harps	171 Covert Ave El Paso, TX 23419	12,110,955	12/12/86
Oscar Blas	1020 Green Rd Dale, IN 23419	9,298,659	09/22/89
Lee Luckas	232 Park Dr Boston, MA	17,400,000	11/10/88
Jane Moor	5 Rivers Dr Vernon, IN 99881	300,061	08/19/86
Barth Gope	11 Sherm Ln Elberfeld, IN 34214	7,400,000	07/07/86
Brynn Mics	3333 Route 2 Dale, IN 34568	1,289,090	05/08/91
Stuart Ste	322 Route 3 Vernon, IN 99881	1,452,890	01/08/90
Ryan Stone	34 Soccer Ave Ferrum, VA 24088	3,889	01/30/88

An inventor has heard that Halin will work with inventors and give them their "fair share," and she is completely out of money. She has approached Halin about a highly innovative furnace. Once the "bugs" are worked out, it should be able to heat or to cool an average-sized house by burning the daily trash and garbage. Halin has hired an engineering firm to evaluate its potential. The engineers think that with some major modifications, it might work although some supplemental energy for heating may be required. Everyone acknowledges, even the inventor, that it is extremely risky. If, however, it can use household trash and garbage for fuel, the profits could be high.

Halin wants to contact only the present stockholders that seem to be risk-takers. She needs a report that includes the names of the stockholders who have invested at least $10,000,000 in her company as well as the ones who invested within the first six months of its existence. (Energies Plus, Inc. was started in June, 1986.) Refer to Table 17.8.

In order to make this database as user-friendly as possible for the office staff, two small program files should be written: one that will call up the file and place the user in the Append mode, the other to print the predesignated reports. Halin expects to use these reports on a frequent basis.

CONCLUSION

Using the Energies Plus, Inc. case study or parts of it within a management information systems class will allow students to acquire meaningful skills. The students will become knowledgeable in the use of the computer and supporting software for decision support and in writing reports to meet information needs. Because the case study requires students to use database programs, write templates, conduct cost/benefit analyses, and develop a data dictionary, they will be well-prepared for employment in the business world.

TransIT and Refocused Strategies in Teaching Advanced Translation

Doug Thompson
Professor/Reader, Modern Italian History and Literature
University of Hull, United Kingdom

The context of a professor's teaching always creates some problems which are unique to one's own university environment, but there are others which are of a more general nature that most classroom teachers encounter. The great majority of my students, being absolute beginners in Italian language when they entered the university, have chosen to spend the third year of their four-year degree course at an Italian university, though a handful of them (usually those with some expertise in the language) have been elsewhere, in France or Germany. This fact alone does tend to create a noticeable imbalance, so that not all students start their final year on an equal linguistic footing. However, in my translation classes this is no longer the great problem it was before we introduced computers, for now my teaching is mainly with individuals in a group and not with the group as a whole. I cannot overemphasize this difference.

The students' final year—in reality, two ten-week teaching terms—is very intensive in terms of classroom hours and written assignments and quite extensive in the range of courses and skills. Consequently, the amount of time devoted to any single activity is very small. Translation is no exception, even though it is one of the core elements of our degree course. The traditional approach to translation (whether to or from the target language) is usually one classroom hour per week in which corrections and assessments of a previous assignment are discussed. However, the student does the bulk of the real work at home in isolation, and it inevitably assumes the aura of a test, even with limitless time as well as free access to dictionaries and other aids.

Another approach is to attempt round-the-class translation of a prepared or unseen passage, letting students complete it as a written assignment at home.

With some exceptions, I have to admit that the majority of my students have found these scenarios arid, not very productive, and less than creative. Unfortunately, the environment places far too much emphasis on public performance, resulting in a heightened sense of competition with the potential for embarrassment and losing face among peers. This detracts from the objectives of the exercise.

CHANGES IN ETHOS AND EXPECTATIONS

Because of what has been happening politically in Britain over the past dozen or so years, there has been a marked shift in the ethos and expectations underpinning our university system of education; indeed, we are continually being urged to emulate the "American model" both organizationally and in our educational aims. Education is now increasingly "big business" and primarily concerned with subjects leading directly to the creation of wealth and technological advancement. Most university modern languages departments have been forced to make concessions of one sort or another to this shift either to survive at all (and some have not) or to be able to continue doing what many of them still believe they should be doing in a modern university—offering a broadly humanistic education rather than job training.

Some of the changes forced on us have been for the better, allowing students greater flexibility in deciding the kind of mix each feels he/she requires. Thus, my own department (Italian) teaches technical translation, interpreting and commercial Italian along with courses on Dante, Laurentian Florence, the history of the Italian language, modern Italian poetry and the novel during the Fascist *ventennio*, something we have accepted as good educational practice. Nevertheless, despite *our* positive response, there has been a noticeable narrowing in student attitudes with regard to what is and what is not worthwhile. Pressures from all sides lead more and more students to choose subjects for which they have no real aptitude or interest—indeed, their choice very often recognizes that interest is being sacrificed to more pressing, utilitarian ends—to become qualified in a subject which will supposedly secure them a profession. This caution also operates inside departments. Typically, now, many students in my own department opt for "applied language skills" rather than for subjects which would intellectually more stimulating and demanding. Among our young people only the more farsighted are capable of appreciating that "applied language skills" cannot exist in an intellectual and experiential vacuum, that there must be all-round intellectual development and expansion of knowledge if any degree of linguistic ability is to be attained. The very terminology itself is misleading ("skills," that is) as though one can learn to manipulate language intelligently in the way that one learns to drive an automobile or to use a word processor—simply by following a set of rules.

METHODS OF TEACHING TRANSLATION

I have found that the traditional type of translation classes in which oral translation of passages takes place, followed by discussion of the merits and failings of a succession of "off-the-cuff" renderings by students, is quite unsatisfactory. There is a tendency for concentration and interest to lapse in almost everyone but the individual currently translating. In such circumstances it is difficult to get students to see the passage as a whole statement and each section of it as an integral part of that whole, often subtly influenced by, or influencing, that overall context. A majority of students really do seem to believe that translation is simply a question of hunting for *the* right lexical substitution counter (which is there, somewhere, if only one were clever enough to locate it) and never think of it as a search for different thought patterns and processes, as one moves between the two languages. This view seems to condone word-by-word, line-by-line translation, which produces a curious hybrid of the lexis of one language and the syntactical structures of the other. General explanations made *ex cathedra* may have interest for some but are often, certainly for the brighter students, usually just another glimpse of the obvious and boring. Per capita productivity rates, are notoriously low in what is, after all, a rather stale, uninspiring atmosphere; most of the real work still needs to be done at home. Absenteeism becomes a problem, which means that some students are effectively receiving no tuition at all.

It is surprising, however, just how much of a hold this time-worn procedure still has in the classroom at all levels of language teaching. Recently, when visiting one of the most renowned university language-teaching faculties in Italy, I was amazed that this was still their unquestioned approach—except that they did it with classes of seventy rather than the fifteen I am convinced is already far too many! It is inappropriate because it teaches by testing what the students already know and by emphasizing (by a crude public exposure) the much vaster area of their ignorance. It is a daunting and offensive ritual.

The problem lies in the wholly artificial, collective nature of the translation class itself; obviously, something can be learned, often is learned, in such an environment, but always a good deal less than the teacher thinks he/she has taught. Translators, usually carry out their trade in solitude, and while we should guard against confusing students who wish to be professional translators, there is a good deal of overlap in the means of achieving their different ends and they cannot really be separated. But in any case, there is some hope that students who have followed an advanced translation course gain a real awareness of what it means to be a translator since is an acquisition not just of skills but, more importantly, of a keen linguistic sensitivity.

INTEGRATING THE COMPUTER INTO ASSIGNMENTS

I was looking for an approach which, within certain limits, would allow students to work at their own individual pace, which would give them access to quite sophisticated levels of grammatical, syntactical and lexical guidance; but which, more importantly, would offer them assistance with individual difficulties in specific contexts that I assumed only a teacher could provide. To my surprise (as a computer-illiterate and latent Luddite), I soon realized that the computer offered the best possibility of creating such a working environment.

TransIT (and now TransLIT) was the outcome.[1] It is, of course, marketable courseware, but rather it is its use as a teaching methodology which answered my particular needs. The course makes use of the word processor (Microsoft Word 5 is the package we use; we are also developing it in Word for Windows, but it will run in most any system), including facilities such as the split screen and the thesaurus, to introduce students to different fields of strictly technical translation. (TransLIT, on the other hand, draws its material exclusively from twentieth-century literary prose texts.) Each of the translation assignments comprises two lessons which, in my own university, are each one hour. It is a mid- rather than high-tech process, which makes it especially attractive to students (and teachers) with little or no experience with computers. Its comparatively slow rate of operation and lack of technological sophistication also make it ideal for classroom use with a teacher present. A more ambitious, hypertext version in Windows, better suited to self-access work, has also been developed.

The first lesson of each assignment presents the students with a passage of Italian on screen, together with two or three questions of a grammatical, syntactical, and occasionally lexical nature. They must study the passage carefully, using the set questions as a guide to their analysis of the more complex features of the passage. If there was more time available, I may even require them to key in answers to these questions because, though their spoken Italian within a fairly narrow range is generally very good, their knowledge of how the language works is still rudimentary. Many of them return from Italy with a very false picture of their abilities in the language precisely because of this oral facility and are often indignant, then depressed, to discover that they are still at the beginning of the learning process rather than at the end.

Students open two windows (or, if they prefer to have the vocabulary list constantly in view, three, scrolling up and down among them as necessary) and type in their English version in the lower window while consulting their source passage in the upper one. They are able to call up a fairly comprehensive vocabulary list for any given passage, and additionally, they may consult dictionaries currently available on CD-ROM. We encourage students to spend about a quarter of the first lesson of each assignment analyzing the passage before they ever type a word, but old habits die hard and many launch into translation without having thought out the problems beforehand. This is generally evident in their first printout. At the end of the hour, they indeed print out as much of the passage as they have managed to translate and hand it in for preliminary correction. This correction consists of indicating, through an agreed set of conventional symbols, how acceptable their translations are. It is a process which takes up very little of the teacher's time. Rarely do I write any words on their scripts at this stage because they will still be expected to make further decisions about their initial solutions during the course of the second lesson. I generally write a percentage mark on each script at this stage.

When the students return for the second lesson of the assignment (at least twenty-four hours later, to give me time to do the brief, initial correction), they receive their semi-corrected printout together with one or two different printed English versions of the same passage. Normally, these versions are radically different in style one from the other; neither of them will be wholly "correct" nor are they presented as any kind of model. Using these versions, which are intended to act as a stimulus to further thought rather than to provide ready-made answers, together with my questioning of their original solutions and with constant reference back to the original Italian text, the students are then asked to correct their own first versions of the passage on screen. At the end of this second lesson, they print out their revised versions and hand them in for more detailed correction wherever this proves necessary. This stage is, in effect, the equivalent of that in which a professional translator post-edits a "dirty," machine-produced version.

This second lesson focuses on a very different set of problems from the first. For most students, it is essentially a refining process in which they resolve the few remaining problems and address the real translator's problems of tone, nuance, and idiom. It is, frankly, much more concerned with expression in English than with understanding Italian, and rightly so, because at this advanced level, it is the poverty of the students' English and not their ability to comprehend Italian which is the main stumbling block. In an era in which audiovisual communications' media, with their prepackaged responses, dominate consciousness from a very early age, the habit of reading can not be taken for granted among students, even students of the humanities. Their spoken and written expression is perhaps more than ever, stereotyped and clichéd. For most, outside their minimal vocabulary, words are a tiresome struggle since not too far down in their minds snuggles the comfortable but erroneous notion that acquiring a language means merely learning to say what one can already say in one's own tongue—which for the average student is regrettably not very much! In one of the early passages in TransIT, the term *quinta colonna* (fifth column) is used but even when they have made the obvious translation, the students remain bewildered because they have never met the expression before! And, needless to say, they are totally unaware of its origins and original significance.

I constantly bring them back to the Italian text, persuading them to compare the syntactical and grammatical differences between the two languages in a further attempt to help them understand that, together, these aspects represent nothing less than the organization of thought processes on the page and that these differ, often radically, from language to language. Not only must the words used be English but so too must the grammar and the syntax and the idiom since "literal" (I prefer the term "dirty," to emphasize their unacceptability) translations are at best only a halfway house, at worst near-gibberish.

Once students are familiar with the computer and the word processing system (between two to five weeks seem necessary for this, depending on the receptivity of the individual—unless, of course, an intensive crash course can be arranged before the course begins), they become wholly responsible for the organization of their time in class. The only requirement imposed on them is that they provide printouts of their work at the end of each lesson. I do not insist that they complete the passage in either lesson, though they must get halfway through it to qualify for a grade; thus, they are free to work at their own pace, though this does not preclude unsolicited interruptions by me. In practice, some students do return in their own time to complete the work of lesson one after they have already handed in their printout, but this does not affect the mark they receive though it may help them to achieve a better grade in lesson two of the assignment. Even in this mid-tech version, TransIT can be used as a fully or partially self-access course. Even without a teacher's minimal corrections to the student's first printout, the two printed versions that come with the second lesson will make students realize that their own first version is lacking, which should stimulate further improvement. The only real objection to using it as a wholly self-access course is that the student has no way of knowing just how successful his/her final version has been. Sometimes, when I am unable to be present at a lesson myself, students operate well enough in my absence but in these circumstances, they will always eventually have the benefit of my comments on their final printout.

The majority of students do manage to complete both parts of each assignment in the two class hours available. However, with longer or linguistically complex passages, the weaker and the more conscientious students tend to do a lot of preparatory work at home, some even going as far as to write out a first version of the passage prior to the first lesson. This is something I try to discourage during the first few weeks, and I absolutely forbid it after the fourth week or so of classes. They are not allowed to bring hand-written notes of any sort into the Computer Assisted Language Learning (CALL) unit. The intention is that they should learn to work quickly and accurately, and most students do, rapidly improving their concentration span, with higher motivation than in more conventional, classroom-based translation groups. If I wished to sacrifice speed and move at a more leisurely pace, there would be nothing to prevent me from doing so; however, in our particular circumstances, the speed element is crucial since the students will eventually be obliged to take a timed examination at the end of their course. Most quickly learn and certainly appreciate, the nearer final examinations come, that a couple hours of concentrated work each week in the unit will suffice and thus free them to deal with other parts of their degree course. In any case, for the professional translator time is money and since with these particular students, career decisions will soon have to be made, we try to simulate the working conditions of the professional so that any who might consider becoming translators will have no illusions about the intensity of such work.

Students know that I am generally available to discuss problems with them. Indeed, I am now free to give help where it is needed; thus, virtually all of my teaching has direct influence on the individual student's thinking and is often applied immediately to his/her work on screen. Often, I see mistakes in the making and can direct students to a particular grammatical rule, to check a word meaning in the CD ROM dictionaries, or to use the online thesaurus, but only rarely do I provide concrete solutions. I find that this kind of prompting, which focuses on the problem of the moment, is a most effective way of getting students to think seriously about linguistic problems and, in time, it probably helps them become aware of language as a precision tool.

Because of the two-lesson structure of each assignment, with its two very different though interconnected objectives, correcting translations is no longer as time-consuming chore. The preliminary marking at the end of lesson one is very rapid (I manage sixteen or so in under half an hour), while the correction of the second stage, though in theory much more detailed, is in most cases also very quick, because of the self-correcting elements which most students recognize and incorporate into their final versions. Thus, very few errors remain to be corrected and only occasionally, with weaker students, do I find it necessary to write detailed comments on their errors or, as a last resort, provide them with answers.

I once had a colleague, a teacher of French, who at the beginning of each class handed to her students a photocopy of her English version of the passage the students had translated and which she had painstakingly corrected. This version was presented in the ensuing class as a superior model to be emulated, regardless of how well or badly the students had performed in their own versions. Her emphasis was, in reality, a negative one, an emphasis on their finished product as a *definable* goal they had *failed* to achieve—a series of more or less "creditable" failures which she then rescued by letting them study something that they could never hope to achieve. I have no doubt that valuable lessons were taught during the course of her classes, but this approach is diametrically opposed to my own. Translation, like any form of creative activity, is open-ended and will permit an endless flow of perfectly acceptable solutions. Students, perhaps in part because of the generally repressive nature of the institutionalized education process, find this hard to accept; many even fear it for it denies the existence of a comfortable, absolute target which they can eventually attain with practice.

There is a sense in which the translations handed in are superfluous to my teaching aims, which are to inculcate in students a complex process of thinking about, and assimilating, language. I make them aware that there is never one single correct way of translating a phrase, a sentence, a paragraph—not even a word. Yet at the same time, they are continually reminded that there are very many inadequate ways of translating what is before them. There is, in short, perfectibility but not perfection.

What factors are at work, then, in the operation of this course? First, there is a radically different use of student and teacher time from that normally associated with this area of language learning. Second, the use of available space is very different: a useful analogy might be that in which theater moves from the confines of the picture-frame stage out into the round. Instead of *standing* before students *seated* in serried ranks—with all the authoritarian implications this has—I move among them, often sitting beside pairs or individuals, helping them achieve our shared objectives. To some extent, this particular use of space requires rather different for teacher and student. For example, while attending to one student I may be "called" by another, to whom I eventually move, and this is one of several quite subtle ways in which the course creates in the student the sense of being much more in control of his/her own academic destiny than was the case in the conventional classroom. That I might discuss something I have noticed on a student's screen, leading to him or her to change it seems to have a reassuring effect—continually suggesting the relative unimportance of the "testing" element of the exercise and reinforcing awareness that they are being taught and are learning as individuals.

Third and very important is the computer itself; despite all the minor irritations it can cause, it is truly a "magic box." Because of the totally interactive nature of the course, the individual controls every aspect of production from first reading to laser-printed copy and I find that in the great majority of cases, this is a source of satisfaction and increasing self-confidence. Far from being a distraction, learning to handle the technology efficiently appears to be a further stimulus; the desire to translate well and the desire to master the means to it seem to interact and feed off each other.

CONCLUSION

Students assure me they enjoy the course and that they learn a great deal. The steady increase of higher grades as the year progresses suggests that their evaluation of their progress is reasonably accurate. Given the overall time constraints on students in their final year of a British first degree course, TransIT provides a better learning environment and motivation than any other method of teaching translation I have ever tried or seen in operation.

The hypertext version of TransIT this has been developed in the context of a nationwide project, funded by the United Kingdom Higher Education Funding Council, under which the national Computers in Teaching Initiative Center for Modern Languages is leading a large consortium of linguists (the TELL or

Technology Enhanced Language Learning Consortium) with already proven expertise in the field. The aim is to produce software and courseware which may readily be transported from one language to another, from one level of learning to another, and even from one computer system to another to institutions across the whole higher education spectrum.

What has happened with TransIT and the teaching methodology it incorporates is that it has been "transported" in its original mid-tech, low-cost form to provide similar courses in introductions to technical translation in French, German, and Spanish. Second, the Italian material in it has been fitted into a hypertext shell (developed in "Toolbook") already developed successfully for German at Coventry Polytechnic (designated a university since September 1992). However, the project, concerned as it is with translation as a language-learning activity (and this is only one part of one of its three main strands), goes much wider than this. It is aiming at facilitating all kinds of language handling through giving online access to translation (and other) aids such as bilingual dictionaries, spell checkers, style checkers, grammar checkers, and thesauri— as well as general and more specialized encyclopedias. It will eventually develop at low cost what might well be called a language workstation in order to make possible independent learning within the broad field of composition, comprehension, and translation skills. Some aspects of this work were already well advanced before the consortium was formed, notably by colleagues at the Universities of Ulster and Manchester (Institute of Technology), and it is this section of the project concerned essentially with language-learning tools that I am coordinating. This and the multiplicity of other activities covered by the consortium and the, nationwide input and huge expenditure it will entail demonstrate that the computer's potential for language learning at all levels is now widely accepted and is increasingly regarded as the keystone in a policy of languages-for-all, whether inside or outside the formal national education system. In the next two to three years we are going to experience a veritable explosion in the use of computers at all levels of language learning because the consortium is addressing every conceivable aspect of that activity in what may prove to be a national policy for CALL.

NOTE

1. *TransIT* (An Advanced [Technical] Translation Course: Italian to English), a course of twenty lessons by A.D. & D.J. Thompson, Department of Italian, University of Hull, U.K., 1991. *TransLIT* (An Advanced [Literary] Translation Course: Italian to English), a course of forty lessons by A.D. & D.J. Thompson, Department of Italian, University of Hull, U.K. (commercially available October 1994).

Chapter
19

Chemistry and Art: Developing a New Course with NSF Grants

John L. Bordley, Jr.
Professor of Chemistry and Computer Science
Johns Hopkins University, Baltimore, Maryland

The University of the South, commonly known as Sewanee, is a rural, residential, highly selective, traditional liberal arts college with 1,080 undergraduates and seventy students in its School of Theology. During the winter and spring of 1986, the university decided to begin to sell, service, and support Macintosh computers, to standardize on Microsoft Word and Microsoft Excel, and to bundle these applications with every computer sold. Development work on software in the various science courses has centered on having the students use Excel spreadsheets and graphs rather than on developing stand-alone applications. The carryover of expertise in Excel from one science course to another has been beneficial. In the fall of 1991, an AppleTalk network with an Ethernet backbone connecting the entire campus, including dormitories, became operational. In many courses students and faculty use a central file server for exchanging files. In conjunction with the network, the university uses KeyServer software from Sassafras Software. This software guarantees that only the proper number of copies of a given application are used simultaneously.

The author and two colleagues, Janet Schrenk of the chemistry department and Pradip Malde of the fine arts department, received a National Science Foundation (NSF) grant (Instrumentation and Laboratory Improvement Program Leadership Projects in Laboratory Development through grant #USE-9153695) to develop a new course for nonscience majors. This course would have a traditional laboratory component and would satisfy the science requirement. To emphasize laboratory work and experimentation even during normal class hours and to decrease the time needed during class time to introduce some topics, the computing network facilities were used. The details that follow represent the ways that the network, file sharing, Excel, HyperCard, and QuickTime are now being used at Sewanee.

AN OVERVIEW OF THE COURSE

The Chemistry and Art course was developed to meet the science requirement for the nonscience majors who make up eighty percent of the student body. Six modules were prepared with the idea that four would be taught during any one semester that the course is offered. The modules represent a variety of artistic processes which permit the introduction of some of the fundamental ideas of chemistry: features, trends, and regions of the periodic table; electron structure; acids and bases; and oxidation and reduction. The modules are glassmaking and coloring; metal casting and patination; pigments, dyes, and binders; photography; papermaking; and printmaking. During each semester there will be an introduction to the visible spectrum and properties of light, color theory and instrumentation, and the use of modern laboratory instrumentation. Scientists will see the course as chemistry with art while liberal arts students will see the course as art with chemistry.

THE COLOR CONTROL PANEL—COLOR AND COLOR SPACES

An underlying theme in the Chemistry and Art course is color. Color can be measured and described by a series of three values in any of a variety of color spaces. A student wishing to understand color and the numerical representations of colors in the different color spaces needs the opportunity to experiment and see the interactions as the color or the numbers change. No application needs to be written for this exercise, as Macintoshes with color monitors allow for this experimenting. Two of the most common color spaces, RGB (red, green, blue) and HSV (hue, saturation, value or lightness), are part of the Color Control Panel (Figure 19.1). The user can move the cursor on the color wheel and adjust the scroll bar to the right to produce a desired color and see the resulting RGB and HSV values, or the user can pick values in either color space and obtain both the values in the other space and the corresponding locations of the cursor in the color wheel and the slide in the scroll bar. In all cases, a large swatch of the chosen color appears in the upper left corner of the dialog box.

EXCEL—COLOR PERCEPTION AND COORDINATES

Color perception is complex, but basically it combines the properties of the light source, the light reflected by an illuminated object, and the properties of the detector. For humans, the eyes are the detector, and the resulting signal is

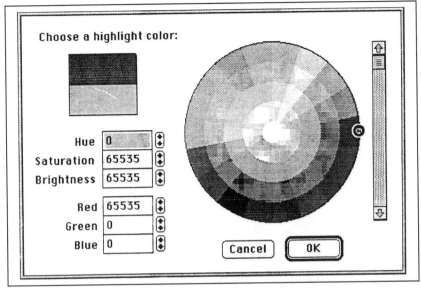

Figure 19.1   The Color Control Panel on the Macintosh

sent to the brain for final processing, i.e., color recognition. Tables of values are available for common light sources. There are also tables for the color matching functions of a standard observer. From a particular experiment, data for the amount of light reflected by an object of interest at each of several wavelength intervals is obtainable. Determining the three color space values is really an integration process. At each wavelength interval the power of the light source and the amount of light transmitted must be multiplied by each of the three color matching function values representing the red, green, and blue sensitive detectors of the standard observer. The three resulting sets of numbers are then added and normalized.

A brief example makes the process much more understandable and also illustrates that a fairly simple spreadsheet can be assembled to perform all the operations. A chart based on the data in the spreadsheet can show the various curves, and a cell containing a sample of the color can be displayed.

Figure 19.2 contains data for eight, fifty-nanometer intervals. For each wavelength interval are listed the power of the light source, the amount of light reflected by the object, and the standard color matching function values. Each cell in one of the product columns is the product at the given wavelength interval of the light source, the sample, and the appropriate color matching function. For example, the value 18.677 in the Prod y column for the 500 nanometer interval is a product of 59.86, 0.966, and 0.3230. Adding the three Prod columns gives the tristimulus values X, Y, and Z, respectively. The normalized chromaticity coordinates, CIE x, CIE y, and CIE z are calculated as shown.

Once the x, y, and z values are calculated, RGB values can be determined by an appropriate algorithm. Once the RGB values are known, a cell in the spreadsheet can display the color.

Since one of several standard light sources would be used and the values at five and ten nanometer intervals are available, and since the standard observer is almost always used, the remaining item to vary is the reflection from the sample. In the lab, students use a spectrophotometer to determine the amount of light transmitted at each wavelength interval. The students enter these results into the spreadsheet and see the X, Y, Z and x, y, z values calculated and the corresponding color displayed. As a computer exercise, however, it is interesting to see the effect on the resulting color when the shape of the reflection curve of the sample is varied. In Excel when a chart and spreadsheet are linked, the curves on the chart change as the values in the spreadsheet change. However, the values in the spreadsheet also change if the points on the curve are changed. In Figure 19.3, some data points have handles. These handles allow a user to grab and move single points. Once the student has reshaped the sample curve to a desired appearance, the calculations are redone in the spreadsheet, and, once again, the resulting color appears in the indicator cell. This interaction between the chart and the spreadsheet allows the student to experiment and to obtain a good understanding of color measurement and color measurement values. In the lab when a colorimeter is used that produces x, y, z values as the output, the student should have an appreciation of the origin of the numbers, their meaning, and last, but certainly not least, what the color is.

HYPERCARD—PRESENTATION OF CLASS MATERIAL

One of the objectives of the Chemistry and Art course is to maximize laboratory time and minimize traditional classroom lecture time. HyperCard stacks developed at the University of the South can be used by the students outside of class time. Since there are the two layers of chemistry and art, each discipline with its own vocabulary, the stacks are designed so that a student can navigate

Wave-length	Light Source	Sample	Color Matching Functions			Prod x	Prod y	Prod z
			x	y	z			
400	14.71	0.120	0.0143	0.0004	0.0679	0.025	0.001	0.120
450	33.09	0.145	0.3362	0.0380	1.7721	1.613	0.182	8.503
500	59.86	0.966	0.0049	0.3230	0.2720	0.283	18.677	15.728
550	92.91	0.169	0.4334	0.9950	0.0087	6.805	15.623	0.137
600	129.04	0.066	1.0622	0.6310	0.0008	9.046	5.374	0.007
650	165.03	0.048	0.2835	0.1070	0.0000	2.246	0.848	0.000
700	198.26	0.030	0.0114	0.0041	0.0000	0.068	0.024	0.000
750	227.00	0.000	0.0003	0.0001	0.0000	0.000	0.000	0.000
						20.087	40.730	24.494
						X	Y	Z
CIE x=X/(X+Y+Z)	CIE y=Y/(X+Y+Z)		CIE z=Z/(X+Y+Z)			CIE x	CIE y	CIE z
						0.235	0.477	0.287

Figure 19.2 Using a spreadsheet to calculate tristimulus values

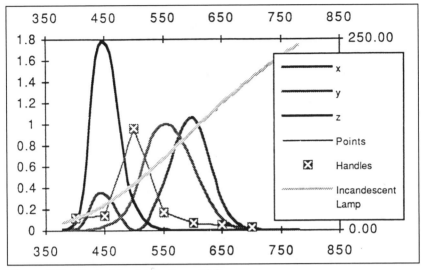

Figure 19.3 Chart of the data in figure 19.2

through an art topic and ask for explanations of the underlying chemistry topics or choose a chemistry topic and see examples from the different areas of art. This course and the stacks prepared for it are an example of a situation in which nontraditional, nonprint "book" seems to be the best medium to present the material.

With HyperCard and the Macintosh, it is possible to leave one application, go to another, and return to the first. Therefore, in the middle of a stack explaining the color calculations shown previously, the student could press a button to go to Excel and actually try the examples and then come back to HyperCard and continue with the explanation.

An extensive glossary is available in the HyperCard stacks to assist all interested users in mastering the vocabularies of the different fields.

HYPERCARD AND QUICKTIME—PRESENTATION OF LABORATORY EQUIPMENT AND EXPERIMENTS

Instructing a number of students in the proper use of an instrument is often difficult. Textbooks often have pictures or diagrams of some instrument, but not necessarily the exact piece of equipment available to the student. Demonstrations are also difficult because it is hard to have a group of students gather around a single piece of equipment and see what is happening.

QuickTime movies or still shots can now be made quickly and inexpensively with a video camera and the VideoSpigot board. These movies and still shots can be incorporated into HyperCard stacks to illustrate specific features of the actual equipment the student will be using. Likewise, proper setups for experiments can be recorded and presented. The stacks are placed on the central file server and thus available for the students to use on computers in their rooms or in the computer laboratories.

HYPERCARD AND FILE SERVER—PRELAB QUIZZES

A common problem with laboratories at all levels is to get students to read something about a particular experiment before they come to lab. Assigning questions to be looked over by the instructor at the start of a laboratory session helps some, but the instructor is then very busy at the beginning of the lab when other things must often be done.

Instead, a HyperCard stack can be placed on the file server. This stack presents a series of questions, one per card. Students can move through the stack at will, skipping over questions at first, changing answers, and reviewing any HyperCard or text information. When the students are satisfied with their answers, they press a HyperCard button which logs them on to the file server from a Macintosh using System 7. Their names and responses are written to a file that the instructor can examine before lab. If the file is a text file, it can be opened in Excel and sorted by student name or by any one of the responses. An instructor can easily spot patterns of responses for the different questions. At the beginning of the actual laboratory period, the instructor will know that the students have done some preparation. During the laboratory lecture, the instructor can concentrate on problem areas and skip over the items that the students showed they understood.

At Sewanee free-form responses are usually used, but multiple-choice, matching, or fill-in-the-blank questions are all possible. The HyperText features of HyperCard allow for dragging possible responses into fill-in-the-blank blanks. Immediate feedback is possible by only allowing the correct answer to be put in a blank. Similarly, multiple-choice questions can be graded immediately if desired. Graded or not, the results for each student can be placed in a text or HyperCard file on the file server for the instructor to look over prior to the laboratory period.

CONCLUSION

All the ideas presented here have been tested. Some will be used in other courses and departments, but all will continue to be developed and expanded. The main idea has been to present some of the kinds of things that are being done with Macintoshes and a campus-wide network at Sewanee. Through the use of computer, the Chemistry and Art course can be a viable learning experience.

Chapter

20

Evolution of the Classroom with New Technology

Abigail M. Thomas

Associate Professor, Department of Mathematical and Computer Science, Lyndon State College, Lyndonville, Vermont

Not all institutions of higher learning can afford state-of-the-art multimedia technology for the classroom. An affordable, and equally effective alternative, however, is the combination of an LCD (liquid crystal display), a PC (personal computer), a dot-matrix printer, and a cart. This transportable unit was utilized in two courses at Lyndon State College, a small rural college in northern Vermont. The focus of this chapter is to review the changes that occurred in the students' classroom performance, in curriculum content, and in the use of the computer facilities from the introduction of this particular combination of equipment.

Lyndon State College, like many other small institutions with limited resources, has found it difficult to meet the ever increasing demands of students for computer time. The campus has two IBM/DOS-based computer labs with approximately twelve computers in each lab, and one Macintosh lab with eight computers. These three labs must accommodate approximately 1,000 students. Given these sparse resources, faculty members are therefore limited and often unable to reserve these labs for teaching classes. Consequently, many courses in which computers are an assumed tool are often taught in a traditional classroom/lecture format, frequently with the aid of a chalkboard and an overhead projector—but *no* computer.

The process of trying to teach computer use without a computer led to a creative exploration of possible solutions beyond the chalkboard and overhead projector. Many alternatives were considered, from the inconvenient setting up/tearing down of a computer for each class to the high cost of a permanent computer in each classroom. The inconvenience of the former and the expense of the latter resulted in the creation of the Mobile Computer Teaching Unit (MCTU).

EQUIPMENT

Design of the mobile unit required consideration of the software and course requirements, as well as the classroom location. In the two courses (FORTRAN and Data Organization) for which this unit was designed, the software could be run on a PC with a hard disk, permitting the use of a cost-effective, "recycled" computer (Zenith-148 PC with a hard disk upgrade) rather than buying a new computer. A computer cart (4 feet long, 2 feet wide) with wheels was purchased to hold the computer and overhead unit with an LCD. An Okidata 192 printer was added to the cart at a later date. In order to transport the printer to the classroom, a small piece of plywood was placed on top of the LCD unit, and the printer, in turn, was stacked on top of the plywood. Once in the classroom, the printer was placed on a nearby desk. The Sharp QA-25 LCD was a low-end model since the classes using the MCTU did not require graphics. Given the equipment mentioned, the transportable teaching unit was both affordable and functional for the classes involved.

CLASSROOM PROCESS PRIOR TO THE MCTU

In order to evaluate the effectiveness of the MCTU, it is important to understand how each of these classes functioned prior to the introduction of the MCTU. Previously, the FORTRAN and Data Organization courses were lecture format using a chalkboard and sometimes an overhead projector but no computer. The FORTRAN class met three times a week including a one-hour lab. Students with no previous computer knowledge found the one hour lab time inadequate and had difficulty following the lectures. Lab time and tutorial time with the instructor had to be increased in order for these students to succeed in the course.

The lecture material was presented primarily on the chalkboard using flow-charts, pseudocode, and actual code. Students took copious notes from the board, often focusing more on copying the FORTRAN syntax than on comprehending the program itself. Students generally struggled to imagine the output of any given program and were unable to apply their understanding to larger programming examples. In addition, their attention span grew shorter as the programs became longer. Students found it difficult to communicate their knowledge which, in turn, reduced the amount of interaction and feedback between the instructor and students.

The other course, Data Organization, required no previous knowledge of computers and met as a two-hour, hands-on lab and a one-hour lecture. During the one-hour lecture, the twenty-four students shared lab/project experiences and ideas and listened to the instructor give an overview of the next lab session while using transparency after transparency of screen displays. The course material, unlike that of the FORTRAN course, was presented primarily during the hands-on lab time. The instructor found the lab component a challenge and at times difficult to teach; the design of the lab sessions allowed for no central instruction. Instead, instruction occurred mostly on student need and demand. The faculty member became reactive rather than proactive; as students asked for individual assistance on the computer, the instructor lost the class at large.

CLASSROOM PROCESS AND TEACHING

The experience in both FORTRAN and Data Organization led to rethinking the course teaching methods and the development and introduction of the MCTU. A brief description of the changes that transpired in each course is presented below with a discussion of the implications of the MCTU use in college teaching. In both courses the MCTU was added as the primary media aid while minimizing the use of the chalkboard/overhead projector and transparencies. What occurred in both classes using the MCTU was refreshing and at the same time surprising.

In the FORTRAN class, the presence of a computer provided an opportunity for students to witness the steps involved in compiling and executing a FORTRAN program. As the instructor typed and edited the lecture programs, students asked a wide range of questions from "Where is the Alt key?" to "How would I link two executable modules?" One particularly helpful teaching technique was for the instructor to verbalize every keyboard move. This technique enabled students with little computer background to follow the lecture and to ask basic questions. The class dynamics changed, participation improved, and interaction with the instructor increased.

The ability to print with the MCTU permitted lecture notes to be created, copied, and made available to students in the library. By reducing the amount of note-taking from the chalkboard, students were able to concentrate on the concepts at hand. Students were invited to demonstrate their grasp of the material by suggesting, for example, that they make modifications to the lecture code, thus providing an interactive dynamic and much needed feedback for both instructor and students.

The introduction of MCTU to the Data Organization course resulted in more dramatic changes. First of all, the format was redesigned: instead of including the lab sessions, all three classes became lecture-based with the MCTU as the primary teaching aid. The rapport between the instructor and students was enhanced through the MCTU. For instance, when the faculty member mistyped a word, students enjoyed correcting the error. The faculty frustration of teaching the earlier Data Organization classes was replaced with humor and a feeling of camaraderie between the student and teacher.

An unanticipated change in the class format occurred when students volunteered to demonstrate their semester projects to their peers. Students learned about each other's ideas and experience by presenting and articulating their work. They began to think critically and creatively. The difficulty level of projects increased along with the level of understanding. The introduction of this new, relatively inexpensive technology, MCTU, brought about an evolution in the teaching of these two courses.

Every piece of technology has its place and limitations. After teaching several courses using the MCTU, it is now possible to address the implications for the classroom. To begin with, the MCTU is appropriate for some but not every course; for instance, courses involving writing process, application software, and programming have benefitted from its use. The decision to use MCTU is dependent on course content and, of course, on faculty teaching preference.

Faculty members who wish to use the MCTU should be aware of some of the pitfalls encountered in the Lyndon State College experience. One major mistake is to overuse this piece of technology. The MCTU may be used for part of a class, perhaps thirty minutes. Silently typing on the keyboard should be avoided: not only does it isolate the instructor, it leaves the student out of the learning process. Two methods to avoid this pitfall are to verbalize the keystrokes as they are performed and to provide students with a handout that associates keywords to keystrokes.

There have been some surprising benefits from the use of the MCTU. The most rewarding is the unexpected rapport that developed between the students and faculty while using the MCTU. Reproducing common errors on the computer, such as mistyping or incorrect commands, can be a valuable class learning exercise. Encouraging students to explore "what if" questions strengthens the creative process and fosters the development of critical thinking skills. The availability of lecture notes in the library enables students to attend to the content of the course and to think about the material at hand. Another positive aspect to using the MCTU was the student presentations, a feature that can be used in unique ways yet to be explored.

CONCLUSION

The college spent little money for the MCTU, and the computer labs were freed from these two classes. In today's economy these are benefits that cannot be overlooked. Lyndon State College did not need to purchase new equipment for this project; the small, informal environment led to the exchange of equipment among departments, thus providing an older PC for the project.

Clearly, the benefits of this project were enormous for both the instructor and students. Teaching effectiveness was enhanced and student performance improved. Students' interest in the course content rose and class participation increased.

The Mobile Computer Teaching Unit (MCTU) introduced to these two classes provided an affordable and valuable resource for the classroom. Indeed, the class did evolve in its structure and content with this new piece of technology.

Chapter
21

CAL Heuristics in the United Kingdom's UMIST

Marie C. Hayet
Lecturer and Computer-Assisted Learning Project Officer
University of Manchester Institute of Science and Technology
(UMIST), United Kingdom

In difficult times for the national economy and shrinking resources for education, Computer-Assisted Learning (CAL) erupted on the United Kingdom's higher education scene with the promise of vast quantitative benefits. The huge investments necessary to develop good-quality courseware and the difficulties posed by the integration of CAL into the existing infrastructure and teaching provision have somewhat tempered the initial enthusiasm and paved the way for broader initiatives at the national level by subject and at the level of the individual institutions through their information technology, teaching, or curriculum policies. The need for further research into all aspects of CAL, especially strategies and scenarios, soon became obvious. At the same time CAL found a place, more modest than may have been anticipated, as a teaching method, alongside other methods. The case of the tuition of the French language in the UMIST context, a British university of technology, follows.

POLITICAL-ECONOMICAL BACKGROUND

Before cuts became a buzz word in the United Kingdom's higher education circles, Computer-Assisted Language Learning (CALL) had been introduced to teach more efficiently those areas of modern languages which have traditionally been learned through repetitive drills: vocabulary, morphology, elementary structures and their transformations, use of aspects, moods and tenses, etc. For those institutions that could afford the hardware infrastructure, CALL represented a useful adjunct to the rest of the teaching and was not perceived as any threat to the teaching work force or the quality of its teaching.

The drastic cuts in education of the Thatcher years resulted, among other things, in a huge increase of the student-staff ratios in universities, to a level particularly damaging for a subject which, as a skill, is largely based on individual learning and practice. In subsequent years, the decision was made to increase the overall number of young people in higher education; by encouraging a significant growth in the yearly student intake, the government wanted to see nearly one in three of all young people in higher education and to provide for between twenty and thirty percent of the adult population in the United Kingdom by the year 2000. Under those circumstances, CALL started to become a substitute for small-group teaching. A recent change of policy will result in future intakes being smaller than the expected growth, with numbers scheduled to level off in 1996. Target undergraduate and postgraduate student numbers have also been introduced, with penalties both for underrecruiting and overrecruiting, while applications for university places are still rising. As science and engineering courses do not attract a plethora of applicants and suffer from the disadvantage that the number of secondary-school pupils reading science has decreased, achieving these targets is difficult, especially when standards have to be maintained. It is therefore imperative that the teaching provision is enhanced and diversified, and that access courses are set up to achieve the imposed targets. In this context of flexible teaching and learning, CAL clearly has a central role to play.

The situation has not been improved by the recent introduction of differential tuition fees, which universities receive from the Local Education Authorities on behalf of their students, according to the type of course. Band 2 fees (Science and Engineering) remained constant, making it a serious disincentive for a university of science and engineering departments to rely too heavily on "home" undergraduate entrants (British and European union students pay the same level of tuition fees in British universities).

Against a backdrop of shrinking resources in real terms, the decision was made to extend the teaching provision to "nontraditional entrants." The United Kingdom lags behind its European partners as far as the educational attainments of its youth are concerned, and a significant proportion of those who leave school enters the working world without adequate qualifications. This move was also meant to compensate for decreasing numbers in the traditional population of university entrants, i.e., eighteen-year-olds fresh from secondary schools. Nontraditional entrants may mean people in employment who wish to improve their career prospects or retrain to adapt to changing needs in their professional field of activity and those in need of continuous training on a part-time basis: unemployed people, women resuming studies after raising a family, homebound people, etc. They may not hold the school-leaving qualifications granting access to higher education, but they can offer relevant professional experience instead. Opening access into the UMIST study program to nontraditional entrants meant adapting to differing learning paces, differing learning patterns, sometimes differing mobility. To fulfill these requirements, CAL provided an obvious solution.

From nontraditional entrants in universities to "traditional workers" in the workplace, it was hoped that CALL systems and courseware could have a dual purpose, university education and corporate learning with continuing education.

In 1992 the first steps towards the modularization of all courses in the United Kingdom were made. The stated aims of modularization were shifted from "a means of overcoming artificial subject boundaries, promoting student choice and clarifying course objectives" to "administrative efficiency, flexible learning, and promotion of credit transfer between courses and institutions." No matter what the true goals were, for all academic departments, this meant packaging all the courses into units which carried similar numbers of taught hours (lectures, tutorials, practical sessions, etc.) and the same number of credits. The first difficulty related to the fact that the new notional units often have to encompass what has previously been taught as several discrete courses and they do not readily combine into a coherent whole. Also, modern languages have traditionally been taught in small groups and have been classified as "arts" courses, even in the case of language engineering, despite the extensive use it makes of computers and laboratories. Traditionally, arts courses have comprised fewer taught hours, leaving more scope for individual study, research, and writing. In those courses which combine scientific or engineering disciplines with modern languages, the number of hours taught in language courses had to be increased to match those taught in the rest of the course in order to carry the same number of credits. This was not possible with existing resources, and in the absence of additional resources, leveling the number of hours taught resulted in mirroring the style of tuition in force in science and engineering degrees, namely in introducing "laboratory" sessions (CALL).

In the second half of 1993, teams of people appointed by the Higher Education Funding Councils embarked on a series of visitations of departments in higher education institutions to assess the quality of their teaching. Until then, universities had been assessed on the basis of their research work and their research ratings regularly published in the national press. Initial reports from these visitations tend to indicate that criteria to achieve the very much sought after "excellence" comprise teaching innovations, a code of practice on teaching, delivery systems for quality assurance, the value which employers lend to the course, any academic staff's commercial and industrial experience (leading to added value in the teaching process), as well as a visible interplay of research with teaching. Among the teaching innovations, CAL has been given favorable reviews, and in the teaching of modern languages, it was seen as a definite plus.

Finally, with the advent of a single European market and the European Union, there is considerable pressure to provide for the teaching of modern European languages for everybody. This "languages for all" policy entails a massive development in the teaching of specialist languages to language learners with specific professional needs.

INCENTIVES

A number of British and European initiatives have been launched to support the introduction of technology in teaching and learning.

In 1986, the European Economic Community (EEC) announced the first phase of the DELTA program to investigate distance and open learning, the usability of existing technologies for learning purposes, existing resources and learners' libraries, the issue of standards, related European legal issues, as well as to design learners' workstations. Other EEC-funded programs, ERASMUS and LINGUA, have supported European collaborative ventures in the development of transnational courses and language-learning technology, as well as language audit techniques. Yet other EEC-funded programs, ESPRIT and EURO-TRA, LRE (Language Research Engineering), MLAP (MultiLingual Action Plan), support research and development in technologies which involve natural language processing; this support directly feeds into CALL developments.

In the United Kingdom, three main initiatives offer immediate support and advice to the development of Computer-Assisted Learning (CAL), in general and CALL, in particular.

In 1991-92, the Information Systems Committee (formerly the Computer Board) of the then Universities Funding Council (UFC)—which then became the Higher Education Funding Councils (HEFC) when universities were merged with Polytechnics—launched a three-year program: Information Technology in Teaching Initiative (ITTI), which consisted of a set of projects to develop multimedia software tools and tutorials to support teaching and learning throughout the United Kingdom's educational community, as well as to define common standards and conventions in the main areas of delivery, presentation; aesthetics, functionality; usability, pedagogy, authoring, and corporate provision.

In 1992, the UFC also launched the first Teaching and Learning Technology Program (TLTP) funded at the minimum level of £5m a year to support the development of courseware and to increase flexibility in the learning provision. In so doing, the UFC sought to "make teaching and learning more productive and efficient by harnessing modern technology"; it states in its circular letter of August 1992 that "the level of funding will reflect the anticipated efficiency gains arising from it." Part of the remit of the TLTP projects is to disseminate benefits and products (software and courseware) throughout British higher education free of charge. The first TLTP products, of variable quality, have just started to trickle down to the higher education institutions.

Another national initiative, the Department of Trade and Industry's (DTI) very active Speech And Language Technology (SALT) Club, has a provision for CALL undertakings, but its areas of interest encompass the whole field of language engineering. The research councils also fund language engineering projects and a number of other, unrelated projects should find useful applications in CAL; for instance, the Science and Engineering Council (SERC) is funding a project on "teleworking."

In order to ease off the diversification of the courseware provision to continuing education, the Training, Enterprise and Education Directorate of the Employment Department, eg., Enterprise in Higher Education (EHE), and the Department for Education, e.g., PICKUP (Professional, Industrial and Commercial Updating) are running various schemes to favor better and broader training in order to increase students' employability. They distribute incentives on a competitive basis, in the form of grants, focusing on issues of vocational courses or vocational course components, industrial involvement in teaching and learning, interpersonal skills, personal transferable skills including information technology, independent learning, etc. "In higher education our aim is to help to facilitate a system which, without diluting academic rigor, is accessible, flexible, responsive and relevant to the present and future needs of individuals, employers, and the labor market." This overall aim has been interpreted in various ways, but it normally translates as the "development of methods of teaching and learning, and curriculum innovation and change, so as to create a student learning environment conducive to lifelong learning." Among these methods of teaching and learning, Computer-Assisted Learning occupies a prominent position, and it is also viewed as a formative method for the acquisition of the necessary additional skills.

Both for the European and for the British programs in CAL(L), the involvement and the support of industry is actively encouraged. Industry is not only expected to feature as the provider of hardware and software and as a source of funding, but also as a full partner in the design and development of CAL(L) products and as a potential client for the resulting courseware products.

To relay the incentives at the national level, an increasing number of Centers for Computer-Based Learning are being established in United Kingdom universities. Computing services departments have come to earmark some of their resources to support CAL(L), and equipment grants are top-sliced for equipping CAL(L) laboratories. At UMIST, Income Generation Funds have for some years been distributed by the Academic Development and Resources Committee (ADRC) as "pump-priming" monies to mature research procedures and development work, which can then be funded by outside sponsors. A number of these grants concerned CAL projects. They helped release the staff from at least some of their teaching duties, thus enabling them to devote more time and effort to CAL pursuits.

TECHNICAL SUPPORT

Created in 1988 and funded by the Information Systems Committee of the Universities Funding Council, the Research Councils, the Polytechnics and Colleges Computer Committee, Combined Higher Education Software Team (CHEST) seeks cost-effective solutions related to information technology (IT) needs. It advises on solutions for common use of software/hardware and negotiates cheap rates with IT suppliers. It publishes a yearly catalogue on paper which is also available online on NISS (National Information on Software and Services) Bulletin Board.

Another source of technical support, the ITTI organizes regular workshops and publishes books, tutorials, and software packages of consistently high quality.

Computers in Teaching Initiative (CTI) centers were set up in May 1989 to promote the use of CAL in the academic disciplines they represent and to act as information centers for software, courseware, relevant projects, and organizational issues. Under the coordination of the CTI Support Service (CTISS), the twenty existing CTI centers produce regular newsletters, publish resource guides, and review courseware. They provide online information via JANET (the Joint Academic NETwork), a wide-area network, which links up all academic institutions in the United Kingdom, as well as some research institutes, with direct access to the European Academic Research Network (EARN) and gateways to the world networks. The centers run workshops and conferences and the staff visits university departments to demonstrate software, to advise on computers in teaching, and to answer individual inquiries. The CTISS acts as a focal point for activities relating to the use of computers in university teaching in the United Kingdom's CTISS publishes topical files on CAL issues (hypertext, CD-ROMs, multimedia, authoring systems, etc.). The CTI centers have also received an extension to their funding until July 1999.

Finally, circulation lists by electronic mail (mailbase@uk.ac.mailbase) are already numerous, and new ones are created all the time. Public domain software archives and FTP sites are also growing in number and contain an increasing proportion of CAL packages and teaching tools. The large number of journals and conferences presently dedicated to CAL(L) clearly shows the highly topical character of CAL(L) and the high degree of involvement of the British and European governments. Among various subject-based associations, the Association for Learning Technology (ALT) created in 1993, seeks to appeal to a wide community of learning technology practitioners in higher education, commercial providers and policy makers, librarians, and publishers. It aims "to promote good practice in the user and development of learning technologies in higher education, to facilitate interchange between practitioners, developers, researchers, and policy makers in higher education and industry, to represent the membership in areas of policy such as infrastructure provision and resource allocation."

INSTITUTIONAL BACKGROUND

CAL in a University of Technology

UMIST is a university of science and technology which is now completely independent from the Victoria University of Manchester. It used to be the faculty of technology of the Victoria University of Manchester although it has had its own funding for many years. Since October 1988, the student population at UMIST has increased by more than 31 percent (+25 percent undergraduates, +70 percent postgraduates). With just under 5,500 now, the target number, somewhere round 5,800, was expected to be reached by 1995. The student population at UMIST is mainly in science and technology departments, but there is also a thriving school of management and a department of computational linguistics which is also in charge of the modern language provision throughout the institution. The overall student number at UMIST has a direct consequence on the tuition of modern languages in so far as a large proportion of these students read degree courses which include a modern language as a compulsory component. Because of the technical outlook of the institution, CAL methods are perfectly suited to its existing policy, its infrastructure, its equipment, and its proposed developments.

It was first decided to investigate the feasibility and the practicality of introducing CAL methods within UMIST during the 1990-91 academic session. This move followed the direct incitements emanating from various national and institutional sources. It also represented an attempt to help relieve lecturing staff of increasingly heavier teaching duties, thus enabling them to redeploy their activities to such areas as research. Until then, "the only way UMIST was coping with the increases in student numbers and more restricted funding was with staff having to work much harder, within sufficient time to devote to their various jobs. It was clearly important that every opportunity should be taken to ensure that the increasing demands on staff were matched by the development of effective and realistic teaching and learning strategies which would safeguard quality and academic standards."

It is debatable whether CAL per se constitutes immediate relief for allegedly overworked staff because generating courseware is a very time-consuming and painstaking activity. However, it was thought that this strenuous process could be helped "centrally" by using appropriate software developed elsewhere or by entering into partnerships to exchange suitable material, which might result in the unification of contents and standards within universities. It was also hoped that the introduction of CAL could, from the onset, yield valuable benefits in connected areas of domain-based research by providing extensive coverage of contents, error analysis, and learners' reactions, over and above the presently required "enhancement in teaching skills." Fortunately, in a university of technology, there was no evidence of any opposition to the idea of computer-based instruction replacing some of the teaching, especially laboratory classes. Computers inspire no threat and if there were some reservations in entrusting them with valued educational activities, the reluctance was due to the shortcomings of CAL techniques, presently endowed with insufficient intelligence. Part of the work in introducing "robust" CAL therefore consisted in isolating those areas of teaching which can be computerized without incurring any significant loss in quality. In the least favorable case,

CAL could free teachers from some of the more repetitive preparation, teaching, and assessment work. Computer-Mediated Communication (CMC), through electronic mail or computer conferencing, would help in providing directly available feedback and trouble-shooting.

At UMIST, the increase in teaching duties was not only due to an increase in student numbers but also to a decrease in the basic knowledge of traditional entrants and therefore the need for remedial tuition in such areas as mathematics, in order to avoid high drop-out rates. This relative decline in the level of the qualifications of new entrants required an institution-wide approach to the learning needs of students, especially those from nontraditional backgrounds. Remedial work and individualized and self-paced learning are well-suited to CAL methods, and it was also hoped that CAL could contribute to raise the quality of the training given to all people learning at UMIST—traditional full-time students as well as others. The Academic Standards Committee of the institution is laying down procedures for quality assurance and for insuring that the institution's high profile in terms of research is matched by an equally respectable profile in terms of teaching.

Infrastructure

Manchester hosts the United Kingdom's National Computing Center, and the university is well-endowed with computing support in a wide range of areas. Manchester is also one of the first few sites to be connected to SuperJanet, the 1000MB per second fiber-optics network due to replace the Joint Academic Network, which is 100 times slower. Alongside the University of Manchester Computing Center, UMIST has its own Support Unit which specializes in computing support and services for engineering disciplines, and each department has one or more computing officers on their staff. The UMIST Computing Services Support Unit houses two CAL-related projects. One project, in Finite Element Analysis, provides CAL supports for a methodology widely used in engineering. The other project concerns the organization of CAL throughout the institution to adapt its educational and training provision. This effort focuses on six directions: heuristics for the learner through hypertext; network delivery of courseware and computer-mediated communication (CMC) through electronic mail and computer conferencing; simulation and "games"; subject-dependent software and authoring for exercises and tests; information technology (IT) in support of learning/teaching and training for CAL techniques; as well as local and remote information storage technology for subject-based resources and reference material.

At UMIST, an Academic Information Systems Committee oversees equipment policies, and an Equipment Subcommittee of the Academic Development and Resources Committee allocates funding. All departments have their own (mostly with Ethernets) networked computing laboratories. The whole campus is networked with a fiber-optic backbone which also links an increasing number of student residences, with network access points in each student's room. In addition, throughout the institution, a number of public access clusters of PC and UNIX workstations, with access to a very wide range of applications software, are being continuously upgraded and can be used for independent learning. In accordance with the recommendations first contained in the Nelson report and maintained in the report of the Working Party on the Provision of Computing Facilities for Teaching (Inter-University Committee on Computing) in 1991, there is approximately one workstation available for five students.

The computers are heavily used as the student population at UMIST has to be computer-literate. For this reason, the use of CAL does not pose any great problem of adaptation and motivation, nor does it require lengthy computer tuition. In addition, within the framework of largely vocational science and engineering courses, the manipulation of CAL techniques is perceived as an added skill in the use of IT related to the main field of study.

A CAL Working Party, a CAL Officer

In October 1991, a CAL Working Party was set up, as a subcommittee of Computing Services, with a few people interested in CAL and some representatives of various relevant UMIST committees (distributed systems, computing support, equipment, academic standards, library and information resources, staff development, etc.), in order to ensure synergy across the management structure of the institution. The terms of reference of the CAL Working Party include the following:

- to promote the development and integration of effective CAL products and systems at UMIST and their distribution and exchange with those of outside users
- to continuously review CAL provision within the institute, seeking and collating information on facilities needed for more efficient, qualitative student learning and greater staff productivity and to advise the Computing Services Committee accordingly
- to advise on appropriate CAL strategies for meeting the developing needs of staff and students and assist with the coordination and dissemination of relevant information within UMIST
- to liaise with CAL users and developers, on and off campus
- to meet at least once per term

Soon after its creation, the CAL Working Party successfully applied for a grant from the Academic Development and Resources Committee which made it possible for this author to renew for two thirds of her time as the UMIST CAL Project Officer, from February 1, 1992. The support was renewed twice, at a reduced level, until the need for a permanent, full-time CAL officer had been proven.

As well as complying with the terms of reference of the CAL Working Party, the work of the first CAL project officer consisted of devising and implementing a permanent structure for CAL, providing continuing CAL support to individual departments or groups, and laying down the foundations necessary to apply for external funding. Information work involved collecting and disseminating data on existing good practice and relevant software. Development work involved investigating teaching strategies and learning scenarios to be supported in hypermedia. All the work was actively supported by the Staff Development Unit (SDU) and the computerized Library Department, both very active in computer-based staff training and information. In the absence of any great upheaval in the national and institutional teaching policies, the present CAL working party and its permanent CAL project officer could well end up as a fully-fledged CAL unit or, more in keeping with the institution, a unit of educational technology, especially if at least part of its funding is brought by research and development grants. CAL could then become an area of independent research and development within UMIST.

Departmental Background

The Department of Language and Linguistics houses the Center for Computational Linguistics. This slant in language study provides a natural environment for CALL as another area of language engineering research and development. In this setup, CALL can be based on an extensive linguistic coverage of the modern language to be taught, a study of error analysis and interferences with English, language generation (for corrections or adaptive courseware), a systematic usage of language analysis and manipulation tools (taggers, text-retrieval systems), including aids to reading and writing, linguistic reference material, in particular lexicographical and terminological tools, grammars, as well as corpora. It also calls for more advanced processing tools to model natural language, as in dialogue systems, aids to indexing or abstracting, machine translation, and diagnostics systems.

A modest first step was taken for French in 1989-1990, with the introduction of two weekly computer-based language course units: sessions of grammar practice based on structural drills and questionnaires helping with the assimilation of theoretical data on the one hand and, on the other hand, an introductory course in computer-based tools for language analysis and manipulation. This first attempt did not prove wholly satisfactory because drills and questionnaires do not *teach* anything. They supported practice and testing, but the capabilities of the software to accommodate timely and relevant explanations were very restricted. The progressions and the "learning" paths consisted of the same linearity for everybody. Students found the CALL sessions tedious overall, even when they came as a direct application of a lecture. As far as the study of computer-based tools for language work was concerned, having to come to grips with cumbersome systems and fiddly procedures did not make their relevance immediately clear, and the simultaneous teaching of the methods of inquiry with the object of the inquiry led to some confusion. A possible remedy was found with the design of a computer-based training package, task-based, covering both the manipulation of the software and the language work it enables. This first stage of CALL undoubtedly helped the students enhance their French language proficiency and gave them indispensable training in the use of the language technologies. However, it still lacked a structured knowledge base from which the students could acquire knowledge at their own pace and in keeping with their individual needs and learning styles, while being helped along by the built-in learning strategies.

Another reason for introducing CALL related to an ever-present concern for course integration. The students of the department read a mixture of specialized linguistic, mathematical, and computational subjects together with two foreign languages. In such a multidisciplinary field, it is of great importance that proper integration of the course components should be maintained and strengthened all the time. This integration is first achieved through syllabus design by strictly tailoring the contents to specific needs and purposes: the linguistic theories taught are those which are most productive in NLP, together with the linguistic areas where formalization still represents a major hurdle; the mathematics course concentrates on set theory and logic; the computational elements focus on high-level programming languages like Prolog and Lisp.

The same methods cannot be applied to modern languages and the integration is less straightforward. Studying foreign languages for the sole purpose of manipulating them in NLP deprives the students of a valuable skill. Besides, it is not clear how much knowledge can be acquired without any practice. Also, studying a language outside the context of its speakers and their culture is linguistically misleading. All these objectives had to be reconciled in some fashion and in an overall language technology program, CALL can be a valuable integrator and simultaneously help towards the acquisition of a skill. In the same way as the institution resorted to heuristics to set up its CAL program, the specificities of the subject and the demands of the educational situation led to the introduction of a strategy for our French language learners based on heuristics through the use of hypertext and hypermedia. The development of a learning shell started with a view to producing not only a readily usable CALL tool, but also as a testbed for research into teaching strategies and learning scenarios supported by software.

LEARNING SHELL FOR CALL AND CAL

When the CAL Working Party made its appointment of the first CAL officer, it sought to give CAL a headstart by capitalizing on the experience gathered with CALL in the French section of the Department of Language and Linguistics. It was decided that the dissemination of good practice should, among other tools and procedures, take the form of a multimedia sample system which would be used to demonstrate the capabilities of that teaching method. It was also hoped that the software implementation could be reused in other CAL systems in other subjects. With this purpose in mind, the demonstrator, exemplifying a French language course, served to experiment with implementation techniques for a variety of teaching strategies and learning scenarios, and for the embedding of both generic tools and subject-specific tools.

Hardware, Software

The hardware configuration which is used for the French language development work comprises a fast IBM PC 486 with 8 megabytes of RAM, a hard disk of 180 megabytes, a SuperVGA graphics card, the sound card SoundBlaster Pro, the video card VideoBlaster, an Ethernet card for access to network services, a CD-ROM drive and a mouse. The hardware used by the learners on campus is hardly less sophisticated.

The development was based on Guide version 3.1, a hypertext package for the PC commercialized by OWL International Inc. Guide runs under MicroSoft Windows 3.1/DOS 5 and provides an authoring environment to create hypermedia documents encompassing text, graphics, sound, animations and full-motion video, as well as the means of customizing one's application and interface. A reader version of Guide is used by the learners. At the time the development started, Guide was a more obvious choice than it may currently be nowadays, with a growing number of competing multimedia authoring packages. Another possible choice would have been Authorware. Guide was preferred for its better capabilities of handling text and the intention of its proprietary company to produce a version for UNIX, an operating system widely used in UMIST given its existing hardware infrastructure. Also, it was important that the multimedia documents generated for the courseware could be ported without too much difficulty to other applications and not imprisoned in a given authoring tool. For that reason, future developments will need to rest on some standard document format. SGML/HyTime are currently being investigated.

For reasons of authenticity, the decision was made to ensure that, as far as possible, the learning interface should be in French. It was not at first clear whether translating the learning tool into French, itself an object of study, constituted sound educational practice. However, we took the view that computational linguists have a definite need for the French metalanguage and that hypertext should feature among the IT tools students would be taught in both English and French.

Embedded exercises have been mounted on numerous packages running as subprocesses of the main application, both commercial packages and packages developed in-house: French versions of the Wida packages (A Demi Mot, A Juste Titre, Autrement Dit, Jeux de Mots, Mot pour Mot, Terme à Terme, etc.); Question Mark of the eponymous company; Méli-Mélo, a package developed in-house using C++ to support the study of discourse structures and text grammar; another, yet unnamed, graphical package developed in-house to visually support reconstructions and identify unifying criteria; as well as some template exercise questions written in the Guide built-in programming language, LOGiix.

Linguistic software tools supporting the language study are directly accessible from within the environment. These include various dictionaries held on the computer hard disk, on CD-ROM, on local hard drive or remote network; an English spelling checker/grammar checker and a French spelling checker/grammar checker, both of which also are used as aids to reading and writing programs; a text-retrieval package (TACT, developed under the direction of John Bradley of the University of Toronto); simpler packages to analyze and classify texts on the basis of statistical data to support such stylistics studies as PC-Style, WordFreq, WordList. Also included are miscellaneous public domain packages: a good text editor, also used as glossary and dictionary maker; a simple lemmatiser (a program which gives the root forms of words); a simple database used for lexicography, terminology and indexing tasks; a spreadsheet; a flow chart for thesaurus building and graphical knowledge representations; a decimal-imperial measure converter (useful in all sorts of sublanguages, from clothing sizes to scientific language via travels and transport); and an extended ASCII codes pop-up table.

Other remote tools are accessed over an Ethernet Local Area Network, a fiber-optic campus network and, in some cases, the JANET Wide Area Network. These support Computer-Mediated Communication by allowing direct access to a text-based electronic mail system (UNIX-based Elm) and to a system of computer-conferencing (PortaCOM, then NIX, both hosted on a Sun3 System). Such facilities enable the learners to submit queries to a question-answer service, to engage in collaborative work, and to participate in discussions with their fellow learners. For the most eager, this type of interaction can be pursued around the clock, logging into the host from outside the university. As hardware becomes more affordable, it is hoped that learners can increasingly use this facility away from the campus.

Coverage of the Domain

The first concern when embarking upon the development related to the thorough coverage of the domain by subject experts. The CALL system was to present high quality contents and to support knowledge, not just to offer practice or testing. Our initial attempt at exploring reusable ways and means of covering a predefined domain was also to serve as a basis for further domain modeling for purposes of diagnosis, intelligent feedback, and later, for adaptive courseware generation. "Adaptive courseware generation" means that each learner is continuously assessed by the system which generates presentation sequences and progressions in keeping with the learner's successes and failures at interacting with the system in the expected way.

As far as the French language was concerned, and from our computational linguistics point of view, a thorough coverage of the domain included courseware units in morphosyntax for sentence grammar and units in discourse structures for text grammar. These were complemented by separate units for practice and testing, courseware units in civilization presented from the point of view of pragmatic knowledge deemed necessary to handle general and specialist language, and courseware units representing various French sublanguages. The notion of "sublanguage" is borrowed from computational linguistics and defines a subset of the "general language," which constitutes a self-contained and autonomous linguistic system. In theory, the sum of all sublanguages equals a general language, but the frontiers are not exactly defined and there are overlaps. A phonetics and phonology course with exercises is presently being developed, and a course on French cinema is at the design stage. As the French language course is intended for language engineering students, it places great emphasis on language structures at all linguistic levels but does not contain any literature or view civilization from a historical point of view.

When courseware development work has reached a sufficient level of completion, the system will be used for a total of seven weekly hours which used to be taught in the form of lectures and seminars—two hours on the morphosyntactic and discourse structures of French, one hour on the culture and civilization of contemporary French-speaking countries, one hour of translation from French into English and from English into French, two hours of theoretical phonetics and practicals, and one hour entitled Electronic Linguistic Tools or IT for French in the first year of the course which presents a number of PC-based tools for computer-aided language manipulation tasks. In addition, through the moderation by the tutors of computer conferences, the study of actual usage by each individual learner, it is hoped that the system can replace a large proportion of individual academic tutoring and significantly change the role of the French lecturing staff.

Learning Support

Another concern of importance to us when we began this development related to learning support. We wanted to avoid producing what would amount to a more or less sophisticated presentation system, as opposed to a learning system. The focus of any such system would have to be on learning issues and this naturally encompassed a meaningful presentation of contents showing their relevance in the field and within the progression.

Hypertext is a popular form of presentation of material for learning purposes. This way of organizing information tends to be more faithful to human intellectual behavior as compared to traditional linear structure. Vannevar Bush, often seen as the pioneer of the concept of hypertext, developed the idea of a filing system whose structure would be inspired from the associative behavior of the human mind. "With one item in its grasp, it snaps instantly to the next that is suggested by the association of thoughts, in accordance with some intricate web of trails carried by the cells of the brain." (Bush, in *Atlantic Monthly*, No. 176, 1945). Our hypertext base is therefore a set of cross-referenced documents where subprocesses have been embedded to support various learning activities. The nonlinear structure of the resulting database integrates course units with the corresponding reference material and exercises. Both sequential and nonsequential navigation within the system can be entirely free or limited to certain progressions or to individual components of the system.

The didactic value of the image, still and moving, brought multimedia to our system, hence hypermedia. However, the field of application for the development, French language for computational linguists, did not easily lend itself to the use of media other than text and graphics, especially full-color photographs at a high resolution (1024 x 768) with 256 colors. Sound was included for the pronunciation of given word or phrase presenting some difficulty, on its own and in context, for the phonetics module, as well as to illustrate the differences between written discourse and spoken discourse. Animations are being added for articulatory phonetics and acoustics illustrations, as well as for some technical languages, (an example would be to feature the movement of a needle, in slow motion, in a unit on the manufacture of textiles). Video documents are being prepared to enhance the study of spoken language structures and of course, for the French cinema course. It will feature selected excerpts as illustrations of the sequences referred to in the study, as well as anthologies. Very much aware that computers are not suited to support the reading of large amounts of text on the screen, we actively researched meaningful uses of nontextual media within our field and this has undoubtedly enhanced our approach to a traditionally text-based subject area.

REFERENCE MATERIAL IN CONTEXT

The core of this multimedia database is made up of authentic French documents to which reference material and various sorts of exercises are linked at several levels. The appearance and the layout of the original documents, if they first appeared in print, are reproduced faithfully. Basic hypertext links are of three sorts and respectively display information by clicking on embedded icons featuring the sort of information given: monolingual or bilingual dictionaries for context-dependent lexicographical information, as opposed to the dictionaries which form part of the language tools available; bespectacled eyes for morphosyntactic information; a flying bird for information about discourse structures; and a world map for pragmatic information. Other hypertext links enable direct access to online resources like terminologies, or primary document sources of immediate relevance. Sometimes, these embedded references consist of a pointer to other "learning media" (paper, audio or videotapes, and other magnetic media). The volume of the reference material, both lexicographical and grammatical, is growing. It is hoped that it will eventually constitute full descriptive works in both these fields and that they can be adapted for use independently from the units for which they were initially developed.

EXERCISES

Embedded exercises are of three sorts: questionnaires strategically placed within a unit and designed to help with the *assimilation* of the material presented, *practice* exercises relating to an extensive coverage of the structures of French, and *testing* exercises as a means of assessing knowledge. Generally speaking, assimilation exercises have been coded in LOGiix and practice and testing exercises have been mounted on separate packages which are activated as subprocesses of the main hypertext process. These subprocesses represent a whole array of questionnaires, gap-fillers, associations and substitutions, memorization and restitution, deconstructions and reconstructions, and reformulations. The answers to the questions in our so-called assimilation exercises cannot be found in the lesson directly; they normally encourage further thought on information contained in the lesson—deductions, inductions, or the contextualization of some general knowledge. One sample question is to ask what the postcode of a given address is, a fact not expected to be memorized. What is being called for in this case is a search of a postcode book entered by clicking on an icon and understanding how it is organized. This presupposes that one has understood the administrative organization of French territories, which was the object of the preceding section of the lesson.

Another type of question in assimilation exercises would be geared to help generalize or particularize a piece of knowledge by establishing a relation with connected pieces of knowledge. For instance, in terminology, the interpretation of a word, or term, requires that the pragmatic context in which it is being used is known. If one says, "Pass me this file," one needs to know whether the request is taking place in a computer lab, in a beauty salon, or in a mechanic workshop to be able to interpret "file" correctly. In order to enable or reinforce the acquisition of such a term, several sentences where one word is missing or several definitions belonging to different spheres of knowledge would be followed by a request to find the word which can fill all these gaps or the word which corresponds to all the definitions.

Yet another type of question in assimilation exercises would be used to emphasize similarities or differences between a given structure in the general language and a deviant structure lifted from a previously presented document. Along the same lines, the topic of a question could be to isolate an intruder among a set whose common characteristic has been presented in the lesson. Answers are entered in dialog boxes or by selecting special characters on a graphical keypad. In multiple-choice questionnaires, differing feedback is associated with the various wrong answers. The correct answer is normally reinforced by some complement of information and the "don't know" option which triggers a further series of questions leading to the answer. The format of all these questions is well-documented and accompanied by the corresponding software, so that the various question templates can be reused in other applications.

HEURISTICS

The navigation within the course units—some of them have complex structures—and across units within the system is performed thanks to a navigation subsystem. At the bottom of all screen displays, a bar of iconized buttons control the navigation: rewind, one step backward, pause, one step forward, fast forward, plus a "back to menu" button, an "exit from the system" button, and a "help" button. Documents are structured into "pages" ("frames" in Guide) and navigation is either sequential (moving forward or backward one frame at a time, moving on to the next document or returning to the previous document) or nonsequential (jumping to the end of a document or back to its beginning, jumping to any other document at any point). The navigation subsystem has the merit of being completely consistent throughout the system and able to handle the addition of news documents in the database without any difficulty. To each document two parameters are attached: its overall number of pages and its relative position within the system. These parameters are managed by an initialization program which drives all the navigation and does all the housekeeping. In those cases where progression is to be made through a specific answer to a question displayed on the screen or through a choice of alternatives controlled by the main windows display, the default navigation configuration can be overruled at the level of each document and the corresponding buttons are disabled on the bottom bar. An absolute indication of "where one is" in the system is given by clicking on a button within the help subsystem; this returns the name of the course module, the name of the course unit within the module, and the name of the document. A relative indication of where one is within a course unit (featured by a stack of documents) is given, as in a book, by a perspective of the pages which have been turned and make the book thicker on one side. A relative indication of where one is in a particular document is given, thanks to the pagination comprising both the current page number and the overall page number in the document.

Within the course modules and the course units, learners are free to go as they please. However, for each course unit, one of the main design issues concerns the compromise which has to be reached between two extremes: complete freedom on the one hand and a totally constrained path on the other. Complete freedom could equate letting a learner loose in a national library or some other temple of world knowledge. This type of situation may lead to knowledge, eventually, but will incur enormous delays and runs the risk of erroneous or patchy acquisitions. A totally constrained path stops learners acquiring knowledge "by doing" and leaves no place to trial-and-error procedures. By and large, a compromise solution was to mix theoretical learning with empirical learning. The presentations of course units, interspersed with assimilation exercises, support a theoretical approach to learning. Empirical learning, driven by situations, case studies, and problem solving, involves either the manipulation of electronic data sources for consultation only or the use of electronic linguistic tools to conduct an experiment, the result of which has to be imported into a dialog box, as perhaps an answer to a question. A help subsystem contains indications of the purpose of the tools embedded in the learning system and of the way in which they should be used. The usage of the more complicated tools is taught separately.

FEEDBACK AND DIAGNOSIS

Each learner is known to the system individually and a record of his/her whereabouts and actions is kept. This contains some feedback in the form of a historical account of sessions, time spent on the system, time spent on specific modules, and scores obtained at exercises. Tutors regularly review these record files and leave comments which the learners can access by clicking on an icon that displays the full account of their interaction with the system. Immediate plans include the plotting on an animated graph of the progress curve for comparison to the rest of the class.

Specific feedback, on exercise questions for instance, is given for each answer, right or wrong, or when asking for help. Useful as this may be, the current state of affairs falls well short of a teaching machine and the learner machine-tutor dialogue is still limited to the predefined stocks of information which can be retrieved in determined ways. There are no means of assessing or correcting individual free linguistic productions, not even translations. Gap-fillers and free-text questionnaires give some scope for limited practice but even state of the art language parsing does not provide the level of accuracy which is required of human learners. Not only does it allow some incorrect utterances, it also rejects correct ones and gives no feedback.

A good feedback system—not even a good machine-tutor—should know "correct" French (whatever this may mean), recognize "incorrect" French (whatever this also means), know the learners' native language in order to be able to detect interferences in French, be capable of analyzing—and synthesizing—"mistakes" made over a period of time, be able to generate natural language to give customized explanations, make corresponding recommendations, and suggest appropriate solutions, as well as "understand" natural language and know the rules of dialogue to respond aptly to learners' queries. A feedback system with fewer features is what we are presently researching. Its first version, robust but unsophisticated, makes use of a set of reference materials in hypertext format and a relatively large database of exercises in morphosyntax (about 600). The diagnosis will be based on a fine indexing of the reference material, on the corresponding exercises, and on a capture of the mistakes made. Captured errors are checked against their indexing descriptor and the computer clock. After so many hours of usage, tentatively three to five, the system returns a verdict in the following vein: "In view of the mistakes you have been making in the last xx days/weeks of use of the system, it would appear (the system cannot afford to be too assertive) that you have failed to understand properly the topic yyy." Then, either the learners are directly taken back to the lesson and given additional, well-targeted exercises or they are presented with a table of the sort of mistakes made consistently, with corresponding buttons which open up the corresponding reference material with exercises.

BENEFITS OF THE PROJECT

As system development continues alongside courseware development, the existing courseware provision, mounted on the present version of the system, is being extensively field-tested. It is still early to decide beyond any doubt whether the benefits suggested have been definitely secured. Nevertheless, our initial explorations of the intellectual, organizational, and practical issues involved in mounting an integrated CAL course and developing modules to be fitted in a hypermedia structure have already shown a number of quantitative and qualitative benefits.

As for quantitative benefits, such a hypertext system can be duplicated and profitably used by larger numbers of students. "Spoon-feeding," which used to be an unfortunate characteristic of the British higher education system has been replaced by a more active and demanding *learning* mode, while the provision remains highly personalized. This move is not always easily accepted by those lecturers who believe CAL to be very demotivating and equate its results to "pile them high and teach them cheap."

The productivity gains envisaged concern staff time released and additional teaching/learning hours obtained. Depending on the subject, it is expected that between 40 and 60 percent of the tuition can be dispensed by means of CAL. If one ignores both the large initial investment and the continued investment in CAL research, development, and supervisory tasks, it is envisaged that the economy realized will at least offset the increase in teaching commitments of recent years and help redeploy lecturers' time. There is every reason to refrain from increasing overall recruitment and staff/student ratios as financial penalties are imposed upon those universities in the United Kingdom that the recruitment targets.

Regarding qualitative benefits, hypertext/hypermedia is being used as an aid to defining and packaging more systematically both the domain knowledge and the knowledge deemed to be acquired by various groups of students. It recreates the cohesion of disciplines which, for reasons of practicality, have often been taught in miscellaneous units. It is also used as an aid towards the formalization of the teaching progression; the project adds value to the courses in terms of contents, richness of approach, and appeal to new generations of computer-literate students. It provides an adequate answer to the necessity of accommodating the learners' widely differing backgrounds, knowledge, levels of proficiency, needs, and learning patterns. Modern language learning relies heavily on individual practice and CALL has allowed some customization of the learning contents, processes, and paces to individual requirements. It is still early to gauge whether this system has increased the quality of the tuition given, but it has certainly increased the students' exposure to the language and, with its built-in remedial provision, those who leave British school are less ignorant of formal grammar.

CAL has made study times more flexible and it will eventually, when the supporting hardware and software can be provided for each individual student living off-campus, have the same effect of flexibility on studying locations. Students acquire knowledge in a more independent fashion, develop their learning skills through the variety of approaches, and become more responsible for their own learning. The "schooling" process is also more positive in character, and failure of the tests doesn't represent anything final. It only means further work towards successful results, when learners feel ready to take them. Eventually, this latitude, properly handled, may contribute to abolish strict examination schedules and reduce the overall failure rate.

In terms of employability, this type of learning is perceived as being closer with the customs of industry and the needs of today's employers. Students offering a broadened range of skills, especially IT skills, alongside the capacity to learn under their own steam, can be made use of more readily and are seen as more adaptable to change. CAL is training them to be trained though not, it is to be hoped, at the expense of academic education. This particular achievement already seems to be proven by the standard of collaboration of which they are capable in their host enterprise during their compulsory industrial placements and by the greater benefits they reap from the experience.

As far as staff is concerned, early results would tend towards some improvement in the quality of their lives. The emphasis has been shifted from labor-intensive teaching to research/development and supervisory tasks. The place and the degree of involvement of lecturers in this new educational setup is changing from being fountains of knowledge and dictators of study to that of academic tutors and facilitators. This type of CALL work encourages teamwork and better communication among the lecturing staff. This, in turn, reduces the damaging isolation of lecturers in their field of expertise or an equally damaging imprisonment in one's own field. It limits the duplication of effort and ensures a more consistent approach. Collective responsibility may end up spreading the burden and make it possible to rely on the team to some extent, thus contributing to reducing stress and creating happier lecturers!

Chapter 22

Medaille College: Integrating Computers into Course Syllabi

Donna Marie Kaputa

Department Chair of Computer Information Systems
Medaille College, Buffalo, New York

in collaboration with
Douglas Anderson, Carol Harrison, and Janice Schlegel

Educators worldwide are experiencing the first major transformation in the transmission and storage of ideas and information since the introduction of the printing press in the fifteenth century in Italy and Germany. Our entire economy is increasingly becoming information-based. Some predictions have been made that by the year 2000, sixty-six percent of all jobs will be information-based. Whether we are talking about the creation, manipulation, transformation, or dissemination of this knowledge does not matter. Rather the fact remains that our life is becoming increasingly global and information-based. We are living in a global community today, wherein nearly everything we do or say has an impact upon other countries as if we were close geographical neighbors. We may not be closely bound geographically, but we are indeed neighbors bound electronically.

Roughly a quarter of a century ago computer technology was first combined with communications to produce one interlocked industry that is transforming our personal lives, our politics, our international relationships, and our educational systems. That industry is telecommunications, or the transmission of data or information through communication channels. The telecommunications technology we have now requires a rethinking of nearly every aspect of higher education.

INTEGRATING COMPUTERS INTO THE CLASSROOM

There has been discussion regarding the integration of computing technology into the classroom. One common assumption is that since the technology is available, should we not integrate it into the classroom? However, the fact that it is available does not mean that it is necessarily a worthwhile tool. Some faculty members don't believe that it will enhance their teaching processes, and for them there is little incentive to incorporate computer technology into their syllabi.

Computers will have a positive impact in the classroom if faculty members realize what changes must occur in their pedagogical approach and what differences may result in how students learn and how they apply what they have learned. Most faculty members would jump at the chance to incorporate other skills acquisition techniques into their syllabi.

Is there a necessity for effecting a change in the pedagogy of faculty? If not a necessity, is there a change tangibly evolving because of the use of computers in the classroom? Let's look at how this change has evolved.

EVOLUTION OF COMPUTERS ON CAMPUS

The time line of computer usage on campuses started with time-sharing (sharing a computer and sharing the cost). Computer gurus or priests (anointed by their technological expertise) knew everyone using the system and what their particular application was. As systems grew and the number of people using the system started to expand, there was a growing need for computers to access information. Computer czars (appointed by administrative authority) started developing campus-wide computing strategies, and the demand for other services such as online bibliographic searches increased. Today there is a growing need for computers on campus to enhance faculty and student productivity. Applications such as word processing, spreadsheets, databases, telecommunications, and graphics are examples of packages used to increase productivity.

Word processing in itself (the manipulation and massaging of text), has been of extraordinary significance for higher education. Professionals can focus on the written expression rather than on how to get it typed and formatted. In many instances word processing has served as a carrot to entice users into other applications. People are able to overcome their "cyberphobic" tendencies and start looking for other ways the computer can aid their productivity. Studies have shown that the use of word processors on campus is able to justify the cost of the computer systems on which they run.

Some campuses are involved in teaching writing on computers using the "process approach." Since this process focuses on the inner workings of each student's own writing, the students work on a single piece of writing over a long period of time doing prewriting, drafting, revision, editing, and proofreading. This technique encourages peer and instructor feedback as an aid to composing. It encourages group participation sometimes and individual interaction with the faculty member sometimes as he or she consults with and facilitates each student's efforts. Using this type of process, the student must assume responsibility for conceptualizing and designing the end product, with a lot of consultation going on in the interim. In this way, the student becomes actively involved in the writing process.

INTEGRATING COMPUTERS INTO MEDAILLE'S WRITING CURRICULUM

At Medaille College writing faculty members are very excited about how the use of computers in the classroom has changed the way in which they teach writing. Medaille is a small, liberal arts college located in western New York. At Medaille, there is a broad spectrum of students with various writing abilities. Before word processing was introduced, the faculty members would assign more papers and spend more time on vocabulary drills and the mechanics of grammar and spell checking. At Medaille there now exists a clear recognition for computer literacy in the classroom. After several initial lessons in word processing, the students are expected to word process all assignments.

One faculty member loves the word processing capability because it is easy for the student to revise, it encourages structural revisions, and it reinforces spontaneous generation of thoughts. His students become truly engaged with the task at hand. Since the student can mark blocks and cut and paste, organization and structure of the essay or paper can be emphasized. He asks for *more* drafts and *more* changes to the students' papers than he would have asked for before computer availability. The use of the computer in his class has actually enabled him to demand more and get more from his students, and they love it.

Other writing faculty members at Medaille have expressed great excitement in discussion of their use of computers in their syllabi. One particular writing course referred to as Advanced Composition is presented with a research orientation to it. Jan Schlegel sees this as an approach unique at Medaille in that it combines computer usage, team problem solving in which the students work together in a collaborative effort, and the portfolio concept for assessment. By using word processing in their classes, the instructors now have structured a portfolio system for the student and the student's assessment. There are now fewer papers asked for with more time to write, revise, and buff.

The Advanced Composition writing course involves a real-life research project which is comprised of four separate papers. First, the students define a problem and sketch its scope. Second, they analyze the problem (this is the second paper). Third, the students are asked to design a data collection instrument, collect data, and analyze them. Depending on the outcome of the data analysis, several options are posed. The fourth paper concerns itself with the student's recommendations and implementation procedures.

Because the students are involved with evaluating alternative solutions to their problem, critical thinking skills are called into play. After each individual paper has been written, a computerized writing style analyzer is used. The style analyzer helps the students to see errors in grammar, readability, punctuation, etc. The students then go back and revise and finally concatenate the four papers together to produce one finished project.

Often hypotheses are restated and ideas are reworked. Statistical packages are used to help in the data analyses, and graphics packages have been used to present the findings in a professional context. All of the faculty members consulted feel that this entire undertaking could not possibly occur without the incorporation of the computer into their syllabi. Finally, the students are asked to do an analysis of the entire process, which has indicated that they have unequivocally enjoyed the research and writing assignments. Faculty members have commented that the student commitment was incredible!

One other way in which the computer had an impact on the writing curriculum is in the area of computer-aided instruction. At the onset of one particular writing course, a grammar checker/tutorial is used to spot weaknesses and evaluate sentence length and structure, readability, punctuation, subject/verb agreement, etc. Faculty members use this as a springboard to decide which problem areas should be emphasized, and this allows them to focus on concepts which are essential to raise student skill levels.

CONCLUSION

It is easy to see that the applications of computers in the writing curriculum at Medaille College have been interesting and varied. All faculty members interviewed expressed a genuine excitement about teaching with computers. It seems as if their whole curriculum has been revitalized through their innovative use of computer technology.

This excitement has been transmitted to their students and the whole college has felt the positive impact of having better writers. It is hoped that the vibrations will continue to spread and the echoes be felt elsewhere on campus in all curriculums.

Computer Information Systems and Art: The Development of a Symbiotic Relationship

Ellen M. Dauwer,
Assistant Professor of Computer Information Systems
College of Saint Elizabeth, Morristown, New Jersey

Until recently, the graphics component of business applications software courses focused primarily on the development of business graphics or presentation graphics. Typically this involved producing pie charts, bar graphs, and line graphs using data from spreadsheets. Usually the graphics component received little emphasis in the software course. With the development of the Macintosh family of computers and other computers with graphical user interfaces, such as Windows, the options for the graphics component of an applications software course have greatly expanded.

Although we may teach in computer labs that are equipped with both the computer hardware and software resources that support instruction in computer graphics, the typical Computer Information Systems (CIS) instructor often lacks the artistic training that is desirable or even necessary for such instruction. CIS instructors may be quite familiar with the operation of the hardware and the many commands of the software, but when it comes to the creative uses of these programs, they may feel quite inadequate. The familiar phrases—"I cannot draw" or "I'm not an artist"—may be their responses to this problem. They need assistance from the artists in this area, not only to produce graphics but also to assist students with their own productions. This may involve helping them to develop an idea for a graphics project as well as assisting them in both drawing and editing it.

Somewhere else on campus there is may find the flip side to this problem. Art instructors are often encouraged to integrate the increasingly sophisticated computer graphics resources that are available into their courses. Their department may be equipped with the computer hardware and software that supports the production of creative graphics, yet they may be unable to operate and use these resources. Additionally, they may find the curricular integration of these computer resources both difficult and intimidating.

Therefore, a two-sided problem exists. On one side there are CIS instructors who lack the artistic expertise to fully utilize graphics software in a creative way in their teaching. On the other side there are art instructors who lack the computer expertise to utilize computer hardware and graphics software and to incorporate it into their instruction. Each lacks what the other possesses; or, conversely, each possesses what the other lacks—thus, the need for a symbiotic relationship.

A symbiotic relationship of this type developed between a CIS instructor and an art instructor at the College of Saint Elizabeth, a small, liberal arts Catholic college for women that is located in northern New Jersey. The problem scenario described above occurred there: a CIS professor was experiencing difficulty teaching the graphics component of a newly-designed applications software course, and an art professor was unable to adequately use her newly purchased computer and graphics software. Both decided to learn from the other in order to enhance their knowledge, their skills, and their teaching. Through their collaboration they found that the skills in one discipline enhanced those in the other. A symbiotic relationship developed between the two persons and their disciplines which enhanced the courses in the two curriculums.

HISTORY OF THE PROJECT

In January of 1990 the College of Saint Elizabeth established a Macintosh laboratory consisting of sixteen Macintosh SE computers with hard drives which were networked together, three dot matrix printers, one laser printer, a scanner, two full-page monitors, four additional 5.25-inch external disk drives, a disk cartridge, a modem, a Macintosh SE/30 which serves as a file server, and a tape drive to back it up. This lab was acquired through funds of a New Jersey Department of Higher Education Computers in Curriculum Grant for the business administration department (see Table 23.1).

Also in January of 1990 the art department of the college purchased a Macintosh IIcx, a laser printer, a scanner, and a wide variety of graphics software including MacPaint, MacDraw, Studio 8, Adobe Illustrator, Aldus Freehand, Cricket Draw, SuperPaint, and FullPaint. These were purchased through the funds of a Challenge Grant of the New Jersey Department of Higher Education, supplemented by college and art department funds (see Table 23.2).

Two sections of a new course, entitled Business Applications Software II, were planned for the spring semester of 1990. The primary components of this course were database management, graphics, and desktop publishing, with a small section on telecommunications. Software for the course included

Table 23.1   Mac Lab

Hardware
16 Macintosh SE computers with 20 MB hard drives and a
    SuperDrive
1 Macintosh SE/30 file server with a backup tape drive
3 Apple ImageWriter II dot-matrix printers
1 Apple LaserWriter II NT printer
1 Apple page scanner
2 Radius full page monitors
4 5 1/4 inch external disk drives
1 disk cartridge
1 Apple modem
AppleTalk network

Software
WordPerfect
FileMaker II
MacDraw II
MicroPhone II
HyperCard
PageMaker

Acquired January 1990 through the New Jersey Department of
Higher Education Computers in Curriculum Grant to the
Business Administration Department of the College of Saint
Elizabeth

WordPerfect, FileMaker, HyperCard, MacDraw, MicroPhone, and PageMaker. It was the intention of the instructor that, through an introduction to each of these applications and to the key features in each software package, students would then be able to master additional features independently at a later date (see Table 23.3).

Training was provided to the faculty of both the business administration and the art departments in the use of the various software packages and the hardware resources through the funds of both grants. This training provided the faculty with the basic knowledge and skill needed which would be enhanced through practice and further training. Recognition of this need led to the development of cross-discipline collaboration between the faculty of the art and CIS departments.

IMPLEMENTATION

In the spring semester of 1990 the art instructor audited the Business Applications Software course that was taught by the CIS instructor. The presence of an artist enhanced the course, particularly the graphics component of it. The art instructor shared with the students the artwork she produced using graphics software. She also assisted them with their graphics projects. Additionally, she gave invaluable artistic advice in teaching graphics to the CIS instructor.

Throughout the spring semester and the summer session of 1990, the CIS instructor assisted the art department faculty with the use of their Macintosh computer, laser printer, scanner, and several of their software packages. Gradually the art faculty acquired considerable expertise with both the hardware and software. Meanwhile, the CIS instructor's knowledge of design, layout, and other artistic techniques was expanding.

In the fall semester of 1990 the Business Applications Software II course was again taught in the CIS department. Drawing was offered during the same semester by the art department. Informal assistance continued between the two instructors, and at different points during the semester each taught a segment of the other's course. The art instructor taught the Business Applications Software students the principles and features of drawing and painting programs and then shared with them some of her own work that had been produced using the graphics packages of the art department. She also assisted the students with their graphics projects for the course.

The CIS instructor taught a segment of the art department's drawing course, introducing the students to the Macintosh lab, demonstrating fundamentals for

---

Table 23.2   The Art Department
Computer Resources

Hardware
1 Macintosh IIcx
1 Apple LaserWriter II
1 Apple page scanner
1 Apple modem

Software
MacPaint
MacDraw
Studio 8
Adobe Illustrator
Aldus Freehand
Cricket Draw
SuperPaint
Full Paint

Acquired January 1990 through the New Jersey Department of Higher Education Challenge Grant and funds of the College of Saint Elizabeth.

---

use of the hardware, and then assisting them in the use of a graphics package. The art students were then able to produce a simple drawing on the computer using several of the features of the software package. This provided them with the experience of using another medium in the drawing course.

The art instructor continued to assist in the graphics component of the Applications Software course in the spring semester of 1991. Informal assistance and collaboration continued between the two instructors.

Table 23.3 Business Applications Software II

Description	This course is an introduction to the Macintosh computer. The applications of database management, telecommunications, graphics, and desktop publishing will be the focus of the course; however, word processing will also be used. There will be extensive use of the Macintosh computers, preceded and supplemented by lectures.
Text	*Macintosh Productivity Tools*—Terris B. Wolff; Boyd & Fraser Publishing Company, 1990
Objectives	1. The student will be able to adeptly use a Macintosh computer.
	2. The student will be able to design and manipulate a database as well as produce reports of it using FileMaker.
	3. The student will be able to produce and edit a simple graphic using MacDraw.
	4. The student will be able to connect with another computer using a modem and communications software.
	5. The student will be able to design, produce, and edit a simple brochure using PageMaker.
Requirements	• participation in lectures/discussions and labs
	• reading assignments from the textbook and supplementary materials
	• four lab assignments:
	1 word processed document
	3 reports from a database
	1 graphic
	1 publication
Components	3 weeks—Introduction to the Macintosh: Its operations, operating system, desk accessories and other tools
	2 weeks—Word Processing: WordPerfect
	2 weeks—Database Management: FileMaker
	1 week—Telecommunications: MicroPhone
Scanner	
	2 weeks—Graphics: MacDraw
	3 weeks—Desktop Publishing: PageMaker

Results of this collaboration were evident in the annual college art show. Many of the art students used the Macintosh computer resources of the business and art departments for their invitations and for labels of their work. The computer graphics projects of several of the business students were also displayed in the show.

The collaboration between the faculty members of the two departments has also affected course registration. Art students are encouraged to take Business Applications Software II, and CIS students who are interested in graphics are encouraged to take an art course.

PLANS FOR THE FUTURE

Both instructors plan to extend this cross-discipline collaboration into future curricular plans. The resources of the Macintosh lab have recently been expanded to include additional graphics packages. Previously, each computer was equipped with only one piece of graphics software, namely MacDraw. Now each computer contains a paint program (SuperPaint), a drawing program (MacDraw), and an illustration program (Freehand). Additionally, the main memory of each computer in the lab has been expanded to accommodate these additional programs. A course in business graphics is also under consideration for the future.

The faculty of the art department is in the process of planning greater integration of computer graphics software into their courses. They are examining their present courses in order to plan for ways to enhance them through the use of available computer resources. Additionally, and most importantly, a new course in computer graphics was designed and taught. Two consultants were assisting them in these ventures; one is providing additional training in the use of their graphics software packages, while the other was helping them to design the new computer graphics course and to enhance their current courses.

CONCLUSION

The symbiosis that began through the auditing of a course has grown into curricular enhancement and design. The teaching of graphics by a CIS professor and the use of computers in an art course no longer seem to be impossible or formidable tasks; rather, they are made possible by the sharing of complementary talents, skills, and areas of expertise. Informal collaboration and assistance continue to provide the backdrop for dreams and plans for future projects. Each professor is able to work with greater confidence, knowing that his or her efforts are supported by the other. Students of both departments gain knowledge and skill across disciplines that were previously seen as unrelated and mutually exclusive.

Chapter

24

Student Information Skills Project

Susan P. Fowell

Project Leader, Information Skills Project
University of Sheffield, United Kingdom

The past few years have seen a rapid growth in the amount of information available in electronic form as well as an increase in the use of such facilities as electronic mail to communicate information between student and teacher. Alongside this growing use of electronic information and data sources is the increasing recognition that information technology (IT) and information handling skills are necessary components in the life and learning skills of the student in higher education.

In order to encourage the development of student information skills, the Information Skills Project was established at the University of Sheffield. The Information Skills Project represents a joint undertaking between the university's two main information providers (Academic Computing Services and the main library) and the Enterprise in Higher Education Initiative.

The main aim of the project is to establish IT as a tool for teaching and learning, to encourage all students to acquire information skills, and to ensure that such skills are integrated into academic courses and into the provision of training by information providers such as the library and academic computing services.

BACKGROUND

There are many changes occurring in higher education in the United Kingdom, with plans for increasing access to greater numbers of students and the provision of a wider range of modes of study. There are to be larger numbers of students on part-time courses and an increase in students being taught through methods of distance learning. This increase in numbers has a significant effect on the demand for resources provided by the library and Academic Computing

Services and also heralds a reduction in contact time between lecturer and student. There will be a greater emphasis on independent study, and information technology holds the key to organizing this independent study through the use of programs of computer-assisted learning.

There is also the feeling, quite rightly, that information technology and information handling are important skills in everyday life and that they will be vital in the future working life of the student. Therefore, all students should be equipped to enter the world beyond the university as competent users of IT.

The need to develop student information skills is twofold. In the first instance the increasing numbers of students entering higher education will stretch existing teaching resources. In this case computers offer a supplementary means of learning as well as providing information bases for the storing of administrative details about courses, modules, assessment requirements, and so on. Secondly, the needs of employers and the world in general demand that students should be capable of using information technology and developing their own information handling skills.

These are both perfectly good reasons why we should encourage the development of information skills; however, we must consider what other value the teaching of information skills might hold for university education. Let us look beyond the restricted view that computers can be used as repositories of self-teaching material toward the ways IT-based information skills can assist us in the development of academic skills and the way they can enhance learning in universities.

As university teachers we focus on the development of intellectual skills at a meta-level. We encourage students to develop their critical faculties and their ability to infer meaning and to convincingly articulate that meaning. If we are to make best use of information technology in these same terms of encouraging academic creativity and enhancing scholarly pursuits, then we must develop the meta-skills associated with information handling. Information skills should be developed which enable the student to gain a better conceptual understanding of the information with which they are dealing. That means focusing on the nature of the information being used and selecting the most appropriate way of visualizing or modeling that information in order to convey meaning.

The teaching of basic IT-based information skills has often been reduced to the teaching of individual software packages. For example, a common approach has been to teach students how to use particular word processing, spreadsheet, and database packages with little regard to when and how such packages might be used by the students in their academic studies. Simply changing the data used in the examples from say financial data for a business studies student to population data for a geography student does not immediately mean that learning how to use a spreadsheet package becomes any more relevant to the student or appropriate in the context of their academic studies.

A fundamental principle of the Information Skills Project is that it is more important to provide the student with a greater conceptual understanding of the role of information, of the ways information can be modeled, and of the generic features of types of software packages than a keystroke-by-keystroke approach to a selection of proprietary software packages.

However, having decided that it is desirable to encourage a higher level of IT-based information skill, we still need to ensure that the student develops the basic technical ability to use the wide range of information handling technology available to them. There are significant problems associated with the teaching of basic IT skills which must be addressed before we can hope to see all students developing their IT-based information skills.

The initial problem concerns the level of IT experience of the students when they arrive at the university. Although there is a much greater use of IT in schools, the number of students who enter higher education as competent users of IT is still small. A survey of history and English literature students found less than fifteen percent of the students had previously used a computer and of that number very few would consider themselves to be confident users of the technology. Discussion with colleagues in pure science and engineering departments reveals that the picture is not very different there, in spite of beliefs to the contrary. As IT facilities are more available to school students, this problem should lessen. However, with the planned increase in nontraditional students, the problem of students entering the university with few basic IT skills could still exist. Therefore, it will be necessary to provide some means of providing these students with the basic IT skills.

At the University of Sheffield, as in many British universities, the range and diversity of use of electronic information and information technology are extremely wide. Some departments have traditionally used IT and have developed their teaching to make use of the facilities available within the university. Other departments are just beginning to introduce IT into the curriculum.

This highlights another problem. Many members of the teaching staff are themselves new users of information technology and are not always aware of the possibilities available to them. Therefore, if we hope to make IT an integrated part of all course provision, there is a need to support teaching staff members in the development of their understanding of IT and of the ways which IT can be integrated into the curriculum.

THE INFORMATION SKILLS PROJECT PLAN

The original project plan was to produce self-teaching materials for the students to enable them to learn how to use the various IT packages available within the university. If we are to make IT-based information handling an integral part of all courses, there is a parallel need to provide training and support for teaching staff on the ways IT can be introduced into the curriculum and to help them address the pedagogic issues surrounding the introduction of IT, such as the assessment of IT-based coursework and the evaluation of courses.

Therefore it was decided that the objectives of the project were to design a basic IT skills program, to support staff in the use of IT in teaching and learning, and to establish examples of IT as a tool in teaching and learning.

The basic program is designed in the form of short tutorials and exercises which can be picked up as self-learning material by individual students or taught by departments. This will enable all students to acquire the basic information handling skills. The philosophy of the program is based on the concepts of information and that IT skills relate to three areas of information handling which are information acquisition, information preparation or visualization, and information presentation. The model for this basic information skills program is outlined later in this chapter.

As support for staff in the use of IT, a series of booklets are planned to help teaching staff map out an effective introduction of IT into their teaching. The initial booklet takes a look at the facilities which exist at Sheffield University and the ways these facilities can be used. Subsequent booklets focus in greater detail on specific types of packages or information-based activities.

In conjunction with the University Staff Training and Development Unit, a number of training events will be staged which address the pedagogic issues of using IT in teaching.

An interest group has been established which draws together teaching staff from a wide range of departments to discuss developments in IT teaching, to demonstrate new facilities and to share project information and experiences. The members of this group also act as information sources within their own department and arrange similar activities for their colleagues.

To establish examplars of IT as a tool in teaching and learning, the Information Skills Project works very closely with a number of departments to help establish examples of good practice surrounding IT in teaching. These exemplars form case studies for other departments considering introducing similar activities, and the material and documentation from each exemplar are made available to all other interested departments.

A MODEL FOR DESCRIBING INFORMATION SKILLS

Before we begin working on the curriculum and the integration of IT skills we need to gain a clearer understanding of the nature of IT-based information skills.

The philosophy of the Information Skills Project is to look at information from a conceptual and functional viewpoint and then to select the most appropriate tools for handling that information. Thus, students must be introduced to the notion of information and then to the tools and techniques which are available to enable them to access and model that information. That is, students must have an awareness of the nature of the information and the possible ways that information can be handled.

The following model is proposed as a means of conceptualizing IT-based information handling and as a framework around which to hang the basic information skills.

The Information Skills Model

Information skills can be divided into three main skill groupings: information acquisition, information preparation/visualization, and information presentation skills. Students must be taught both how and where to acquire information, how to convert information into usable forms, as well as how to present it effectively.

Information Acquisition Skills

These are the skills involved in searching for and acquiring information stored in electronic form. This could involve the searching of databases of bibliographic information or the searching of full-text databases for particular articles or academic papers. It could involve the retrieval of data from data sets, ie., the United Kingdom Census or government statistics on economic indicators and voting patterns. Students need to be aware of what information is available and how to retrieve that information; thus, they must learn to use electronic mail, to search for and retrieve information from locally and remotely located databases, and to discover what electronic information is available and where it can be found. The skills needed in acquiring information involve students in finding information, selecting what is appropriate, and saving that information locally so they can begin to use it in their own work.

Information Visualization/Preparation Skills

These are the skills involved in the modeling of the raw data, be it text, numerical, graphical, audio, or video. The skills involved are those concerned with deciding how to model the information and with selecting the most appropriate tools for the task. Also, students must learn about the interchangeability of data between packages and the conversion of data from one form to another, such as converting numerical data into graphical representations that organize text-based information into structured databases.

Information Presentation Skills

These are the skills involved in transforming the visualized information into a suitable format for presenting that information to others and conveying the meaning of that information. These could be the skills involved in word processing, publishing documents, creating a hypertext system, or selecting the most appropriate form of a graph or mathematical model.

INFORMATION SKILLS APPLICATIONS

Information technology is not simply an alternative means of doing existing tasks but a very enabling technology. This must be highlighted so that students can make the most of the available technology and electronic information to enhance their learning.

Information skills can provide the student with a new freedom to think about the nature of information as well as the means to manipulate and model that information.

Information skills can enable students to gain access to previously restricted information. For example, one of the curriculum projects at Sheffield University involved the development of courseware which contained tables of British social attitudes and British election survey data which was previously only available to users with access to a mainframe and network connections to the University of Essex mainframes. This placed data in the academic public domain which has previously only been available to a restricted number of specialists. The data allows undergraduate students to consider the social values and electoral influences of the Thatcher decade in a way previously unavailable to them. They can view the tables of raw data, download the data and create new cross-referenced tables, and load the data into a statistics or graphics package to visualize the underlying trends. From this they can use the information to answer questions and pursue general themes of political science. While developing skills as political scientists, students are acquiring the basic transferable skills of information acquisition, visualization, and presentation from within the context of their academic discipline.

Other examples of the way IT-based material can be used to exploit intellectual questions can be seen in the CD-ROM-based packages such as CD-WORD, the Patrologia Latina Database, and the English Poetry Full-Text Database in which the student can view documents, commentaries, and dictionaries. The related software makes searching for the relevant information much less time-consuming than looking through the paper-based documents. It allows students to concentrate on the nature of the information, as well as to carry out statistical analyses, concordances, and searches for concepts. There are many other examples of how information technology can help students view information in a more holistic manner and thus increase their conceptual understanding within their chosen academic domain.

CONCLUSION

By adopting a more abstract view of information skills, students are encouraged to think about what they are trying to do with the information and to acquire a wide enough knowledge of methods and techniques available to make an informed choice about the selection of a method of visualizing or presenting that information. This enables students to gain a better conceptual understanding of information and the role that information plays in their academic work.

By focusing on information skills as a vital set of tools for enabling students to handle information in a more effective way, we are beginning to overcome the cultural barrier where many arts and social sciences students have viewed information technology as something either for number crunching and engineering drawing or, at best, as an alternative to using a typewriter.

By taking the training of teaching staff into account, the Information Skills Project has harnessed the enthusiasm of some extremely imaginative teachers who have helped to spread the use of information skills in academic departments which previously made little or no use of information technology in their teaching. The Information Skills Project, Academic Computing Services, and the university library produce a wide range of material to help the students acquire the basic IT-based information skills, allowing the academic departments to focus (with the assistance of the Information Skills Project) on the ways electronic information can be most appropriately used to support the academic development of each student.

It is encouraging to see that the views of teaching staff towards the teaching of information skills have changed and that it is now more widely appreciated. With the integration of IT into the curriculum, students not only acquire vital transferable IT skills but also have the opportunity to develop their intellectual skills further by viewing their subject area from a higher level of abstraction.

25

A Case Study in the Use of Union College's Teagle Writing Lab

Najmuddin Shaik

Associate Professor of Computer Information Systems
Union College, Barbourville, Kentucky

Dianne Ferris

Chairperson, Humanities Division
Union College, Barbourville, Kentucky

Long ago—so long ago that no one remembers—a college curriculum contained no such a thing as Freshman Composition. Those who went on to higher education came, as a rule, from educated families, read books for recreation, and needed no particular instruction in the use of language. But that time has utterly vanished and the writing course now stands for most freshman as the initial, little loved but much needed foundation of future college success.

That these courses are labor-intensive is well-known and that computer technology can diminish the labor is equally established. To be sure, some studies, such as those of Gail Hawisher and Richard Collier, have cast doubt on the value of computers to actual improvement of student writing. Another recent study suggests that the "toy-like" nature of the computer can actually be detrimental to student writing (Halio). Yet the burgeoning use of these tools in one writing course after another, in one school after another, suggests that they do indeed help, but in remarkably different ways. Every effort to integrate the computer into the writing course represents a unique experience, a particular mix of existing conditions and practices. The effort described in this chapter simply adds to the catalog. It will be of value, we hope, to institutions with features that, in one respect or another, match our own—institutions with a limited budget for computer resources, with a student population drawn to some extent from a rural area with poor schools, and with composition courses taught by the English faculty rather than by graduate assistants.

This last feature is worth emphasizing. When composition courses are entirely the responsibility of the full-time English faculty, there can be no proscription. These will be people with established modes, favorite procedures, and a healthy mistrust of panaceas. Thus, the study described here was very much an exploration of possibilities. It was undertaken, during a five-week summer session, by one English professor and one member of the computer science faculty at Union College, in the spirit of an initial step designed to see what our setup could do.

In November 1991 the Union College English department, thanks to a grant from The Teagle Foundation, installed a computer lab dedicated to the facilitation of teaching freshman English. Equipped with twenty-one Mac LCIIs, a laser printer, and an overhead projector, the entire lab is networked using TIMBUKTU. We chose MacWrite II for our writing software, but limited resources precluded adding any of the myriad of other programs and aids now available (see Robert Kozma for an overview and analysis of these tools). Since the English department decided that all composition students would be expected to use the lab for at least part of the composition process, the choice of a user-friendly system was deemed essential.

The idea behind networking, on the other hand, was to create a facility that can be used not just for simple word processing (i.e., as a writing lab), but also as a teaching station should individual instructors so choose. The intention was not to standardize every section of composition. Rather we hoped to furnish a flexible tool, an environment that could respond to the various styles of a full-time English faculty. The networking, furthermore, will accommodate later purchases of the increasingly sophisticated programs coming onto the market.

PURPOSES OF THE TEAGLE WRITING LAB

Union College, a small, private college, is located in the mountains of southeastern Kentucky, part of the infamous fifth congressional district. Relatively few of our local students come from homes likely to have a computer, and their schools are just beginning to purchase adequate equipment. Thus, computer literacy for all of our students constitutes one of the goals of installing this facility. Furthermore, many of our students enter from schools in which writing is little stressed. If assigned at all, papers tend to be modeled on the old idea of creating an outline and then filling it in—writing as a linear process rather than a recursive one. So a second goal is to instill in our students the habit of thinking of writing as a process in which revision and rethinking becomes habitual every time they write. This process, of course, is what the computer facilitates. The third goal is to assist the teaching of composition, to whatever extent it proves possible, through a networked system. These aims are, relatively speaking, quite modest compared to the more elaborate experiments going on at many institutions. However, we believe a simple beginning is a suitable one, indeed a possible one, given the nature of the student body and resources of the college.

The first systematic use of the facility to work toward all three goals occurred during the first summer session of 1992, in a small section of freshman composition described below.

PROFILE OF THE STUDENTS

The class consisted of only eight students. Seven were "high school specials," students who had just completed eleventh grade. The eighth has just completed his senior year. All eight attended the same high school and all, in spite of differences now apparent, could be called successful in their studies. All intended to continue on to college with this summer course constituting their first experience of higher education. It is simply happenstance that no one in the class had previous experience in college courses or in use of the computer for writing.

Thus we had a homogeneous group, with its attendant advantages and disadvantages relative to a study. The small size permitted detailed analysis of what occurred, both in student writing and in the use of TIMBUKTU. Furthermore, homogeneity meant that we could more closely gauge the impact of the computer, since this was the only major variable in the situation. On the other hand, we had no way to measure its impact on the weak vs. the strong student, on those with and without previous college experience, on younger vs. older, etc. These kinds of measurements would be considered in the fall with nine to ten sections of twenty students each.

A prominent advantage of both small size and homogeneity is something that might be called class solidarity and interaction. These students knew each other already and quickly became willing to talk and share their work and their ideas. As one student wrote in her exit essay, " . . . all my fears subsided when I walked into the classroom. All of my friends were here from high school and I knew I wouldn't be alone."

PROFILE OF FRESHMAN ENGLISH

At Union College all students take three semesters of English. The latter two carry through Volume I of the *Norton Anthology of World Literature*, with several longer papers assigned to reinforce what is learned in the first semester. That first semester, Freshman Composition, combines instruction in writing the 500-word essay with an introduction to essays and poetry, using *The Borzoi College Reader* (see syllabus in Appendix A). The course also includes a library use component, conducted and scored by one of the college librarians.

Since habitual reading is a major factor in successful student writing, the literary component of the course is of prime significance. It is not simply there to provide examples of expert essay writing. For that matter, such models, if presented as something to imitate, often prove more daunting than inspirational. So, first and foremost, we present the text as an exposure to the world of ideas. It serves as the beginning of any academic effort to help students furnish their minds, to achieve a brain inhabited with thoughts others have found valuable. In other words, it is a part of the course that cannot be shoved into the background as we experiment with ways to make Freshman Composition more effective.

In the fall or spring semesters there is time for as many papers as the individual instructor chooses to assign. However, in a five-week summer session, even though the contact hours are the same as the rest of the year, four papers (not including the diagnostic essays at the beginning and the end) are a more reasonable load. This is especially true when the intention is to have every student take a paper through at least three drafts.

Peer review has long been part of Freshman Composition at Union, and some instructors also assign journal writing. Some include instruction in exercises contained in the handbook, but the need for such inclusions depends very much on the particular grammatical problems of one set of students to the next.

Working within this framework, in this five-week session that met for an hour and a half every day, the students read twenty-five selections from the text, some short and some longer, and wrote essays on the following topics:

Diagnostic Essay (first day)—The me no one sees or knows
Topic 1—Fear of failure
Topic 2—Conditioning yesterday and today (raising boys vs. raising girls)
Topic 3—Users and usee (the dynamics of manipulation)
Topic 4—Issues (one global and some local)
Exit Essay (Last day)—Analysis of the course

PROFILE OF THE STUDY

We conducted this study as both exploration and analysis. It was a "trying out" of the facility as the course proceeded and, at the same time, a charting of the results. The best description is in terms of purposes and results.

Purposes

1. To train students in recursive writing, using the computer as a tool for self-editing, rethinking, and rewriting
2. To train students in peer review as a technique for improving writing
3. To see what can be readily taught in Freshman Composition using a networked set of computers and overhead screen

4. To determine what can and cannot be measured by computers in the way of improvement in writing, using manual measurement now in anticipation of computerized measurement in the future
5. To determine what proportion of class time should be spent in the computer lab and in the regular classroom

RESULTS

All the students learned to use their computers very rapidly (within the first class period). Those who caught on fastest were asked to help the others, a technique that reinforced learning and very quickly established rapport among the students.

Recursive Writing Process

Students tend to assume that writing is a sequential process, where one sentence after another goes down on paper until the end is reached. This assumption becomes even stronger if they have been taught to outline a paper before writing it (as if students know before they write exactly what they have to say on a given topic). Studies show, however, that good writers circle back on their prose, reworking, rearranging, removing, and adding, as the effort to find words allows them to discover what their thinking on the subject actually is. This principle is nowhere more articulately stated than in the words of Collete Daiute:

> Writing is a dynamic process. It combines thinking, feeling, and talking silently to readers and to oneself. Writing is a process of discovery as writers develop ideas and create texts. Like all discoveries, the process of creating a text often surprises even writers—who, after putting words on paper, see new ideas that lead them to refine a piece or start a new one (p. xii).

Indeed, some of the best papers are "discovery" papers, in which the writer by the end realizes that the position adopted at the beginning is not in fact what he or she really thinks. If there is a motto for writers it might well be "how do I know what I think until I see what I can say." Yet the business of redoing a page by hand is so laborious that beginning writers, especially if encouraged to see perfect mechanics as the major task, will resort to platitudes—what could be called "the sun rises in the east" papers. Such essays are most seductive, for the student rarely needs to do more than one clean copy to turn in.

In the matter of encouraging students to rethink and rewrite there can be little doubt that the computer is a boon. Our students willingly sat down to draft after draft, often unaware that the end of the period had arrived. At first, however, their tendency was to simply add more words at the end rather than circling back to rethink and revise. Yet by the third and fourth papers, seven of the eight had become, in various degrees, critics of their own work. They were spotting inadequacies even though sometimes at a loss about how to mend the prose. One could almost describe them as becoming fussy about small improvements.

The eighth student revealed an aspect of the process we had not anticipated. If faced with the screen for a first draft, this student seemed unable to produce more than a sentence or two. What evidently was needed, as a first step, was a paper and pencil draft, preferably performed alone. Once that was accomplished the student could comfortably enlarge and revise the prose at the computer. (Interestingly enough this individual proved from the beginning to be the most skilled, the most specific and helpful, in peer review.)

Peer Review

The value of peer review has long been established and for several years has been a component of Union College's composition courses. However, as McDougal and Littell point out, this technique has its greatest impact when the writer has time to respond to the suggestions of peers. Here again, the computer as a tool to conserve time, energy, and patience is of major value. Where a student might be reluctant to accept suggestions when it means redoing even one page, the ease of altering on the screen is of primary value.

The advantages of the lab to peer review are, in fact, several. The first and obvious one is ease of revision. The second has to do with our networking. We created a set of peer review questions (see Appendix B)—and mailed a copy to each student by electronic mail. A hard copy of the draft under review was handed to the reviewer, who in turn read the draft and typed answers to each question on the computer. A hard copy of the peer review was given to the students to take home, even though a soft copy could have been mailed on the network. The whole process proved intriguing, and perhaps for this reason the reluctance one usually meets in introducing peer review simply was not there.

A third benefit was equally unexpected. From the very beginning, seated side by side, our students had become accustomed to helping each other ("How do I get out of this window?" etc.). From such informal assistance it was only a small step to the more formal task of answering a set of questions designed to assist a fellow student in seeing how his/her prose reads. In other words, the physical proximity of the lab setting, plus the challenge and readability of the screen, served as an introduction to peer review.

A further benefit was, and always will be, that lamentable handwriting does not impede the process of reading another student's words. It is of course a major benefit of word processing bestowed on the instructor who must read thousands of students' words each semester. There seems to be little mention of this blessing in current studies, perhaps because it is so elementary. Yet, anyone, students as well as instructors, expected to read and comment upon another's prose, cannot but feel the task is less difficult when that prose is in print.

What should also be mentioned is a subtle but unmistakable alteration in class psychology. As Dawn Rodriguz comments, the use of the computer "strengthened the bonds among [her] students and encouraged more willing collaboration during revision sessions" (p. 385). This was certainly true for us. Instead of seeing themselves as separate individuals, struggling alone with a paper, our students evolved a group sense of "we are all in this together." Although we made no attempt to introduce collaborative writing in a short semester, there was indeed a collaborative atmosphere. This in turn induces relaxation, a lessening of any sense of failure.

The peer review questions can be applied by students to their own prose, and we encouraged them to do this too, both on the screen and with the printed drafts they took home. In the future, perhaps we may use the split screen, with questions on one side and the prose to be edited on the other, and the whole projected on the wall as a way of training students in the technique of analyzing prose.

What Can Be Taught in a Networked Computer Lab?

The lab facilitates composition and revision, peer review, and testing. An effort to use the network to have students take turns editing a mangled piece of prose was inconclusive. The prose was on the screen and students took turns using the instructor's machine and mouse to correct slang, punctuation, etc. The rest of the class was encouraged to suggest verbally what the editor might do. It would take a much longer space of time than a summer semester to give this technique a sufficient trial.

What is not easily handled in a lab setting is discussion of literature at least in the traditional way. A united group, addressing each other and the words in the text in a single act of consciousness, cannot be achieved. The screen, indeed the computer itself, distracts students from focusing on each other or on remarks and responses that have an impact on the whole. So one of the decisions to be made by each instructor would have to be allocation of time.

What Can Be Measured from Draft to Draft?

In order to know how effective this approach to teaching writing is, we needed to select some aspects of good writing that can be counted from draft to draft. We recorded the number of paragraphs, sentences per paragraph (PS), conjunctions used (C), and compound sentences (CS). In addition, we selected some errors to be counted to see if subsequent drafts helped diminish or eliminate them such as comma splices and run-ons (CR), fragments (F), punctuation errors (PE), and spelling errors (SE). Capitalization errors and errors in verb forms were initially to be part of our count, but this group of students simply was not making errors of this sort.

These are some basic aspects of writing an instructor looks at in the process of helping students achieve a successful paper. Only the value of conjunctions might be considered an eccentric choice. However, it can be argued that conjunctions and conjunctive phrases present one measurable facet of strong writing.

They served as the connectives which show how one sentence relates to the next and act as signposts indicating the writer's logic. Students who learn to steer their reader carefully through the progress of an argument are students who have learned to be conscious that writing is not the fulfillment of an assignment, but rather the crucial art of making themselves articulate to others.

The conjunctions, and words used as conjunctions (such as "while") were counted manually, and we don't yet know if software is available to do it by computer. At any rate, manually counted and expressed in graphs (Figures 25.1 and 25.2), the use of connective words did indeed rise as students reworked their prose towards a completed essay.

Similarly the number of satisfactory paragraphs, ones with at least five to seven sentences, has long served as one measure of competent student writing. An adequately developed thought requires, unless one has Samuel Johnson's

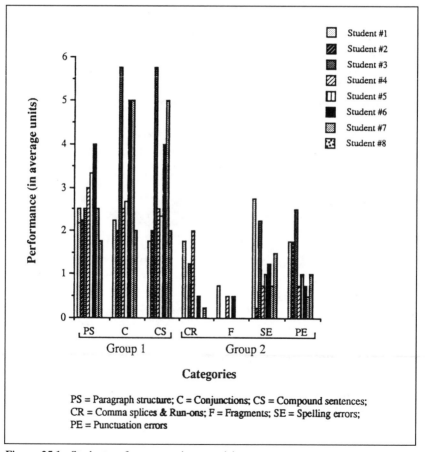

Figure 25.1 Student performance prior to revisions

command of the periodic sentence, more than three or four sentences. Few beginners can present a point clearly and persuasively with so few lines. Yet the fully developed paragraph has almost become an endangered species in a world of sound bites and the format of the newspaper column. Here again, the computer as a tool facilitates rewriting. Furthermore, this is a tool that allows students to see their sentences in print form. Large handwriting can make three sentences appear to be a paragraph, but reduced to type, the inadequacy becomes quickly apparent.

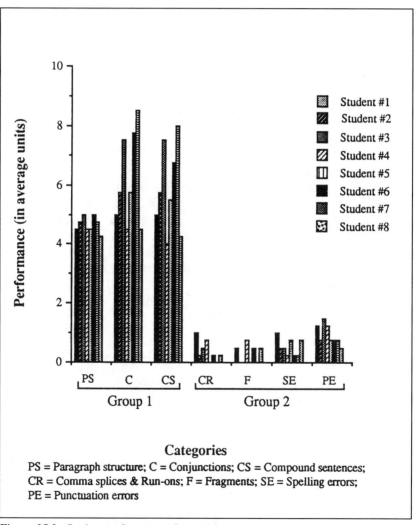

Figure 25.2 Student performance after revisions

In the matter of eliminating errors, we quickly discovered that this particular batch of students had little trouble with capitalization or verb tense. Furthermore, some were already strong enough writers that they had little trouble with the major errors—comma splices, run-ons, and fragments. Others, however, did have to wrestle with these and except for one setback (in the paper on "Users and Usee"), experienced by one student, the graphs show improvement.

Spelling was to some extent helped by the spell checker, even though it is by no means a foolproof tool. Both spelling and punctuation improved over the course of multiple drafts. With *The Holt Handbook* there is now available software to be used for checking grammar, so we planned on trying it out that fall.

The values of each variable were averaged separately for the first and the final drafts, for each student. These values were graphed. Comparing the graphs, it is evident that the values of group 1 variables (PS, C, and CS) showed improvement after revisions and the values of group 2 variables, (CR, F, SE, and PE) showed a marked decline (see Figures 25.1 and 25.2). A paired one-tailed t-test was performed on the data using the Statview 512+ program (see Table 25.1). Values of PS, CS, CR, and SE variables are not significant while the values of C, F, and PE variables are significant. However, due to the small sample size these results need to be interpreted with caution.

Using a computer to compile metrics to measure improvement can be a considerable savings of labor. Nevertheless, it will always be only a partial component of reaching a judgment about the quality of a piece of writing. The intelligence and balance of any student essay, the degree to which a point is clearly and persuasively made, the management of language, the subtleties of tone—these are things which require a trained mind to reach a fair estimate both of the final outcome and of the improvement from draft to draft. However, some things can be measured by a computer: specific kinds of errors, number and length of paragraphs, and to some extent the use of connectives. The statistics within this chapter are therefore of value, but must be seen only as a part of the foundation of judgment.

What Percentage of Course Time Is in the Lab?

In this matter, the tendency in the first two weeks was to spend more and more time in the lab. This was partly the result of putting the quizzes on the network and partly a matter of trying out the various possibilities of the facility. With increased time, however, came the realization that the eye-to-eye contact, the chemistry of any given class, was being lost. For a composition course strictly devoted to composition such a loss might not matter. However, for any introduction to essays or short stories or poetry, the traditional classroom format, however modified, seems essential. As a result, in the third week the instructor returned to devoting more consistent blocks of time to regular classroom lecture and discussion.

For the future, our sense of a workable ratio between use of the regular class-room and use of the lab is 3:2. For lecture, discussion, and other activities sixty percent, or two hours out of a three-hour week seems appropriate, and for work-ing in the lab, forty percent. Students would then use open lab hours to contin-ue working on their papers. However, we can readily see an even division of time as both possible and suitable.

ADDITIONAL NOTES

A writing course which uses a lab for student essay writing has one benefit that cannot be stressed enough. One knows that the students are writing their own papers rather than buying them. This is undoubtedly a huge plus for using a lab. Of course students may take a draft home or to the dorm and get help, but that kind of help is radically different from using someone else's papers to ful-fill the requirements of a course.

The students' exit essays were extraordinarily positive about their experi-ence with this approach to writing. Even the individual who felt the need of a handwritten draft for a start responded positively to the process as a whole. Some—and they perhaps speak for all—indicated a new attitude towards a sub-ject that is rarely a favorite: "To be honest and truthful I actually like English better now that I've taken a college course. English isn't as boring as everyone says it is."

CONCLUSION

The value of a lab such as ours to the teaching of composition lies in five large areas:

1. the ease of revision and of instilling in students understanding and appli-cation of recursive techniques
2. the ease of initiating students into the uses of peer review
3. certain applications of a networked lab such as administering quizzes
4. application of recursive techniques
5. the absolute, unquestionable benefit of ensuring that students write their own papers

The comment of one student on the exit essay provides a suitable conclu-sion because it is typical of the response of the whole class. "I have usually dreaded taking English classes because they were always the hardest for me. This class has definitely changed my view on reading and writing. The meth-ods of recursive writing, and the writing process, which are fairly new to me, were and will be very helpful. With the introduction to these methods I have spent more time actually thinking about the topic rather then just trying to get words down on paper."

APPENDIX A

Instructor: Dianne Ferris   Course: Freshman Composition
Credits: 3 Hours   Semester: Summer I Session
Text: *The Borzoi College Reader*, Muscatine and Griffith
      7th Edition
      The Holt Handbook, Kirszner and Mandall, 3rd Edition
      A standard college dictionary

Course Objectives

1. Competency in writing short essays (approx. 500 words) that are grammatically correct, coherent, and organized into well-developed paragraphs:
   a. Grammar: no run-ons, comma splices, or fragments; proper use of verb tense, apostrophes, and capital letters; correct spelling; use of standard English instead of local dialect
   b. Coherence: one sentence logically follows another and the essay is a completed statement
   c. Paragraphs: each paragraph has at least 5-7 sentences and a central point which determines where it begins and when it ends
2. Ability to use a Macintosh computer for the purpose of composition, revision, proofreading, and completed copy, as well as for development of writing skills in general.
3. Ability to identify and express one's own experience (including the experience of other people's writing and thinking).
4. Recognition of composition as a process, with several stages which can recur before paper is ready to hand in.
5. Introduction to library resources.

Teaching Strategies

1. We will meet at least three days a week in the Teagle lab for the purpose of instruction and for working on papers.
2. A quiz each day on the reading assignment in *The Borzoi College Reader*.
3. Peer review
4. In-class discussion of assigned reading.
5. Diagnostic essays, written in class on the first and last day.

Students are required to attend every class period and to bring their *Borzoi College Reader* and *Holt Handbook* and a notebook each time.

Method of Evaluation

Final grade is based on essays, quizzes, and class participation.

APPENDIX B

Peer Review Sheet
Freshman Composition Course
Summer I Session
Name of Reviewer:

Essay Topic Reviewed:
Essay Written by:
Date:

1. What point is the essay making? Is there one sentence that could be called a topic sentence?
2. What part do you find most convincing? Clear? What might be added?
3. What part need(s) more development or explanation? Can you suggest ways to strengthen the essay?
4. What specific examples or illustrations are given? Can you suggest more?
5. Do you see any areas of mechanics the writer should work on?
6. Is there any place where the logic could be clearer?
7. Do you see any reference to or quotation of outside sources? (This could be anything printed from the Bible to yesterday's newspaper; famous sayings or folk wisdom; song lyrics; etc.)

REFERENCES

Bickel, Linda L. "Word Processing and the Integration of Reading and Writing Instruction." in Collins and Sommers (ed) *Writing On-line: Using Computers in the Teaching of Writing*. Boynton/Cook Publishers, Inc., 1985.

Collier, Richard M. "The Word Processor and Revision Strategies." *College Composition and Communication* 34.2 (1983): 146-8.

Collins, James L. and Elizabeth A. Sommers. *Writing On-line: Using Computers in the Teaching of Writing*. Boynton/Cook Publishers, Inc., 1985.

Daiute, Collette. *Writing & Computers*. N.Y.: Addison-Wesley, 1985.

Evans, John F. "Teaching Literature Using Word Processing." *Writing on Line*. Boynton/Cook Publishers, Inc. 1985. 83-88.

Halio, M. P. "Student Writing: Can the Machine Maim the Message?" *Academic Computing* (January 1990): 16-19;45;52-53.

Hawisher, Gail E. "The Effects of Word Processing on the Revision Strategies of College Freshmen." *Research in the Teaching of English* 20.2 (1986): 141-59.

Kozma, Robert B. "Computer-Based Writing Tools and the Cognitive Needs of Novice Writers." *Computers and Composition* 8.2(1991): 32-45.

McDougal, and Littell. *Teaching and Evaluating Student Writing*. Illinois: McDougal, Littell & Co., 1988.

Rodriguz, Dawn. "Computers and Basic Writers." *College Composition and Communication* 36.3(1985): 336-9, 385.

Sommers, Elizabeth A. "Integrating Composing and Computing." in Collins and Sommers (ed). *Writing On-line: Using Computers in the Teaching of Writing*. Boynton/Cook Publishers, Inc., 1985.

Chapter

26

Using Computer Software in a Literature Class: Rereading a Text with SEEN by Conduit

Nancy Enright

Director of Computer-Assisted Instruction Center
Seton Hall University, South Orange, New Jersey

As an English teacher and director of the English department's Computer-Assisted Instruction Center, I have been working with computers in English classes since 1988 when I began work at Seton Hall. At that time the English department did not have its own local area network (LAN); in fact, no LANs existed on campus. For my computer-assisted classes, I used a lab run by the Department of Academic Computing. CAI classes were either in basic skills English or Freshman Composition. However, as we slowly but surely progressed at Seton Hall, we obtained a Computers in Curricula Grant from the New Jersey Department of Higher Education. With this grant we set up the first LAN on campus and installed WordPerfect 5.1 onto the hard drive of the server. For the last several years we have begun using computers in literature classes as well as in composition classes.

THE USE OF SEEN BY CONDUIT

One useful tool in literature classes is SEEN by Conduit. This text analysis program, designed by Helen Schwartz, allows students to analyze a text by prompting them with a series of generic questions geared to a variety of topic choices. Students select one of six tutorials: Essay Analysis, Art History, Historical Conflicts, Character Analysis, Plotting in Fiction, and Exploratory. SEEN is interactive, so students' responses are fed back to them in follow-up questions. Being generic, it can be used for almost any kind of text fitting one of the six categories. In my second semester freshman class, College English II, we have used Character Analysis, Plotting in Fiction, and Exploratory.

College English II is an introductory course to literature and the research paper. Students read texts in three genres (short fiction, poetry, and drama) and write two short papers and one longer research paper. In past semesters I have used SEEN to help prepare for these papers by having students analyze the text they have chosen for their papers. Though we are again using it this way this semester, I also recently tried SEEN in a new way that showed its usefulness in helping students to re-examine a text found difficult or uninteresting.

STUDENTS' RESPONSES TO SEEN

Prior to going to the CAI Center for this exercise, I told my students to re-read the one short story they liked least or understood least of all the selections read for the short fiction component of the course. Then they were to use SEEN to analyze this text that they had either disliked or not understood very well before. Afterward, I asked them to tell me in a brief paragraph whether or not they found the exercise helpful.

Their responses were encouraging. Out of nineteen students who did the exercise and handed in the paragraph, all but three considered the experience helpful. Five considered it somewhat or "a little" helpful. The other eleven, the majority of those students responding, found it decidedly helpful. Comments from them are revealing. One student said, "The exercise helped me understand the story more. I[sic] raised questions that allowed me to [go] into more depth. . . . Questions that I normally do not raise." Another student explained:

> I used SEEN for the story "I Stand Here Ironing" by Tillie Olsen. It really helped me a lot. Before I started I knew little about what the author was trying to say, but after it really helped me grasp a better understanding about the struggle between mother and daughter.

One aspect of SEEN praised by a student is the way its prompting questions can help break a story down into its component parts. She said, "It helped break down the story into different categories and helped me interpret it much better. Step by step, it made the story more clear."

The fact that SEEN uses generic questions forces students to do their own thinking. They are not being led according to an agenda to a "correct" response. Students must simply think carefully about a text in order to answer these questions that are carefully designed to prompt in-depth thinking. Some students were bothered by the lack of guidance. One student, who said the exercise was somewhat helpful, acknowledged "the questions the computer asked me did make me think about the story but didn't really help explain anything." And one of the three students who found the exercise unhelpful was bothered by this fact also. Another student says, "SEEN helped me out a little by helping me to break down the story so I can understand it better. It would help me more if I was told whether or not I was on the right track with my answers."

However, these (usually qualified) negative comments do not negate the force of the positive responses of the majority of students. It seems that the students who liked the exercise found the stimulus to their thinking worthwhile even though they never found out if their thinking was now "correct." I was pleased to see that students said the stories now "made more sense" or that they approached them now with "a better, more focused outlook." One student said she actually came to enjoy the story more. This sort of response indicates that students benefitted by having their critical thinking strategies honed even though they never found out from the software if they were "right" or "wrong."

CONCLUSION

As for those students who were helped only a little or not at all, I feel that part of the problem was my fault in that I did not prepare them properly for the generic quality of SEEN. I probably should have explained to them in more detail exactly what SEEN is and isn't so that false expectations were not raised and let down. Some students may think of computers as "magic" machines which can tell them "answers." We see this attitude in its extreme form in students who rely overmuch on the thesaurus function of their word processor instead of genuinely expanding their vocabulary or who misuse the spell check as a substitute for overcoming repeated errors (like "there" for "their" or "to" for "too"—errors, by the way, that a spell checker cannot catch). However, my students' desire for text specific and guided questions indicates that such software designed to accompany literary anthologies might be an asset to at least a portion of students and could be used in conjunction with (not instead of) software such as SEEN. Overall, this exercise confirmed my belief that computers are useful in the literature as well as the composition classroom.

Part Four:
Software/Hardware

Chapter

27

Professors as Developers: Exploiting the NeXTstep Environment

Joel M. Smith

Director of Academic Computing and Information Technology
The Claremont Graduate School, Claremont, California

In the 1989-90 academic year, the administration, faculty, and educational computing staff at Allegheny College, a traditional liberal arts college, began planning the restructuring of its use of computer-based tools to support instruction. The early research, organization, and planning which led to the implementation of this program is a story unto itself, one involving vision on the part of the administration, innovative thinking by educational computing staff, and the commitment of a small group of professors to take pedagogical risks in the hope of enriching their teaching.[1] This chapter refers to the products of these early planning efforts, focusing on the details of the eventual implementation of the instructional computing program at Allegheny. This chapter also discusses the assumptions behind adopting an ambitious program of instructional software development at a small liberal arts college. It gives details about the software technologies employed, outlines the approaches to using these technologies that made large-scale development of customized software at a small college a reality, and draws out the rather significant implications of this experiment for future designs of instructional computing.

REDEFINING COMPUTER SUPPORT: THE GOALS

Allegheny's experimental program in educational computing was goal-driven from the beginning, with an insistence by both administrative and faculty participants that the effort be one in which teaching objectives and methodologies drive the choices of technology and the integration of that technology into the curriculum. The reverse often occurs; technological trends, vendor contributions and alliances, and commercial software availability are often allowed to constrain decisions about teaching with computers. Such technology-driven programs seem, *prima facie,* to have less chance of success in improving instruction than those driven primarily by pedagogical considerations. The fact that the implementation of academic computing programs has often been shaped by questions of vendor price concessions and corporate viability may explain in part why computer-based instruction has never lived up to its original promise to make major contributions to the quality of American education. Pedagogical viability should be the overriding concern.

To get a clear map of pedagogy at Allegheny, the faculty committee on computing conducted a series of interviews with faculty to learn about their teaching goals, difficulties, and styles. This work culminated in an extensive "Report on Pedagogy and Academic Computing at Allegheny College" issued in early 1990.[2] On many items there was general agreement among the faculty:

1. Difficulty in writing effective, well-argued papers is an ongoing problem for students at all levels.
2. Students tend to compartmentalize both factual knowledge and analytical skills by course and discipline, so that they are unable to transfer what they have learned in one disciplinary area to another.
3. Students often have difficulty in tracing the implications of hypotheses or opinions, especially their own.
4. All teachers are confronted with almost an unmanageably wide range of learning skills and styles in every class.
5. Students prefer a passive approach to learning, especially listening to and taking notes on a lecture, over the kinds of active and collaborative learning that are considered by many professors to be more effective.

In addition to pedagogical problems shared by all, professors identified many discipline-specific challenges, ranging from teaching the concept of a limit in calculus, to explaining the subtleties of plagiarism, to finding ways to illustrate the process of abstraction to a logic class, to getting students to explore the role of syntax in the meaning of poetry. When these discipline-specific difficulties were added to the list of common problems, it became clear that for computers to help with teaching, an institution must deal with the diversity of pedagogical problems that exist across an entire college curriculum. This diversity of need is compounded by the different teaching styles and emphases of professors within a single discipline. While one strength of American colleges and universities lies in the variety of teaching methods and disciplinary interpretations that a student encounters, this variety makes supplying computer-based support for instruction a daunting task. As David Drew has suggested, making educational technology appropriate to the task is a key in achieving its adoption.[3] Diversity of need clearly increases the challenge of achieving this match. In the face of this challenge and limited resources, there is a tendency by those involved in educational computing services to withdraw to supplying basic productivity tools, leaving individual departments and professors to cope by themselves with finding appropriate instructional software.

The administration and educational computing staff at Allegheny decided to experiment with an ambitious strategy to address both the common pedagogical challenges and the great diversity of needs and teaching styles identified in the committee's report. To accomplish this, we decided that the content of instructional software used would need to be dictated by our professors, for they know the strengths and weaknesses of their students and their institution's educational style. Only a program of local software development would permit this kind of customization. The previous strategy for academic computing at Allegheny had been to maintain basic productivity software (word processors, spreadsheets, and flat file databases) and to suggest that professors identify for themselves commercially available software to use for specific disciplinary needs. Even though the college had the hardware facilities that would permit the use of such third-party instructional software, virtually none was employed.

A good example of the failure of this strategy was in the area of writing instruction. During the course of the development of a new writing program at Allegheny from 1988 to 1990, the directors of the writing program and the writing center reviewed a wide range of software for writing instruction. These professors rejected each of the packages they assessed, sometimes because of poor quality but more often because the software did not fit the design of the individual writing program they were creating for Allegheny. In general, there had been little response by faculty to efforts to encourage use of third-party instructional software. A survey of instructional computing literature in general quickly reveals that the most significant use of computers for teaching is almost always by those who have developed their own applications in some way, even if that is by using a standard package like a spreadsheet program to create algebraic modeling tools that fit the class they are teaching.

In light of these facts, educational computing services at Allegheny decided to make instructional computing a more effective, and therefore attractive, means of helping professors get their ideas across by finding a way to let them design and create their own computer-based tools and lessons—to get their own ideas on the screen. This decision was based on the following beliefs:

1. Pedagogical design rather than hardware or software availability should drive the design and application of instructional computing.
2. Computer services at colleges and universities will always face a great diversity of ever-changing needs for computer augmentation of instruction.
3. Because of the variety of teaching strategies and styles, individual professors must be party to the design of computer-based instructional tools to support their efforts.
4. Involving professors from a wide range of disciplines in the design and production of instructional software increases the field of ideas working

their way into software, thereby increasing the overall quality of any instructional computing program.

5. Professor involvement in the design of lessons for a particular course can create a feedback loop for enriching and improving both the computer lessons and the overall teaching in that course.

Based on these assumptions, Allegheny implemented a program to encourage and support the design and creation of instructional software by professors across the entire curriculum.

THE TECHNOLOGY THAT MADE THE PROJECT

The clear difficulty with asking professors to create their own software was the apparent lack of feasibility. In 1990, Milton Glick estimated that "It takes 100 to 1,000 hours to develop one hour of courseware." [4] Taking the more conservative figure of 100 hours for each hour of courseware, and assuming that we were to develop ten hours of homework lessons for ten different courses, this would mean 10,000 hours of development time or about a full year of work for each of five full-time programmers. This level of personnel support is clearly beyond the capacity of a small liberal arts college. It is beyond the resources of almost all institutions. Moreover, effective applications in many disciplines require the use of sophisticated graphics and graphical user interfaces, and these tasks would threaten to push us toward the higher end of Glick's estimates.

This is where the ideas behind Steve Jobs' NeXTstep operating system and development environment made such a difference to our plan. NeXTstep is the name that NeXT Computer, Inc. uses for the combination of the graphical user interface, the Mac operating system, and the object-oriented development environment that are the bundled software components of NeXT's UNIX workstations.

The key for our project was the development environment, based on Objective-C, an object-oriented extension of the C programming language. Included in the set of tools provided to NeXTstep developers on every machine in version 2.1 are (1) an Objective-C compiler, (2) a large library of user interface and utility objects and custom C functions in what NeXT calls the Application Kit library, and (3) Interface Builder, a program with an unusual combination of interface design, project management, and visual programming tools. Equally important is the complete integration of Display PostScript, the powerful graphics language from Adobe Systems, Inc. that NeXT has achieved in its development tools and operating system.

It may well be that it was NeXT's corporate strategy to create this unusually powerful set of software development tools to encourage commercial developers to create applications for their machines. We at Allegheny saw something altogether different—development tools of sufficient power to obviate the need for third-party programmers. We saw a set of tools that would, and did, allow us to realize exactly the kind of custom-tailored, professor-designed instructional software program that we had envisioned. For our purposes, the most important concepts behind NeXTstep as an educational computing environment are its use of object-oriented programming and its integration of that programming language with tools for modifying the characteristics of objects and combining them into applications *without writing additional computer code.*

Object-oriented programming languages are built on the paradigm of integrated circuit chips, mass-producible units of functionality that can be combined in different ways in different settings to create different overall systems. In Objective-C, for example, each conceptually distinguished unit of functionality, or "object," is made up of two files: an interface file and an implementation file. Almost all the code in any software application is compartmentalized into these objects. The interface and implementation files of each object taken together specify the set of data structures used in the object, called "instance variables," and define a set of "methods" that the particular object can execute when asked to do so.

The interface and implementation files are more accurately described as templates or "factory objects," which include methods for generating clones of themselves. These clones or "instances" of the object will contain all of the data structures and execute all the methods of the factory object when asked to do so. Any number of clones of a factory object can be created for use in an application. The characteristics and behavior of these instances can vary, depending on the values given their instance variables (the internal data structures). For example, there can be two instances of an object designed to draw a window on the screen which are identical in all ways save that the instance variable that defines the size of the window has a different value in each. The windows would then be drawn with different sizes on the screen but would behave identically in all other ways.

Object-oriented languages are designed so that instances of objects perform the actions specified in one of their "methods" only in response to a message from another object (or itself) directing it to execute that particular method. The syntax of the language always includes a way for objects to send messages to one another. A message sent to an object from other objects must exactly match the syntax of one of its methods, or the object will ignore the message. If it does match, the object will, in response to the message, execute the code that defines the method requested. Applications created in this paradigm are made up of a collection of objects that do different things in response to messages passed from one to another. Applications are usually written so that some messages are sent in response to user actions such as clicking a mouse or typing on a keyboard. This is how the user interfaces with the object-oriented application.

In some ways objects are just collections of subroutines; however, there are important technical differences when it comes to the capacity of the object-oriented paradigm to reduce development time. First, the messaging paradigm, followed by all object-oriented languages, allows objects to be added to an application without being integrated with existing code. This means that integration of a new object into an application need not be accompanied by efforts to match data types and structures passed throughout the code. The result is that objects are highly portable from application to application and easily reusable. Moreover, once an object is debugged, the isolation of its code from other objects through the messaging paradigm assures its reliability. A library of objects can therefore cut programming time more effectively than a library of subroutines.

Second, object-oriented programming languages include a characteristic known as "inheritance." This is a structure which allows the programmer to define a new object as a "subclass" of an existing object. The new object will inherit all the functionality, that is, all the data structures and methods, of the object of which it is a subclass. Subclassing is a syntactically trivial step in object-oriented languages. This means that a programmer can take an object that does most, but not all, of what he/she wants, define a new object to be a subclass of it, and write only the additional methods desired without rewriting the entire object. The new object will automatically do all the things the object it inherits from does. Code only has to be written for methods that embody the additional functions desired. This characteristic is completely foreign to subroutines.

The object-oriented approach to programming inherent in the NeXTstep development environment promises to cut development time for instructional software significantly only if a library of reusable objects is available. Fortunately, part of NeXT's development support package is a large library of objects for user interface and programming utility functions. NeXT calls this library the Application Kit.

For example, the Application Kit contains a "Window" object. In response to a message, this object is designed to draw a window on the screen and give this window a standard set of characteristics: the capacity to be moved, resized, closed, miniaturized, drawn in, track mouse events, etc. In fact, this Window object responds to 141 messages, which gives application developers a great deal of prepackaged control over this most fundamental unit of the graphical user interface. NeXT's Application Kit in NeXTstep version 2.1 currently contains sixty objects providing user interface, programming utility (like storing data on disk), and sound functions. It is a library of frequently used objects which greatly reduces development time.

Perhaps most significant is the NeXTstep development system's programming tool called Interface Builder which realizes a latent potential of object-oriented programming to make much of the application building process entirely graphical. The behavior of an object is modified in two ways: by setting its internal data structures or "instance variables" to different values and by sending it messages to execute one of its methods.[5] NeXT has exploited these features of object-oriented design in its Interface Builder tool to allow programmers to modify the visual characteristics of instances of objects that draw to the screen (objects that draw windows, buttons, sliders, switches, etc.) and to arrange for the sending of certain kinds of messages simply by making a graphical connection between the sender and receiver.

NeXTstep applications, like all object-oriented applications, are made up of a collection of objects. Usually, some of the objects are taken from the Application Kit library and some are written by the programmer. The Interface Builder tool is used to manage the building of the application by allowing assemblage of objects and arranging for messaging among them graphically. Each object can be given a visual representation using Interface Builder. The programmer can then use these visual representations rather than the code itself to create much of the application.

In order to create these lessons in NeXTstep using Interface Builder, the programmer need write no code at all. Interface Builder has a set of graphical palettes which hold graphical representations for the Window object and the ScrollView object as well as many others included in the Application Kit library of objects. To get a window with a scrolling text on the screen, the programmer simply uses a mouse to drag the graphical representation of the Window object out of one of the palettes, places it where it is to appear in the final application, sizes it to the desired dimensions, drags the graphical representation of the ScrollView out, places it inside the instance of the Window, sizes it to fit the Window, and starts typing the text that is to appear in that scrolling view.

Many user interface objects can be graphically manipulated using Interface Builder in this way. For example, the control panel for drawing the graphs of two linear equations can be created using the palette of visual representations of TextView, Button, Title, Box, and Scroller objects—all part of the Application Kit library. The bottom line is that a great deal of the user interface, often the most difficult programming task, can be created by graphical manipulation rather than by writing C code.

By allowing graphical representations of all the objects in an application, including new objects written by the programmer, the designers of Interface Builder have made it possible for programmers to arrange for objects to send messages to each other without writing code at all. This capability in combination with a library of already created objects opens a very unique opportunity for educational computing: the possibility of letting anyone create computer-based lessons without needing to know programming languages. Obviously the combination of developer's tools provided by NeXTstep greatly reduced development time.

NEXTSTEP: A DEVELOPMENT TOOL FOR AN INSTRUCTIONAL COMPUTING PROGRAM

While NeXTstep appeared to be a technology that would allow us to support local development of customized, professor-designed software with a limited educational computing staff, that fact was established only through progressive experimentation. After attending a NeXT developers instruction course in early 1990, I began creating a series of lessons for my introductory philosophy course and a few experimental lessons for a developmental writing course in the English department. Somewhat to my surprise, it was possible to create graphically sophisticated, interactive software to use for homework lessons as the course was being taught.

This was a long way from another of Milton Glick's accurate characterizations of traditional development of courseware as requiring that "You have to plan no later than August what you will teach in October, or the software will not be ready." Glick describes this situation because in university teaching "We rely heavily on improvisation, on freedom to follow up ideas that excite interest, and on unexpected happenings that illustrate the problems we discuss."[6] Indeed, I found one of the great values of being able to produce software as the course proceeded was the ability to include in lessons material that students had submitted earlier in the class, to develop applications to address problem areas that became evident only as the class progressed, and to use insights from class discussion to modify lessons to make them more effective for that particular group of students. Similar successes were experienced by professors in the writing program using lessons created to their design.

Based on these results and our growing conviction that the concepts behind NeXTstep were the right ones for turning all academic users into courseware developers, in the fall of 1990 we inaugurated more ambitious experiments in locally created software. I wrote a set of twelve computer-based homework lessons for a new course entitled Models of Human Reasoning, and five professors from the English department designed an ensemble of ten lessons for English 100 created in collaboration with a full-time programmer from the educational computing staff. Once again, both sets of lessons were created as the courses were taught. The lessons we created were not intended to replace teaching.

The lessons that were created were functional in that they displayed texts and graphics and asked students questions about the information. The ease with which these lessons were created—development of a lesson never took more than one week—allowed the professors to tailor the content of the computer-based instruction to the individual classes and to the texts they were using.

Some of the pedagogically important, network-based aspects of these lessons were developed in short order and frequently reused thanks to the object-oriented nature of our development tools. For example in a window titled

"Untitled" there is an electronic notebook in which students doing this lesson would write answers to questions. This notebook is drawn by and is the interface to an object, a subclass of the Application Kit's ScrollView object, to which I added methods that provide text formatting, spell-checking, and the capability of being saved and retrieved from any directory on Allegheny's computer network. It is its own text-processor tailored for use in instructional applications at Allegheny. It allowed students to save their work on the network where professors could access and grade it. Developing this Electronic Notebook object in NeXTstep required only about twenty-five hours of programming time. Moreover, once developed, it has been reused many times in applications for subjects ranging from physics to philosophy to religious studies. Incorporating it in each of these lessons required about two minutes of work using Interface Builder.

The success of these experiments in local software development prompted us in the spring of 1991 to expand the experimentation which was rapidly becoming implementation. Several members of the mathematics department and one member of the chemistry department attended NeXTstep developers school, and educational computing services added a full-time developer, Dr. Charles Fleming, using funding from a private foundation. Two members of the biology department began exploring the possibilities for development there. In the summer of 1991, thanks to funding from the National Science Foundation and private foundations, the number of NeXTs on campus was increased to around 160. That summer, educational computing services began offering regular workshops in NeXTstep programming for faculty and students. During that summer and the fall of 1992, a great deal of instructional software was produced by faculty, staff, and now students for biology, chemistry, physics, mathematics, and geology.

For example, Dr. Fleming collaborated with Dr. Anne Kleinschmidt and Dr. Glen Wurst, members of the biology department, during the fall semester to create an ensemble of thirteen lessons to support laboratory instruction in an introductory biology course. Here again, the lessons were developed during the semester as the course was being taught. By the spring of 1992, the English, geology, philosophy, chemistry, biology, mathematics, physics, and religious studies departments were all using applications developed at Allegheny to support their instruction. Faculty in psychology, sociology, political science, and economics are now designing a set of objects to be used in the creation of individualized lessons to teach concepts of probability and statistics in all of these disciplines.

IMPLICATIONS FOR FUTURE COMPUTING

Space does not allow the description of or depiction of screens from even a significant fraction of the over 120 computer-based lessons and tools developed by or to the design of Allegheny College professors over the last two years.

What is most notable about the history recounted here is the exponential rate at which computer lessons and tools have become a part of the educational infrastructure at Allegheny. This is due to a combination of the powerful modeling and presentation capabilities offered by the workstations used at Allegheny and the fact that professors were offered the opportunity and resources to put their own ideas into practice on the screen. Professors have used these workstations in a great variety of ways: to create applications allowing students to see multiple representations of data on the screen at one time and draw conclusions about the relationships among those representations, to see diachronic processes and relationships in real time, and to perform experiments that would otherwise not be feasible because of time or safety considerations.

Because we controlled the production of the software ourselves, we were able to directly address many of the general pedagogical challenges identified in the faculty computer committee's original report on pedagogy. For example, the English department, through the software developed for English 100 and through the design of journal-keeping software for use in Liberal Studies 200—the required, sophomore-level, multidisciplinary writing course that is a significant feature of the new writing program—was able to use computer technology to address faculty concerns about student composition. Through the creation of a now widely-used bulletin board tool called No-Problemo, students were encouraged to collaborate on raising issues and giving answers to one another. Applications were created with textual, visual, and auditory representations of information to capture the wide range of learning styles that professors reported having difficulty coping with. Lessons were made highly interactive and experimental, giving students tools to solve problems rather than merely presenting them with information so as to obviate their preference for passive learning. The entire project, now underway, in the development of software for teaching statistics is designed to show the use of probability and statistics theory in a wide range of disciplines so as to help break down student tendency to compartmentalize application of statistical knowledge and skills.

Perhaps one of the reasons why instructional computing has not had the impact that many of us hoped it would is because only those professors who had both the desire to use the unique capabilities of computer-based representations *and* the technical skills to produce them could use this tool. Even working with a programmer who has the technical skill but who doesn't know the discipline in question proves a frustrating and time-consuming task for many professors. The design concepts behind the NeXTstep development environment offer a design path to changing this state of affairs. Since vendor loyalty often plays too big a role in computer planning, I want to emphasize that, while Allegheny employed NeXTstep because it offered these capabilities long before any other development tools have, the concepts behind it are what are really important. The combination of the object-oriented programming paradigm, a large library of objects, programming applications allowing visual representation of software projects and the objects that make them up, and tools within those applications to modify and arrange for messaging among objects can literally allow any professor to create computer lessons in the same time that he/she would create a text lesson.

There is a considerable amount of work to be done by educators and computer hardware and software vendors to make this a widespread reality. First, educators must work on collaborating to produce libraries of objects that are likely to be common building blocks in educational applications. Second, educators can encourage commercial software developers to work less on turnkey instructional packages that try to play to the least common denominators among institutions and provide instead the objects and tools for putting them together to synthesize our own, individualized lessons. Finally, we must design, engineer, and test objects and the tools for combining them so as to maximize the amount of programming that can be done simply by graphical manipulation of visual representations of the objects.

What I am suggesting here, and what the Allegheny experiment shows to be a genuine possibility, is a fairly dramatic redefinition of the notion of a software developer, in instructional settings.[7] The technology exists even today to allow professors who will never write a single line of code to be instructional software developers and those who know some programming to make much more sophisticated applications than they ever imagined they would have time to. This would increase the diversity of ideas on using computer technology to improve instruction. It would also enhance the probability that feedback from constructing computer-based representations of a subject or problem would affect the general understanding of that subject or problem. To accomplish this, we will have to think in different terms about what we want vendors to provide by way of hardware and software. We will also have to challenge ourselves to exploit these tools to gain new insights into our disciplines. These are the challenges that many administrators and professors at Allegheny College accepted to produce a glimpse into a possible future for educational computing.[8]

NOTES

1. The central figures in conceiving of and starting this program were Dr. Edward J. Barboni, Vice-President for Planning and Information, Ms. Lynda Barner-West, head of Computing Services, and Ms. Ginger Willis, a member of the academic computing staff. The faculty who participated in the earliest development stages were Dr. Susan Smith, director of the expository writing program; Ms. Bethany Reynders, director of the writing center; Dr. James Sheridan, chair of the philosophy department; Dr. Michael Barry, a member of the mathematics department, and myself.
2. The members of this committee were Ms. Bethany Reynders, Dr. Mary Bivens, Dr. Shafiq Rahman, Dr. Alec Dale, Dr. Behrooz Afrasiabi, Dr. Doug Lanier, and myself. Dr. Edward Barboni was a an ex-officio member as Vice President for Planning and Information and was a central force in keeping the committee focused on teaching as opposed to technology for its own sake.

3. David Eli Drew, "Why Don't All Professors Use Computers," *Academic Computing*, October 1989, 12-14; 58-60.

4. Several of these same assumptions are expressed by William Graves, "Personal Computing and Liberal Education: A Higher-Education Case Study," *Education and Computing* 2 (1986): 215- 222.

5. Strictly speaking, messaging is the only way objects in Objective-C are affected. Instance variables are given initial or new values only through messages that cause the performance of methods which reset them.

6. Glick 38.

7. Actually there is no reason why the concept of user/developer wouldn't be equally valuable in all domains in which computers are used to address diverse and unique problems.

8. The professors at Allegheny who produced or designed software for this project who were not mentioned in this chapter are Dr. Benjamin Haytock, Dr. Sally Hair, Dr. Brian Reid, Dr. James Lombardi, Dr. Shafiqur Rahman, Dr. Benjamin Slote, Dr. Steve Bowser, Dr. Mark Lord, Dr. Laura Quinn, Dr. Diane Goodman, Ms. Diane Brautigam, Dr. Michael Cartwright, Dr. Tom Goliber, Ms. Nancy Lowmaster, Mr. Paul Howell, and Dr. Judy Halchin. A special thanks goes to Dr. Andrew T. Ford, Dean and Provost of the College, who was properly skeptical of the project at the beginning while supporting those faculty who chose to be involved and who came to be a key to sustaining the efforts as it grew and proved its pedagogical worth.

Chapter

28

Establishing a Networked Lab with Focus on Integrating Computers into the Writing Curriculum

Constance Chismar

Associate Professor of English Education and
Computer Writing Center Director
Georgian Court College, Lakewood, New Jersey

Since 1988, members of the English department at Georgian Court College have been revising syllabi, rescheduling courses, implementing collaborative learning methods, and handling in-service programs for new and experienced writing instructors. We were not motivated by program review, nor a new department chair, nor by accreditation requirements; no, the culprit was a seemingly harmless piece of equipment: the computer. In 1988, we worked under the principle "Ignorance is bliss." As of this writing we began our sixth year of computer-integration, and we realize how much we have learned about the potential of computers in the writing curriculum and how difficult the struggle toward computer integration really is. The one "blissful" fact remaining as we continue to learn is that we have taken the first painful steps; the rest is not a struggle but a challenge!

This case study may be helpful to small colleges in the early stages of setting up a computer lab or of integrating computers into existing writing courses. The establishment of a small Computer Writing Center, its subsequent growth, and the integration of computer applications in writing courses are discussed as well as faculty and student training, curricular adjustments, and specific examples of software applications in writing courses.

HISTORY

Georgian Court College is a four-year, Catholic liberal arts college with a women's undergraduate day division, a coed undergraduate evening division, and a coed graduate division with total enrollment of about 2,000 students. The college is located in Lakewood, New Jersey, about one hour north of Atlantic City, an hour and a half south of New York City.

The campus, originally the estate of George Jay Gould, a turn-of-the-century railroad tycoon, was purchased by the Sisters of Mercy in 1924. The original buildings are in the National Registry of Historic Places, and the campus itself is designated a National Landmark. Modern dorms, offices, and classroom buildings blend with historic structures, vast areas of manicured lawns, gardens, and statuary. The entrance of technology through these historic gates has been an interesting phenomenon to observe and experience.

A COMPUTER WRITING CENTER BEGINS

Until 1987, the college had one academic computer lab, shared by the mathematics and business departments. Students used this lab for computer science and business applications only, but during spring 1987, a pilot training program introduced volunteer faculty to word processing and to the philosophy of Writing Across the Curriculum. The project, Computer Writing Across the Curriculum (fondly called CWAC), resulted in positive attitudes toward computers and integration of word processing in two faculty members' writing classes.

During the summer of 1988, the Dean of Academic Affairs asked this author to research hardware and software necessary for a second computer lab, which would serve writing courses primarily. With the help of an outside consultant, the work began.

Renovation of a building, which at one time had been part of the Gould family stables, was completed that summer. New electricity, central air conditioning and heating, flooring, drop ceiling, fire and security systems were installed.

At that time the Computer Writing Center housed fifteen IBM PS/2 Model 30 computers, networked to a Model 80 server, three Epson dot-matrix printers, and two Hewlett-Packard laser printers. We received a Novell Education Grant for Novell SFT NetWare, version 2.15. We also installed IBM's I-CLAS to make Novell more user-friendly. Since then, we have deleted I-CLAS and upgraded Novell and hardware, maintaining an IBM campus standard.

We based our decision to establish a networked lab rather than a room of stand-alone computers on several factors: (1) the long-range administrative goals called for campus-wide networking, and this lab would be the beginning of the academic component; (2) sharing and managing software are easier on a network, especially as the number of available computers grows; and (3) online communication through e-mail and similar programs is possible with a network.

We also had to select a word processing program. After reading software reviews and talking with writing and computer lab directors on other campuses, we selected WordPerfect 5.0 as the standard word processing program for the writing courses. In 1991, we upgraded to the 5.1 version. The academic units of the college adopted this program as the standard as we moved toward networking the entire campus. Students find this program relatively easy to use, with sufficient orientation and in-house manuals and it offers a comprehensive selection of features to integrate into customized training sessions as needed.

Training sessions for English faculty are held at the beginning of each semester and during the summer as needed. Instructors learn basic network concepts and receive a basic WordPerfect orientation. They are also introduced to other writing-related software programs, which they can choose to learn at their convenience during the semester.

THE WRITING COURSES

Four writing courses are usually scheduled in the Computer Writing Center. The college offers two levels of freshman writing courses into which freshmen are placed through testing: Fundamentals of English Composition and College Prose Composition. Approximately fourteen sections of these courses are offered each semester, with one or two sections offered during summer session. In addition, Journalism and Creative Writing are offered during the fall and spring semesters respectively. All sections meet twice a week: one 100-minute period in the computer lab, and one fifty-minute period in a classroom. Instructors alternate lab and lecture activities within the scheduled periods.

Until 1993-94, the director of the Writing Center scheduled WordPerfect orientation sessions for each writing course at the beginning of the semester. She or the English department's computer lab assistant presented WordPerfect and printer basics during a 100-minute class period. Orientation topics related specifically to the basic writing/revising needs of students in these writing courses: formatting disks; keyboard basics; adding and deleting text; moving text; centering, bolding, underlining; spell checking; thesaurus; saving and retrieving; printing. Also included was a brief network orientation, including instruction on logging on to the network, selecting appropriate software and printers, and logging out.

In fall 1994, the information in that orientation would be included in a one-credit pilot course that presented a broad overview of computer and multimedia applications. Since this course would be voluntary, we would still need to offer support in the writing classes. The computer lab assistant, experienced in network and software applications, would be available to writing instructors during lab periods.

At that time, writing instructors had available several other programs besides WordPerfect: Writer's Helper, SEEN, and Grammatik V, Practical Composition, and Write On! They received information about the features of these programs as we added them to the network and could arrange with the director of the Writing Center or the computer lab assistant to receive training any time during the year or in the summer. We have found, however, that we cannot overwhelm instructors with training. Until they are comfortable with integrating basic WordPerfect features into their courses, we suggest but not intrude with more sophisticated features and additional programs. Instructors are made aware of the nature of each program and have received suggestions about how to integrate these programs into their courses. They also share ideas and experiences with one another. We made training available upon request.

OPEN LAB FOR WRITING

From 1988 through 1992, in addition to the weekly 100-minute scheduled lab time, the Writing Center offered supervised, open lab hours. Student assistants, many of whom had already taken a writing course, were familiar enough with WordPerfect to help with basic software problems. Students also had access to a networked WordPerfect tutorial and a printed in-house manual.

One indication of the growing popularity of the open lab, which students used primarily for written assignments in any course, came in the form of student-hours: the number of hours of student use (calculated from sign-in sheets) quadrupled from academic year 1989-90 to 1990-91. Student use increased further in 1991-92 as instructors in other departments encouraged students to use the computers for written assignments.

Good news and bad news accompanied this growth. The good news was that students were using the computers for help in creating and revising text. This encounter with technology would benefit them not only in their college courses but also in their careers, since most students enter fields requiring computer experience. The bad news was that the popularity of computers was now outpacing their availability on campus. About three weeks before finals, students were waiting in line for computers during open lab hours.

By fall 1992, the campus had four computer labs, each with open lab time. This expanded availability of time and computers relieved some of the pressure. Unfortunately, the continued development of the Computer Writing Center, with its supervised open lab hours, reference materials, and supplemental software, has been put on hold as the new Information Systems office attempts to meet the needs of the entire campus. We continue to support the English classes, however, by building an online collection of reference and supplemental texts and software. Along with our computer lab assistant, I work with the writing faculty to help them learn and integrate those programs into their courses. As the campus adjusts, a space for the Computer Writing Center should emerge.

APPLICATIONS IN THE WRITING CURRICULUM

The benefits of integrating computers into the writing curriculum becomes increasingly evident as our experience grows. In the freshman writing courses, instructors use the computers as effective teaching tools for presenting and reviewing concepts and for responding to student writing. They also see the computers as effective tools for students to generate ideas and revise text. Instructors encourage students to write to learn; the computer aids in integrating that technique easily.

Another benefit of using the computers to present and review concepts occurs early in a semester: these activities give students practice using the computer in a nonthreatening, controlled way. Instructors sometimes have students work in pairs to eliminate some "technical trauma" and to encourage collaborative learning.

We have also observed that, with computers, as opposed to dittoed handouts, students can practice and receive immediate feedback from the instructor or from within the program itself. Students can correct/revise on screen and print out a clean copy for future reference.

Some instructors have also begun to use the computer to respond to student writing, using a feature of WordPerfect 5.1, called Document Comment, which allows instructors to insert boxed comments in student text. Others insert comments in bold and/or underline format so they stand out from student text.

We surveyed one class in which this technique was piloted and received some interesting feedback:

- "I think the handwritten comments were much more helpful. There were no comments on grammar, and that is my problem."
- "I liked the old way of giving comments . . . When you write directly on our essays it's easy to tell exactly where we need correction."
- "I liked the idea of using the computer to evaluate . . . It was very clear to read. The suggestions were in the text right after the area which needed work . . ."
- "I enjoyed getting my corrections on disk. Sometimes seeing red on my essay for the third revision makes me feel full of anxiety. This was much better."
- I think that the comments are neat; however, I prefer reading your comments on paper—my eyes don't adjust to looking at a computer screen for a long time. But since we were able to print out the comments within the essay, reading them along with my [paper] was easier."

The first few comments exemplify what we know from research conducted by Mina Shaughnessy and others. Students may find surface errors easier to correct, so they look for those comments, often ignoring substantive changes. The purpose of the writing courses, however, is to provide a scaffold of good writing by using teacher feedback and to encourage students to construct their own scaffold, gradually removing the teacher's. Use of the Document Comment feature, or text-editing programs such as Grammatik V or Writer's Helper, should help students strengthen their revising and editing skills.

Students can use the computer as a tool for generating ideas. Writing instructors use two programs available for that purpose: Writer's Helper and SEEN, both from Conduit. Writer's Helper contains prewriting and organizing activities that help students generate ideas and organize them. For example, audience is a particularly difficult concept for beginning writers, so early in the semester instructors introduce an activity that helps students think about their identified audience. The questions focus students on writing for a particular audience and help them begin to generate ideas for their essays. After students have written a draft, they can use the revision activities in Writer's Helper to evaluate organization of ideas, as well as sentence structure and word choice. The program can also introduce literary style. For example, students can analyze various aspects of a particular author's writing style and then try to model selected aspects in their writing. As of fall 1994, we have upgraded to Writer's Helper 3.0 which has even more features.

In one of the writing courses, students use a text containing readings upon which they base their writing assignments. Some instructors use the SEEN program to help students generate ideas and organize their thoughts as they do these readings. SEEN is a series of guided reading tutorials that can easily be adapted for writing and literature-based assignments. The questions in the Essay Analysis activity, for example, allow students to transfer the knowledge they gained from analyzing a model essay to their own writing and, subsequently, into an understanding of elements of literature. Another tutorial, called Art Analysis, guides students through an analysis of a work of art. Students can use the answers to these questions as a basis for an analytical essay.

After students respond to the questions in any of the activities, they can post their work on program bulletin board. Other students can then retrieve those responses, read them, and add their own comments; students have not only their original ideas, but also those of others, including the instructor. This feature can be helpful in generating ideas and receiving feedback on written drafts.

The basic concept of electronic mail is a feature of networked computers that has great potential for teaching and learning, especially in a writing course. Instructors can send and receive information to and from students, setting up an online dialogue. Our English department purchased enough e-mail licenses to pilot their use in two writing courses during the 1991-92 academic year. Since the college is moving toward a campus-wide e-mail system in the near future, we will not purchase additional licenses. We plan to purchase or develop a program that allows for "real-time" interaction, so students and instructors can dialogue in or out of class. As a step in that direction, two instructors were scheduled to pilot the Norton Textra CONNECT software in fall 1994.

The possibilities are exciting; we will not, of course, replace human interaction, but we can add another dimension to communication and collaboration.

The most popular feature of computers in a writing class is probably the ease of revision. Students from a few writing classes shared what they liked about computers, and most responses related to revision:

- "I notice my mistakes more easily. I feel I have become a better writer."
- "My writing has improved. I've never really revised essays as many times as I do now. The computer makes it a lot easier."
- "My writing has become more spontaneous and confident. Also, it's become tighter because of my ability to move around and make changes that create more fluency in my work."

OBSERVED CHANGES

At Georgian Court College, the role of the writing instructor has changed as the writing courses moved from classroom to computer lab. We have experienced and observed many positive changes in the dynamics of teaching and learning because of this shift.

Classes are scheduled for two meetings weekly: one single period in a classroom and one double period in the computer lab. Instructors have worked together, readjusting syllabi to accommodate the shift from three single-period meetings.

Because all instructors were somewhat new to computers when the transition took place, a unique camaraderie has developed. Writing instructors rely more on sharing successful activities and teaching techniques that incorporate computers and on helping each other with computer snags. More in-service instruction concerning computers and software takes place and provides a logical segue into more discussion of writing and learning.

In the typical classroom setting, instructors lead and dominate the lecture/discussion. The lab setting allows for more collaborative learning. Students feel free to ask instructors how to use the computers or software, but the freedom to ask questions flows over into academics—"How does this sound?" or "Is this the right word?" or "Should I move this paragraph to the end?" Students seem less afraid to get feedback from an instructor who is circulating and moving on, rather than grading.

Students also have control over text changes at this point. They see no "red marks" or extensive instructor writing on their papers with these suggestions; at this stage all is verbal, spontaneous, easily changed or replaced. The computers appear to be tools of empowerment for students who are learning about their own use of language.

Not only do students feel freer to talk with instructors during lab time, but they also seem more comfortable sharing their work with their peers. Students ask one another to read the text on their screens and make suggestions; they also ask each other for help with software commands, which takes pressure off instructors to know all those answers. The atmosphere of the lab encourages collaboration and allows the instructor to become a facilitator rather than a lecturer. The language of the classroom changes quickly during the semester from a high percentage of "how to use computers" talk to "how to write" talk. Some computer talk is always evident because students can move paragraphs, spell check, or retrieve ideas from other files; however, the commands quickly become secondary to the primary focus of the class, which is learning to write more effectively.

In the computer lab, the clustering of workstations and availability of a conference table contribute to a collaborative form of learning, with students at workstations, or grouped at the table, or rolling their chairs to read their neighbor's work. Instructors are free for small group or individual conferences or instruction.

THE FUTURE OF COMPUTER-INTEGRATION

The most difficult part of establishing this computer-integrated writing lab was moving from paper plans into action. Now that the transition stage is behind us, we are ready to face new challenges.

We anticipate many changes, including a move toward a "dedicated" computer writing center that offers assistance not only in writing-related software but also in basic writing skills. We see the continued need for ongoing faculty training, not only in WordPerfect but also in the other programs and in new programs. We hope to introduce faculty to the concept of multimedia within the next few years. As a result of observing students at work in the Writing Center during open lab time, we see the need to maintain ongoing communication with other departments, to learn their writing needs, and to accommodate those needs via the Writing Center.

In fall 1992, the Writing Center was relocated, the hardware was upgraded, and we became part of a growing campus-wide academic network. We now have access to a color liquid crystal display (LCD) panel for overhead projection of computer images. Faculty can demonstrate various writing and revising techniques on the computer to an entire class. We have a scanner with an Optical Character Recognition (OCR) program that copies typed or printed text and transfers it to WordPerfect so students with typewriters or non-IBM-compatible computers can transfer their work easily and quickly and have it available for use in the class. Faculty have network access to the library's online catalog and to various bulletin boards through Internet and Compuserve.

We continue to grow, and we are acutely aware of the changes taking place in our department and in the college. These changes are exciting and challenging for both faculty and students as we move together toward the future.

Chapter

29

The Value of Portable
Computers in the Classroom

Garrett Bozylinsky
Associate Vice President for Computing
Indiana University of Pennsylvania, Indiana, Pennsylvania

William Creighton
Director of Academic Computing
Indiana University of Pennsylvania, Indiana, Pennsylvania

"The computer, like paper or electricity, is a tool and resource that enables people to create and use other tools and resources. It is therefore a medium with a vast collection of uses, whose power, viability, and value for education we are just beginning to discover and assess" (Diane Pelkus Balestri et al., *Ivory Towers, Silicon Basements: Learner-Centered Computing in Postsecondary Education*, Academic Computing Publications, Inc., McKinney, Texas, 1989, p. 1). Use of computing to improve the quality of teaching is an area which has produced more promise than results. Yet, at the same time, many institutions already provide, or are in the process of providing, each faculty member with a personal computer. At Indiana University of Pennsylvania (IUP), providing each faculty member with the opportunity to acquire a personal computer is part of the long-range strategic computing plan.

BACKGROUND

IUP is a comprehensive, public university. It is the fourth largest university in the Commonwealth of Pennsylvania with an enrollment, at the time of this writing, of nearly 15,000 students and 750 faculty members. The undergraduate curriculum is presented through IUP's six teaching colleges: Business, Education, Fine Arts, Human Ecology and Health Sciences, Humanities and

Social Sciences, and Natural Sciences and Mathematics. Graduate studies are administered through the Graduate School and educational opportunities for adults and nontraditional students are coordinated through the School of Continuing Education.

PROVIDING COMPUTERS FOR FACULTY USE

IUP, like many other institutions, has been faced with meeting the challenge of providing computers for faculty use while, at the same time, experiencing a diminishing base budget. With declining budgets and increasing pressure to graduate computer- and information-literate students, it is extremely important that each new computer purchased provide the institution with a maximum return on investment.

In the classroom, faculty are becoming increasingly expected (and, in our experience, generally anxious) to make use of computing to augment their lectures. Many institutions have classrooms specially equipped with a computer and overhead projector. As image processing and networking mature, such classrooms can be used to project any graphical image that has been stored electronically: perhaps collections from the university library, computer manuals and documentation, or images and information stored in other locations, even off-site. Any such images can then easily become part of a classroom presentation.

However, there are serious obstacles to faculty use of such equipment. Lectures are prepared using a computer at home or in the office which most likely differs significantly from the classroom computer. There may be specialized software, large amounts of data, or special hardware requirements that are essential to the presentation. Can a faculty member be certain that the application run on a home or office computer will run without incident on the classroom computer? Does it have enough memory? Is the graphical interface the same? Does he or she have to hunt for keys on a strange keyboard? Is there enough disk space? If the classroom is not part of a campus-wide network, is there time to load software or application data from floppy disk(s) in the short amount of time before class begins? Or, if the software is on the classroom computer, is it the same version; is it configured similarly; and does it behave as the one used by the faculty during preparation? How can teachers be expected to embrace and utilize computing in the classroom in the face of such obstacles?

There are even more obstacles. Before a lecture is delivered in the classroom, it is first prepared in the office and/or at home. Those faculty who do not have a computer at home are forced to develop all of their computer-related material in the office. Realistically, the consequence is that faculty will develop far fewer computer-assisted classroom lectures.

For those faculty members who have acquired a personal computer for use at home, many obstacles still remain. The same hardware incompatibilities noted above with regard to classroom use usually exist between office and home computers. The same software may not be on both machines or may not be the same version. If a campus-wide network exists, the home computer is not likely to be connected to it. Data must be carried back and forth or downloaded via modems. The same software may not perform similarly on both machines.

Given these difficulties, it is in many respects surprising that faculty use of computers in the classroom is as high as it is. The current level of classroom usage in light of these obstacles may, in fact, be evidence of the significant contribution faculty believe computing can bring to the classroom environment. Would the opportunity for faculty to use the same computer in the classroom as elsewhere increase faculty use of computing in the classroom?

STUDY OF FACULTY USE

In order to answer this question and others relating to the value to faculty of portable microcomputers, a study involving twelve faculty members at IUP was initiated. The study was directed by the associate vice president for computing and coordinated by the director of Academic Computing Services. A proposal defining the parameters of the study was funded by Zenith Data Systems of Groupe Bull who agreed to provide six desktop computing units (three 286 and three 386sx machines) and six portable computing units (three 286 and three 386sx laptops during the first semester and six 386sx notebooks during the second semester). In addition, a color monitor was provided with each portable and positioned at the faculty member's primary work location.

The study was conducted at IUP over a period of two full academic semesters: fall 1991 and spring 1992. Prior to the start of the fall semester, twelve faculty members (two from each teaching college) agreed to participate in the study. For the first semester, six received Zenith laptop computers and six received similarly configured Zenith desktop computers. The faculty also attended an instructional workshop which provided information about the equipment and software. Prior to the start of the spring semester, those with laptop units were given desktops but those who had desktops were now given Zenith notebook computers to evaluate the impact of size and weight based upon feedback from the first semester laptop users who generally found them to be too heavy.

Support staff and participants maintained open communications throughout the study. Communication between participants was also encouraged. Staff facilitated and provided training as necessary in the use of electronic forms of communication (e-mail and electronic conferencing). Throughout the study, participants were encouraged to use the equipment as though it were permanently assigned to them, in essence to treat it as though they owned it.

Data for the study was gathered through the use of individual interviews, open discussion in informal social gatherings, electronic conferencing and e-mail, and, most significantly, a series of four questionnaires. The questionnaires were administered at four critical points in the study to ensure the integrity and consistency of the data being gathered. These points were prior to the start of the study, after the period of portable use, after the period of desktop use, and at the conclusion of the study. The questionnaires were designed to allow a range of responses from zero to ten, in most cases with ten representing a much more intense opinion. Responses were grouped at various stages to facilitate analysis and reporting.

While the study dealt with many aspects of portable computing, only those which relate directly to teaching and classroom use are reported here. Specifically, this chapter addresses the hypothesis that faculty with portable computers will be significantly more inclined to use them in the classroom than faculty with desktop computers. Given that portable microcomputers are generally more costly than equivalent desktop models, if an institution is to allow or encourage faculty to choose the portable unit over the desktop, it should expect to see, among other things, a corresponding increase in classroom computing.

In terms of general background, the participants' years of service ranged from five to twenty-five years with a median of 13.5 years. Years of computer usage ranged from two to fifteen, with a median of 7.5 years. On both dimensions, the twelve participants covered a fairly broad background. The median self-assessment of computer literacy was 6.5 on a scale of zero to ten with only one participant ranking himself low, five as moderate, and six as high on this scale; again, a fairly broad background. The group was subject-matter knowledgeable, experienced, and generally aware of at least basic microcomputing concepts.

Most of the participants (seventy-five percent) had none or extremely little previous experience with portable computers. This finding is consistent with our understanding of the general climate of faculty computing in higher education today. The portable microcomputer still appears to be a relatively new and nontraditional device which is not frequently considered by faculty.

There were several questions which dealt explicitly with the classroom use of portable computers *vis à vis* desktops. Prior to beginning the project, participants were asked how frequently they used computers in the classroom. After their use of the portable and desktop computers, participants were asked how much they used it for classroom presentation, and how much it impacted their teaching. In addition, at the end of the study, participants were asked to compare which computer they made greater use of in the classroom.

About two-thirds of the participants made some use of computing in the classroom. The frequency of actual use of the portables in the classroom however, was very modest and remained virtually the same throughout the duration of the study. On a scale of zero (very little) to ten (very much), more than one half rated their classroom use at one and one third in the two to three range. Only one participant rated himself above the midpoint on frequency of use in the classroom. While it would have been gratifying to validate the hypothesis directly with an increase in actual use, realistically, the short duration of the study made dramatic change in behavior unlikely.

Yet, when participants were asked at the end of each semester of use how much each machine was used in the classroom, differences between portable and desktop users began to emerge. Seven participants made use of portables in the classroom while only four desktop users did so. Clearly this would largely be due to the difficulty of moving a desktop into the classroom, although several departments on campus have desktops available on carts that can be wheeled into classrooms. But to some extent, that is also the point of the hypothesis. If faculty have personal control over the computer they use in the classroom and, for example, are not dependent on arranging to make use of one available to several faculty, they are more likely to make use of computing in the classroom.

In addition, participants were asked to evaluate the impact each type of computer had on their teaching. They rated both desktops and portables similarly and moderately high. On a scale of zero (low impact) to ten (high impact), the median rating for desktop users was six compared to 5.5 for portable users.

Weight, however, appears to have been an important consideration. Of the six participants who were provided notebooks (weighing seven pounds), five of them felt it had a moderate or high impact on their teaching. But of the six participants given laptops (weighing fifteen pounds), only three felt similarly. In another view of the same information, of the eight participants who felt the portable computer had a moderate or significant impact on their teaching, five of them were notebook users. Conversely, three of the four participants who felt the portable computer had little impact on their teaching, were users of the laptop models. These users likely saw fewer differences between the laptop and desktop.

One participant commented, "I felt cheated in never really getting the advantage of the portability. It was too heavy to really move around." Another commented, "So far I have not found much advantage to using a laptop because I have not taken it out of my office. The darn thing is not that light." But the most colorful characterization of the impact of weight on portability came from a faculty member who even coined a new acronym: "The laptop was invented by a computer whiz whose brother specialized in abdominal surgery for aging faculty. We are his next unwitting victims. Check your BC/BS for a category called CHIPS: Computer Hernias in Professional Subjects."

The simple conclusion is that if a computer is to gain any added value for its portability, it must be truly portable. It is safe to conclude the laptops used were too heavy for faculty to move them easily enough to make them more valuable than desktops. A notebook size computer is minimally required.

At the end of the study, participants were asked to make a point-to-point comparison of which computer they made greater use in the classroom. Only two (seventeen percent) preferred the desktop; four (thirty-three percent) were clearly undecided or had no preference, and six (fifty percent) preferred the portable in varying degrees. This seems to corroborate our original hypothesis. But would all faculty agree that portables would be of greater benefit than desktop micros? "Certainly not all faculty!" was the way one member of the group answered that question. Among the comments expressed was that "the older, heavier portables created a stigma of sorts that must now be overcome." Although he used it in class several times, one faculty member felt his discipline (English composition) did not lend itself to heavy use of computing in the classroom and, therefore, saw less utility in the ability to bring his computer to class.

This comment reinforces the fact that hardware is only one part of the equation for increasing computer use in the classroom. Faculty must also be encouraged to begin creatively assessing the opportunities computing provides them for enhancing their classroom presentations. In addition, software must be made available. One participant noted that all of her overheads were on her micro, but she lacked a graphics software package to project them in the classroom. That addition for her, she felt, would have enabled her to make much greater classroom use of the portable.

We believe the most responsible conclusion is that for a significant number of faculty, the hypothesis that faculty with portable computers will be significantly more inclined to use them in the classroom than faculty with desktop computers, will be true. Other obstacles emerged regarding portable computers in the classroom (and computing in the classroom in general).

One obstacle which arose in using the portables was, as one participant put it, "But when is a laptop no longer a laptop? . . . I have my 'laptop' connected to the VGA monitor, the telephone, the printer, and, of course, to the ubiquitous surge protector." Other participants reported similar frustrations. If portables are to be of maximum utility, a docking port in which the computer can be quickly and easily attached and detached from the plethora of "home" office devices and peripherals is probably essential in most cases. It is certainly important in making a portable computer truly portable.

"Knowing that the equipment will work" was how one participant described another important issue. It is essential for faculty to have confidence in the technological devices that will be used to support their classroom presentation. More than a few faculty have related their horror at walking into a classroom expecting to use a computer that had been removed by a colleague or which had been sent out for repair. Equally frustrating is finding that the overhead projector is not working, or that the LCD panel does not have the proper cables for attaching to the computer. Faculty members, in order to maintain their credibility and the respect of their students, must not fumble about or flounder as they make their classroom presentation. If technology is to become integral to the classroom process, it must be a natural fit. Only after faculty are convinced that their most basic concerns regarding the dependability of technology have been addressed in a satisfactory manner can they begin to consider how technology can improve classroom outcomes.

In the classroom, teaching effectiveness frequently requires faculty to respond immediately to student questions. Many times an answer will require material for which the need could not have been anticipated. If the response is delayed until the next meeting, the dynamic nature of the classroom has been compromised, rather than enhanced, by technology. Use of portable computers can increase this responsiveness through increased availability of software and data on the unit in the classroom. The portable becomes, in essence, an extension of the faculty member's office. The significance of this in the classroom is related in the following manner by one of the participants, "Although I may not need the equipment each day in class, I want it available to me in order to be responsive." By actually carrying the faculty member's computer into the classroom, the likelihood is increased that the software or data needed at any given time, in any given situation, will be available for use. Such convenience cannot be expected from single or multiple desktop units without losing the spontaneity of the response.

CONCLUSION

The portable microcomputer is a technology that provides faculty members with additional freedom and options which allow them to be more comfortable and confident using computers in the classroom. As a technology, portable microcomputing can, for some faculty, reduce the obstacles of using computing to enhance the classroom experience. Based upon the feedback of the participants in this study, the lighter weight and more powerful notebook computers already available can make an important contribution to computing in the classroom. In view of the internal and external pressures to bring computing into the classroom and to teach more effectively, it is hard to ignore the impact of portable computers for some faculty. Our findings would indicate that faculty should at least be provided with notebooks as a serious option.

ACKNOWLEDGMENT

The authors are grateful to Zenith Computer Corporation of Groupe Bull for providing the computers used in this study.

Chapter

30

Music, Computers, and Learning at New England Conservatory

Paul Burdick
Music and Computer Studio Director
New England Conservatory, Boston, Massachusetts

Lyle Davidson
Theory Department Chairperson
New England Conservatory, Boston, Massachusetts

Wednesday afternoon and the New England Conservatory's (NEC) Music and Computer Studio is full—at first glance overfull. Students fill both of the studio's two connected rooms. In the front room, students work individually at separate Macintoshes: a composition student stares intently at the orchestral score filling the screen. As he enters notes from a Musical Instrument Digital Interface (MIDI) keyboard, pitches fall across the screen and into the score. There is a liberal arts paper due today, and students working in MacWrite and Microsoft Word are looking at notes and typing. Some are tentative, others work with seemingly clear purpose, typing deliberately, pausing, typing some more. One student is working in a draw program to create a concert announcement for a recital.

In the studio's second room, a counterpoint class is in process. Fifteen students sit scattered around five of the studio's computers, three to each Mac. The level of noise in the studio's classroom resembles a busy workshop and indeed everyone is highly focused on the task at hand—completing a two-part species counterpoint exercise above a cantus firmus used by Mozart.

In one group, a student moves the cursor to the counterpoint on the screen and begins to implement yet another revision of the melody-in-process, while another student points and sings the line, saying this is how it should go. The group sitting next to them begins to play the most recent version of their work,

and as the melody sounds, a spirited debate about the effectiveness of a particular note ensues. Once the melody is played through, they immediately play it
again, and then still a third time, working to settle their aesthetic differences and
get it right.

If we look closely at the situation that occurs regularly on Monday-
Wednesday-Friday afternoons for every freshman at the conservatory, we will
find that deliberate choices have guided the unique structure and design of
NEC's computer studio. This chapter discusses the design of a computer studio
around the double function of word processing and music processing, the deliberate building of collaborative learning as a model for classroom use of the studio, and the flexibility that allows a range of use, including student résumés,
papers, program notes, concert announcements, simple four-voice harmony,
species counterpoint, jazz arrangements, chamber ensemble transcriptions,
orchestral scores, and music composition.

PRACTICAL AND ADMINISTRATIVE ISSUES

This section briefly discusses practical and administrative issues. It includes a
brief history of the facility, a summary of current resources in terms of hardware
and software, the current staffing and hours of the studio, and funding. Following
this discussion of practical concerns, we will address the use, support, and impact
of the studio on students, faculty, pedagogues, and course planning.

Brief History of the Studio

The music and computer studio at NEC was informally established on a pilot
basis in 1983 with two Apple IIe computers. Careful research demonstrated that
the studio could be an important tool in students' musical development. Over
the next several years the studio grew slowly, adding three more Apple IIes, one
Imagewriter Printer and a Kurzweil 250 MIDI keyboard. In 1986, the studio
was more formally organized, and an acting director appointed. At this time, the
switch to Apple Macintosh computers was made because of the available music
software for notation and sequencing, allowing for arranging and composition.
As resources and funding became available, more computers, as well as MIDI
and peripheral equipment (printers, hard drives) have been added.

Space and Layout

At present, the studio occupies two large, adjacent rooms in the basement of
the conservatory, with a third room available for storage and equipment repairs.
All three rooms are connected with doors that can be left open or closed as the
organization of classes and students requires throughout the day. The larger of
the two rooms is often used for classes meeting in the studio, as well as for general use when there are no classes convening.

A low-budget operation, all the equipment in the studio is arranged on tables
running along the walls of the studio, with enough space around each computer

for at least three people to be able to sit and see the screen comfortably. Extra chairs are stacked in the corner of the room, and can be added or subtracted as the number of persons in the room warrants. The space in the central part of the room is important to allow for easy movement of students and instructors, facilitating over-the-shoulder comments and group discussion.

Equipment

Presently, there are twelve Macintosh computers available for student and faculty use; eleven of these are Macintosh Plus computers (or equivalently modified Mac 512s) and one Macintosh LC. The 20 MB hard drives are connected to each computer, and there are external floppy drives on approximately half of the computers. Three AppleTalk Imagewriters and one PostScript laser printer are available for printing throughout the studio, connected to the computers with an AppleTalk network in a simple bus configuration.

Three of the Macintoshes are connected to MIDI peripherals with MIDI interfaces. (The MIDI protocol is the basis for digital communication between synthesizers and computers.) These include one Casio CZ 101 keyboard, a Korg MIRex rack mounted synthesizer, controlled by an Akai MIDI control keyboard, and a Kurzweil 250 keyboard. The MIDI interfaces used are made by PASSPORT and Opcode, and are of the simple 1 in/1 out or 1 in/3 out variety.

Five more Macintoshes are equipped with simple headphone extension boxes. These boxes plug into the headphone output on the back of the computers and lead to a set of eight 1/4-inch phone jacks, each with a separate volume control. These phone jacks can then be used for individual headphones for one or more persons at each computer. Headphones are provided as requested. In addition, small speakers are also plugged into the phone jack boxes, one per box. The volume of the speakers can then be adjusted as needed if a more public performance or playback is required. This arrangement has the effect of making the playback out of the computer much more audible than the playback from the Mac speakers.

Software

The studio offers a modest range of software, with an understandable emphasis on music applications. MacWrite and Microsoft Word are used for word processing; SuperPaint is available for graphic applications. Music software falls into three categories: notation, sequencing, and ear-training/teaching.

Notation software provides the user with the means to manipulate conventional music notation on screen. Most notation software packages also allow for some kind of score playback as well, either MIDI or computer based.

The use of notation software is roughly similar to the typical use of word processors: musical ideas are entered in notation and can be subsequently printed in a more formal score as desired. As with the range of word processors from the humble to the full-featured, notation programs also span a similar range. High-end music notation programs allow for true music desktop publishing. The studio uses three such packages: Deluxe Music Construction Set (DMCS), Music Prose, and Finale.

Sequencing software provides the user with a synthesizer-based recording tool, roughly analogous to a multitrack tape recorder. Such software must be used in exclusive conjunction with a MIDI synthesizer connected to the computer using a MIDI interface. The studio uses EZ Vision, made by the Opcode company.

Ear training/teaching software generally presents a fairly narrow set of musical goals in each package (e.g., hearing intervals, knowing key signatures). These goals are generally pursued using a drill and practice model. The studio uses Listen and Practica Musica.

Faculty have also generated materials for use in the studio. These include dictation materials, a graded set of melodies based on the materials of the solfège classes, and historical examples of counterpoint exercises by a student of Mozart, Thomas Attwood, and Beethoven.

Staffing and Availability

The studio is managed by the director of the Music and Computer Studio, and he works twenty-five hours per week. In addition, students from the conservatory's work study pool work as studio assistants. The studio is staffed by a single student worker for the hours the studio is open.

The studio is open an average of fifty hours per week during the school year: forty-six of these hours are from Monday to Friday, with the remaining four hours on Sundays. Typically, the studio is open from noon until 10 P.M. from Mondays to Thursdays, from noon until 6 P.M. on Fridays, and from 1 to 5 P.M. on Sundays.

The studio is available for use by students and faculty on a first-come, first-serve basis and as the number of available computers permits. Additionally, the studio is also available for classroom use, with classes convening in the studio.

Typically, there are about ten hours of classes in the studio per week. Usually they are convened in the larger of the two rooms with the door shut between them to minimize interruptions. The smaller of the two rooms can then remain open to serve students and staff in the normal manner.

Funding

As powerful as the impact of the studio is, its cost per student is relatively low. With an enrollment of approximately 700 students, the average cost per student is about $40 per year. The greatest expense is staffing and labor. Relatively inexpensive equipment is purchased incrementally by the studio as funds are available. This equipment includes Macs at the bottom of Apple's product line, synthesizers and MIDI equipment, upgrades to current equipment, and peripherals.

Funds for the studio come from the administration of the conservatory. These funds are also supplemented by a student activity fee, a portion of which is allocated to the studio. The annual budget is around $29,000. Typically, about $22,000 per year is spent on labor, $5,000 on new hardware, software, and upgrades, and another $2,000 on supplies and operating expenses. The school also provides a maintenance contract for the hardware in the studio, above and beyond the funds budgeted.

STUDIO USE

The studio is used by students and faculty for both direct and indirect classroom use.

Student and Faculty Use

Students and faculty are free to use any available computers at any time the facility is open. Classes can reserve a portion of the studio in one-hour time blocks for class use. When classes are in session, there are typically five to six computers available for student use; when there are no classes, there are twelve.

Students use word processors, graphic programs, and music software. Word processors (MacWrite, Microsoft Word) are used in a manner typical of most higher education settings: for papers, notes, letters, bulletins, etc. Graphic programs (SuperPaint) are used for making concert announcements, graphs for papers, bulletin board announcements, and recreation.

The music software used includes programs for notation, sequencing, and education. The notation software is used extensively, and the three different packages the studio offers (DMCS, Music Prose, and Finale) provide a range of applications based on the user's needs and goals. Typically, DMCS is used in class room settings and for persons who are not already familiar with notation applications. Music Prose fills a midlevel niche, providing relatively extensive possibilities with a relatively short learning curve. Finale offers the widest range of capabilities in a complex application.

Generally, people with very simple goals will use DMCS, while those with more extensive needs (e.g., bigger scores, complex piano parts, big band charts) will use Music Prose or Finale. DMCS is commonly used by students doing simple homework assignments in counterpoint or harmony; it can also serve students unfamiliar with computers or notation software.

Composers working on scores in the studio invariably end up using Finale. Common applications for Music Prose are singers doing transpositions of scores, jazz students working on arrangements, and instrumentalists working on chamber transcriptions. These two applications are both made by Coda and have the virtue of compatible file types; files made in one program can be opened, used, and worked on in the other application. As a result, students are usually encouraged to begin working in Music Prose and move to Finale only when they have needs that the lesser program cannot accommodate.

Sequencing software used in the studio is limited to Opcode's EZ Vision software. Sequencers commonly are used towards creating synthesizer performances in popular idioms (rock, jazz, hip-hop) In this regard, sequencers are well-suited as a compositional tool in these idioms. Such software can also provide a means of exploring scores, working with orchestration, arranging ideas, and dealing with issues of shaping, phrasing, and articulation in the body of more classically based music.

Class Use

Classes at NEC make use of the studio in two ways: indirectly, by requiring that coursework be performed on a computer outside of class time, or directly, with classes convening in the studio.

Indirect Class Use

Classes in the liberal arts department require students to use word processing and to hand in computer printout for writing classes. Students are free to use any computers at their disposal, with the large majority of them relying on the school's Music and Computer Studio. For students working in the studio, peer assistance is available to provide the students with student feedback and advice. (Peer assistance is provided by work study students working for the liberal arts department in that capacity.)

In addition, students commonly use the studio for creating papers for other classes, in particular classes in music history and musicology. Although none of these classes explicitly require that students use computers, students choose to use them, almost without exception.

Direct Class Use

Classes in the undergraduate theory department convene regularly in the studio. These include classes in species counterpoint and harmony.

Species counterpoint is the practice of writing a melody that can "go along with" another melody. Typically, the teacher provides the student with a simple melody, called a cantus firmus, and the student writes another melody, called the counterpoint to work with the cantus. Students use sets of rules, called species, in writing their melodies. Each species increases the range of the student's expressive possibilities, as well as the number of possible difficulties.

The harmony taught in the studio is conventional nineteenth-century harmony. Students work through successions of chords in a four-voice texture as instructed by the teacher.

Classes that meet in the studio rarely meet there exclusively. Typically, classes will meet in the studio for a series of two to four class sessions and then meet in a classroom for one to four sessions. All class sessions in the studio are one hour in length.

All of the music classes taught in the studio have implemented a collaborative learning model as a way of structuring their use of the studio. Students work in groups, with two or three working on each computer. The largest class meeting in the studio totals twenty students, with fifteen as a common class size. As such, the average class claims five to seven of the twelve available computers in the studio, leaving the rest open for general student use. While the need for fewer computers is an advantage of the collaborative learning model, the decision to use this model is not born of mere efficacy.

STUDIO SUPPORT

The studio provides support for students and faculty in numerous ways from introductory first sessions in the studio through help with class development.

Introductory Sessions

At the beginning of each school year, the studio provides one hour introductory sessions for all interested students. These sessions are limited to no more that twenty students at a time. All incoming freshmen are required to attend these introductory sessions by the liberal arts department as a way of introducing them to the studio. Any student may attend these sessions, and sessions are held as needed throughout the first two weeks of the semester. Typically, about twelve sessions are held.

In these introductory sessions, the basics of the Macintosh interface are demonstrated and explored: the mouse and cursor, windows, pull-down menus, disks, files, etc. In addition, MacWrite is explored as an introductory application. These sessions are not intended to be comprehensive, but to have the students become comfortable with the computers and the environment.

Ongoing Support

A student assistant is working and available for all hours that the studio is open. The primary responsibility of the studio assistants is to help other students learn software and solve problems as necessary. Emphasis is placed on teaching and fostering resourcefulness, with a priority placed on helping students understand how to work in the software environment of their choice, rather than giving "just follow the recipe" advice. As a result, a great deal of informal support is provided by other students on a peer-to-peer basis as well. Students who are very active in this fashion frequently grow to become studio assistants.

Support for Classes

Classes use the studio in two ways: by requiring that work be done on computers in the studio or by meeting in the studio itself. Classes in both of these groups have been intentionally designed to incorporate the studio into their work and activities. Support for all of these classes comes in various forms, and from sources both internal (the studio director) and external (faculty and administration) to the studio.

For classes that require that work be done in the studio, the primary issue for smooth operation is that of coordination. Since most incoming students are required to take writing classes, it is critical that the scheduling of due dates for drafts and revisions be coordinated to allow for a smooth flow of traffic in the studio.

Students are required to use the studio to write papers in both the undergraduate theory and liberal arts departments. Both departments propose a set of deadlines and due dates for each of the papers they will assign for a given semester. Then, at the beginning of each semester, a meeting is held with the faculty of both departments in order to make final decisions, taking into consideration due dates and class sizes.

Classes Meeting in the Studio

With assistance in class scheduling from the administration, there are very few classes competing for the same time slot in the studio. If a class that will meet in the studio has no other class to compete with, arrangements for studio time are made with the director as little as a day in advance of the class. Frequently instructors will work out a schedule two to three weeks ahead of time, planning their studio and classroom times, and provide the studio with this schedule. This flexibility is important because it allows instructors to respond to changes in classroom issues and dynamics by working in whichever venue—classroom or computer studio—can best serve the issues at hand.

All of the classes meeting regularly in the studio are taught by members of the undergraduate theory department. The department holds regular (weekly or biweekly) faculty meetings where pedagogical issues and any remaining scheduling issues can be addressed. Meetings are commonly organized by class assignments (that is, meetings will be held for all counterpoint teachers). As such, meetings can focus on very specific pedagogical issues for the class at hand, both regarding the use of the studio and the general shaping of the class itself.

Class Development Support

Support for class development is also provided as needed. Initially, the species counterpoint classes were the only ones to meet in the studio. After these classes were established, a harmony teacher at the school became interested in designing a harmony class around the studio. He visited counterpoint classes in session, and conversations were held with the director of the studio and with faculty currently teaching in the studio.

A wide range of issues were explored in developing the class: what materials were appropriate, how assignments could be structured, what changes collaborative learning would bring to the class, timing for assignments, how to schedule class and studio time, etc. After several months of thought and discussions, a harmony class was developed that implemented and expanded on the model initially outlined in the counterpoint classes (Hoffmann 1991).

STUDIO IMPACT

Collaborative learning and the integration of aural knowledge are two areas of studio impact on the student.

Collaborative Learning

A model of collaborative learning forms the basis for classroom organization in the conservatory's computer studio. All of the classes that meet in the studio use some form of collaborative learning. Work groups of two or three students are created. Typically, the instructor will assign the class a relatively open-ended task to approach and complete within a single class. Each group must work together on the task at hand.

With the collaborative learning model serving as a guide for organizing the classroom and making assignments, emphasis is then placed on working with students to explore, experiment, discuss, and revise. Students evaluate their own work in the course of the class, debating differences of opinion and modifying their efforts and decisions as they continue to work.

Each group must work towards a consensus as to the best approach for the given problem; students soon learn that they must find ways to discuss the virtues of their decisions in the face of alternatives presented by others in the group. In this light, the successes shared by the group have been tested and verified first and primarily by the students themselves. The instructor is then approached with music that has not just been created to conform to a set of abstract rules; their work can now stand as a "sonic object" with virtues and liabilities that can be discussed, argued, and verified. The instructor can then participate in a discussion that is already in progress, serving to arbitrate, observe, and verify as the situation warrants.

Integration of Aural Knowledge with Rules of Music Theory by Application

With the coupling of the resource of the computer studio and the classroom model of collaborative learning, a critical change in emphasis takes place. Specifically, with the integration of playback and notation provided by music notation software (in the classroom, most commonly DMCS), the aural results of decisions made by students and represented in conventional notation can be placed at the center of inquiry.

This circumstance facilitates the integration of perceptual knowledge (aural) with conceptual knowledge (rules of music theory) in the course of an active application (writing counterpoint) where the efficacy of generalized rules and personal judgments can be personally verified in an immediate and tangible way. In this fashion, both rules and judgments come to be tested and finally, personally held as sensible, true, and useful.

Without the kind of application found in the studio, research done at the conservatory shows that few students play their work before handing it in to be graded by the instructor. Students understand the task involves following a set of rules; they do not think personal evaluation is critical, neccessary, or even desirable.

With the kind of application found in the studio, the results of the students' work can be more objectively placed at the center of discussion as a sonic object to be examined and evaluated. All students hear what they write continuously in the course of making decisions. This process can then happen interactively with the teacher and with other students.

WORKING METHODS AND DYNAMICS

Because of the grouping of students into teams, the dynamics of the classes change and with it the traditional role of the teacher. For best instruction, both classroom and studio are used for each class.

Setting Up Student Groups/Teams

For each class, students are organized into groups or teams. It can be helpful to work in informal groups for one or two sessions to start, to allow for both students and teacher to explore how different individuals work together. Once there is a sense of the individuals and personalities involved, more concrete groups can be formed. This organization can be based on student preference, or directed by the teacher. Groups of two or three seem to be most desirable; more than this may allow students to coast too easily without participating in the enterprise.

Once established, groups typically stay together for a period of time. Commonly groups will be reorganized one or two more times throughout the semester. By keeping groups together for more than one or two sessions, students can develop an understanding of and appreciation for personal differences in approach and aesthetics. As groups work through more than one session together, they will evolve a working and aesthetic style particular to the group.

After a significant period of working together, the groups should reorganize. Typically, this will happen once at mid-semester. This reorganization can provide the teacher with the possibility of matching or contrasting personalities and learning styles. In addition, a new point of view provided by a new work group can serve to restimulate students' interest and involvement.

Working with Student Groups

Once student groups are established, it is helpful to assign each student within each group a clear and individual role to play. This is particularly important in groups of three people, in which a strong personality can dominate and a more timid student can pull back or coast. The group itself or the instructor can decide on the role assignments.

In the species counterpoint classes, students work in groups of three and are assigned roles as follows: rulekeeper, aesthetician, and producer. The rulekeeper is charged with the task of ensuring that the group's efforts comply with the rules of species counterpoint. The aesthetician is charged with judging "CIA"—Coherence, Independence, and Aesthetics. These give the student a beginning criteria and conceptual framework for making decisions about individual judgments. Finally, the producer is in charge of production—in this case, seeing to it that the group's ideas are entered into the score on the screen, making modifications, and playing back as the group sees fit.

These roles can be reinforced or softened as deemed helpful by the teacher. With specific student roles assigned, it can be helpful to question a particular student on his/her area of responsibility as a way of directing the group's work (e.g.,"Tom, are the rules OK in measure 5?", "Sue, what do you think of the motion from A to F in the 7th measure? Do you like it?").

Teacher as Coach

A new role for the teacher unfolds in the context of this new model. This new role asks that a teacher be flexible, adaptable, and experienced. The instructor must demonstrate confidence in his/her own decision-making processes, above and beyond any single decision.

Teachers working in this new model will find that less of their time is occupied with the dispensing of information, and more time is spent evaluating decision making while it happens. This places an emphasis on teachers as thinkers and creators, and not merely as sources of information.

John Stein, a graduate student in education at Harvard University, performed a case study of the Computer Studio at NEC and of the models of teaching used there. In his study he observes the following:

> Working in the computer lab requires a major shift for both the instructor and the students. In normal classroom situations the teacher is the primary arbiter and dispenser of knowledge. An experienced and capable teacher, especially, will create familiar routines, exercises, examples, anecdotes, in short, a self-contained world for transferring subject matter to students. The process revolves around the teacher and within the classroom ultimate power rests there. In the lab, the process creates a dramatic shift in the nature of teacher/student interaction. Power and responsibility

for what transpires travels closer to the student end of the continuum and away from the teacher. This shift is serious and profound. The teacher must be willing to relinquish the unquestioned authority and control of the educational process which he [or she] is accustomed to wielding. Correspondingly, the students must be willing to shoulder more responsibility.

Since so much of what transpires in the computer lab is initiated by the student, the teacher must develop a new set of skills. Lyle Davidson, the first teacher at the conservatory to teach a counterpoint class in the computer lab: "The first time working in the studio is a trip, because it just turns all your strategies upside down. For example, when I had fifteen people down there working, one of the big problems was getting everybody's attention. You move from station to station around the room about as fast as you can, and when you hear or see a really strong example of something, you have to whistle to get everybody's attention. And then you have that group play the example, you talk about it for a minute, and then everybody goes back to work. So it's living examples, right there, on the spot. The style of teaching is a major change; you become a coach. You're constantly hovering around, making suggestions. It requires different abilities. It requires quick analysis of a problem, an ability to offer instant solutions, on the spot, on your feet, thinking about how you can provoke your students." (Stein 1992, pp 14-15)

Course Development and Mechanics

All of the classes that meet in the studio will also meet in a conventional classroom setting. Typically, the classroom is used to impart information and discussion in a more conventional manner, while the studio is used to explore and personally test rules, judgments, and ideas. (Since the conservatory's computer studio is in the basement of the building, and the classrooms are on the upper floors, we have come to think of this as the upstairs/downstairs effect.) John Stein further notes the following:

> The contrast between the normal classroom sessions and the time in the lab is instructive. Classroom sessions are used by Paul (Burdick) to introduce new material, and to discuss homework assignments and the musical journals he has each student keep. In the classroom instruction tends to fall into familiar patterns of lecture/note-taking. Even in the case of an educated, thoughtful, energetic, and sincere teacher like Paul, the weight of classroom habit and tradition creates an inertia that is hard to break. Students sit with their chairs arranged in a circle around the perimeter of the room (Paul: "I always make sure the chairs are arranged in a circle, not

those scary little rows.") A few of the students are very active participants in the session, asking questions, making comments, volunteering information. Most of the class, however, hold themselves apart from the activity, participating only when called upon. When the period is over, these students gather their belongings, walk out the door, and one wonders what they have appropriated.

In the computer lab, students are asked to use the new material they have been studying to compose counterpoint projects. Lab time is spent actually manipulating the information and creating music with it. In a traditional counterpoint class, which does not make use of a computer lab, this process of creating with the new material is typically done on an individual basis as homework. Here, Paul also assigns individual homework, but the process of personal composition has been added to class meeting-time as well. Since half of the class meetings occur in the lab, much more of the educational process consists of personal manipulation by the student. Students seem to participate more enthusiastically as more of the burden falls on their shoulders. Paul senses the difference in the two meeting places and he says: "A lot of what transpires in the classroom depends on my personal state. There are times when I can go into the classroom and explode, and the class just kicks. The classroom is much more dependent on my own performance and energy level than is the lab, where students are personally more responsible for what gets done." (Stein 1992, pp 13-14)

CONCLUSION

New England Conservatory's Music and Computer Studio functions in a relatively small space, with a modest budget and little funding. Off-the-shelf software is used with low-end Macintosh computers and supported by a student staff. And yet, when humble resources are coupled with ideas, enthusiasm, and innovation, it is possible to construct a computer studio which will make a major impact on an institution. At New England Conservatory, these ideas include new models of classroom organization, new models of teaching academic subjects, greater cooperation across departments, and a successful way of integrating different forms of information and knowledge. In music, the computer studio makes it possible to bring together the past aural knowledge each student brings to class with the more discursive, verbal knowledge typical of music theory. Computers are thereby cast as genuine educational tools of the late twentieth-century—facilitating interaction and questioning, collaboration with others, critical thinking, and the individual exploration of the differences and value of information, knowledge, and skill.

REFERENCES

Hoffmann, James A. "Computer-Aided Collaborative Music Instruction." *Harvard Educational Review*, Vol. 61, No. 3. August 1991.

Stein, John. "The Use of Music Notation Software and the Computer in Species Counterpoint Classes." A case study prepared for Harvard School of Education, Spring 1991. Unpublished.

Chapter

31

Academic Computing Case History: Establishment of Microcomputer Access at a Community College

Dick W. Birkholz

Coordinator, Academic Computing
Sheridan College, Sheridan, Wyoming

The focus of this case study is on the successes and setbacks of providing microcomputers for the students and faculty in the academic area at Sheridan College, a small community college in Sheridan, Wyoming. The college has approximately 1,400 students and generates 1,300 full-time equivalents (FTEs) on the main campus and has approximately 1,200 students and generates 650 FTEs on a branch campus (outreach program) at Gillette, Wyoming. Discussion of the planning and funding processes provides useful information for those interested in providing more access to microcomputers in the academic world.

In the spring of 1988 the need for microcomputer accessibility at Sheridan College was discussed by the Academic Council. Composed of division chairs and academic support personnel, the Wyoming Higher Education Computer Network (WHECN), a consortium of the seven community colleges and the University of Wyoming, had requested a five-year computer plan from all Wyoming community colleges. The plans were to be used to determine the needs of the colleges since the Harris minicomputer at each college was being phased out for both the academic and administrative functions. After purchasing Sequel minicomputers for the administrative functions at each college, WHECN decided to develop a new system around local area networks (LANs) and file servers for the academics and for office use by the staff because of the cost of a minicomputer and terminals for each college and the lack of standard applications software for the minicomputers. Sheridan College had a laboratory of sixteen IBM PCs, twelve Apple II+s, and a lab of Harris terminals but there was a need to expand. The biggest question that kept surfacing was "Why should we (faculty and staff) spend the time developing a microcomputer needs and priorities list, when we don't have any money to spend on such a project?" Even though the outlook for funding was bleak, the faculty and staff developed a list of needs and established priorities for the academic area. It was combined with the administrative plan to produce the all-school, five-year plan.

The list of needs was compiled from individual desires, needs, and/or dreams. Every faculty and staff member was asked to submit what they would like to be able to do in the classroom and what hardware, software, and development time would be needed to change the curriculum. The needs were compiled for each division and priorities were made within the divisions. The Academic Council approved the priority list for the entire academic area.

The list represented a dream to be accomplished over a five-year period with completion in fiscal year 1994. The list included two microcomputer labs of sixteen PCs for microcomputer application courses, an AutoCAD lab, a mathematics lab, a microcomputer for every faculty member, software training, a LAN network and a fiber-optic backbone connecting four buildings into one network on the Sheridan campus. A lab of twenty PCs and a file server were proposed for the Gillette campus. The estimated cost of the plan was $400,000 for the hardware, software, and the fiber-optic backbone. The plan was the dream of a few and the future for many.

How was a small rural community college able to accomplish such a project? In the beginning, the WHECN was a key ingredient for the initial funding for the plan. Also, WHECN provided technical support in the form of engineers and software consultants, hardware and software acquisitions, and vendor contacts. The Zenith microcomputer had been established as the standard for the community colleges and the university through a Request for Proposals (RFP) written by the staff of WHECN and the computer services department at the University of Wyoming. The RFP provided the opportunity to establish a standard for two or three years at a reasonable cost so an institution does not need to bid every purchase nor receive several kinds of hardware within a short period of time. For small institutions with limited technical support, 100 percent compatibility is very important. At the time, Sheridan College had a Computer Services Center with a director and two technicians to provide administrative and academic support.

In the fall of 1988, a coordinator of academic computing (0.2 faculty release time) was appointed to direct the academic side of the plan. The coordinator was instrumental in working closely with the faculty through ad hoc committees and the Computer Services Center in the implementation of the plan. An important ingredient in the success of the project was that the coordinator was a faculty member who understood the needs of the classroom and the faculty.

Ad hoc committees were established for the various specialty areas, i.e., humanities division, allied health programs, microcomputer computer applications programs, engineering, and mathematics. The coordinator of academic computing worked with the division chairs and faculty to establish the committees which functioned only until their objectives were fulfilled. All of the input from the ad hoc committees was then used to support the acquisition of software and hardware through grants or foundations and to recommend changes in the curriculum. The various committees functioned from three to twelve months.

As the faculty and ad hoc committees began to discuss acquisition and use of microcomputers on the campus, a clear division in faculty skill levels and interests became apparent. The faculty could be categorized into two groups. The first group was comfortable using a microcomputer and had either taken applications courses or were self-taught in applications software. This group demanded the most and knew what they wanted regarding hardware, software, and how they planned to use the materials. The second group had avoided the microcomputer but were interested in using the microcomputer in their offices. This group needed a lot of guidance, and the coordinator developed a list of questions to draw these faculty into the discussions during the ad hoc committee meetings. The questions included the following:

- Have you ever used a microcomputer? If yes, for what purpose?
- Would you like to learn how to do word processing? Examples of various uses were discussed.
- Are you available to take a word processing training workshop or an introduction to microcomputers workshop?
- Are there any presentations you could do in your classroom on the microcomputer if one were available?

AD HOC COMMITTEES

Most of the ad hoc committees functioned during the first two years of the plan. A summary of their activities follows. These committees were vital in involving the faculty and keeping the curriculum and students as the central focus of the five-year plan.

Humanities Division

The Humanities Division Committee was formed to evaluate the needs of the entire division regarding the use of microcomputers. The areas involved in the discussion were English composition, language courses, music, and art. The English department decided all English composition instructors needed to be microcomputer and WordPerfect literate and suggested that the instructors enroll in a WordPerfect workshop. Two English composition instructors who were comfortable with microcomputers have encouraged their students to use word processing to write their papers. A goal of the English department is to eventually have most of the composition classes taught using the microcomputers.

A dilemma facing the students and the English faculty in the beginning composition courses is training the students in the use of WordPerfect within the first three weeks of each semester so they can use the microcomputers as word processors. Basic WordPerfect workshops of eight contact hours have been designed but have not been fully implemented because of scheduling and staffing.

The Spanish instructor was interested in using computers in her Spanish lab and found software for Apple II+ microcomputers. Since the college has mostly Zenith microcomputers, she plans to switch to IBM-compatible software as soon as she can select and purchase software.

The music department has used Macs accompanied by synthesizers for music courses for several years, particularly in the improvisation and composition courses. Currently the department has a lab of five Macs. The goal is to establish a lab of sixteen Macs with synthesizers to be shared with the art department. The music department plans to use the Macs for college courses and to provide continuing education workshops for junior high and high school music educators during the summer. The art department is just beginning to be interested in the use of computers in its design courses.

Allied Health Division

Initially, the faculty of the allied health division, i.e., dental hygiene, dental assisting, and nursing, were interested in taking introduction to microcomputer and basic word processing workshops to become microcomputer literate. In the last two years, most of the allied health faculty have requested microcomputers for their offices, have taken WordPerfect workshops, and are using the microcomputers in their course preparations. In addition, the nursing department has selected software involving dosages, records, communication, evaluation, and nutrition to be used in the classroom.

Microcomputer Applications Programs

The microcomputer applications programs include the CIS program, office skills/secretarial program, Learning Center business courses, and the continuing education/community services courses in the microcomputer applications area. A benefit to the committee was that all members were already using microcomputers. The function of the committee was to evaluate and streamline the curriculum in the microcomputer applications area so there were no duplications, credits matched the class time and content, and the courses were in sequence. New course numbers were assigned to the new sequence of microcomputer applications courses and two new courses were added to the curriculum: Desktop Publishing (using PageMaker) and an Integrated Software course (using Enable).

The committee met weekly for one hour during the fall of 1990 and it took about ten weeks to complete the process, including the preparation of course number changes and new course descriptions for the curriculum and standards committee. The microcomputer applications committee functioned the best of any of the ad hoc committees because it met weekly; minutes were provided to all committee members between meetings, and members volunteered to complete part of the duties of the committee.

Engineering

The engineering ad hoc committee was formed to complete a survey for a Carl Perkins Grant. It included engineering, surveying, and drafting faculty and four engineers from the community. The committee determined the new student training needs in the areas of surveying and CAD and in retraining of community members for the new technology. The information generated by the committee was used to obtain a $26,000 grant with an equal institutional match to upgrade the AutoCAD and surveying programs.

Mathematics

In August 1991, the mathematics committee was formed to help implement a $99,000 Wyoming Educational Trust Fund grant, which was used to incorporate microcomputers into the mathematics curriculum. The committee evaluated the curriculum for the incorporation of the National Council of Teachers of Mathematics standards into all levels of mathematics from College Prep Math, a remedial course, to Differential Equations. Committee members reviewed and selected hardware and software and were responsible for the incorporation of microcomputers into the curriculum.

The mathematics ad hoc committee was formed after the other ad hoc committees and when the computer overview committee was functioning. The mathematics ad hoc committee provided a response to a specific need. It is anticipated that other ad hoc committees will function as the need arises.

Formation of an Overview Committee

In the spring of 1990 a computer overview committee was formed at the recommendation of the coordinator of academic computing and the academic council. The committee meets monthly and is composed of faculty representatives from each division, the director of computer services, and representatives from media services, continuing education, student services, the business office, student senate, and Gillette campus. The committee recommends microcomputer lab policies and the purchasing of supplies, hardware, and software from the student computer fees. In addition, the committee evaluates and modifies the five-year plan periodically, recommends training sessions, supervises the student lab assistants, and makes recommendations on the needs of computing to the deans. Through a reorganization of the governance system, the overview committee is now a standing committee under the Dean of Administration and Dean of Instruction.

FUNDING THE PROJECT

Using the five-year plan and suggestions from various committees, proposals were written to acquire hardware and software and provide development time to make changes in the curriculum. By having a plan formulated, numerous sources of funding were used. The following sources helped make the project a success:

- Carl Perkins vocational grants
- WHECN funds via the Wyoming Legislature
- Student computer fee funds ($1 per credit hour up to 12 credits)
- Sheridan College Foundation
- Local philanthropic foundations
- Current operational equipment budget
- Wyoming Educational Trust Fund
- Local one-mill levy for capital equipment

The following sources should also be considered:

- Title III grants
- National Science Foundation
- Local corporations including matching funds
- Local individuals
- National corporations
- Fund drives

In the fall of 1988 less than six months after the five-year plan was developed, WHECN distributed legislative funding to help with academic computing. Since Sheridan College had a complete plan, we received $154,000 to establish a lab of sixteen PCs, received software licenses for WordPerfect, Lotus, and dBase for the LAN file server, and provided the LAN backbone, a fiber-optic network between buildings on the Sheridan Campus. Also, a file server and ten PCs were purchased for the Gillette campus.

In the spring of 1989, the coordinator of academic computing (a 0.2 release time position) received a $42,000 Carl Perkins grant with an equal institutional match to expand the computer information system and office skills programs. An additional microcomputer lab of sixteen Zenith 286s with an HP LaserJet II printer was established and six faculty microcomputers were upgraded. Microcomputers were shifted to form a lab of twelve microcomputers. The grant also provided development time to make curriculum changes. Six microcomputers were placed in the library as an open lab courtesy of both grant and institutional funds. In addition to the Carl Perkins grant, institutional funds were used to complete the 20 PC lab on the Gillette campus. Additional funds from the standard operational budget were used to purchase two Macs for the music department, software upgrades, and five PCs for faculty offices. Within the first year of the plan, $258,000 had been expended on networking, installation, microcomputers, software, training, and course development.

In 1990, a Carl Perkins Grant for $26,000 and a $26,000 local match were used to expand the AutoCAD lab to Version 11 for sixteen microcomputers and to purchase a plotter and a 4 x 4 digitizer. The Perkins grant also provided a theodolite with a recording device and Wildsoft software to expand the use of software in the surveying program. Funds were also available to provide training for instructors in both the AutoCAD and surveying programs.

A local philanthropic foundation has contributed $20,000 annually to academic computing since 1990. The first gift was used to provide three nursing faculty with Zenith 386 microcomputers, six Zenith 386 microcomputers for an open student lab, and software for the nursing program.

In 1990, the Board of Trustees passed a one-mill levy for capital equipment which added about $75,000 per year to the equipment and acquisitions budget. About $30,000 of the total was expended for microcomputers and printers for microcomputer labs, faculty microcomputers, and one additional Mac and synthesizer for the music department.

A fee of $1 per credit up to twelve credits was approved by the students and the Board of Trustees in the spring of 1991. The fee raises about $30,000 per year and is used to help pay for student microcomputer lab supplies, lab hardware, and software upgrades. In addition to lab supplies, four lab microcomputers and two laser printers were purchased in the last year. One microcomputer to be used for CD-ROM library access was also purchased. Software upgrades for the Sheridan campus LAN have been made with WordPerfect 5.1, Lotus 1-2-3, dBase IV, DOS 5.0, and PageMaker 4.0 in recent years. On the Gillette campus the student fees have been used to purchase microcomputers, printers, and software for that campus.

In 1991, additional software was purchased using Carl Perkins funds. The nursing department spent $5,000 on software for the classroom on nutrition, communication, evaluation, dosages, and records. The political science department spent $4,000 on a CompuSketch software package to help train students in making composite drawings of suspects.

In August 1991, the Natural Science Division received a $99,000 Wyoming Educational Trust Fund Grant to incorporate microcomputers as instructional tools into the mathematics curriculum. The grant included about $55,000 for hardware and software. A total of nineteen Zenith 386 microcomputers with numeric co-processor and 3 megabytes RAM were purchased for labs, faculty, or classroom use. The two classroom microcomputers are equipped with In-Focus LCD projection pads to help with presentations. The remainder of the grant was used for curriculum development and planning and the incorporation of DERIVE and MAPLE V mathematics software into the curriculum. Other software which is being used in the math curriculum includes MiniTAB for statistics and

TKSolver for the Calculus II lab. A second grant of $12,000 has been received to complete the mathematics project.

In the fall of 1991 an open lab of sixteen Zenith 386 microcomputers with 3 megabytes of RAM and numeric co-processors was completed using $14,000 of institutional funds, $7,000 of Carl Perkins funds, and $2,000 of student fee money. Only two courses, Desktop Publishing and sections of AutoCAD, will be taught in the lab with the remainder of the time as open student lab time. All software available on the LAN will be accessible to the students.

With the increased enrollment over the last two years, enough excess tuition funds were available to replace one lab of sixteen Zenith 159s on the Sheridan campus and one lab of twenty Zenith 159s on the Gillette campus with Zenith 386s during the summer of 1992. The Zenith 159s from the two labs will be placed in faculty offices during the fall of 1992.

The original five-year plan had been completed by the fall of 1991, two years ahead of schedule. The exception was that about twenty-five faculty microcomputers were still needed. By the fall of 1992, all faculty offices would have microcomputers, and Zeniths 386s have replaced Zenith 159s in two of the microcomputer labs.

Within four years the college was able to complete the five year plan and continue to move forward. About $600,000 has been spent on the computer project for academics and more than 250 microcomputers have been connected to three LANs for student, faculty, and staff use.

Since the initial five-year plan, new items have been added to the needs list. A Mac lab for music/art will be expanded from five Macs to sixteen, and a central lab of fifty to eighty PCs with a trained assistant for every twenty PCs in use is proposed.

CONCLUSION

It is very important to have a plan (dream) in place because funding opportunities sometimes have a very small window of opportunity for application. A director or grant writer may only have a month or less to put a request or grant proposal together. The funds for hardware and software are available if faculty members know what they want and what materials they need to implement their objectives.

The ideal outcome is to acquire a complete lab all at once, but only one microcomputer and software can be used to develop a pilot project. The faculty can try different modes of instruction and experiments which can be helpful in determining what may or may not work in the classroom. These examples and the trial runs are important in convincing a grant reader or donor that the institution can be innovative in the use of microcomputers and software.

All faculty and staff need to dream and be creative. There will be some risks and setbacks in any project but those involved need to focus on the positive aspects and to keep trying to implement technological advances.

32

Development of an Advanced Technology Classroom

Eugene P. Buccini

Professor of Management
Ancell School of Business, Western Connecticut State University,
Danbury, Connecticut

Ronald G. Benson

Professor of Management and
Chairperson of Management Department
Ancell School of Business, Western Connecticut State University,
Danbury, Connecticut

For centuries teaching has remained a relatively stable art. From Socrates and the Socratic method to quantum physics, students have learned in basically the same fashion. Teachers stand in front of a room and lecture to students who may ask questions, take notes, or just listen and absorb. The first major change came about with the printing press, which made books available to the students themselves. In the twentieth-century, the style of teaching changed at universities to a more student-centered environment. Yet for the most part, classrooms are still designed for the industrial age. With the advent of the computer, however, vast change in how we teach and how students learn is now occurring.

WESTERN CONNECTICUT STATE UNIVERSITY

Western Connecticut State University is a public university in Danbury, Connecticut, consisting of the Ancell School of Business, the School of Arts and Sciences, and the School of Professional Studies. The Ancell School of Business offers a full undergraduate curriculum leading to a B.B.A. degree and master's degree programs in business (M.B.A.) and health care administration (M.H.A.).

The use and development of technology is one of the key principles at Western Connecticut State University, and during the past several years the school has been making significant strides in this area with substantial computer facilities and labs, MIS instruction, and the development of an Advanced Technology Classroom.

THE ADVANCED TECHNOLOGY CLASSROOM

The Advanced Technology Classroom at Western Connecticut State University was initially a joint project with IBM. The classroom itself consists of a "smart lectern" built around pen input technology, a rear projection system, remote keypads, computers with specialized desks, decision support software, and audiovisual support components.

The Smart Lectern

The Smart Lectern is the core component of the advanced technology system. It consists of an IBM PC-AT, audiovisual electronics, software that coordinates and manages all other hardware and audiovisual support, and a pen input plasma panel. The computer in the lectern has a keyboard which allows the instructor to show or modify information on the rear projection screen. The plasma panel provides classroom options for the instructor. One of these options is the use of the electronic blackboard. By using a light pen on the plasma panel, the instructor can write or draw in four colors; execute circles; squares, or rectangles with just a touch of the pen; or annotate information on the screen. The panel also shows the instructor's notes, the sequence of graphics, video and keyboard responses, and a configuration of the classroom. There are also additional special effects available.

Rear Projection System

The rear projection system consists of a 3-foot by 4-foot screen in the front of the classroom, recessed into the wall along with stereo speakers on either side. Presentations are controlled via a hand-held remote unit.

Keypads

A cornerstone of this classroom is the keypad response system. Each student has an alpha-numeric keypad at his/her desk which is connected to the smart lectern. Keypad questions are asked either verbally or are authored into the lesson and appear on the large screen. Students indicate their answers for multiple-choice, true-false, yes-no, scale, or numeric questions. The concept of the keypad is threefold. First, keypads increase interactivity by keeping students active throughout the class period. Second, unlike the traditional classroom environment where the instructor asks a question and one person answers it (with many of the remainder of the students "tuned out"), answering with keypads involves everyone simultaneously. Finally, the results are shown instantaneously in the form of bar charts. This gives immediate feedback to instructors and students alike. The instructors can see whether the students understand the material and if not, they can remediate. For the students, they don't need to feel embarrassed to give their answers (and perhaps get them wrong). The keypad system provides anonymity.

The computer in the smart lectern also can capture data. If students are assigned seats, the keypad system can provide real-time testing. Data can be stored so instructors have a history of how well particular students answered questions. They are able to know who is struggling with the material and can provide the necessary intervention. Historical data can also be shown on the screen allowing the present class to see how students in the past answered a particular question. Finally, the plasma panel itself has the option of showing who answered the question and who did not, as well as what answers each student gave. This is meant to provide a means of helping students and not to monitor or embarrass them.

Computers and Desks

The room itself is set up in a U-shape with students having their own desks. The desks are connected to one another and they face the rear projection screen. Each student has a computer recessed in the specially designed desk. The computers contain various software packages and are networked together. In addition, one station serves as the coordinating station and is connected to the rear projection screen as well. On the top of each desk is a plexiglass square which allows the students to look down and see their computer screens without the monitors having to be on top of the desks, thereby restricting visibility and inhibiting cross discussion by students.

Decision Support Software

The latest addition to the Advanced Technology Classroom is the group decision support software, Visionquest, by Collaborative Technologies, Inc. This software expands the Advanced Technology Classroom into an electronic meeting room. The software allows the students to do electronic brainstorming, to rate, rank, allocate points, and to vote on the results of their brainstorming. This information is on every student's monitor as well as projected on the large screen in the front of the room. This addition allows students to answer questions using longer responses than merely true-false, yes-no or numeric entries. It also can be used for case study analysis by the entire class as well as an inventory of options for action to be taken. It also enables students as well as professionals to conduct electronic meetings.

Group decision support systems enhance group discussion by providing everyone equal access to the discussion. Students who are inhibited or non-assertive can feel free to add their ideas to the list of ideas generated by others.

At the same time, those who are overly assertive can no longer monopolize the discussion or impose their ideas on others.

Audiovisual Support Components

In addition to the above hardware, the classroom contains additional audiovisual support: a laser disc, a 3/4 inch VHS player, a 1/2 inch VHS player, an audiocassette player, and a Videoshow player that plays the computer graphics shown on the screen. A printer is connected to the coordinating computer which provides immediate hard copy of group discussions using Visionquest software or any other information on the computer screen.

COURSEWARE

Courses were specifically developed or adapted for use in the Advanced Technology Classroom (ATC) and are currently being utilized there; the ATC allows for a multimedia presentation of course content in an exciting, interactive environment.

Course Presentation

The courses in the ATC consist of a series of graphic images: icons, word charts or both, presented in a sequenced fashion interspersed with video clips and/or music. As instructors go through their lessons, a series of images are projected on the screen. The benefit of such conceptual visualization is well documented in the literature. Unlike a transparency or slide, the technology allows for one bullet of information to be projected at a time. It also offers the opportunity for animation. Video clips can be authored into the presentation and automatically activated using the remote unit without having to start and stop the equipment each time. By careful selection of such clips, actual visual examples can be given for each of the points presented. Keypad questions can be asked to get student responses to the actions taken or not taken. The net effect is to have a seamless presentation with the instructor free to roam the classroom using nothing more than a remote unit to activate every part of the multimedia presentation.

Courseware Development

Each course was developed by its own instructor who designed the course, selected all images, selected the graphics software used, developed all the graphics, and authored the course. The course literally consisted of hundreds of computer graphic images. Each course was field-tested during its development and is currently used on a regular basis in each semester. Two of the business courses developed and used include Operations Management and Negotiation and Conflict Resolution.

PRODUCTION/OPERATIONS MANAGEMENT COURSE

Courseware was developed for a course entitled Operations Management which is a required course in the B.B.A. program. The purpose of the course is to give students a survey of current managerial approaches utilized to efficiently and effectively produce goods and services. This includes such topics as quality, production planning, project management, materials management, work methods and measurements, and capacity management. While the course is problem oriented, it would not be characterized as "quantitative." Problems or cases are used to illustrate management problems, potential solutions, and management approaches.

Courseware

The courseware was designed closely around *Operations Management*, first edition, by Vonderembse and White and published by West Publishing. The transparency masters that are supplied with the book were extensively used as guides in making computer visuals. Some of the videotape segments provided with the book were also used. All computer visuals were developed using the Freelance graphics software.

The courseware was developed in an interactive and incremental manner over several semesters. During the first semester, computer visuals and keypad questions were prepared as time permitted as part of normal course preparation. Approximately twenty hours per week were devoted to this. By the end of this semester, standard formats and procedures for developing the courseware were derived. These included standardized color schemes, type fonts and heights, and visual labeling and naming. The latter became critical as the number of visuals exceeded 750.

The second semester was one of extensive additions and revisions which probably consumed as much time as the original iteration. There was little resemblance with the end products of the first two semesters. In particular, many text charts were converted to pictorial representations, problems solutions were divided into many small steps, and keypad questions were made more challenging and extensive. For instance, many bullet charts were converted into multiple charts with an illustrative drawing for each. Keypad questions became more subjective in nature where the students would be quizzed, "How would you handle this problem?" or "What is the real problem?" rather than "Which is the correct answer?" End of chapter problems were encoded into computer visuals and then the solutions were incrementally developed through multiple visuals and keypad questions.

The third semester was used to refine and reorganize. Segments of the course were altered based on problems noted in the previous semester.

Assessment

During the second and third semesters, one section of the course was taught in the ATC utilizing the courseware and one was taught in a normal classroom setting. The same professor, syllabus, etc. were used in both sections. The differences between the two sections were the ATC hardware and courseware and use of computer-generated visuals rather than simplified transparencies. Student achievements, interest in the subject, attendance, and opinions were recorded.

Students nearly unanimously preferred the ATC approach. They found the course easier and had better attendance. The same material was often covered in less time in the ATC. But surprisingly, no significant difference was found in terms of student performance on exams. The students claimed to have spent less time learning the material but this was not converted into higher attainments. Students appear to work just hard enough to get their desired grade. Instructors plan to add more material and depth to the course now that additional time is available in the ATC environment.

NEGOTIATION AND CONFLICT RESOLUTION

Negotiation and Conflict Resolution is a graduate-level course in the MBA curriculum. Graduate students in nursing, education, and health care administration also use the course for their programs. The purpose of the course is to teach students how to negotiate collaboratively in order to solve work and interpersonal conflict. The course content consists of understanding conflict, competitive negotiation tactics, collaborative negotiation techniques, planning and preparation, using power, negotiation communication techniques, personality and negotiation, alternative dispute resolution techniques, and the effect of groups on negotiation. The nature of the course requires that students first learn the techniques of negotiation, then apply and practice them by actually negotiating cases with each other. Consequently, it is a very experiential course.

Use of Technology

The ATC proved to be an ideal environment to teach an advanced-level experimental course such as Negotiation and Conflict Resolution. The multimedia environment allows students to view examples of different negotiation styles. The keypads provide the opportunity for students to choose which tactics are most appropriate for different situations. The group decision support system allows teams to identify various options that may be acceptable to their opponents. In fact, such software is a key tool in moving negotiations from a competitive approach to a collaborative problem-solving model. The computer graphics allow the important didactic part of the course to be taught with creativity and excitement. The conceptual visualization aids students in understanding and remembering complex theories and applications. The software employed is Pictureit which is used with the Videoshow unit for presentation of visuals.

Assessment

A review of the Negotiation and Conflict Resolution course taught in the ATC leads to a number of conclusions. The first is that such an environment allows for more material to be covered than if presented in a regular classroom. The general consensus is that between ten percent and fifteen percent more material can be covered in each teaching session. However, these results cannot be realized unless the images presented by the computer graphics are distributed to the students. When they are not, students are too busy taking notes or spending their time trying to copy complex images presented on the screen. By providing hard copy of these images, students in effect "get the notes." This allows students the opportunity of listening, participating, and just annotating their notes.

In addition, student attention and involvement increases due to the involvement with keypads and the group decision support software.

Reaction of Students

Based on research conducted, students appear to be very pleased with the course. Their reactions are extremely positive and the course is closed out each semester it is offered. Students rate courses in the ATC consistently higher than similar courses that do not make use of the ATC. The students rate the keypads, course organization, audiovisuals, and computer graphics consistently high.

CONCLUSION

The use of the Advanced Technology Classroom at Western Connecticut State University enhances the educational process for the student as well as for the instructor. It offers a more exciting learning experience and has shown real gains in productivity, satisfaction levels, and information learned. It is also an evolutionary system. As new software and hardware are developed, the ATC will continue to be modified to meet the needs of the students, the instructors, and the community. In short, it is a very effective means of providing a twenty-first century education for tomorrow's students.

Chapter

33

The Advanced
Technology Classroom

Marla J. Fischer

Professor of Management Information Systems
Ancell School of Business, Western Connecticut State University,
Danbury, Connecticut

Advancements in computer and information technology are having a profound effect on the manner in which instruction is delivered in a growing number of university classrooms. High-tech, multimedia, instructional delivery systems are gradually eclipsing conventional methods of instruction and will soon replace the lecterns and blackboards that have been the hallmark of university classrooms the world over for several centuries.

My introduction to the "new age" classroom began in the summer of 1988 when the IBM Corporation funded our grant proposal for a university-based rendition of their Advanced Technology Classroom, also hailed as the Classroom of the Future.[1] The Advanced Technology Classroom (ATC) is an innovative, computerized, instructional delivery system used by IBM for training corporate executives at their Management Training Center in Armonk, New York. Prior to awarding the grant, IBM had used the ATC exclusively for in-house training. Under the terms of the grant award, Western Connecticut State University received the ATC system at cost, together with supervised instruction on its use, in return for developing courseware for the ATC, field-testing the ATC's effectiveness in a university setting, and serving as a demonstration site for this futuristic classroom.

I was fortunate in being among the first faculty members at the university to have classes scheduled in this new and revolutionary electronic classroom. It is from this perspective, as a novitiate in instructional delivery systems, that I provide the following account of what these high-tech classrooms are like, using as a prototype WestConn's ATC. In addition to describing the technical and pedagogical features of the system, and student and faculty reactions, I also identify some of the issues and challenges that must be addressed in order for high-tech, instructional delivery systems to become successfully integrated into university settings.

DESCRIPTION OF THE SYSTEM

The ATC is an integrated, multimedia, interactive, instructional delivery system. In the ATC a large (4 ft. x 4 ft.), high-resolution video screen replaces the traditional blackboard. A specially designed electronic podium containing a central microcomputer serves as the master control panel for the classroom. From this podium, the instructor can control and coordinate all components of the system.

What makes the podium unique is its ability to orchestrate seamless, multimedia presentations without requiring the instructor to independently activate each component of the instructional sequence. The instructor can, for example, present information either on the electronic blackboard using a sonic pen or on the video screen where computer-generated graphics, videotape, or material from laser disks can be used to illustrate key concepts and ideas. Without leaving the podium, the instructor can, as an example, present introductory information from an audio cassette, follow this immediately by a video tape/laser disk segment illustrating the concept, and follow this with instructor-prepared visuals and graphics that highlight the key points which were introduced. The instructor can access scanned images, full-motion video, digitized images, and computer-generated graphics from the podium as well as from a remote, hand-held unit.

Each student's desk in the ATC is equipped with a student response unit to respond to variable-choice formatted questions posed by the instructor. These student keypad units are not designed to take the place of normal pupil-instructor interaction but are used instead to keep the instructor apprised of how well each student is comprehending information during the course of the lesson. The microcomputer built into the podium informs the instructor of each student's response to the keypad questions and provides summary data on the performance of the class as a whole. Access to these data allows the instructor to make "online" decisions regarding the pace of instruction: whether to move on to new information or to provide further explication of topics. This feature of the system eliminates the need for instructors to scan the faces of the class in search of nonverbal cues that might signal frustration or confusion.

The design of the ATC also allows the instructor to share the keypad question results with the class. The instructor can display on screen not only a histogram indicating what percentage of the class answered a particular keypad question correctly (or incorrectly) but also comparison data showing how the class compares to previous classes responding to the same question.

An additional feature of WestConn's ATC is that each student's desk contains a personal computer. The PC unit is mounted under a specially designed desk.[2] A glass top on the desk allows the student to view a recessed screen; a slide-out drawer contains the keyboard. The advantage of this design is that the visual field in the classroom is not obstructed by PC hardware that might otherwise prevent normal viewing and interaction. The PCS in the ATC are networked within the classroom (LAN) and connected to the university mainframe which provides both local and campus-wide connectivity.

PEDAGOGICAL FEATURES OF THE SYSTEM

There is a paradox in the fact that while learning theorists long ago identified the critical elements essential for facilitating learning (Gagne, 1979; Hilgard and Bower, 1966), these elements are often ignored in the design and delivery of instruction, particularly at the university level. Perhaps, it is because most faculty at the university level hold a Ph.D. degree and Ph.D. programs are not structured or intended to prepare teachers (Lewis and Altbach, 1992). For optimal learning to take place, there has to be a careful marriage between the structure of the lesson and established principles of learning. Perhaps the greatest virtue of the ATC is its capability for weaving basic principles of learning into the fabric of a lesson/course.

One example of the ATC's capability for capitalizing on established principles of learning is its provisions for interactivity (Horowitz, 1988). Basically, interactivity refers to the dynamic exchange that takes place between the learner and other components of the system and the extent to which the learner becomes an active participant in the learning process. Interactivity may include several kinds of engagement: a learner may engage the content/materials of the lesson, a learner may engage the instructor who is directing the lesson, or a learner may engage other students participating in the lesson. Each form of interactivity plays an important role in maximizing opportunities for learning.

The design of the ATC enhances opportunities for all forms of interactivity. In the ATC students interact with the instructor not only through the traditional questions and answers but also through the use of keypad response units and student PCS. The incorporation of periodic keypad questions into a lesson forces full participation by all members of the class and provides the instructor with a more accurate indication of student progress than voluntary responses. An inherent benefit of the keypad units is the confidentiality they provide to students, since responses to keypad questions are essentially confidential (only the instructor knows). This means that students can respond to questions without fear of being publicly embarrassed by an incorrect answer. In a conventional classroom a sizeable number of students may withdraw from participation for this reason.

Interactivity with the content/materials, the instructor, and other members of the class also occurs through the personal computers. There are, for example, numerous software packages that enable students in math classes to analyze data that the instructor has provided as part of a lesson. There are also software programs that let students type in their own thoughts or comments on a particular topic which can then be released by the student for inspection by the instructor or by the class as a whole. Classroom PCs can be used for library searches and for a multitude of other instructional purposes during the course of a lesson.

A related pedagogical virtue of the ATC is that it allows students to monitor their own progress. The increased opportunities for interactivity provide students with steady feedback on whether their responses are correct. This immediate feedback serves to either reinforce prior learning or, alternatively, signal the student that more study and practice are necessary.

The ATC is also ideal for assisting the instructor in making the lesson relevant and meaningful. With its capability for utilizing multimedia, the ATC can make the learning experience dimensionally richer. With much greater facility than would be possible in a conventional college classroom, the ATC can open the door to a wide range of experiences. Students can be taken to distant locations around the globe to see "first-hand" the events and conditions they are studying. They can meet the experts in their discipline and hear personal accounts of their contributions. They can be exposed to broad applications of the principles and theories they are studying. In short, the learning experience can be made to transcend the classroom. By transcending the boundaries of space and time, the ATC provides access to a larger body of information in ways not possible in a traditional classroom. The end result is an enriched experiential base for learning.

The ability of the ATC to present first-hand information is by no means trivial. Since the beginning of time, instruction has centered heavily on information handed down from an indeterminable number of sources. The person acting as instructor served both as the repository for information and the conduit through which that information was communicated to the student. In serving in this dual role, the instructor (not the information) was the focus of the lesson, as well as the interface through which the learner came in contact with information. The depth and purity of the information presented rested entirely on the accuracy of the instructor's sources (whatever they might be) and on the instructor's ability to communicate the information with minimal distortion. With instructional systems such as the ATC, education moves closer than ever before to the purest form of information transfer, to instruction that is firsthand and experiential, as opposed to second-hand and anecdotal.

Yet another pedagogical virtue of the system is it can cater to individual differences in learning styles. First, the very nature of the system encourages the instructor to present information both auditorily and visually. Though it is customary for instructors in traditional classrooms to periodically backup their spoken lectures with a variety of visuals, there is a tendency to rely primarily on auditory presentation. The design and operation of the ATC tends to strike a better balance in how information is communicated. In doing so, the ATC manages to accommodate both auditory as well as visual learners. Indeed, there is a body of literature suggesting that for all students, learning is facilitated when abstract concepts are visually broken down into more concrete, digestible units (Arnheim, 1969). Through what has been termed "conceptual visualization," the learner can comprehend concepts that would remain unclear in the absence of visual dissection.

A second way in which the system meets the needs of students with different learning styles is its capability for accommodating both extraverted and introverted learners. While extraverted learners tend to be comfortable participating in classroom interactions, their introverted counterparts are usually more reluctant to engage either the teacher or their fellow classmates (Eysenck, 1976). The incorporation of the keypad units into the ATC affords an opportunity for introverted students to participate covertly in the lesson without having to sacrifice their anonymity.

A final pedagogical benefit of the ATC, and one that is extremely important, is its impact on the structure and organization of the lesson. Since the use of the ATC requires preprogramming the system for the presentation of instructional materials, the instructor is obliged to pay strict attention to the structure and orchestration of each lesson. As a consequence, instructors using the ATC tend to have a greater awareness of the structural integrity of their lessons than those whose presentation format allows them to be more casual about how course content will be presented.

STUDENT AND FACULTY REACTIONS

Given the many pedagogical features of the ATC, the question remains, is it effective? To answer this question, faculty participating in the ATC project at WestConn administered a survey to students taking courses in the ATC.[3] The survey asked students to evaluate specific features of the ATC and to rate the overall effectiveness of the ATC as compared to a more traditional classroom setting. The features that were examined included the effectiveness of the computer-based visuals, the impact of the ATC on the organization and sequencing of instruction, the effectiveness of the keypad response units, and the effectiveness of the ATC in fostering interest and motivation.

Students were asked to respond to each survey item by indicating their rating on a seven-point Likert scale. Three points on the scale were prelabeled to assist students in arriving at their decisions. A low rating of "one" indicated that, for the feature under consideration, instruction in the ATC was "much less effective" as compared to a regular classroom. A rating of "four," the mid-point on the scale, indicated that the two instructional environments were perceived as being "the same." A high rating of "seven," indicated that the ATC was perceived to be "much better" with regard to the feature under consideration.

The results of the survey indicated a high degree of student satisfaction with the ATC. For each feature examined, ninety percent (or higher) of the students rated the ATC as being better than the traditional classroom with the majority of responses clustering around "six" and "seven" on the seven-point scale. Anecdotal remarks from students included comments such as "sparks interest," "sticks in your mind," "keeps all students involved," "allows maximum participation," and "shows us things we wouldn't see otherwise."

Like students, instructors teaching in the ATC also had positive reactions to the instructional system. All of the instructors involved with the ATC project felt that the electronic classroom stimulated student learning. They reported increased attentiveness from their students and a greater number of unsolicited statements extolling the virtues of the classroom. Instructors reported, in addition, that the system enhanced their instructional effectiveness by promoting greater classroom efficiency. They found less of a need to repeat information and received fewer requests from students for clarifying examples. The time that would otherwise have been allocated for these activities was therefore available to use for other purposes, such as providing additional instruction or engaging in other class activities. Although the time savings reported varied across instructors, it ranged from five to fifteen minutes of additional time per class period.

Indeed, the ATC was so well-received by students, faculty, and administration it served as a catalyst in initiating campus-wide interest in information technology systems and provided the impetus for the installation of additional hi-tech classrooms at the university.

ISSUES AND CHALLENGES

The many positive features of the ATC and other high-tech instructional systems will not by themselves guarantee that these innovative systems will automatically find their niche on today's university campus. Corresponding adjustments in the university ecosystem, in the pedagogical and administrative infrastructure, must also be made in order for these systems to become ecologically rooted. While some of these adjustments are trivial and can be made quite easily, others are more challenging and require new modes of thinking.

Safeguarding the System

Because a high-technology classroom represents a considerable financial investment, special security provisions are required to ensure that the system will remain intact and in working order. In our own case, we found it necessary to keep the more portable components of our system in cabinets within the classroom. In addition, we installed a more comprehensive security system including an alarm, so that only specific individuals would have access to the classroom. However trivial this may seem; nonetheless, it represents a provision that is not necessary for more traditional classrooms.

Using the System

Challenges relating to the use of the system fall under two distinct categories: those that relate more broadly to the role of the instructor in the educational process and those that pertain to the software/hardware associated with instructional delivery systems.

The first of these challenges is entirely new and has to do with the impact that high-tech instructional delivery systems will have on traditional modes of instruction. In a conventional classroom it is the instructor who is the focus of the lesson: the instructor typically presents and explains the content of the lesson and describes the conditions or events under study. In this capacity, the instructor serves as the repository, the filter, and the funnel for virtually all information. If we are to truly take advantage of what instructional delivery systems havé to offer, we must begin to redefine our role as instructors. Where possible, we must engage the technology to provide our students with first-hand accounts and observations of the topics they are studying. Source-based presentations should take precedence over instructor-based presentations. In implementing this change, the intent is not to diminish the importance of the instructor's contribution to the learning process, but instead to underscore the pedagogical value of providing students with more direct experiences with the subject matter. With this shift in role, the instructor assumes the responsibility for orchestrating and directing the lesson and relinquishes the responsibility of serving as the sole provider of information. Along with this shift in role, the instructor continues to highlight and clarify information and to provide focus and perspective to the overall lesson.

Making this transition and learning to use these systems appropriately is apparently no simple matter. Too often, fledgling users get sidetracked by the graphics capability of these systems and come to see them as nothing more than high-tech replacements for the overhead projector. Misled by this perception, new users will devote virtually all of their instructional planning time to the development of computer-generated visuals to punctuate their instruction. While the introduction of snazzy visuals into a lesson may have legitimate pedagogical value, the indiscriminate use of visuals prevents the user from fully exploiting the powerful learning tools within the system.

To take full advantage of these powerful instructional systems, we must avoid fixating on a single feature and must try instead to design lessons that tap the entire range of features engineered into these systems. This would include, but not be limited to, provision for the presentation of source-based instruction and materials, provision for various forms of interactivity, provision for ancillary visuals that help to clarify and consolidate learning, and provision for incorporating established principles of learning. Only when used in this way, can these systems live up to their promise of leading us into a new age of learning.

Having said something about the role of the instructor in using these systems, we can now turn to considerations that relate to the hardware/software. When we first began the project at WestConn, it took approximately forty hours of preparation time to prepare the courseware materials for a one-hour lesson. Because the software available for this purpose was both intricate and cumbersome, a considerable degree of technical expertise was required in order to develop materials independently. Although courseware development packages are gradually improving, much of the software currently available on the market continues to be unnecessarily complicated rather than user-friendly. There is a pressing need for software that can be used by people without a degree in computer science. There is also a need for publishers to offer courseware materials predesigned by content and instructional systems specialists, particularly materials that can be later customized to suit the specific needs of the instructor. Until these materials become available, it may be necessary for universities to offer some form of assistance, such as reassigned time or courseware development services to faculty who need to prepare materials for instruction in high-technology classrooms. Other avenues might include the establishment of user-groups/consortia across universities through which materials might be jointly developed and shared.

A separate, but related, challenge concerns the fact that much of the existing software used for creating and authoring instructional courseware interfaces only with the hardware/software of specific instructional delivery systems. As a consequence, a user cannot take advantage of available software packages (however powerful they might be) unless those packages happen to be compatible with the platform requirements of the instructional delivery system in use. The problem of incompatibility not only limits one's ability to freely select software for courseware development, but also, in the event of a modification in the system's platform, renders unusable any courseware developed using the previous system. After spending literally hundreds of hours developing materials for a given course, instructors are understandably reluctant to introduce new software/hardware that would require them to trash their instructional materials and begin all over again, even though the newer platform may offer distinct advantages. There is, therefore, a critical need for industry standards that will allow for greater compatibility of hardware/software across the various manufacturers.

Supporting the System

Machines sometimes totally break down or more subtly fail to function in the manner in which they were intended. Given the number of high-tech devices associated with an instructional delivery system, and the interdependency of many of these items, the possibility of a system malfunction needs to be anticipated. Apart from outright mechanical failures, there is also the possibility that another instructor using the classroom might change or adjust something to suit a particular need and later forget to restore the modification to its original condition. Whether due to mechanical failure or human oversight, system malfunctions can have disastrous consequences for a scheduled lesson. The price we pay for the benefits provided by the technology is that, to an extent greater than ever before, instructors are at the mercy of the system. When the entire lesson is authored into the computer, together with whatever exercises or activities are planned for the students, it is exceedingly difficult to salvage the lesson in the event of a system failure. For this reason provisions must be made to respond to sudden breakdowns.

The most obvious provision is to have technical support services available to respond to such emergencies, like calling road service to handle automotive emergencies. Indeed, it is often the case that malfunctions can be rectified expeditiously by a knowledgeable technician familiar with the elaborate workings of the system. The challenge is to get a technician to the classroom within a time frame that would make it feasible for the instructor to resume the lesson once the problem is corrected. Recognizing this need, some institutions have adopted operational guidelines for responding to such emergencies. In some institutions, support personnel are required to address and correct a problem within fifteen minutes after the report of a dysfunction. Of course, there will be occasions where more time is needed, but the existence of operational guidelines ensures, at the very least, that an entire class presentation won't be scrapped for a malfunction that might take five minutes to rectify.

Modifying the System

As with all technological products, the components of instructional delivery systems are constantly being redesigned and upgraded with each new generation offering advantages over their predecessors. Accordingly, there is always the temptation, so long as the funds are available, to upgrade the existing system to remain on the cutting edge of technological innovation. How often and in what manner systems should be modified are critical decisions. If a system is updated too frequently, users may be forever relearning how to operate the system or redesigning existing courseware for use in the system. Frequent changes may also compromise ongoing instructional research on the system. One way to prevent this is to designate time frames during which users would agree to maintain the system in its current configuration without changes or upgrades. Such agreements would allow those working with the system to use their time more productively. When the time for modification does arrive, decisions regarding specific changes ought to be made primarily by the instructional faculty using the system, in concert with the technical support team that maintains it. There are many instances where a proposed upgrade may have technical merit but may fail to meet the specific instructional needs of those using the system. If the primary objective of these systems is to improve the effectiveness of instruction, then instructional considerations must be the overriding factor in decision making.

CONCLUSION

Spawned by advances in computer technology, the information age is now upon us. With the dawn of the information age comes the capability for immediate access to vast funds of human knowledge and experience. Recognizing the potential value of information retrieval in instruction, scientists and engineers have begun to develop computerized classroom systems that may ultimately revolutionize the educational process.

High-tech instructional delivery systems, such as IBM's Advanced Technology Classroom, are designed to maximize opportunities for learning. The technology engineered into these systems not only allows users to have immediate access to multiple forms of information but also allows for the creation of learning environments that both engage the student and exploit established principles of learning.

To take maximum advantage of these innovative instructional delivery systems, educators need to make fundamental changes not only in their approach to instruction, but also in the administrative and organizational infrastructures that support and nurture the instructional process. Taking these measures help ensure that future students will be successful in acquiring the knowledge and skill they will need to be productive citizens of the twenty-first century.

ACKNOWLEDGMENTS

Faculty participating in the ATC project included R. Benson, G. Buccini, M. Chalmers, J. Cilliza, and L. Kershnar. The ATC Project would not have been possible without the support and effort of numerous individuals. The author would like to acknowledge A. Stewart, J. Hancock, and S. Feldman for their role in making the project a reality; as well as P. Steinkrauss, F. Leuthauser, and B. Blaylock for their contributions to the project. Technical support services were provided by B. Clement and A-V Services of New Jersey. The project team is especially indebted to H. Horowitz, S. Rolando, E. Katz, M. Daily, and their colleagues at IBM for the training and guidance provided in the use of this facility.

NOTES

1. IBM awarded the Advanced Technology Classroom Grant to Western Connecticut State University as the result of a proposal submitted in April of 1988 by Drs. R. Benson, G. Buccini, and the author.
2. The personal computers and special desks for the ATC were acquired through a State of Connecticut, Department of Higher Education, High Technology Program Grant awarded to the author in August 1989.
3. The results reported here are based on data collected by Drs. G. Buccini, J. Cilliza, and the author.

REFERENCES

Arnheim, R. (1969). *Visual thinking.* Berkeley, CA: University of California Press.

Eysenck, H.J. (1976). *The measurement of personality.* Baltimore, Maryland: University Park Press.

Gagne, R.M. (1979). *The conditions of learning* (2nd ed.). New York: Holt, Rinehart & Winston.

Hilgard, E. & Bower, G.H. (1966). *Theories of learning.* New York: Appleton-Century Crofts.

Horowitz, H. (1988). "Student response systems: Interactivity in a classroom environment." Paper presented at the Sixth Conference of Interactive Instructional Delivery, Society of Applied Learning.

Lewis, L. & Altbach, P. (1992). The new civil rights law and doctoral education. *Academe*, May/June, 12–14.

Part Five: The Web

Chapter
34

A Syllabus for a World Wide Web Writing Workshop

Jack R. Kayser
Educational Technology Specialist
Lafayette College, Easton, Pennyslvania

The development of the World Wide Web, or Web for short, has challenged the academic community to master a new medium of communication. Using the Web to explore knowledge is easy, but presenting knowledge is more difficult. It is possible for individuals to teach themselves how to write Web pages; however, the constraints of time or limited computer experience can inhibit such learning. Many students and faculty want to learn how to write their own Web pages but they need some guidance to get started.

In order to provide an organized format for teaching Web writing at Lafayette College, a syllabus has been developed, and it has been successfully used in a number of Web writing workshops involving students, faculty, administrators and alumni. The workshop takes approximately two hours, after which time all participants have created their own home page. An outline of the syllabus is presented in this paper, along with a discussion of the knowledge and hardware necessary for conducting a Web writing workshop.

PREREQUISITES FOR TEACHING

Several elements should be in place before attempting to instruct others to create Web pages. These prerequisites can be divided into three areas: computer literacy, hardware, and software.

Computer literacy is a definite prerequisite. It should be required that all participants in a Web authoring class be familiar with using a word processor and managing computer files. Knowledge pertaining to computer languages or programming is helpful, but not necessary. Participants should also be familiar with a drawing or graphics package if they intend to create or modify images.

Computer hardware should be in place and accessible. A computer workstation should be available for every participant. Students learn best by doing, not by watching. Each workstation should be operating with a graphical user interface such as Windows or Macintosh. These computers should be connected to a local area network, which also includes a computer that is running a Web server. The server acts as a host for storing and distributing the Web documents. In order to access the Internet, the local network should be connected to a regional network, which in turn is connected to the Internet at large.

Web pages can be created and viewed on a computer that is not attached to a network. In such an instance, a Web browser is used to view disk or hard drive files in the local mode. This method is adequate for basic Web documents that are composed of just graphics, text, or local hyperlinks.

There are some software essentials as well. Computers which are connected to a local area network must be running Transmission Control Protocol and Internet Protocol software (TCP/IP), while the Web server must be running a Hypertext Transmission Protocol (HTTP) server. Individual workstations must also be running a browser program in order to display Web documents. Several Web browsers are available at no cost for educational purposes.

A basic word processor is required to write the Hypertext Markup Language (HTML) that makes up a text Web document. Programs exist that assist an author in writing HTML; however, since basic Web pages are straightforward and brief, a simple text processor is sufficient.

A graphics package is required if images are to be created or modified (cropped, resized, or reformatted). Several basic shareware programs are available to carry out such tasks. Many sophisticated image and graphics programs exist to carry out more advanced creation or manipulation work, however, simpler programs are less likely to overwhelm a beginner.

The final group of programs that must be in place include Telnet, for controlling the computer that hosts the Web pages, and a program that uses File Transfer Protocol (FTP), for sending or deleting files.

With these elements—computer literacy, hardware, and software—in place, an instructor can proceed to teach a group to create their own Web pages. Before taking such a step though, some thought should be given to establishing the goals of the workshop and the outline of the syllabus.

GOALS

The goal of each participant in the workshop should be to create and store a home page on the network's server. The content of these home pages should be basic, with only text, hyperlinks, and graphics. In order to accomplish this, each participant must have a pre-existing user account on the host computer. Since the HTML and graphics files are created on a workstation, but stored on a host, some means of file transfer must take place. Account access and file transfer will require learning Telnet and FTP skills.

SYLLABUS

A general introduction to the Internet and the World Wide Web is appropriate at the beginning of the workshop. A demonstration of the World Wide Web through the use of a projection system can then outline the items that will be discussed during the presentation. During this demonstration an explanation of what a Uniform Resource Locator (URL) is, as well as how the host computer communicates with a workstation, will help the students understand the distributed nature of the Internet. Once a basic background is established, a more specific presentation can proceed, beginning with HTML.

It is useful to have an HTML tutorial up and running on the server for use during the presentation. This tutorial should delineate all the major examples of text and formatting, as well as in-page and out-of-page hyperlinks. The tutorial should also contain examples of in-line images, hyperlinked images, and images that act as hyperlinks. The tutorial serves as both a presentation tool and a reference for the participants.

After explaining how basic HTML documents are created, it is appropriate to discuss the various file formats that may be encountered on the Web. Although this syllabus only covers text, hyperlinks, and graphics, other elements can appear in a Web page, such as sound and video files. Presenting a list of the extension names will prepare the participants for the inevitable encounter with, or usage of, such files.

It is at this point in the instruction that the participants should be capable of constructing their first Web page. It is suggested that a simple pre-existing Web page be hyperlinked from the tutorial. This basic page (header, body, hyperlinks, and formatting tags) can serve as a template for the participants to modify by adding their own individual information. Participants should be encouraged to create hyperlinks to Web sites that are of personal interest. This initial assignment should contain several format styles, graphics, and at least one hyperlink. Approximately thirty minutes should be devoted to this writing activity, during which time the instructor can assess progress and offer advice.

Once the basic Web page is created and stored on a disk, the workstation browser can be used to view the document in the local mode. It is important to stress that new pages be checked over in the private local mode before sending the documents to the host computer, where anyone on Internet can view them.

After the Web pages have been reviewed and corrected in the local mode, they should be sent to the host computer. Before sending the files though, participants should be instructed to open up their accounts on the host and change their passwords. Each participant should be given his or her account address and original password, in addition to a set of instructions for running a Telnet program. If a display system is available, a demonstration of logging in, changing the password, and logging out, should be given. Many people who are unfamiliar with UNIX are reluctant to execute Telnet commands and should be given encouragement and guidance.

After changing their passwords, participants should be directed in the use of an FTP program to transfer their Web documents from the workstation to the host computer. It is advisable to discuss good FTP skills such as directory structure, how to list or change directories, and how to rename or delete files. These skills will improve Web page management and reduce the possibility of inactive files on the server.

The final step is the use of the Web browser in the URL mode to view the newly created pages. Once the participants see their pages via Internet, they are usually impressed and realize the utility of writing for the Web. From here on, it will be their personal interest that motivates them to improve their writing skills and develop more advanced Web pages.

CONCLUSION

This chapter has focused on the mechanics of teaching a two-hour workshop on writing Web pages. No attention has been given to the details of how Internet works or even defining the various HTML tags. It is likely that the individuals responsible for teaching the workshop will be familiar with these details. The intention here has been to outline the method and content of a syllabus that has worked on several occasions, for both faculty and students.

NOTES ON CONTRIBUTORS

James F. Aiton has been a physiology lecturer in the School of Biological and Medical Sciences, University of St. Andrews, Scotland, for fourteen years and is the organizer of the Animal Physiology and Histology course. His other computer-related responsibilities include acting as chairperson of the university computer users committee and also serving on the management boards of both the BioNet Teaching and Learning Technology program and the Computers in Teaching Initiative Center for Biology.

N. Faye Angel is assistant professor of business at Ferrum College, Ferrum, Virginia. She received an M.B.A. degree from Virginia Polytechnic Institute and State University. Since that time she has actively promoted computer use at all levels of education and has published in the area of employee computer monitoring.

Dorine Bennett, RRA is an instructor for the medical record programs at Dakota State University, Madison, South Dakota. Ms. Bennett also provides consulting services to a number of health care facilities and presents workshops on medical record topics. She received an A.A. in medical record technology and a B.S. in medical record administration from Dakota State University. She has completed coursework in the Master of Business Administration/Management of Information Systems program at the University of South Dakota, Vermillion, South Dakota. Prior to entering academia, Ms. Bennett worked with medical record departments in the long-term care and community health fields.

Ronald G. Benson is a professor of management and chairperson of the management department at the Ancell School of Business at Western Connecticut State University, Danbury, Connecticut. He teaches courses in the areas of operations management, total quality management, strategic planning, materials management and organizational behavior. Previously, he was employed by the General Electric Aircraft Engine Group, Magnum Electric Corporation, the Bendix Corporation, and the Sheller-Globe Corporation. He also has taught at Oregon State University and the University of Toledo. His education includes a B.S. in industrial engineering and an M.A. and Ph.D. in business administration, all from the University of Iowa.

Dick W. Birkholz received his B.S.E. in 1966 and master's in biology in 1968 at Emporia State University and his Ph.D. in botany at the University of Kansas in 1970. He came to Sheridan College, Sheridan, Wyoming, as an instructor of biology in 1971 and has taught biology and genetics for twenty-two years. During the last eleven summers he has taught general biology at the University of Wyoming. He became involved in microcomputers in 1981 when Apple II+ microcomputers were used in testing for the self-help modules for biology developed with an NSF CAUSE grant. Since 1984, Dr. Birkholz has served on various computer committees at Sheridan College and since 1988 he has served as coordinator of academic computing. From 1978 to 1991 he served as the chair of the natural science division. In the last ten years he has received numerous grants for science and math teacher education workshops, high technology equipment grants, and curriculum development grants.

John L. Bordley is professor of chemistry and computer science at Johns Hopkins University and has taught at The University of the South, Sewanee, Tennessee. He is director of academic computing and teaches a chemistry or computer science course each semester. He is interested in the use of computers in higher education and in interdisciplinary studies involving science.

Garrett Bozylinsky has served as the associate vice president for computing at Indiana University of Pennsylvania (IUP) from 1987-94. Since January 1994, he has served as the associate provost for information technology. Prior to his work at IUP, he served as the director of academic computing at Western New England College; assistant director for computing at the University of Maine at Orono (SSRI); and director of research and development at the University of Maine at Orono (BPA). Mr. Bozylinsky holds a B.A. in political science from Elizabethtown College and an M.A. in political science from George Washington University.

Drake R. Bradley is Charles A. Dana professor of psychology at Bates College, Lewiston, Maine. Dr. Bradley has published articles on visual perception, statistical simulation, and computer-assisted instruction in *Nature, Science, Perception and Psychophysics, Psychological Bulletin, Vision Research, Perception,* the *American Journal of Psychology,* the *Italian Journal of Psychology,* and *Behavior Research Methods, Instrumentation, and Computers.* Based on his use of computer technology, Dr. Bradley was awarded the Nan Weinstein Merit Award for innovation in teaching in 1987. In 1991, his statistical simulation program, DATASIM, was awarded first prize in True-BASIC's Best-of-BASIC competition. An aviation enthusiast and part-time aerobatic pilot, Dr. Bradley has recently developed courses which employ computer flight simulators to teach mathematical, spatial, navigational, and perceptual-motor skills.

Eugene P. Buccini is a professor of management at the Ancell School of Business of Western Connecticut State University, Danbury, Connecticut. He teaches courses in the areas of negotiation and conflict resolution, human resource management, human resource development, organizational behavior, and health care management. He has over eighteen years experience both in consulting and direct line responsibility in executive and employee relations positions. He received a Ph.D. from New York University specializing in human resource management, an M.B.A. from Pace University in personnel and labor relations, and a B.A. in economics from New York University. He is also the author of *Personal Policies and Procedures for Health Care Facilities* and various articles in the field.

Jeanne Buckley, Ed.D. received her doctorate in educational technology from Columbia University and her master's in instructional design from Syracuse University. She served as educational technologist for the Title III grant at Bucks County Community College, Newtown, Pennsylvania, from January 1991 to May 1992. Dr. Buckley has taught at Columbia University, St. Joseph's University, and Bucks County Community College and is currently an adjunct professor of instructional technology at Penn State Great Valley and Philadelphia College of Textiles and Science. Dr. Buckley's book *Multimedia Technologies and Instructional Design: Responding to the Challenge* is published by Educational Technology Publications.

Paul Burdick is a composer and teacher, specializing in the area of music and technology. A member of the theory department at New England Conservatory, he also serves as the director of its Music and Computer Studio. Mr. Burdick has composed chamber, orchestral, and computer music for film, television, and live performance. His music has been heard on PBS, New England Sports Channel, and in live concerts in Boston and New York. In addition, Mr. Burdick has worked in conjunction with the Soundtrack Recording Studios (Boston, New York) as a software consultant, developing algorithmic compositional environments. Music developed by Mr. Burdick at Soundtrack Studios is now broadcast on Cable Television throughout New England.

Carole Carmody is director of information technology at Bloomfield College in Bloomfield, New Jersey. She also teaches computer literacy and sociology. Dr. Carmody holds a B.A. in sociology from Marymount Manhattan College and an M.A. and Ph.D. in anthropology from New York University. She has done field research on political change in the Caribbean and is currently doing research on African-American communities.

Constance Chismar has taught English and writing courses for over twenty years. She has a B.A. in English from Georgian Court College, New Jersey; an M.A. in reading, with reading specialist certification, from Montclair State College, New Jersey, and she received an Ed.D. in English education from Rutgers University, New Jersey. She is currently associate professor of English education and director of the Computer Writing Center at Georgian Court College. Her primary concern is the influence of computer integration on language and learning in college classrooms.

S. James Corvey is director of educational computing at Mountain View College, Dallas, Texas. He holds a B.A. and M.Ed. from Florida Atlantic University and M.L.S. from State University of New York, Geneseo. His background in education includes work at Florida Atlantic University, State

University of New York, Geneseo; Miami Dade Community College; Houston Community College; and Mountain View College of the Dallas County Community College District. He has presented papers and workshops at national and international conferences on learning and cognitive style and has consulted at scores of colleges and universities, as well as for the ARAMCO schools in Saudi Arabia.

William Creighton is the director of academic computing services at Indiana University of Pennsylvania (IUP). He currently serves as a governing board member for the Consortium for Computing in Undergraduate Education (C-Cue) and has presented professional papers about computing-related topics at various national conferences. He has twenty-five years of experience as a computing professional and has served IUP in a number of computing service capacities for nearly twenty years. He holds a B.A. in computer science, a M.A. in adult and community education, and is committed to lifelong learning.

Ellen M. Dauwer, S.C., Ph.D. is an assistant professor of computer information systems at the College of Saint Elizabeth in Morristown, New Jersey, where she teaches courses in application software, database systems, programming, and statistics. She received her doctorate in management of computer resources from New York University. She has had extensive experience teaching mathematics and computer science on the secondary level and conducts in-service programs for teachers in both elementary and secondary schools. A member of the Sisters of Charity of Convent Station, New Jersey, she is an avid photographer, a hobby that further links computer information systems and art.

Lyle Davidson is a lecturer on education at the Harvard Graduate School of Education and a member of Harvard Project Zero. He is currently working with the Lincoln Center Institute. He writes on portfolio assessment, musical cognition in child development, and pedagogy. A composer, he is chairperson of the theory department at the New England Conservatory of Music, Boston, Massachusetts, and a member of the composition and music education faculties. He is a member of the new music ensemble, Dinosaur Annex, and his music is published by E.C. Shirmer Music Company and recorded on CRI.

Wayne Draznin is assistant professor and Computer Arts Program coordinator at the Cleveland Institute of Art. He holds an M.F.A. from the School of Art and Design, University of Illinois at Chicago. His artwork has been exhibited nationally, and his writings on issues and practices in contemporary art have been published in *Art and America, New Art Examiner, Dialogue,* and elsewhere.

Patricia Ericsson is an instructor of English and director of writing at Dakota State University, Madison, South Dakota. She has published articles and presented papers about computers and composition and the ethical concerns of computers and composition. She is a member of the editorial board of *Computers and Composition* and *TEXT Technology*.

Marla J. Fischer has been teaching at the university level for the past twenty years and is currently a professor in the management information systems department in the Ancell School of Business at Western Connecticut State University in Danbury, Connecticut. For the past five years, Dr. Fischer has been a member of the IBM/WCSU Advanced Technology Classroom (ATC) project team responsible for developing and demonstrating ATC courseware and for providing instruction in the ATC. In conjunction with the ATC project, Dr. Fischer has also served as the ATC Research Coordinator and has presented papers on instructional technology systems at both national and international conferences. During a recent sabbatical leave Dr. Fischer studied instructional delivery systems in university and corporate settings both here and abroad.

Susan P. Fowell is currently a lecturer in the Department of Information Studies at the University of Sheffield. She holds a B.Sc. in geography (1980) and Postgraduate Certificate in education (1981) from the University of Sheffield, an M.Sc. in computer studies (1987) from Sheffield City Polytechnic and a Ph.D. from Leeds Metropolitan University. She worked as project leader on the Information Skills Project at the University of Sheffield and has a wide experience of teaching in higher education. Her main research interests are in the areas of knowledge acquisition, the pedagogic and methodological issues surrounding the development of computer-assisted learning material, and computer-supported collaborative work.

Marie C. Hayet is a lecturer in the Department of Language and Linguistics—Center for Computational Linguistics, UMIST. Since February 1992, Ms. Hayet has been seconded for part of her time to the UMIST Computing Support Services to promote computer-assisted learning within the institution and advise on development. Her academic interests include French linguistics, sublanguages, computational methods for language analysis, computer-assisted learning, multimedia, and she has a number of publications in these areas.

Clive Holtham is Bull Information Systems professor of information management at City University Business School, London, England. Following professional training as an accountant (he was Young Accountant of the Year in 1976), he has been an active innovator in the use of IT for improved management. He moved to the business school after six years as a director of finance and information technology. His research centers around the top management use of IT and the application of IT for strategic advantage. He is a consultant to major organizations in the public and private sector and lectures widely to academic and business audiences, both in the United Kingdom and abroad. He has been actively involved in the United Kingdom.'s Computers in

Teaching Initiative, and is a regional director of the Center for Finance, Accounting, and Management.

Punnipa Hossain is an assistant professor in foundation studies and also contributes as technology consultant for the Computing Center at Lock Haven University, Lock Haven, Pennsylvania. She holds a B.Ed. from Srinakarinwirot University in Bangkok, Thailand. With a master's in educational technology from the University of the Philippines, in Diliman, Philippines, she also holds a doctoral degree in educational technology from Southern Illinois University, in Carbondale, Illinois. Her research and teaching interests include media needs assessment, application of hypertext in education, and design and implementation of instructional delivery systems.

Eric Johnson is professor of English and dean of the College of Liberal Arts at Dakota State University, Madison, South Dakota. He is the editor of *TEXT Technology: The Journal of Computer Text Processing*. He has written or edited nearly one hundred articles, monographs, and papers about computers, writing, and literary study.

Donna Marie Kaputa received her B.A., M.B.A. and is soon to receive her Ph.D. in higher education from the State University of New York at Buffalo. She has been teaching for about fifteen years in the computer-based management information systems area at a variety of colleges and universities. Currently she is department chair of computer information systems at Medaille College. She is interested in educational technology and ethical implications of computing and computing technologies.

Jack R. Kayser originally began his career in architecture but switched to engineering in order to understand the underlying nature of structures. After working for several years as a designer, he returned to academia to earn a master's and Ph.D. in structural engineering. Upon completing his degree he worked as a consultant and a professor of civil engineering. Since 1994, Dr. Kayser has avidly promoted the use of the World Wide Web at Lafayette College. His activities have included teaching several workshops on writing for the Web and developing Web resources to assist in teaching engineering mechanics. Dr. Kayser currently is serving as Lafayette's Educational Technologies Specialist.

Robert O. Little is the director of the Lock Haven University Computing Center, Lock Haven, Pennsylvania. He graduated with high honors from the University of Texas at Arlington, receiving a B.B.A. in accounting; he then attained a master's of business information systems from Georgia State University in Atlanta. He has a certificate in data processing and is a Certified Systems Professional. Mr. Little is active with CAUSE (the National Association for the Management of Information Technology in Higher Education), and currently serves as a member of the national editorial committee. He has published articles in *CAUSE/EFFECT* and *Systems Development* magazines, is listed in Who's Who Worldwide, and has worked in management systems consulting, with Andersen Consulting. He planned and implemented a $26 million dollar, 5-year management information system for the University of Miami (Florida) and managed the systems development activities for the nation's largest mutual fund records processing service, before moving to Lock Haven University.

Les Lloyd is the assistant vice-president of information technology at Rollins College with responsibility for academic and administrative computing as well as networking, and he previously spent eight years at Lafayette College with similar responsibilities. He has also edited *Campus-Wide Information Systems and Networks, Using Computing Networks on Campus I, Using Computer Networks on Campus 2,* and Administrative Computing in Higher Education and currently is editor of the quarterly journal *Campus-Wide Information Systems.*

W. Brett McKenzie has worked at Bryant College, Providence, Rhode Island, as an instructional support specialist since completing a master's in interactive technology in education at Harvard Graduate School of Education. He first worked with integrating networks for teaching writing while an instructor at Naval Academy Preparatory School in Newport, Rhode Island. He is completing his doctorate in education at Clark University, Worcester, Massachusetts.

James S. McKeown is an instructor in the College of Business and Information Systems at Dakota State University in Madison, South Dakota, where he teaches computer science and computer education courses. He is currently enrolled in the instructional design and technology program at the University of Iowa where is he working on his Ph.D. in instructional design with emphasis in CAI. He has a M.A. in computing in education from Teachers College/Columbia University and a bachelor's in history from South Dakota State University. Mr. McKeown has taught at the high school and college levels in South Dakota and New Hampshire for twelve years.

Lynette Molstad is an assistant professor of business and information systems at Dakota State University in Madison, South Dakota, where she teaches business and information systems courses. She received a B.S. in business education and a B.A. in business administration from Dakota State University. She also has an M.A. degree in business education and an M.B.A. with emphasis in management information systems from the University of South Dakota. Ms. Molstad has taught at the high school and college levels in South Dakota for over twenty years.

Nils S. Peterson is an instructional software designer and is now coordinator at the Center for Development of Educational Technologies. The work on MacCycle was carried out during the tenure of a Maitland Ramsey Research Fellowship which was awarded by the University of St. Andrews. His special interests include physiological simulations and open-ended problem solving as a teaching medium. Recently published teaching simulations include the "Cardiovascular Function Laboratories." Mr. Peterson was also a founding member of Project BioQUEST.

Marilyn Puchalski, received her master's in information science from Drexel University. She is currently director of academic computing at Bucks County Community College, Newtown, Pennsylvania. Ms. Puchalski also holds a position as senior associate professor of computer science at BCCC and has taught a wide spectrum of credit and noncredit computer courses for fifteen years. One of the principal authors of the Title III grant, she also worked as a systems analyst in business and industry for several years.

Martin Rich, B.Sc. (London) M.B.A. (City) is a lecturer in information Management at City University Business School, London, England. He worked for over ten years as a consultant and project manager, predominantly in an information systems development environment. This included contributions to the Alvey collaborative research project. He then received an M.B.A. at City and subsequently joined the business school as a lecturer. His research interests include the relevance of information technology to management education, and the organizational issues raised by the changing use of technology, particularly data communication networks. Mr. Rich also has a B.Sc. degree in applicable mathematics from Birkbeck College, University of London.

Robert A. Saldarini is a full professor of information science at Bergen Community College. He was released from instruction in 1988 to head up a 1.3 million dollar technical grant. As director of applied technology, he was responsible for planning and implementation of a complete networked desktop publishing laboratory, a CAD laboratory, and a CAM/SIM laboratory. Currently he is working on the implementation of expert systems software, and he serves as chair of the academic vice president's task force on multimedia. Robert has been trained in multimedia and AVC at the IBM Training Campus in Atlanta and in laser disc design at the University of Nebraska. His professional credentials include a textbook entitled *Analysis and Design of Business Information Systems* (Macmillan Publishing, 1989) as well as multiple articles and national presentations on information systems topics.

Najmuddin Shaik studied at Osmania University (India) and Northern Illinois University where he earned an M.A. in economics and an M.S. in computer science. He has also completed advanced graduate course work in economics leading towards a Ph.D. He is involved in teaching senior-level computer courses and is currently an associate professor of computer information systems at Union College, Kentucky. His major areas of interest are computer security, object-oriented analysis and design, C programming, object-oriented database, UNIX operating system, and microcomputer applications.

Alan Shuchat is professor of mathematics at Wellesley College, Wellesley, Massachusetts, and recently completed a term as associate dean of the college. As an administrator, he was active in promoting the use of technology in the curriculum. With Fred Shultz, he was codirector of a National Science Foundation grant to establish a mathematics graphics classroom at Wellesley and is coauthor of some of the mathematics software described in his chapter. His chapter is based on a talk delivered to the Faculty SIG of the New England Regional Computing Program (NerCOMP) in April 1992.

Joel M. Smith, formerly assistant professor of philosophy and director of educational computing services at Allegheny College, Meadville, Pennsylvania, is currently director of academic computing and information technology at The Claremont Graduate School, Claremont, California. He earned bachelor's and master's degrees in both philosophy and physics from Baylor University, and he earned his Ph.D. in history and philosophy of science from the University of Pittsburgh. Smith has taught at Baylor, the University of Pittsburgh, Indiana University, and Allegheny College. He has published papers and reviews on topics in the philosophy of science in *Studies in History and Philosophy of Science*, and *Nous*. He has given numerous presentations and lectures on educational computing at a variety of institutions, including the Conference on Science and Technology for Education in the 1990s in Moscow, the University of Michigan, and the University of Notre Dame.

Abigail M. Thomas is an associate professor of mathematical and computer science at Lyndon State College, Lyndonville, Vermont.

Doug Thompson is currently professor/reader in modern Italian history and literature at the University of Hull, United Kingdom. He is author of books on Pavese, Pirandello, and the Italian fascist state and together with his wife, June (center manager of the CTI Center for Modern Languages based at Hull), author of two advanced translation courses (Italian/English). He was to lead a team of researchers drawn from the United Kingdom and Italy in the production of a fully comprehensive language workstation under the auspices of the British government-funded Teaching and Learning Technology Programme, in the fall of 1992.

Susan Whiten, trained originally as a reproductive physiologist, is now a lecturer in the School of Biological and Medical Sciences. Ms. Whiten organizes the Human Anatomy course and has particular responsibility for teaching both regional anatomy and histology. Although not a computer expert, she recognizes the need to modernize these areas of teaching and sees computer-aided instruction as one of the best ways of integrating anatomy, histology, and physiology.

Paulette Wiesen, RRA is director of the Medical Record Programs at Dakota State University, Madison, South Dakota. She received B.A. in medical record administration and psychology from the College of St. Scholastica, Duluth,

Minnesota. Prior to entering the field of education, Ms. Wiesen managed medical record departments in acute care hospitals.

Jo Ellen Winters, senior associate professor of English at Bucks County Community College, Newtown, Pennsylvania, has been teaching freshman composition (and literature) for over twenty years. She has been teaching computer-augmented composition for the last three years as part of the college's Title III grant. She is developing a discipline-based English Composition II course (Psychology and Gender) under a grant from the Pew Charitable Trust. Coordinator of faculty development for her department and editor of the faculty newsletter, she has participated in an NEH Summer Seminar for College Teachers, given a paper on computers and technology at the Myrtle Beach Computers on Campus Conference, and published a paper on Faulkner in the *Community College Humanities Review.*

INDEX

3M Corporation, 77
3M Multi-Function Record,
   Systems Management, 160-3
116 DOS platform, 26
80286 DOS, 87

Addison Wesley Company, 133
Adobe Premiere, 69
Aiton, James F., 63, 345
Aldus Pagemaker, 6
Allred, R., 24, 33
Alson, D.R., 25, 33
American Health Info. Management
   Association, 158
Amiga, 78
Amiga A1000, 44, 48
Amiga A2000HD, 48
Anderson, Douglas, 237
Angel, N. Faye, 185, 345
Anhorn, Judy, 20
Apple, 28, 37, 69, 76-78, 243
Apple II, 26, 30, 58, 176
Apple IIE, 4
Apple Macintosh, 26
Apple Macintosh, LC, 64
AppleWorks, 4
Arts and Letters, 59
Aspects, 132-33
Aston University, 142
AT&T, 5, 37
Audio Visual Connection (AVC), 77
Autodesk Animator, 59

Baldwin-Wallace College, 85, 87-88,
   90-1
BASIC, 7
Bates College, 93
Beach, Richard, 14, 20
Bennett, Dorine, 157, 345
Benson, Ronald G., 345
Bergen Community College, 73
Birkholz, Dick W., 345
BITNET, 142, 176-7
Bloomfield College, 3-55, 11-12
Bordley, Jr., John L., 207, 246
Bozylinsky, Garrett, 346
Bracey, G., 24, 33
Bradley, Drake R., 93-94, 109-110,
   112, 114, 116-7
Bridwell, 14, 20
Bright, G.W., 25, 33
Brown, A.L., 128
Buccini, Eugene P., 346
Bryant College, 119, 128
Buckley, Jeanne, 129
Bucks County Community College,
   (BCCC), 13, 129-31, 133, 135-7
Burdick, Paul, 347
Burley, Tom, 154, 156
Bush, 231

C++, 6, 229
CAD, 43
CAL, 217-28, 235-6
California State University, 155

CALL, 205, 217-22, 226-7, 229, 236
Cambridge Multimedia Systems, 72
Campione, J.C., 128
Carmody, Carole, 3, 347
Carson, 142
CHEST, 221
Chismar, Constance, 347
City University Business School,
    143-4, 150, 153, 155
Clark, Andrew, 142, 156
Cleveland Institute of Art (CIA),
    43, 46, 48
CLV, 59
College of Saint Elizabeth, 241-4
Collier, R., 20
Commodore, 44, 78
Commodore Business Machines, 48
Computer Select, 176
Cooper, M.M., 128
Corel Draw, 6, 10, 59
CSUNET, 155
Covey, James S., 49

Daedalus Integrated Writing
    Environment, (DIWE), 168-70
Dakota State University (DSU),
    157-163, 165-73, 175-7, 183
Dallas County Community College,
    District (DCCCD), 56-57
Darley, 106-111, 117
DATASIM, 93-96, 98-99,101, 103-
    111, 113-116
Dauwer, Ellen M., 241, 348
Davidson, Lyle, 348
dBase III Plus, 158, 161, 177-8, 181-2
DEC, 78
Department of Employment, 142
Department of Trade and Industry,
    (DTI), 220
DeltaGraph Professional, 69
Desktop Publishing, 9-10, 29-32, 43,
    51, 59, 245

Dobrin, David N., 14, 20
DOS, 4, 7, 10, 29-31. 81, 126, 144,
    158,176-8, 181
Draznin, Wayne, 43
DRG/ASC, 162
Dynix Corporation, 27

EDUCOM, 37-38
EGA, 58
EHE, 221
EKG, 7
El Centro College, 56
English as a Second Language,
    (ESL), 6-7
ERIC, 176
Ericsson, Patricia, 165, 348
European Economic Community,
    (EEC), 220

Ferrum College, 185
First Search, 176
Fischer, Marla J., 349
Fleit, L.H., 32, 33
Flores, F., 128
FORTRAN, 214-5
Fowell, Susan P., 247, 349
FTP, 170

Gillespie, R., 24, 33
Gopher, 170
Gordon, Barbara, 14, 20
Greene, B.B., 32, 33

Hakken, D., 25, 33
Halio, Marcia Peoples, 14, 20
Halio, Marcia Peoples, 14, 20
Hanka, R., 72
Hardy, Ginny, 141, 156
Harman, D., 24, 33

Harrison, Carol, 237
Harvard Business School, 141
Harwisher, Gail, 20
Hayet, Marie C., 217, 349
Hazari, S., 32, 33
Heim, M.L., 128
Hemstreet, R.L., 117
Herrmann, Andrea, 14, 20
Higher Education Funding Council, (HEFC) 220
Hiltz, S.R., 156
Hodgson, 141, 156
Holdstein, Deborah, 20
Holligan, Patrick J., 154, 156
Holtham, Clive, 139, 145, 147, 156
Hossain, Punnipa, 23, 350
Hunter, B., 33
HyperCard, 38, 39, 66, 70, 72, 136, 208, 210-2
HyperCard 2.1, 64
HyperText, 212

IBM, 28-31, 35, 37, 74, 76-78, 142
IBM 4381, 176
IBM/DOS, 213
IBM M57 SLC, 77
IBM PC, 4-5, 28-31, 35, 58
IBM PC 486, 177, 228
ICONAUTHOR, 54
ICONGRAPHICS, 54
ICONWARE, 54
InfoTrack, 176
Internet, 10, 29, 31, 155, 170

JANET, 142, 154, 229
Johns Hopkins University, 207
Johnson, Eric, 165, 350
Joint Photographics Experts Group, (JPEG), 66-67

Kaputa, Donna Marie, 237, 350
Kaye, Anthony, 141, 156
Kearsley, G., 25, 33
Keisler, Sara B., 156
Keyboard Publishing, 72
KeyServer, 207
Kulik, J. A., 25, 33
Kwikstate, 6

Latane, 106-11, 117
Lewis, Ralph, 156
LHU, 26, 28-32
Lillian, 20
Little, Robert, O., 23
Lock Haven University, 23
LOGiix, 229, 232
Lotus 1-2-3, 4, 6-7, 10, 14, 130, 134, 158-9, 161, 177-8, 181-2
Lyndon State College, 213, 216

Mabbett, Alan, 154, 156
MacCycle, 63, 65, 67-72
Macintosh, 28, 30, 35, 38, 48, 66-7, 132-33, 176, 207-9, 211-2, 241-2, 244-6
Macintosh II series, 66
Macintosh IIci, 116
Macintosh IIcx, 242, 244
Macintosh LC, 64-6, 132
Macintosh SE, 242-3
Macintosh SE/30, 242-3
Manchester Business School, 142
Manchester University, 142
Mason, 141, 156
MathCad, 37-38
McClure, P.A., 24, 33
McConnell, David, 141, 156
McKenzie, W. Brett, 119, 128
McKeown, James S., 175
McNair, Malcolm, 141, 156
Medaille College, 237, 239-40

Microsoft Windows 3.1/DOS 5, 228
Microsoft Word, 27, 29, 31, 132, 207
Microsoft Word for Windows, 31
Microteck, 68
MicroVAX, 176
Minitab, 130, 133-34, 137
MINSQ, 38
MIT Sloan School of Management, 147
Modianos, D., 24, 33
Morehouse, D.L., 25, 33
Mountain View College (MVC), 49-50, 56-59, 61-62
Mosaic, 170
MPC, 76-77
MS-DOS, 132, 137, 177-8, 182
MS-DOS 286, 58
MS-DOS 386, 58
Mueller-Lyer, 115
Multimedia, 76
Multimedia PC Marketing, Inc., 76

National Information on Software and Services, (NISS), 222
National Science Foundation (NSF), 37-8, 207
NIX, 229
Noel/Levitz, 10

Olson, J., 25, 33
OmniPage Professional, 6
OS/2, 81, 182
OWL International Inc., 228

Panasonic, 78
Papert, S., 128
Paradox, 31
ParScore, 57
ParTest, 57
Pascal, 6

PC, 6,10, 14, 17, 37-38, 55, 57, 61, 140, 143, 146, 150-1, 176, 213, 216, 225, 228
PC-DOS, 27
PCX, 54-55
Penn State Great Valley, 129
Pesnia, 39
Peterson, Nils S., 63, 72
Philadelphia College of Textiles and Sciences, 129
Photoshop, 69
PhotoStyler, 6
PICKUP, 221
PICT, 66, 69
Plan-It, 150
PODIUM, 77
PortaCOM, 229
PowerMac, 66
Professional Write, 14, 16, 132
Puchalski, Marilyn, 129

Quattro Pro, 27, 31, 37, 193
QuickBASIC, 172
QuickTime, 64, 66-7, 71, 208, 211

Rawson, James, 141, 156
Ready-to-Run, 135-36
Reynolds, Michael, 141, 156
Rheiter, J.A., 128
Rich, Martin, 139
Riesenberg, B., 25, 33

Saldarini, Robert A., 73
SAS, 32, 38
Sassafras, 207
Schlegel, Janice, 237
Selfe, C.L., 20, 128
Senko, 114, 116-117
SGML/HyTime, 228
Shaoul, Jean, 142, 156

Sheffield University, 142
Show Partner, 59
Shuchat, Alan, 35
Siedel, P., 33
Siegal, L., 24, 33
Slattery, 145, 156
Sloan, D., 24, 33
SmartText, 55
Smiley, Tex, 142, 156
SNOBOL4, 172
Southwell, Michael G, 20
Sproull, Lee S., 156
SPSS, 6-7, 9-10
Stanton, D., 20
Statistical Analysis System,
    (SAS), 29, 31
Stewart, 114, 116-117
Stockdill, S.H., 25, 33
Strathclyde University, 142
Sullivan, Christopher, 85
Sun3 System, 229
Sun Microsystems, 78
SuperCard, 38
SVHS, 48
System 7.0 for Macintosh, 31

TACT, 229
Tandy, 78
TELL, 204
Thomas, Abigail M., 213
Thompson, Doug, 197
Thompson, P., 72
Toffler, A., 24, 33
Tolman, M., 24, 33
ToolBook, 38
Tools Optimization, 193
Tools Optimizer, 193
TransIT, 197, 200-2, 204-5
TransLIT, 200
Turner, J. A., 21
Turoff, M., 156

Understanding Systems Ltd., 150
University of Essex, 252
University of Hawaii, 142
University of Hull, 197
University of Manchester, 205, 217
University of Maryland, 141
University of Sheffield, 247, 249-50,
    252
University of the South, 207, 210
University of St. Andrews, 63
University of Ulster, 205
University of Warwick, 142
University of Western Washington,
    126
UNIX, 5, 35, 142, 144-5, 148,
    225, 228-9
U.S. Department of Education, 129-
30

VAX, 36, 38
Ventura, 6
Ventura for Windows, 59
Ventura Publisher Desktop
    Publishing, 59
VGA, 52
Victoria University of Manchester,
    222
Video Interactive Technology (DVI),
    75
VideoLogic, 67
Video Spigot, 67
Vipond, D., 128
VRAM, 64

WAIS, 170
Washington State University, 63
Watkins, B.T., 21
Watson, 145, 156
Wellesley College, 35, 38, 40
West Chester University, 27
Whiten, Susan, 63, 72

Wiesen, Paulette, 157
Williams, P., 24, 33
Windows, 5-6, 30, 182, 241
Winer, B.J., 117
Winograd, T., 128
Winters, Jo Ellen, 13
WordPerfect, 6, 10, 14, 77, 158-9,
    177, 181-2243, 245
WordPerfect 5.1, 177
WordPerfect for Windows, 59
WordStar, 6-7, 10
WordStar 3.3, 4

Wresch, William, 21
WWW, 170

X-Acto, 43
XT clones, 5

Zenith-148 PC, 214
Ziegenhagen, S.T., 117
Zuboff, Shoshana, 153, 156